Ethnobiological Classification

Ethnobiological Classification

PRINCIPLES OF CATEGORIZATION
OF PLANTS AND ANIMALS
IN TRADITIONAL SOCIETIES

Brent Berlin

PRINCETON UNIVERSITY PRESS

PRINCETON, NEW JERSEY

Library of Congress Cataloging-in-Publication Data

Berlin, Brent
Ethnobiological classification : principles of categorization of
plants and animals in traditional societies / Brent Berlin.
p.   cm.
Includes bibliographical references and indexes.
1. Folk classification—Cross-cultural studies. 2. Ethnozoology.
3. Ethnobotany. I. Title.
GN468.4.B47 1992   574.6'1—dc20   91-25245

ISBN 0-691-09469-1

To all those who have seriously contemplated the wonder of Nature's plan

"What's the use of their having names," the Gnat said, "if they won't answer to them?" "No use to *them*," said Alice, "but it's useful to the people that name them, I suppose. If not, why do they have names at all?"
—Lewis Carroll, *Through the Looking Glass*

The frequent occurrence of similar phenomena in cultural areas that have no historical contact suggests that important results may be derived from their study, for it shows that the human mind develops everywhere according to the same laws. The discovery of these [laws] is the greatest aim of our science.
—Franz Boas, 1888

Contents

Preface

IN THIS MONOGRAPH I will present evidence in support of a number of widespread regularities concerning the categorization and nomenclature of plants and animals by peoples of traditional, nonliterate societies. My major claim here is that the observed structural and substantive typological regularities found among systems of ethnobiological classification of traditional peoples from many different parts of the world can be best explained in terms of human beings' similar perceptual and largely unconscious appreciation of the natural affinities among groupings of plants and animals in their environment—groupings that are recognized and named quite independently of their actual or potential usefulness or symbolic significance to humans. This claim might first appear trivial to biological systematists whose own system of classification, since the time of Aristotle and Theophrastus, is also based primarily on perceived affinities among organisms. For anthropology, however, a discipline caught up in a renewed romance with its cultural relativist foundations, such a view flies in the face of those who would see reality, in both its natural and its social forms, as a set of culturally constructed, often unique and idiosyncratic images, little constrained by the parameters of an outside world.

The empirical generalizations and theoretical explanations outlined here are presented in a comparative context, drawing data from a large number of full-scale descriptions of ethnobiological classification. I obviously make no claim that the generalizations capture all that is or can be known about how systems of ethnobiological classification actually work; only that the patterns that emerge are sufficiently regular as to require explanation by any theory of human categorization that purports to be general and comprehensive. Whether the explanations I offer ultimately prove to be totally satisfactory has little bearing on the striking regularities that have motivated these explanations in the first place.

I originally drew up the outlines of a general monograph on the nature of ethnobiological classification some twenty years ago. Significant portions of what I had hoped to say there were subsequently published in professional journals or as parts of descriptive monographs, and the synthesis that I envisaged never saw manuscript form. Additional factors contributed to the delay in producing a book-length manuscript. Studies in ethnobiology, especially those dealing with ethnobiological classification, flourished in the 1970s and 1980s. Many of these works were monographic in scope and increased considerably the number of descriptive treatments on which a broad survey of ethnobiological categorization and nomenclature might be based. Several of these studies provided data relevant to aspects of my earlier statements that led me to revise some of these statements and simply reject others. Furthermore, my own research on systems of ethnozoological classification helped to broaden my earlier understanding of the principles of ethnobiological categorization and nomenclature that had been developed primarily on the basis of work in ethnobotany. Finally, the passage of two decades has helped me develop a more coherent view of the complexities of ethnobiological classification than the one I held when I first set out with a plant press in the Chiapas highlands, then as much concerned with making botanically acceptable herbarium vouchers as with the problems associated with the cognitive underpinnings of ethnobotanical classification.

In ethnobiology, as in other branches of science, knowledge is cumulative, and I have attempted to incorporate the new data of recent research along with the subsequent modifications in my theoretical interpretation that these new data demand. I have also taken this opportunity to evaluate the major criticisms that have been launched against my earlier proposals on the general principles of ethnobiological classification given the new materials available now. I have concluded that the fundamental outlines of the original framework are basically sound, allowing for the easy and natural accommodation of new data and new ways of thinking about them.

I am aware that this conclusion will not be universally shared, and it is of course possible that the patterns described in the following pages might be better understood in terms of some different typology. However, it is appropriate to require of one's critics the formulation of an alternative general analytic framework that accounts for the empirical formal and substantive generalizations in at least as satisfactory and parsimonious a fashion as that proposed here. Thus far, no such alternative proposals have been presented that claim to account for the full body of data now available for ethnobiological classification in general.

I have divided the monograph into two major sections. Part One, "Plan," focuses primarily on the structure of ethnobiological classification as can be inferred from an analysis of descriptions of individual systems. The first chapter reviews earlier attempts to outline the generalizations about ethnobiological classification and presents a recent revision of these views. The next three chapters focus on the major ethnobiological ranks that make up folk systems of biological classification, beginning with the folk genus, moving on to folk species, and then on to taxa of life-form and intermediate rank.

Part Two, "Process," focuses on the underlying processes involved in the functioning and evolution of ethnobiological systems. Chapter 5 addresses the central role of cognitive variation in ethnobiological classification, showing how pattern emerges from regularities in diversity. Chapter 6 deals with the vibrant properties of ethnobiological nomenclature as a reflection of certain perceptual and behavioral features of the organisms to which the names of animals and plants refer. In the final chapter, I outline some of the substantive regularities that can be observed in the content of ethnobiological categories, at least for one biogeographical region of the world, and discuss the evolution of ethnobiological categories and the likely emergence of taxa of folk specific rank as a direct result of the domestication of plants and animals.

As with my earlier published versions on the principles of ethnobiological classification, I have organized my generalizations in the spirit of a series of hypotheses to be tested. Most of the generalizations outlined here are based on a body of empirical evidence drawn from field studies in many diverse parts of the world. Several others are more appropriately treated as hunches based on personal experience about how systems of ethnobiological classification seem to work. Overall, they combine to produce what Morris Swadesh liked to call a "progress report" about one's best current evaluation of what has been learned and to what problems we have to direct our research efforts in the future. I will be more than satisfied if the present report on where we have come can serve to stimulate other scholars to carry out some of the challenging comparative fieldwork needed to bring the emerging picture of ethnobiological classification into clearer, if not perfect, focus.

. . .

Ethnobiological research is by its nature collaborative research, and none of the ideas presented here has been developed in isolation. I owe the most to my Tzeltal, Aguaruna, and Huambisa informants who were willing to participate with me as collaborators in this long journey. They are the ethnobiologists who provided the data that underlie the theory of ethnobiological classification sketched here. It is through their commentary, explanation, and patient teaching that I was first led to seriously contemplate the wonder of nature's basic plan.

In the pine-oak forests of highland Chiapas, my longtime collaborator Dennis E. Breedlove trained me in the fundamentals of field botany. He led me to appreciate the meaning of old-fashioned biological systematics and the inherent pleasures of botanical collecting. In a world where departments of what Thomas Duncan calls "nonprofit biology" are being replaced by molecular and cellular biology multimillion dollar research kingdoms and where increased specialization leads inevitably to increased ignorance, Breedlove's holistic view of the plant world remains one of remarkable importance for ethnobiology as a discipline.

In the rain forests of Amazonian Peru, James L. Patton made it possible for me to begin work in ethnozoology. With Patton, along with John P. O'Neill, John Cadle, Roy McDiarmid, and Camm Swift, I began to appreciate the complexities of conducting vertebrate field zoology in the tropics. Much of the ethnozoological data described here is a result of their collaboration. Their personal support during some of the most difficult times of my research career goes far beyond mere formal scientific collaboration.

Other colleagues have been kind enough to read and comment on my work over the last several decades, and I owe much to their individual perspectives and helpful criticisms. Conceptually, as is clearly seen in the pages that follow, I owe a major debt to Paul Kay, who has helped me develop my thoughts on the nature of ethnobiological categorization since I first started to think seriously about the subject nearly twenty-five years ago. H. C. Conklin's cognitive ethnoscience inspired my first consideration of universal principles in ethnobotany. The standards of excellence he laid down for ethnographic fieldwork have guided modern ethnobiological research since the mid-1950s. I owe much of my current theoretical formulation to the work and collegial commentary of the late Ralph Bulmer. Although we differ in major respects, Bulmer independently began to sketch his own views on the general principles of ethnobiological classification in the early 1960s, and his arguments served to help me clarify my own over two decades of productive debate.

A. Kimball Romney trained me to think comparatively and provided me with an appreciation of the importance of the accumulation of knowledge as a major part of the scientific enterprise. The intellectual mark made in the early 1960s by Romney and his research group at Stanford, including Charles Frake, Roy D'Andrade, and Duane Metzger, continues to guide my basic research orientation. Norman A. McQuown helped me acquire the patience necessary for systematic descriptive linguistic research, and Terrence Kaufman gave me an appreciation of the diachronic dimensions of linguistically informed cultural historical inference. Scott Atran, William Baleé, Cecil Brown, E. A. Hammel, Terrence Hays, and Paul Taylor have consistently been willing to freely exchange data and ideas with me.

My current and former students have made their mark on these pages, and each has influenced my thinking in major ways. I have not always agreed with their interpretations and have not always followed their suggestions. These very disagreements have helped me focus my own views on the subject more concisely. I want specifically to thank Eugene Hunn, who was one of the first ethnobiologists to argue for a perceptually based theory of ethnobiological classification. While I take issue with many of his interpretations on the nature of ethnobiological classification, his views have contributed to the positive development of the field as few others. More recently, James Boster and Luisa Maffi have provided detailed positive criticisms of my current views on the nature of ethnobiological classification, and a number of their ideas are reflected directly in my present position.

That this work should finally be written owes much to my partner and colleague Elois Ann Berlin. She was finally able to move me from dead center and to urge me to take up the task of putting down my ideas in book form. Her encouragement and sacrifice in keeping me moving helped change badly organized mountains upon mountains of data into the synthesis presented here. She has also led me to examine and appreciate the ways in which research on ethnobiological classification could contribute to and be complemented by much broader themes of plant-animal-human relationships, especially in the areas of human health and nutrition. While the exploration of these complex relations is not the major focus of the present work, my current research on medical ethnobotany and ethnomedicine results in great part from her encouragement in expanding my horizons.

Most of the research reported here represents results of work generously supported by the National Science Foundation's programs in anthropology and systematic biology (Grants 64-383, 66-1183, 76-17485, 79-2280, 87-03838, 90-44523), the National Institute of Mental Health (Grant 22012), the Wenner-Gren Foundation for Anthropological Research, and the University of California Consortium on Mexico and the United States (UC MEXUS). This support is gratefully acknowledged.

The monograph was initially drafted in East Lansing, Michigan, in the quiet winter months of 1988, primarily as the result of the freedom provided me by awards from the John Simon Guggenheim Foundation and the Humanities Research Program of the University of California at Berkeley. I am most grateful for this financial support. Paul Kay agreed to read a first draft of the manuscript in its entirety, and his suggestions have helped me strengthen unclear arguments and rephrase otherwise ambiguous claims. The comments of anonymous reviewers have also helped me organize the text more coherently. I especially appreciate the efforts of Luisa Maffi, who provided detailed editorial corrections on the final draft and helped me clarify a number of major substantive issues in the whole presentation. Finally, my editor and long-term friend, William E. Woodcock, has given me sustained editorial support over two decades and has seen to it that the book be published in its present form. It should be clear that I alone, however, am responsible for any errors of content and interpretation.

DETERMINATIONS OF PLANT AND ANIMAL SPECIES FOR TZELTAL, AGUARUNA, AND HUAMBISA ETHNOBIOLOGY

Ethnobiology is nothing without the active collaboration of systematic biologists in many fields whose expertise allows for the accurate scientific determinations of one's collections. The biological determinations of the plant materials associated with the examples cited from Tzeltal ethnobotany result from my collaboration with Dennis E. Breedlove (California Academy of Sciences) and Peter H. Raven (Missouri Botanical Garden). A full list of the names of other specialists who have participated in this effort are given in Berlin, Breedlove, and Raven (1974).

No monographic treatment on Aguaruna and Huambisa ethnobiology has yet been published. However, it is appropriate to indicate here the names of those specialists with whom I have worked closely and who are responsible for the determinations of the major portion of the biological collections from Amazonian Peru that are mentioned in the present monograph.

Mammals: James L. Patton, Museum of Vertebrate Zoology, University of California, Berkeley.

Birds: John P. O'Neill, Museum of Natural History, Louisiana State University.

Amphibians and reptiles: Roy W. McDiarmid, Museum of Natural History, Smithsonian Institution; John C. Cadle, Museum of Natural History, University of Pennsylvania.

Fishes: Camm C. Swift, Division of Ichthyology, Los Angeles Museum of Natural History; Donald Stewart, Department of Ichthyology, Field Museum of Natural History.

The large amount of plant material associated with field expeditions among the Aguaruna and Huambisa have been processed at the Missouri Botanical Garden. I am grateful to Peter H. Raven and the herbarium staff who have facilitated the determinations of many of these collections. I am especially grateful for the collaboration of Ronald Liesner, Thomas Croat, Alwyn H. Gentry, and John Dwyer, who have been primarily responsible for the curating of my collections, providing determinations in the areas of their specialties, and for coordinating the distribution of thousands of collections to numerous other specialists. These latter collaborators are too numerous to mention here but will be acknowledged when a full monographic description of Jívaro ethnobotany is completed.

ACKNOWLEDGMENT OF ARTWORK USED THROUGHOUT TEXT

The artwork found on page 1, PLAN, is that of Alonzo Méndex Girón, my longtime Tzeltal Maya collaborator from Tenejepa, Chiapas, Mexico. The originals of this series of flies are rendered in colored pencil and represent part of a more complete set of ethnozoological illustrations that he produced for me in the late 1960s (see Hunn 1977:288–289 for provisional descriptions of individual creatures). The short-horned grasshopper (Acrididae) shown on page 197, PROCESS, is also taken from this series of penciled drawings.

Alfredo Pague, a young Aguaruna Jívaro from the community of Huampami on the Río Cenepa in Amazonian Peru, produced the drawings of the large toads, *Bufo marinus*, found on the dust jacket (and one reproduced on page 197), as well as the series of Amazonian toucans that illustrate the endpapers of the book (*Ramphastos cuvieri, R. culminatus, Pteroglossus castanotis, P. pluricinctus, Selenidera reinwardtii*). The originals were produced as colored felt-pen illustrations in the mid 1970s.

Finally, the small inked drawings of medicinal plant species that introduce the first page of each chapter are reductions of larger 11″ x 16″ botanical illustrations drawn in 1986 by Antonio López Hérnandez, also of the Tzeltal community of Tenejapa, and form part of a major series of botanical drawings that will appear in several volumes in 1992 as *La Enciclopedia Médica Tzeltal-Tzotzil: Persistencia y Transformación de la Medicina Maya en los Altos de Chiapas*. The encyclopedia represents work carried out by researchers associated with PROCOMITH, A.C. (Programa de Colaboración Sobre Medicina Indígena Tradicional y Herbolaria), a nonprofit organization dedicated to the study, conservation, and promotion of the knowledge and uses of medicinal plants among the indigenous peoples of Chiapas, Mexico.

ORTHOGRAPHIC CONVENTIONS

In the main, I have tried to avoid the use of technical linguistic orthography for the rendering of the indigenous names of plants and animals throughout the monograph, preferring to use instead practical orthographies that are nonetheless phonemically accurate. The three linguistic groups most commonly referred to in the book are the Tzeltal, a Maya-speaking people of southern Mexico, and the Aguaruna and Huambisa, two Jívaro-speaking populations of the Peruvian Amazon. In general, the vowels of each of these languages are pronounced much like those of Spanish, with the exception of the Aguaruna and Huambisa unrounded, midcentral vowel [ɨ] ("barred i"). This sound is rendered something like the last vowel of the English word *sofa*, but with the lips pulled back. In Jívaro words, this sound is written as *e*, as in *ete* 'wasp species'.

Speakers of English will not be familiar with the Tzeltal Maya "glottal stop," indicated by a single apostrophe, as in the Tzeltal word for 'tree', *te*', and 'stem', *te'el*. This is pronounced in a manner similar to the medial glottal "catch" in English expressions such as *uh-uh*, or *oh-oh*. Other unfamiliar sounds in this Maya language are the "glottalized consonants" (p', t', k', ch', and tz'). These consonants are pronounced as their nonglottalized equivalents with the addition of a rapid, explosive "click" or "pop."

English glosses of plant and animal names are indicated by single quotes. Glosses for bird species differ from that of standard ornithological usage and are given here in lower case, for example, *Sarcoramphus papa* 'king vulture', *Piaya cayana* 'squirrel cuckoo'. In general, all indigenous names are set apart from the rest of the text in **bold italics**.

May 1991
El Cerrito, California

ch'ujch'ul
us

PART ONE

Plan

yax tonja

niwak
us

tzotz it
us

sankúro
xenen

untik
xenen

ijk'al xkach
xenen

k'anal
xenen

ijk'al
xenen

k'anal xkach
xenen

k'anal
xut

ijk'al
xut

yusil
satz'

CHAPTER ONE

On the Making of a Comparative Ethnobiology

1.1 Intellectualist and Utilitarian Approaches in Ethnobiology

As its name implies, ethnobiology as a discipline combines the intuitions, skills, and biases of both the anthropologist and the biologist, often in quite unequal mixtures. There is no generally accepted definition of the field, although most practicing ethnobiologists would probably agree that the field is devoted to the study, in the broadest possible sense, of the complex set of relationships of plants and animals to present and past human societies.

Almost any topic dealing with plants, animals, and human beings falls within the realm of the field. Consider the listing of some recent Ph.D. dissertations of interest to ethnobiologists compiled by Hays and Laferriere (1987): "Physiochemical Properties of Tepary Bean Starch," "Taxonomy and Evolution of Mexican Maize," "Subsistence Patterns of the Chulmun Period: A Reconsideration of the Development of Agriculture in Korea," "The Ethnobiology of the Haitian Zombi," "Feasting and Fasting: The Meaning of Muslim Food in Delhi," and "The Principles and Concepts of Thai Classical Medicine."

To this list, add the table of contents of a recent (1987) issue of the *Journal of Ethnobiology*, the official journal of the Society of Ethnobiology: "A Palynological Approach to a Chronometry Problem on the Colorado Plateau," "Seeds of Discontent: Implications of a 'Pompeii' Archaeobotanical Assemblage for Grand Canyon Anasazi Subsistence Models," "Taphonomy and Archaeologically Recovered Mammal Bone from Southeast Missouri," "Virtuous Herbs: Plants in Chumash Medicine," "The Folk Subgenus: A New Ethnobiological Rank," and "Survey of Vertebrate Remains from Prehistoric Sites in the Savannah River Valley."

In spite of these varied foci, at least two major questions, or families of questions, in ethnobiology may be recognized that serve to bring some order to the diversity of the field. The first question is basically economic and asks: "How and in what ways do human societies *use nature*?" The second is fundamentally cognitive and asks: "How and in what ways do human societies *view nature*?" Economically motivated questions occurred first in the field's short history, while more cognitively oriented works were not to appear until the mid 1950s.

Questions of how human beings use nature, especially plants and animals, can be traced to the late 1800s in America (Harshburger 1896). The economic bias was explicitly incorporated into one of the earliest definitions of ethnobiology as the study of the "utilization of plant and animal life by primitive peoples" (Castetter 1944:158). In the United States, almost all of the ethnobotanical and ethnozoological research in the first half of this century was motivated by this single purpose (see Ford 1978 for a useful survey). The early American ethnographer, John P. Harrington, made the economic emphasis clear when he stated, in reference to ethnobotany, that "a small part of the study consists in determining the native names of the plants . . . and the classification of these names [*sic*]. What should be a larger part of the study consists in determining the uses of plants for material culture on the one hand and for food or medicine on the other" (1947:244). The typical format of such utilitarian descriptions was essentially a series of lists, often presented in an arbitrary order, alphabetical by genus or arranged in their presumed phylogenetic sequence by biological family. As Conklin has stated, such research— and there was much of it—"might more accurately be said to treat of botany [or zoology] with notes on ethnology" (1954:10).

Answering questions concerning the ways that human beings view or conceive plants and animals stems from essentially anthropological and psychological biases. The major impetus for cognitively oriented ethnobiological research is relatively recent in ethnobiology and can be clearly traced to Conklin's influential, landmark doctoral dissertation, "The Relation of Hanunóo Culture to the Plant World" (Conklin 1954). This monograph was the first ethnographically and botanically sophisticated description of a full ethnobotanical system of classification for a nonliterate society. Conklin's research, stressing the importance of discovering native categories for plants and their conceptual relationships to one another as a complete, self-contained system, figured prominently in the methodological approach to cognitive ethnography known as American ethnoscience in the 1960s.

Without depreciating the importance of the economic aspects of ethnobiological investigation, the cognitive view of ethnobiology suggests that the "small part" of ethnobiological inquiry that Harrington allocates to classification represents a much more significant area of scientific study than might have been imagined by strict utilitarians. Before human beings can utilize the biological resources of a local environment, they must first of all be classified. As the botanical historian and philosopher Edward Lee Greene was to state in reference to botanical classification, "A genus is first *recognized* and afterwards *defined*" (Greene 1983:55). People must be able to recognize, categorize, and identify examples of one species, group similar species together, differentiate them from others, and be capable of communicating this knowledge to others. Who would deny the validity of Simpson's claim that "classification . . . is an absolute and minimal requirement of being or staying alive" (1961:3)?

Today, all ethnobiologists recognize the value of both the economic and the cognitive aspects in ethnobiological research. While particular emphases may vary, no adequate general study of a society's relation to its biological environment would fail to include detailed information on the ways human beings classify as well as utilize their plant and animal resources. This patently self-evident and hardly controversial observation needs no clarification, despite claims that recent cognitive approaches have concentrated on "what people think of their flora, to the virtual exclusion of how they use it" (Sillitoe 1983:2; also cf. Hunn 1982, Ellen 1986).

Nonetheless, modern research in ethnobiological classification is currently confronted with an important debate that is not so much concerned with the relative importance of economic versus cognitive factors in ethnobiological description as with a third question that unites the two faces of ethnobiology inextricably: "Why do human societies classify nature in the ways they do?"

1.2 WHY IS IT NOTABLE THAT NONLITERATES "KNOW SO MUCH" ABOUT NATURE?

Anthropology, like most other scholarly disciplines, has its fair share of anecdotal tidbits, most of them with a strong basis in fact. Some have been told and retold so often that they have passed out of academia into the main stream of public consciousness. The well-known example of Eskimo "words for snow" comes to mind as perhaps one of the most famous.[1]

Ethnobiology has its own small inventory of pat, standard pieces of common wisdom. Professor Lévi-Strauss, in introducing his famous Chapter 1 in *The Savage Mind*, provides a good sampler of ethnographers' first impressions on the detailed complexity of understanding that nonliterate peoples possess about plants and animals, citing the lucid account of Smith-Bowen's awe at the Tiv's extensive ethnobotanical knowledge and Conklin's record of a short trek with one of his Hanunóo informants, which reads more like detailed comments from the guidebook to some tropical botanical garden than ethnographic

[1] For the true bibliophile, I believe that the original source for Eskimo classification of white ice crystals is Boas (1911). The validity of this piece of folk wisdom has recently been reviewed by Pullum (1989), who provides a delightful discussion on the making of linguistic just-so stories.

field notes (cf. Lévi-Strauss 1966:6–7; Smith-Bowen 1954:15–16; Conklin 1954:115–117).

I have been able to uncover several additional descriptions to add to the list, all of which relate to Western scientists' first impressions of the significance and importance of ethnobiology to the people with whom they work. For example Holmberg, writing on the Sirionó of Bolivia, states that "knowledge of plants and animals is most extensive. When the plants flower, when they bear their fruit, which ones are good to eat, etc., are known by every child of ten. The habits of animals—what they eat, where they sleep, when they have their young, etc.—are common knowledge to every boy of twelve" (1969:120–121). Descola provides a Conklinian description for the ethnobotanical knowledge of the Achuar of Ecuador:

> During a walk in the rainforest, it is very rare that an adult Achuar can resist indicating to the ignorant ethnologist the vernacular name of any random plant. An experience repeated many, many times with patient informants proves that a man can name nearly all of the trees encountered along the full extent of a trajectory of various kilometers, or within an extensive piece of land destined to be cleared [for a swidden]. We have been able to record 262 different indigenous names for wild plants, but this list is certainly limited and undoubtedly would increase by carrying out systematic ethnobotanical investigation. (Descola 1988:144, my translation)

Diamond, an ornithologist who conducted a brief study (Diamond 1966) of the ethnoornithology of the Fore of New Guinea, was, like Mayr before him, greatly impressed with these people's knowledge of birds. In a larger monographic work, Diamond states that

> the Fore [have] a name for every bird that occurred regularly in the area. Usually each species had a separate name, and even sibling species as similar as two *Sericornis* warblers or the two *Macropygia* cuckoo-doves were distinguished (cf. Bulmer 1969 ms). In a few cases (*Gerygone* warblers . . .) related species were lumped under the same name but might then be distinguished by an added epithet. . . . Towards the end of my first season, Paran, my best informant, gave me names and descriptions of 30 birds which he knew but which I had not yet collected. . . . Many of the birds he described were not only rare but small and indistinctive. . . . Fore knowledge of local birds was sufficiently exhaustive that in cases where I showed the Fore a specimen of a bird and they stated that it did not occur [in the area], I [felt] that this information can be relied upon. (Diamond 1972:91)

Finally, I offer, somewhat hesitatingly because of the purple prose, my own rather naive first impressions of the ethnobotanical expertise of the Aguaruna Jívaro written during my first field trip to the area twenty years ago:

> Data collected during our short field survey indicate unquestionably that the Aguaruna's appreciation of the tropical forest is nothing less than phenomenal. Walking

through the tropical forest with an Aguaruna guide is an awe-inspiring experience. One is quickly provided with a separate name for what appears to be each botanically distinctive tree. On numerous occasions, our guide would come to a tree, take a piece of its bark, smell it, taste it, and then firmly provide us with the plant's name. From a resting spot on a jungle trail, one Aguaruna listed the names of no less than forty distinct trees visible from his place on a fallen tree trunk. Reports from the naturalist José María Guallart, a Jesuit priest who has resided among these people for fifteen years, indicate that the group recognizes at least fifty distinct classes of palms. One recently discovered species of *Chamaedorea* recognized by the Aguaruna proved to be new to science. (Berlin 1970:11)

Each of these personal impressions, independently produced at different times in various parts of the world, indicates how vividly native peoples' understanding of nature—particularly their classification of plants and animals—strikes the ethnographers involved. Why should this be so? Why is there no comparable record of personal impressions on the curious ways in which different peoples classify their kinfolk, or their pantheons of cosmological beings, or any other interesting cultural domains that may show equally detailed and extensive classificatory treatments?

The line of reasoning seems to go as follows. It is hardly news that primitive peoples have elaborated exotic ways of classifying their relatives or their supernatural beings. After all, these are quintessential social and cultural domains, subject to the unique imprint of each individual human group. To find "simple savages" controlling an extensive body of knowledge akin to the scientific fields of botany and zoology, however, is truly remarkable. Hence, our growing body of ethnobiological anecdotes.

But how might this extensive classification of nature have developed, and more importantly, how could it be maintained, considering again the nonliterate condition of our primitive brethren? Along the same line of reasoning, the most obvious explanation lies in the utilitarian significance that the myriad plant and animal species must possess for the amazing primitive classifier of nature. As evidence for this claim, consider Diamond's straightforward conclusion on the bases of Fore ethnozoological knowledge:

The purpose behind Fore animal names appears to be utilitarian. The only large animals to serve as sources of meat are the pig, the cassowary, and (formerly) man, so that even the smallest birds are hunted and eaten, as are mice, lizards, bats, and beetles. . . . As a result, many Fore, particularly boys and men, possess an incredibly detailed knowledge of the habits and voices of birds and other animals in their area. (Diamond 1972:91–92)

This argument has, of course, been challenged admirably by Lévi-Strauss (1966),[2] who argues that primitive peoples' "extreme familiarity with their

---

[2] Bulmer claims that the publication of Lévi-Strauss's book in "one stroke conferred respect-

biological environment . . . can scarcely be of much practical effect [because] its main purpose is not a practical one. It meets intellectual requirements rather than . . . satisfying [pragmatic] needs [because] classifying has a value of its own" (1966:9). According to this view, there is an "intellectual need" to classify the natural world because of human beings' inherent "demand for order" (ibid.:10). Unfortunately, the plausibility of Lévi-Strauss's response to neo-Malinowskian functionalism is to a large degree dependent on the inherent beauty of his argument and is in the main unsupported.

In the chapters that follow, an alternative position to the strictly utilitarian view is presented, one that is close to that of Lévi-Strauss but which differs significantly in interpretation. It will be shown that the striking similarities in both structure and content of systems of biological classification in traditional societies from many distinct parts of the world are most plausibly accounted for on the basis of human beings' inescapable and largely unconscious appreciation of the inherent structure of biological reality.

1.3 THE BASES OF ETHNOBIOLOGICAL CLASSIFICATION

One of the main claims in this book is that human beings everywhere are constrained in essentially the same ways—by nature's basic plan—in their conceptual recognition of the biological diversity of their natural environments. In contrast, social organization, ritual, religious beliefs, notions of beauty—perhaps most of the aspects of social and cultural reality that anthropologists have devoted their lives to studying—are *constructed* by human societies. The complexity of this cultural construction of human experience has led a growing number of anthropologists to view cultural and social phenomena as "texts" subject to multiple readings, little constrained by ethnographic facts (cf. Geertz 1973; Marcus and Fischer 1986).

When human beings function as ethnobiologists, however, they do not construct order, they discern it.[3] One is not able to look out on the landscape of

---

ability and legitimacy [to ethnobiological] inquiry, so that, at least in the British anthropological tradition, the specialist in ethnobotany or ethnozoology was made to feel no longer that he was merely indulging himself in idiosyncratic and peripheral pastimes, but was somewhere much nearer to the mainstream of social anthropological development" (1974a:10). Such was not the case in the United States, where the cognitive anthropological tradition, and by implication cognitively focused work in ethnobiology, was, and continues to be, rejected as irrelevant and theoretically vacuous by the majority of American cultural anthropologists (see Murray 1983 for a history of the rise and fall of classical ethnoscience, and Harris 1968 whose famous chapter 20 is now taken as accepted dogma on the inadequacies of idealist approaches in anthropology).

[3] Starr and Heise, in challenging the views of Wagner (1969), note that " 'constructing a classification' seems . . . to . . . entail . . . that our concepts and conceptual techniques are the sole source of the classes that constitute a constructed classification. 'Discerning classes', on the other hand, means that the classes or the traits for forming classes are given or presented in nature" (1969:92).

organic beings and organize them into cultural categories that are, at base, inconsistent with biological reality. The world of nature cannot be viewed as a continuum from which pieces may be selected ad libitum and organized into arbitrary cultural categories. Rather, groups of plants and animals present themselves to the human observer as a series of discontinuities whose structure and content are seen by all human beings in essentially the same ways, perceptual givens that are largely immune from the variable cultural determinants found in other areas of human experience.

However, if nature's plan is unambiguous, it is not exclusive. Ignoring for the moment the discredited nominalist position of Locke and its expression in biology, for example, "species have no actual existence in nature. They are mental concepts and nothing more . . . species have been invented in order that we may refer to great numbers of individuals collectively" (Bessy 1908:220), it is clear that biological diversity can be organized in several different ways.

Some of these different ways, though, are more revealing than others. A classification of plant species based on but a few characters, such as the presence or absence of presumed medicinal properties in the plants, will surely capture a portion of the patterns of variation in nature. However, a much larger fragment of nature's structure will be revealed when greater numbers of more general characters are focused on in the formation of groupings of organisms. In other words, some classifications will be more general than others in that a greater number of possible perceptual parameters will have been used in recognizing the affinities of any particular group of organisms in nature. These more general systems of classification will be largely unconscious because they reflect groupings that suggest themselves to the human observer as perceptual givens, as clusters and clumps so well defined in their overall structure and content as to be immediately obvious and, in the main, perceptually unambiguous.

Thus the ethnobiological data to be presented in the following sections will lend support to the claim that, while human beings are capable of recognizing many distinct patterns in nature's structure in general, in any local flora or fauna a single pattern stands out from all the rest. This overall pattern has been referred to by systematic biologists as the *natural system*. The natural system becomes manifest presumably because of the human ability to recognize and categorize groups of living beings that are similar to one another in varying degrees in their overall morphological structure, or morphological plan. This pattern-recognizing ability is probably innate. However, the answer to this larger ontological question has little bearing on the manifestation itself of pattern recognition in actual systems of ethnobiological classification.

Consider the following informal experiment that I have conducted for several years in my course on ethnobiological classification. Museum skins of several species of brightly colored Amazonian birds—tanagers, barbets, euphonias, puffbirds—all from the rain forests of northern Peru, are dumped from a basket in a heap on a table. Two and sometimes three specimens of each species are included in the pile of skins. The birds all represent different monotypic genera, save one, *Euphonia*, which is represented by two species. A student volunteer is called from the class and asked to simply "classify" the collection.

The student's efforts always result in a series of neatly stacked groups of individual birds, usually lined up in a row. The piles correspond perfectly to the groupings recognized by scientific ornithologists, as well as to those of the Huambisa and Aguaruna Jívaro from whom the specimens were collected. Quite often, the two euphonia species are placed together in a single pile. When asked if the euphonias are "the same," the student will reply that they are different, but seem to "go together" or that "the difference is not very marked, so I put them together." When asked if larger, more inclusive groupings can be formed, the student balks, studies the groups carefully, perhaps separating the tanagers from the barbets and euphonias, but just as often finds it exceedingly difficult to form superordinate categories.

This informal exercise, later redesigned and conducted as a formal experiment by Boster (1987), points out several facts about how humans discern the natural clusters and clumps of biological reality—clusters that are perceivable, one might say, from *distinct perspectives*, or with different *degrees of resolution*. In our informal experiment, one segment of biological reality literally jumps out at the viewer, something like a series of snow-covered mountain peaks on an exaggerated relief map. These peaks represent such obvious perceptual units as to be recognized almost automatically. Recognition of finer distinctions by the process of *differentiation*, as in the case of the eventual discrimination of the two species of *Euphonia*, is possible, though this is markedly secondary and, as we will see later, occurs only after close study. *Generalization*, leading to the formation of higher-order groupings from those natural groupings already instantaneously established, is also possible, but again only with considerable effort.

The evidence to be presented in the materials that follow will build on this feature of the plan of nature and its appreciation by the human observer, stressing the relatively easy recognition of certain groupings of plants and animals that are the most distinctive (groupings that will be called "folk generics") and the more active processes required in the recognition of both superordinate and subordinate categories, (groupings that will be called "life forms" and "folk species"), and that represent diachronically later developments in the codification by humans of the plan of nature. In many ways, our student's recognition of the patterns seen in the set of Amazonian bird species recapitulates a fundamental element in the evolution of ethnobiological classification in general (see Berlin 1972).

1.4 RELATIVIST AND COMPARATIVIST APPROACHES IN ETHNOBIOLOGY

Utilitarian versus intellectualist arguments in ethnobiology form part of a larger dichotomy in anthropological theory that has a long history in the discipline, namely, that of cultural particularism and relativism versus cross-cultural generalization and comparison. Recently, Ellen has characterized this larger debate as a "caricature . . . an entirely false opposition sustained through ideological mystification and polemic" (1986:93). I may have engaged in a bit of polemic in my life, and Ellen himself has demonstrated a good deal of talent in this regard. Neither of us, I would claim, are very good at ideological mystification. As I will show, however, the debate, both in anthropology in general and ethnobiology in particular, is hardly a caricature.

The relativist view, now increasingly in vogue in interpretivist and postmodernist approaches to anthropology, adopts the scientifically nihilistic position that cultures are different in manifold, if not innumerable, ways; that description, if possible at all, provides one with but an imperfect and biased glimpse of individual, unique instances of the human experience; that scientific comparison among cultures is an exercise in vacuous futility.

The contrasting view of the comparativist, while recognizing the broad range of inter- and intra-cultural variation in human societies, nonetheless seeks to discover and document general features of cross-cultural similarities that are widely if not universally shared, and ultimately to develop theoretical explanations that underlie the empirical generalizations one observes. While this search for empirical generalizations may be philosophically uninteresting, even repugnant, to the relativist, there can be little argument that such generalizations present themselves and continue to be sustained by additional new data. To claim, as Ellen does, that "our attempts to tease out convincing domain-specific semantic universals, other than for color [which he discounts as semantically uninteresting] have not yet met with much success" (1986:94), amounts to a gross overstatement.

Focusing more specifically on ethnobiological classification, the major relativist/comparativist split can be seen as a special case of the enduring debate in biological systematics on the reality of the species. Ethnobiologists taking a relativist position ultimately place themselves in the same camp as many population biologists, numerical taxonomists, and theoretical ecologists, who, following a view expressed early by Locke (1848), argue that species are products of the human imagination, mental creations comparable in their reality to any other social or cultural construct.

In ethnobiology, Ellen has been the most vocal advocate of this view, in curious contrast to some of his earlier careful work where the objective nature of species plays a central part in his descriptions (see Ellen, Stimson, and Menzies 1976, 1977). More recently Ellen has declared that "no clear boundaries between species [can be found] by straightforward inference from empirical facts" (1979a:3), and "nature is ultimately a continuity made discontinuous by taxonomic science on the basis of certain selected criteria" (Ellen 1978:154). To argue otherwise is to be caught up in "the confusion of the order of nature with that imposed upon it by man" (Ellen 1979a:1).

On the other side, ethnobiologists holding a comparativist, cross-cultural orientation find themselves aligned with many conservative, orthodox biological systematists who hold that biological species are real.[4] Whether they are the essentialist species of Linnaeus and Ray or the biological species of Mayr's and Simpson's evolutionary biology, these naturally occurring groupings are considered to represent objective, well-defined clusters of plants and animals, even more so in the locally restricted habitat generally exploited by a particular traditional society. These well-defined clusters will not always, of course, exhibit clear-cut boundaries, but will most generally be characterized by a prototypical member surrounded by less typical exemplars of the class. These prototypical centers or foci (following Berlin and Kay 1969) serve as the anchors of the ethnobiological system of classification in terms of their overall salience and perceptual distinctiveness.

For Linnaeus, species reflected the handiwork of God; for Mayr, they are the result of evolution and not the product of the human mind, a position he has defended for over the last half century (cf. Mayr 1942, 1969, 1982). In spite of the insurmountable difficulties in providing a clear-cut definition of the species concept, the undeniable perceptual validity of these biological chunks of reality, readily identified by local natives as well as by visiting taxonomists, led systematists such as Simpson to proclaim "the simple fact [is] that readily recognizable and definable groups of associated organisms do really occur in nature" (1961:57).

The implications of these well-defined and opposing views for ethnobiological classification are clear. For the relativist, the description, or, more accurately, the "creative account" of the ethnobiological knowledge of some particular society, is an end in itself, another ethnographic contribution to the picture of the multifarious cultural diversity of the human species. Since nature is ultimately a "continuum" that is arbitrarily subdivided according to the particular cultural bent of each society, one must be motivated to search for the specific cultural and social factors at work in any particular human group's construction of biological reality. When larger, theoretical issues are tackled, the goal of the relativist is to demonstrate how the contextual and symbolic complexities of sociocultural variation make broader comparative statements impossible or, when some few are arbitrarily wrenched from their cultural

---

[4] Ellen, in apparent approval of Leach's (1976) parody of such biologists as viewing "things juxtaposed in the rigid spaces of cabinets, herbaria, and zoological gardens; not in real life" (Ellen 1979a:2), appears to be involved in a bit of caricaturing himself.

matrix, so trivial and self-evident as to be of little value (cf. Bousfield 1979; Gardner 1976; Ellen 1979a, 1986).

Contrary to this particularist view, a cross-cultural perspective takes descriptions of individual systems as the first and most essential steps in studies of ethnobiological classification, but then adds that these descriptions are but the initial, necessary phase of a larger intellectual inquiry. Since, in any local habitat, biological reality is *not* a continuum but a series of readily definable chunks that can be described in terms of the objective methods of biological field botany and zoology, one is motivated to discover what portions of this reality are cognitively recognized in any particular folk biological system and why. Individual descriptions are then examined from a cross-cultural perspective in the search for general features of both structural and substantive similarities between and among the various systems being compared. To the extent that this examination leads to the formulation of empirical generalizations that are confirmed on the basis of new evidence, steps toward the development of an explanatory theory can be taken, and hypotheses can ultimately be tested.

1.5 General Principles of Ethnobiological Classification, 1966–1976

Perhaps the most important paper in the development of cognitively oriented ethnobiological description is Conklin's "The Lexicographical Treatment of Folk Taxonomies" (1962). In this article, Conklin outlines a number of general structural and semantic features of folk taxonomies that were to be corroborated in the large number of studies in ethnobiology that this work was to inspire, one of the most important being his observation that "the presence of hierarchically arranged . . . folk taxonomies is probably universal" (1962:128).

An even more important impetus in the quest for cross-cultural regularities, however, can be seen in a work that Conklin produced several years earlier, a work that was never published. When I first began to focus on Tzeltal ethnobotany, I had not yet read Conklin's dissertation. One October morning, after having spent several months of ethnobotanical fieldwork in Chiapas, and after having established an abundant correspondence with Conklin dealing with problems of ethnobotanical description, I was pleasantly surprised to receive in the mail a dog-eared xeroxed copy of "The Relation of Hanunóo Culture to the Plant World" (Conklin 1954). As I began to read it, especially the section entitled "Native Classification of Plants," I was suddenly confronted with an unlikely problem in culture history: *transpacific ethnobotanical contact between the Philippines and southern Mexico, direction of cultural transmission not yet determinable!*

I could not fail to notice that Conklin's description of the basic structure of Hanunóo plant classification was strikingly similar in many fundamental respects to that of the Tzeltal Maya (or vice versa, depending on one's focus). Nomenclatural features in the formation of plant names of differing degrees of specificity appeared to be highly regular and essentially identical in the two languages. Plant categories were organized conceptually as a taxonomic hierarchy in both systems, more elaborated in areas of greater cultural significance (e.g., cultivated plants) and relatively shallow in other, less culturally relevant regions. The broad typological similarities between the two systems of ethnobotanical classification were unmistakable and, when pointed out, undebatable—or so I thought at the time. I gradually began to see one of the tasks of ethnobotanical (and later ethnobiological) description and analysis as the delimitation of those areas of similarity among historically unrelated systems of ethnobiological classification and the development of a set of typological principles on the nature of ethnobiological classification in general.

By the late 1960s and early 1970s, a number of papers on the general nature of ethnobiological classification had begun to appear. A recognition of the importance of unnamed taxa in ethnobiological systems of classification was proposed in Berlin, Breedlove, and Raven (1968), although the full implications of these categories for the overall structure of such systems was still unclear and quite poorly understood. The significance of what was then called the "folk genus" was being recognized about this time, and I reported in 1969 on the initial findings in a paper called "Universal Nomenclatural Principles in Folk Science" at the annual meetings of the American Anthropological Association.

Kay's critical paper on the formal taxonomic properties underlying systems of ethnobiological classification appeared in 1971 (Kay 1971). In the same year, the first proposal for universal ethnobiological ranks (earlier called categories, following then standard botanical usage) was published, with an eye to its implications for modern systematics (Raven, Berlin, and Breedlove 1971). This was followed by a paper dealing with the hypothesized historical processes involved in the linguistic recognition of taxa of the several ranks that were claimed to characterize all ethnobiological systems (Berlin 1972).

Finally, comparative efforts to bring together materials from a wide number of ethnobiological sources available at the time led to the statement of general principles of ethnobiological classification and nomenclature outlined in Berlin, Breedlove, and Raven (1973), and exemplified for one complete system in Berlin, Breedlove, and Raven (1974), a statement that was to represent our guiding set of research hypotheses through the next several years.

At about the same time, and to a large extent independently, Ralph Bulmer was himself developing a set of proposals on the nature of ethnozoological classification based on extensive fieldwork among the Kalam (referred to as "Karam" in early works) of the New Guinea highlands (Bulmer 1967, 1968, 1969, 1970, 1974a, 1974b; Bulmer and Menzies 1972–1973; Bulmer and Tyler 1968). In a series of perceptive papers, he argued for the central importance of the "specieme," as well as other features of structure in Kalam ethnozoology. It is appropriate to review briefly Bulmer's suggestions and the proposals of Berlin, Breedlove, and Raven as a preface to a more detailed examination of how the patterns recognized nearly two decades ago must now be restated in light of new evidence and new theoretical insights that have emerged since that time.

Berlin, Breedlove, and Raven's General Principles, 1973

Berlin, Breedlove, and Raven's 1973 paper outlined nine major features of ethnobiological classification and nomenclature that were somewhat immodestly referred to as "principles." With hindsight (and age), it is now apparent to me that a number of these statements were poorly formulated, ambiguous, or simply unclear. I list them in their original order (some slightly paraphrased) and then discuss them in sequence.

1. In all languages it is possible to isolate linguistically recognized groupings of organisms (referred to as taxa) of varying degrees of inclusiveness. Taxa designated by names such as *plant, tree, oak* and *bird, jay, Stellar's jay* are examples of such groupings.

2. Taxa are further grouped into a small number of classes referred to as taxonomic *ethnobiological categories* similar in many respects to the taxonomic ranks of Western zoology and botany. These categories number no more than five or six. In 1973 they were named as follows: *unique beginner, life form, intermediate, generic, specific,* and *varietal.* The rank dubbed "intermediate" was proposed cautiously and tentatively, its validity to be determined only by future research.

3. The five (or six) ethnobiological ranks are arranged hierarchically and taxa assigned to each rank are mutually exclusive. There is but a single taxon of the rank "unique beginner."

4. Taxa of the same ethnobiological rank characteristically, though not invariably, occur at the same taxonomic level in any particular taxonomy, as seen in figure 1.1.

5. In any system of ethnobotanical or ethnozoological classification, the taxon that occurs as a member of the rank "unique beginner" (*plant* or *animal*) is not (normally) named with a single, habitual label.

6. There are usually but a handful of taxa that occur as members of the category 'life form,' ranging from five to ten, and among them they include the majority of all named taxa of lesser rank. These life-form taxa are named by linguistic expressions that are lexically analyzed as primary lexemes, for example, *tree, vine, bird, grass, mammal.*

7. The number of generic taxa ranges around 500 in typical folk taxonomies and most are usually included in one of the life-form taxa. A number of generic taxa may be aberrant, however, and are conceptually seen as unaffiliated (i.e., are not included in any of the life forms). Aberrancy may be due to morphological uniqueness and/or economic importance. Generic taxa are the basic building

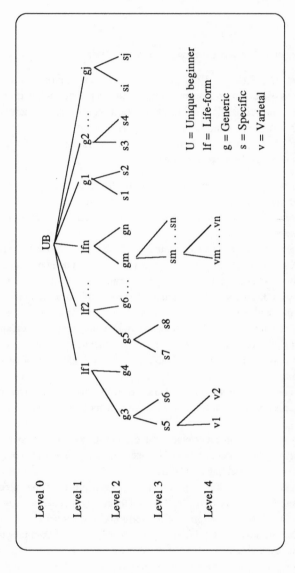

Figure 1.1 Schematic relationship of five of the six proposed universal ethnobiological ranks (*née* categories) and their relative hierarchic positions as shown in an idealized system of ethnobiological classification as proposed by Berlin, Breedlove, and Raven (1973).

blocks of any folk taxonomy, are the most salient psychologically, and are likely to be among the first taxa learned by the child.

8. Specific and varietal taxa are less numerous than generic taxa, and occur in small contrast sets typically of two to three members. Varietal taxa are rare in most folk biological taxonomies. Both specific and varietal forms are distinguished from one another in terms of a few, often verbalizable characters. Finally, taxa of the specific and varietal rank are commonly labelled by secondary (versus primary) lexemes, e.g., *red-headed woodpecker*, *small-mouthed bass*, *white pine*.

9. Intermediate taxa occur as members of the category "intermediate," usually include taxa of generic rank, are rare in folk taxonomies, and are seldom named, leading Berlin, Breedlove, and Raven to refer to them as "covert categories" (1968).

DISCUSSION AND INITIAL REACTIONS

The first principle asserts that groupings of plants and animals constitute a semantic domain or *lexical field* in that (a) these groupings are named, and (b) they are semantically related to one another in some structured, principled fashion. The empirical observation that plants and animals are named in all of the world's languages might well be considered a truism and surely is not a topic for much discussion. The claim that these named taxa constitute a semantic domain or lexical field, however obvious this might seem at first glance, has instead generated debate. In the first place, as noted in principle 5, the domain of 'plant' or 'animal' is often not named. A number of critics were skeptical of allowing for the existence of such unnamed categories and for semantic domains to be established on this negative linguistic evidence alone (see Brown 1974, in reply to Berlin, Breedlove, and Raven 1968, and rebutted in Berlin 1974).

A more controversial aspect of principle 1 concerns the claim that plant and animal taxa are systematically related to one another in terms of the taxonomic relation of set inclusion (e.g., tree > oak, bird > woodpecker, fish > bass). A number of critics have suggested that "taxonomic structure" is probably an inappropriate and empirically unjustifiable way to speak about the semantic structure of ethnobiological systems of classification (see Hunn 1976, 1982; Ellen 1986; Randall 1976). Others (e.g., Hunn and French 1984) have suggested that, while taxonomic relationships may be found in ethnobiological systems of classification, hierarchic ordering is not the primary semantic principle uniting the taxa in any particular folk system.

Principles 2, 3, and 4 assert that plant and animal taxa are distributed in a finite set of ethnobiological ranks. (The term "category" was used originally in 1973, following traditional botanical usage for the recognized levels of the Linnaean hierarchy. "Rank," the preferred term in zoology, was subsequently employed and is used here because it is less ambiguous). A finite number of six ranks was proposed, although it was not claimed that all folk systems would exhibit taxa at each rank (cf., "The number of ranks . . . is probably not more than six and not less than three [kingdom, life form, and generic]," Berlin 1978a:11). It had been claimed earlier (Berlin 1972) that the members of taxa of each rank may develop historically in a definite developmental progression and that it would be possible to find some languages lacking taxa of a particular rank as a reflection of form of subsistence (e.g., the absence of taxa of varietal rank in societies of foragers).

The remaining five principles outlined particular nomenclatural, biological, taxonomic, and psychological characteristics of ethnobiological taxa at each of the six proposed ranks. These characteristics play a major role in assigning taxa to their respective ranks in any particular system. As with the proposal for the recognition of rank in the first place, a number of the characteristics associated with taxa of different ranks have also been controversial, for example: Are taxa of the rank of folk genera special in that they are inherently of greater psychological salience than taxa of some other rank (Dougherty 1978)? Can nomenclatural features serve as a near perfect guide to taxonomic structure (Bulmer 1974a)? Or, does the presence of a folk generic taxon necessarily imply its subdivision into folk species (Bulmer 1974a; Panoff 1972)? These reservations, along with others that will be discussed in subsequent chapters, are best characterized as differences of interpretation of the data by myself and others, sometimes due to poorly formulated presentations of mine. Other major reservations, however, call into question the whole comparative enterprise (Ellen 1986; Sillitoe 1983).

Bulmer's Principles, 1974

At about the same time that my colleagues and I were developing our proposals on ethnobiological classification, Ralph Bulmer was independently elaborating a set of principles on folk biology that are similar in a number of respects to those outlined above. Although Bulmer (1974a) had reservations about a number of the propositions stated in Berlin (1972) and Berlin, Breedlove, and Raven (1973), the fundamental issues raised in his own work are highly consonant with those of our own, and provided the first independent corroboration of the striking similarities among ethnobiological systems of classification.

Furthermore, while Bulmer based his observations on data primarily drawn from his mainly ethnozoological research experience among the Kalam of New Guinea, it is clear that he envisaged his proposals as completely general. I believe that part of his convictions derived from the striking parallels he found between his own personal understanding of what he was to call "natural taxonomy" as a classic "old fashioned . . . naturalist and trophy-collector" (Bulmer 1974b:98) and the understanding of the Kalam—parallels that could be explained only because humans everywhere recognized nature's structure in essentially the same way.

Bulmer outlined five major "principle[s] of natural taxonomy," as follows:

1. [Natural taxonomies] consist of hierarchically arranged sets of contrasting taxa which are generally, though not necessarily entirely, mutually exclusive (i.e., taxa of equivalent order do not overlap in content, or overlap only marginally) (1974b:94).

Bulmer's first principle coincides closely with principles 1, 2, and 3 of Berlin, Breedlove, and Raven (1973). In both proposals, taxa are mutually exclusive and, most importantly, given the objections of critics that were to follow, are organized taxonomically.

2. All but certain lowest order and highest order taxa are 'natural' . . . in that they are perceived as actually . . . multidimensional . . . and . . . 'general' or perhaps even 'abstract,' in the sense that they are used in many different contexts and indeed spontaneously in the context of discussion of their domain in the abstract, i.e., without immediate reference to utilitarian or other particular contexts (ibid.:95).

This second principle coincides with Berlin, Breedlove, and Raven in that both recognize the centrality of a selected set of taxa that are natural and form the core of the taxonomy. Bulmer refers to these multidimensional taxa as *speciemes*, while I and others prefer to use the term *folk generics* for reasons that will be fully justified shortly. Bulmer's second principle furthermore anticipates the emerging debate on the intellectualist-utilitarian bases of ethnobiological classification and comes down squarely on the side of the intellect, a position elaborated in Berlin (1972, 1976a) as well as in Berlin, Breedlove, and Raven (1973).

3. The names applied to taxa are in a high proportion of cases exclusive to that domain (ibid.:95).

This third principle adds support to the criteria of specialized ethnobiological vocabulary proposed by Berlin, Breedlove, and Raven (1973) as evidence for the recognition of the domain of 'plant' or 'animal' as legitimate cognitive categories even in the absence of a name indicating that domain.

4. The language used in discussion of the relationship of taxa of similar order (i.e., within the same contrast set) is the language of kinship and descent—'brothers', 'one father', 'one lineage' (ibid.:95).

While this is not mentioned specifically as one of the principles outlined in Berlin, Breedlove, and Raven (1973), we noted that Tzeltal informants often referred to several conceptually related taxa in the same contrast set as 'relatives' or 'companions'. Just as often, Aguaruna and Huambisa Jívaro informants stated that plant X belonged "together" with plant Y in that they were 'companions', 'brothers' or 'members of the same family' (see Berlin 1976a; Berlin, Boster, and O'Neill 1981; Berlin, Swift, and Stewart, in prep.).

> 5. Such totemic . . . identifications as exist are phrased, if categories rather than individual plants or animals . . . are concerned, in terms of taxa within this 'natural' system (Bulmer 1974b:95).

The exploration of Bulmer's fifth principle has not been carried out cross-culturally to my knowledge. With the exception of his last proposition, Bulmer's principles fit nicely with those offered earlier by Berlin, Breedlove, and Raven and reinforce their plausibility. Nonetheless, neither of these early proposals is now sufficient to characterize the general complexity of ethnobiological classification. The original generalizations must be restated, qualified, and revised in light of new data that have been collected over the last two decades. It is to this restatement that I now turn.

1.6 BAND-AIDS OR TUNE-UP? GENERAL PRINCIPLES, 1992

In any new summary of the patterned ways in which people think and talk about plants and animals, it is important that a clear distinction be made between the *psychological conceptualization* of plants and animals and the *linguistic reflections* of this underlying conceptual structure. This is a difficult issue to deal with in that our best entry into a society's system of classification is through language; ethnobiological classification is most easily recognized through the linguistic web of ethnobiological nomenclature (cf. Frake 1962). Nonetheless, I have organized the current reformulation in terms of those principles that reflect general patterns relating to the *categorization of plants and animals* as distinct from those principles that reflect general *nomenclatural rules for the naming of plants and animals.*[5]

I outline in the following sections twelve general principles that characterize a wide number of ethnobiological systems of classification from diverse parts of the world. Seven specify regularities of ethnobiological categorization and five refer to patterns of ethnobiological nomenclature. Some are refinements of those proposed earlier, having been corroborated in their basic form in a number of subsequent studies; they are restated here in what I believe to be a more concise and less ambiguous form. Other principles are new, reflecting modifications required by additional data that were not available earlier or, if

---

[5] It would be more accurate to speak of empirical generalizations rather than principles, inasmuch as the latter suggests the appropriateness of some formal logical exposition. While this might be possible, and has been attempted for ethnobiological categorization (not nomenclature) by both Kay (1971, 1975) and Hunn (1977), and before them by Gregg (1954) and Buck and Hull (1966) for biological taxonomy, I am not able to offer my own formal treatment, nor do I think that such an effort, even by someone more qualified to do so, would add much to the basic presentation. I will continue to use the term "principle" in its commonsense usage of "general or natural tendency or quality."

available, not understood by me clearly enough at the time to incorporate them in the first formulation. I reiterate that these proposals are to be considered as hypotheses for testing against new empirical data. Their usefulness will be ultimately determined by how well they allow for the ready description and interpretation of as yet undescribed systems of ethnobiological classification. Nonetheless, I believe it noteworthy that the principles be so few in absolute number inasmuch as their applicability is claimed to be totally general.

Ethnobiological Categorization

1. *Traditional societies residing in a local habitat exhibit a system of ethnobiological classification for a smaller portion of the actual plant and animal species found in the same area. This subset is comprised of the most salient plant and animal species in that local habitat, where salience can be understood as a function of biological distinctiveness.* (Following traditional biological usage, recognized groupings of species of whatever degree of inclusiveness will be referred to as *taxa*.)

Principle 1 codifies the obvious empirical observation that in folk systems of ethnobiological classification not all the potentially knowable species of any particular habitat are given conceptual recognition. While Western science may in turn have failed as yet to provide, in some instances, complete faunal or floral inventories of the living organisms in given local habitats (say, some area of the Amazon rain forest), research employing the methods of modern field botany and zoology make such a task possible if not practical.

Principle 1 furthermore implies that it is theoretically possible to predict which species of plants and animals, of the thousands that may be present, will be given conceptual recognition in the folk system (cf. Hunn 1977, who has made a similar proposal). The notion of the "biological distinctiveness" of some taxon, *x*, is most readily understood as a function of both its *evolutionary divergence* and its *internal phenotypic variation*.

2. *The categorization of plant and animal taxa into a general system of ethnobiological classification is based primarily on observed morphological and behavioral affinities and differences among the recognized taxa.*

Principle 2 asserts that the organizing principle of any ethnobiological system of classification will be people's cognitive assessments of the gross perceptual resemblances observed among classes of organisms. While a number of additional organizing principles are at work in conjunction with those of the recognized perceptual affinities of plants and animals, for example, pharmacological properties in medicine, economic significance as food, symbolic salience in ritual, these features relating to the cultural evaluation of biological taxa are secondary in almost all systems for which we have complete descriptions.

3. *Recognized plant and animal taxa are grouped into ever more inclusive groups to form a hierarchic (taxonomic) structure comprised of a small number of taxonomic ranks.*

Principle 3 states that in ethnobiological systems of classification, in a way comparable to that of Western taxonomy, degree of affinity is expressed hierarchically, a reflection of the empirical fact that *biological taxa exhibit varying degrees of inclusiveness* and that human observers recognize this inherent structure. The taxonomic ordering of classes of plants and animals is surely one of the primary features of biological classification in general, having been noted first explicitly by Aristotle and Theophrastus, and has been recognized by all systematic biologists since that time.

Of course, other logical relationships have been described for the conceptual organization of living things in folk systems of classification. Hunn and French (1984) outline the importance of the relationship of coordination in Sahaptin ethnobotanical classification. However, such systems are rare, and in any case do not supplant the notion of natural taxonomy.

4. *Recognized ethnobiological taxa are taxonomically distributed as members of six mutually exclusive ethnobiological ranks comparable in content to the ranks of Western zoology and botany. Taxa of each rank share similar degrees of internal variation as well as being separated from each other by comparably sized perceptual gaps. The six ranks, in descending order of taxonomic inclusiveness, are the* **kingdom, life-form, intermediate, generic, specific,** *and* **varietal.**

Principle 4 follows from 3 in that it recognizes that the decreasing resemblance found between and among groupings of plants and animals, especially those in any restricted habitat, is not psychologically perceived as a continuum. Rather, taxa of rank *x* are, in the main, thought of as representing comparably sized portions of ethnobiological reality.

The structural relationships of the five major ethnobiological ranks (for clarity's sake excluding that of varietal) and their respective taxa are seen schematically in figure 1.2, which illustrates the taxonomic relations among taxa of different ranks as well as the horizontal affinity relationships of taxa of the same rank. For purposes of exposition, the same names will be used to refer to individual taxa as well as the particular rank of which those taxa are members.

5. *Across all folk systems of ethnobiological classification, taxa of each rank exhibit systematic similarities in their relative numbers and biological content.*[6]

[6] Linguistic patterns of nomenclature for taxa of each ethnobiological rank will be discussed in a subsequent section. Taxa are also likely to exhibit differential patterns of psychological salience, a parameter given considerable importance in the general principles set forth in the early 1970s. The current restatement of principles treats matters of psychological salience in a more discursive fashion, since our measures of psychological salience of ethnobiological taxa are, at best, hardly adequate.

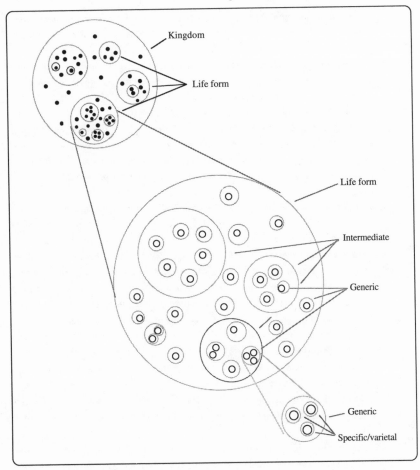

Figure 1.2 Highly schematic telescoping representation of the five primary ethnobio-logical ranks and their respective taxa. *Biological species* are indicated by small black circles. *Ethnobiological taxa* are indicated by faint gray circles. Folk generics are members of one of the life-form taxa but may also be included by no taxon other than of the kingdom. Relative position is meant to convey degree of affinity, where closer proximity signifies greater similarity. Conventions used in this figure are described fully in this chapter.

a. *The most numerous taxa in folk biological taxonomies will be taxa of generic rank. In both ethnobotanical and ethnozoological systems of classification, the number of folk generics reaches an upper limit at about five hundred to six hundred taxa in systems typical of tropical horticulturalists. Roughly 80 per-cent of folk generic taxa in typical folk systems are monotypic and include no taxa of lesser rank. While most folk generics are taxonomically included in taxa of life-form rank (see b below), a small number is conceptually unaffil-*

iated due to morphological uniqueness or, in some cases, economic importance. Generic taxa are among the first taxa learned by children as they acquire their society's system of biological classification.

b. *Taxa of the life-form rank mark a small number of highly distinctive morphotypes based on the recognition of the strong correlation of gross morphological structure and ecological adaptation. Life-form taxa are broadly polytypic and incorporate the majority of taxa of lesser rank.*

c. *Taxa of intermediate rank are found most commonly as members of life-form taxa, and are comprised of small numbers of folk generics that show marked perceptual similarities with one another. Data are inadequate to indicate the relative numbers of such taxa in actual systems of ethnobiological classification.*

d. *Taxa of the rank of folk species partition folk generic taxa into two or more members; in those systems where they occur, folk varietals further subdivide folk species. Subgeneric taxa are less numerous than folk generics in all systems examined to date. There is some evidence to suggest that the recognition of subgeneric taxa is loosely associated with a society's form of subsistence. The conceptual recognition of subgeneric taxa appears to be motivated in part by cultural considerations, in that a major proportion refer to domesticated species of plants and animals. There is some evidence that foraging societies have poorly developed or lack entirely taxa of specific rank. No foraging society will exhibit taxa of varietal rank.*

e. *The rank of kingdom is unique in that it includes but a single member. Taxonomically, the kingdom incorporates all taxa of lesser rank. For ethnobotanical classification, the kingdom corresponds approximately to the biological taxon* Plantae; *in ethnozoology the corresponding biological taxon is* Animalia.

6. *Taxa of generic and subgeneric rank exhibit a specifiable internal structure where some members of a taxon, x, are thought of as being more prototypical of that taxon than others (i.e., are the best examples of the taxon). Taxa of intermediate and life-form rank may also show prototypicality effects. Prototypicality may be due to a number of factors, the most important of which appear to be taxonomic distinctiveness (as inferred from the scientific classification of the organisms in any local habitat), frequency of occurrence, and cultural importance (i.e., salience).*

Earlier principles have focused on the external relationships that hold among taxa of any ethnobiological taxonomy. Principle 6 makes a claim about the nature of the internal structure of recognized taxa, and complements recent work in cognitive psychology on prototype theory in which comparable properties of human categorization have been discussed (see Rosch 1973, 1977, 1978, 1981; Rosch, Mervis, et al. 1975; Lakoff 1973, 1987). The observation that some members of a biological taxon are better examples of the category than others has a long history in philosophy and linguistics as well as biological systematics. In the 1950s Max Black moved to abandon traditional set theoretic definitions of semantic classes specifically in his discussion of natural kinds. Black noted that the object of a semantic definition of biological categories "is to have an extensive range of variation grouped around some *clear cases*. . . . If we examine instances of the application of any biological term, we shall find ranges, not classes—specimens [i.e., individuals or species] arranged according to the degree of their variation from certain typical or 'clear' cases" (Black 1954:25–26, 28).

Chafe elaborated a similar set of ideas in the early 1960s as part of his ingenious but unfortunately largely ignored theory of semantic structure. Chafe envisaged the universe of experience as "an infinite space with an infinite number of potential units and potential patterns" (Chafe 1965:24). Within this space he recognized "target areas" that represented the foci of important experience: "Whatever is close to one of these target areas is significant; whatever is far from any of them correspondingly lacks significance. We can think of such target areas as the manifestation of semiological units. They are multidimensional clusterings of particular experiences around certain nuclei [i.e., foci]" (ibid.:24).

In biological classification, a recognition of the importance of prototypical definition can be traced to the so-called *type concept* of classical taxonomy (see Greene 1983; Mayr 1942, 1982; Simpson 1961). A modern statement of this principle is found in Cowan, who notes that for any taxon one can recognize a "[proto]type acting as the centre of the unit . . . the less typical individuals being grouped about the [proto]type, their distance from the centre being inversely proportional to their community with the [proto]type" (Cowan 1962:437).

In ethnobiology, Berlin, Breedlove, and Raven first described similar properties of folk botanical taxa in their treatment of Tzeltal ethnobotany, noting that "some plant [species] are clearly seen as focal members of a category . . . ; other plants may be within the boundaries of the category . . . but still not be seen as the best example of the category in question" (Berlin, Breedlove, and Raven 1974:56).

7. *Of those taxa recognized in any system of ethnobiological classification, a substantial majority corresponds closely in content to taxa recognized independently by Western botany and zoology. In comparison with taxa of other ranks, those of the rank of lifeform show the lowest degree of correspondence in their biological content with recognized taxa of Western biology, taxa of subgeneric rank greater correspondence, and taxa of generic rank the highest correspondence. Taxa of intermediate rank correspond rather closely with portions of taxa recognized by Western science at the rank of family. For the higher vascular plants and larger vertebrate animals, generic taxa often approximate in their content the genera*

and species of Western scientific biology. For the smaller vascular plants, lower cryptogams, smaller vertebrates, and many invertebrates, the correspondence of folk generic taxa more closely approximates scientific taxa of the ranks of family, order, or class.

Principle 7 makes the claim that for species of plants and animals in any restricted habitat, ethnobiological and biological systems of classification will be highly similar, in that each selects essentially the same groupings for conceptual recognition. It is theoretically true, of course, as Hull has pointed out, that "there are indefinitely many ways of describing the patterns of variation in nature, and in each way there are indefinitely many patterns to be recognized" (Hull 1970:45). However, the empirical comparative data between Western scientific and folk scientific systems of biological classification, as well as among the folk systems themselves, point to a single, preferred ordering that is primary and fundamental in humans' appreciation of nature's plan, lending credence to Gilmour and Walters's assertion that in the classification of living things "one way is more natural than any other" (Gilmour and Walters 1964:4–5). This plan is, in the main, so striking in its presentation that human observers are highly constrained in the ways that they may choose to deal with it. Biological reality allows for few options.

Ethnobiological Nomenclature

While the principles of *ethnobiological categorization* deal with the conceptual organization of plants and animals into a coherent cognitive structure, principles of *ethnobiological nomenclature* focus on those patterns that underlie the naming of plants and animals in systems of ethnobiological classification. In Western scientific biology, nomenclatural concerns have become essentially legalistic, pedantic, and tedious. Many systematists treat nomenclatural problems as a necessary evil. As Simpson notes, biological nomenclature is merely the labeling of the taxa of classification and is essentially arbitrary. It provides "a way for writing and talking about [plants and] animals, . . . but . . . has no scientific interest in itself" (Simpson 1961:34).

The study of *ethno*biological nomenclature, however, is quite a different story. One of the goals of the present monograph is to demonstrate that ethnobiological nomenclature represents a natural system of naming that reveals much about the way people *conceptualize* the living things in their environment.

The following principles claim that the formal linguistic structure of plant and animal names is basically similar in all languages. Furthermore, the linguistic properties of plant and animal names may indicate much about the cognitive status of the taxa to which they refer. There is growing evidence that suggests a much closer, nonarbitrary assignment of plant and animal names to their respective referents than had heretofore been suspected. It now seems likely that salient morphological and behavioral features of plant and animal species are often encoded directly in the ethnobiological names used to refer to these species. It will be suggested that this nonarbitrary, iconic assignment of names to plants and animals may have adaptive significance because such terms will be less difficult to learn, easier to remember as well as to utilize, thus reducing the cognitive effort required of peoples of nonliterate traditions who must control rather sizable ethnobiological vocabularies. (See chapter 6 for a fuller treatment of these topics.) Finally, a comparative analysis of the mapping of names onto taxa has revealed that, while a name is an unambiguous indicator of the existence of some particular taxon, absence of a label does not necessarily imply the absence of a category. These principles are stated as follows:

1. *Intermediate taxa and the taxon marking* 'plant' *or* 'animal' *at the rank of kingdom are generally not named in systems of ethnobiological classification. Some small number of taxa of life-form rank may also be covert, that is, unnamed.*

Principle 1 codifies the empirical observation that the kingdom, as well as most intermediate taxa, are nomenclaturally distinct in that the taxa occurring as members of these ranks are usually not labeled. There is, furthermore, mounting evidence from recent studies that some life-form taxa may also lack linguistic designation. On first reading, claiming the existence of unnamed categories may appear to be counterintuitive and highly improbable and leads immediately to questions about how the conceptual validity of such categories could be established. The supporting evidence for these observations will be provided in chapter 4. It must suffice for now to point out that the data are drawn from systems of ethnobiological classification found in quite different parts of the world that have been carefully studied.

However, when taxa that are usually covert are named, it is common that these terms will be polysemous, that is, will have two or more senses. Examples are Hanunóo *kayu* 'tree' and 'plant in general', and Aguaruna *yámpits* 'white-winged dove' and 'dove in general'. This points to the phenomenon of prototypicality in higher-order categories outlined in classification principle 6.

2. *In ethnobiological lexicons, the names for plant and animal taxa are of two basic structural types that can be referred to as* <u>primary</u> *and* <u>secondary plant and animal names</u>. *Each structural type can be distinguished on the basis of linguistic, semantic, and taxonomic properties.*

   a. *Linguistically,* <u>primary plant and animal names</u> *may be simple (e.g.,* **louse, frog, oak**) *or complex (e.g.,* **skunk cabbage, forget-me-not, catfish**). *In contrast,* <u>secondary plant and animal names</u> *(exemplified by words such as* **sugar maple, large-mouthed bass,** *and* **Stellar's jay**) *are always linguistically complex.*

b. *Semantic and taxonomic criteria show linguistically complex primary names to be of two structural types, productive and unproductive. Productive forms include a constituent that labels a taxon superordinate to the form in question* (e.g., **catfish, bluebird, bullfrog**). *In contrast, none of the constituents of unproductive forms marks a category superordinate to the form in question* (e.g., **prairie dog** is not a 'kind of dog', **silverfish** is not a 'kind of fish', **buckeye** is not a 'kind of eye').

c. *Secondary plant and animal names are linguistically complex expressions, one of whose constituents indicates a category superordinate to the form in question* (e.g., **red oak, fox terrier**). *However, secondary forms differ from primary productive expressions in that the former occur, with predictable exceptions, only in contrast sets whose members share a constituent that labels the taxon that immediately includes them.*

Nomenclatural principle 2 capitalizes on the important semantic notion of *contrast set* first proposed by Conklin (1962) and Frake (1962), but only later given a formal definition by Kay (1966, 1971). Kay defines two taxa as being members of the same contrast set if they are immediately included in the same superordinate taxon (e.g., *Monterrey pine* and *Ponderosa pine* are members of the contrast set *pine*). Knowledge of the contrast set of which a particular taxon is a member is crucial in determining the structural type of that taxon's name. Thus, *sugar maple* can be shown unambiguously to be a secondary plant name in that (a) one of the name's constituents, *maple*, is also the name of the taxon that immediately dominates the category labeled by the expression *sugar maple*, and (b) *sugar maple* occurs in a contrast set whose members are also labeled by names that include that same constituent (*red maple, Norway maple, Oregon maple, vine maple, . . . n-maple*). In contrast, complex primary names such as *tulip tree* or *catfish* do not show this distributional pattern. These expressions occur as the names for taxa in contrast sets some of whose members are labeled by simple primary names such as *hickory, ash*, and *poplar* (all kinds of *tree*), or *bass, crappie*, and *carp* (all kinds of *fish*).

Principle 2 was first recognized explicitly by Conklin (1962) in discussing the properties of semantic fields in general. However, in Conklin's analysis all linguistically complex forms are recognized as *composite lexemes*, without regard to their semantic or taxonomic status. Thus, the expressions *tulip tree* and *silver maple* are, in his characterization, structurally and semantically identical. Principle 2 shows that the two forms are only superficially similar.

It is important to note that principle 2 applies to the habitually necessary components of the labels by which ethnobiological taxa are named. It might be claimed that *hickory (Carya* spp.) can also be referred to as *hickory tree*, and that *ash (Fraxinus* spp.) can be called *ash tree*. While such expanded names do occur in some dialects of American English, the presence of the constituent *tree* is not necessary. On the other hand, one cannot refer to the tree *Liliodendron tulipifera* as *tulip*; the full form *tulip tree* is obligatory as the taxon's habitual label. In contrast, secondary names may be abbreviated, and often are, for example, *winesap apple* can often be referred to simply as *winesap* (cf. Conklin 1962:122).[7]

3. *Generic taxa, and those life-form and intermediate taxa that are labeled, are generally labeled by primary plant and animal names, while, with specifiable and notable exceptions, subgeneric taxa are labeled by secondary names.*

Principle 3 codifies the empirical generalization that the rank of a taxon predictably governs the ways in which that taxon gets named. Thus, primary names mark the American folk biological life forms *bird, fish, tree*, and *vine*. Generic taxa are also labeled by primary names, as the following examples illustrate: *snipe, woodcock, oak, redbud, jackass, cockroach, ironwood, breadfruit, tapeworm, bedbug, earwig, mudpuppy*, and *bullfrog*.

Subgeneric taxa are generally labeled by secondary names, as seen in the forms *blue spruce, spotted salamander, California quail*, and *band-tailed pigeon*. These expressions are structurally identical to the binomials of standard scientific nomenclature, which are comprised of a *generic* appellation and a *specific* epithet. As will be described below (principle 4) there are notable exceptions to the application of secondary names for subgeneric taxa. These exceptions are explainable partially but not totally in terms of a set of additional abbreviation rules based on considerations of prototypicality and cultural importance.

4. *Under certain conditions, subgeneric taxa will be labeled by primary plant and animal names. The empirical data indicate two widespread conditions that can be readily understood in terms of general principles of ethnobiological classification.*

   a. *A subgeneric taxon, x, may be labeled with a primary name when x is thought of as the prototype of the genus. In these cases, the primary name used to designate the prototypical taxon will be polysemous with the name of the superordinate generic taxon. Nonetheless, in situations of discourse where the prototypical subgeneric taxa must be unambiguously distinguished from other congeneric taxa, the prototypical taxon will be named by a secondary name containing a modifying expression that might be most appropriately glossed as 'genuine', 'real', 'original', or 'ideal-type'.*

[7] This observation should be taken as indicative of a general tendency and not as without exception. In rural Oklahoma, one might often hear expressions such as, "You shoulda seen the 40 pound *cat* that ol' Billy Bob Hallpaine caught in Wild Horse Creek last night," in obvious reference to *catfish*.

b. *A subgeneric taxon, y, may be labeled with a primary name when y is a plant or animal species of major cultural importance. In such cases the name used to designate the subgeneric taxon will be linguistically distinct from the label of its superordinate.*

Principle 4 outlines two well-documented conditions under which subgeneric taxa are not labeled by secondary names. The first condition is satisfied when one of the subgeneric taxa of some generic category is considered to be *prototypical*, for any of a number of reasons. In most cases, the primary name used to designate the prototype is polysemous with that of its superordinate generic. (See chapter 3 for a fuller discussion of this principle.)

The second condition under which primary names are found to label specific taxa occurs when the biological species involved are imbued with high cultural importance. Examples from the Aguaruna Jívaro classification of manioc varieties illustrates this situation, as shown in table 1.1.

While principle 4 accounts for the nomenclatural properties of subgeneric names in a wide range of distinct ethnobiological systems of classification, a number of studies describe the labeling of subgeneric taxa with primary names that satisfy neither the condition of prototypicality nor that of cultural importance (see especially Headland 1981, 1983, for the Agta Negritos of the Philippines; Hays 1979, 1983 for the Ndumba of highland New Guinea; and P. M.

TABLE 1.1

Examples of Aguaruna Folk Specific Manioc Taxa (*Manihot esculenta*)

Folk Species Labeled with Secondary Names	*Folk Species Labeled with Primary Names**
yakía mama 'high manioc'	*puyám* 'thin (one)'
shímpi máma 'Shimpi's manioc'	*suhíknum* 'stingy stick'
yusanía máma 'Yusania's manioc'	*kanús* 'Santiago River'
piampía máma 'sandpiper manioc'	*suhítak* 'stingy (one)'
saké máma 'Euterpe palm manioc'	*unáim* 'waterfall'
suín máma 'dark manioc'	*chikím* 'maranth'
ipák máma 'achiote manioc'	*shámping* 'small toad'
kángka máma 'boca chico manioc'	*dapím* 'snake'

Source: Data from Boster 1980:62–65 and personal files.

* There is some evidence that several of the monomial terms for manioc may, in fact, be abbreviations. Boster reports that "most of the monomial Aguaruna manioc cultivar names can be analyzed as contractions of secondary lexemes. . . . For example, *shímpi máma* . . . was used alternately with *shimpím* and *dápi máma* was an alternative of *dapím*. The final 'm' in both *shimpím* and *dapím* seems to be a contraction of *máma*" (Boster 1980:60). The total number of specific manioc taxa ranges upwards to one hundred forms, although no one individual knows all folk species.

Taylor 1990 for the Tobelo of the Moluccas in Indonesia). Possible explanations for these nomenclatural facts will be discussed in chapter 3.

5. *Names for plants and animals commonly allude metaphorically to some typical morphological, behavioral, ecological, or qualitative characteristic feature of their referents.*

This principle codifies a growing body of empirical observations on the non-arbitrariness or iconicity of plant and animal names (more extensively discussed in chapter 6). Primary names of all subtypes, which on first analysis might appear to be semantically opaque, often reveal metaphorical associations of the name with its referent. In ethnozoological vocabulary, this feature is commonly associated with onomatopoeic representations of typical vocalizations of a particular animal species; morphological features are often focused on in both ethnozoological and ethnobotanical vocabulary. Examples are given in table 1.2. In addition, a substantial portion of complex primary names is formed on the basis of analogy with another generic name that labels a conceptually related taxon. This highly productive process might be called *generic name extension*. Examples of primary plant and animal names formed by analogy can be seen in table 1.3. In secondary names, the modifying constituent often marks obvious morphological features of color, shape, size, texture, smell, or taste, or ecological features of habitat or presumed origin, as seen in table 1.4.

1.7 SUMMARY OF GENERAL PRINCIPLES

A summary of the proposed twelve general principles of ethnobiological categorization and nomenclature can be stated as follows.

I. *Categorization*

1. In ethnobiological systems of classification, conceptual recognition will be given to a subset of the existing flora and fauna. This subset will be comprised of the biologically most distinctive (hence, salient) species of the local habitat.
2. Ethnobiological systems of classification are based primarily on the affinities that humans observe among the taxa themselves, quite independent of the actual or potential cultural significance of these taxa.
3. Ethnobiological systems of classification are organized conceptually into a shallow hierarchic structure.
4. Recognized taxa will be distributed among from four to six mutually exclusive ethnobiological ranks, with taxa of each rank sharing similar degrees of internal variation and separated from each other by comparably sized perceptual gaps. The six universal ranks are the kingdom, life form, intermediate, generic, specific, and varietal. There is some evidence that foraging societies have poorly

TABLE 1.2
Examples of Primary Names Indicating Onomatopoeic Association of Name and
Striking Character or Feature of Biological Referent

Aguaruna Jívaro of Peru

sáásá	'Hoatzin' *Opisthocomus hoazin*, where name of bird is onomatopoeic—[sã.sã.sã.sã] 'the bird's call']
káyák	'Red-bellied macaw' *Ara manilata*, where name of bird is onomatopoeic—[kãyák.kãyák.kãyák.kãyák]

Aguaruna and Huambisa Jívaro

suákarep	'Frog species' *Hyla lanciformis*, onomatopoeic representation of name—[suákarep. karép. karép. suákarep. karép. karép]
kuwãu	'Frog species' *Phyllomedusa tomopterna* known for its call [kuwãu.wãu.wãu. kuwãu.wãu.wãu]

Sources: For *sáásá* and *káyák*, Berlin and O'Neill 1981. For *suákarep* and *kuwãu*, personal data files.

TABLE 1.3
Examples of Pairs of Primary Names Illustrating Generic Name Extension

Tzeltal of Mexico

k'ewex	'Custard apple' *Annona cherimola*
k'ewex max	Lit. 'monkey's custard apple' *A. reticulata* (a smaller, less desirable *Annona)*
tzu'um	'A large grass' *Lasiacis divaricata*
tzu'um ak	Lit.'*tzu'um* grass' *Panicum* spp. (a smaller similar grass)
ch'aben	'A small herb' *Crotalaria longirostrata*
ch'aben ch'o	Lit. 'rat's *ch'aben*' *C. maypurensis* (a smaller, inconspicuous herb of the same genus)

Aguaruna Jívaro of Peru

kéngke	'New World yam' *Dioscorea trifida*
kengkengkéng	Wild species of *Dioscorea*
inchín	'Sweet potato' *Ipomoea batatas*
inchínchin	Wild species of *Ipomoea*
papái	'Papaya' *Carica papaya*
papáinim	Wild species of the genus *C. macrocarpa*

Sources: For Tzeltal, Berlin, Breedlove, and Raven 1974. For Aguaruna Jívaro, Berlin, personal data files.

TABLE 1.4
Examples of Secondary Lexemes Exhibiting Semantically Productive Modifying
Constituent

Tzeltal of Mexico	
tzajal wirin	Lit. 'red *wirin*' *Pyrocephalus rubinus* (vermilion flycatcher) [marked red color]
ijk'al wirin	Lit. 'black *wirin*' *Sayornis nigricans* (black phoebe) [marked black color]
Secoya of Ecuador	
suara bia	Lit. '*Prochilodus*like *bia*' *Capsicum annuum* (metaphorical reference to shape of fruit with that of the fish, *Prochilodus* sp.)
wea bia	Lit. 'maize pepper' *Capsicum annuum* ("name refers to similarity of size between kernel of maize and the fruit of this cultivar")
Huambisa Jívaro of Peru	
intásh karachám	Lit. 'hair *karachám*' *Monthichthys filamentosus* (long-bodied armored catfish, modifier focuses on distinctive hairlike appendage extending from the tail)
wichí karachám	Lit. 'tree trunk in river *karachám*' *Rhineloricaria* spp. (long-bodied armored catfish, modifier focuses on habitat in which the species is found)

Sources: For Tzeltal, Hunn 1977:xxv. For Secoya, Vichers and Plowman 1984. For Huambisa Jívaro, Berlin, Swift, and Stewart, in prep.

developed, or lack entirely, taxa of specific rank. No foraging society will exhibit taxa of varietal rank.

5. Across systems of ethnobiological classification, taxa of each rank show marked similarities as to their relative numbers and biological ranges.

   a. Taxa of generic rank are the most numerous in every system, with rare exceptions number no more than five hundred classes in each kingdom, are largely monotypic (roughly 80 percent in typical systems), and, with notable exceptions, are included in taxa of life-form rank.

   b. Taxa of life-form rank are few in number, probably no more than ten or fifteen, are broadly polytypic, and include among them the majority of taxa of lesser rank. Substantively, life-form taxa designate a small number of morphotypes of plants and animals that share obvious gross patterns of stem habit and bodily form.

   c. Taxa of intermediate rank generally group small numbers of generic taxa on the basis of their perceived affinities in overall morphology (and behavior). Intermediate taxa are included in taxa of life-form rank.

d. Specific taxa subdivide generic taxa but are fewer in absolute number. Folk varietals are rare; when they occur, they subdivide folk species. Unlike taxa of superordinate rank, a major portion of subgeneric taxa in ethnobotanical systems of classification is recognized primarily as a result of cultural considerations, in that such taxa represent domesticated or otherwise economically important species.

e. The taxon marking the rank of kingdom in ethnobotanical as well as ethnozoological systems of classification is comprised of a single member.

6. Ethnobiological taxa of generic and specific rank exhibit an internal structure in which some members are thought of as prototypical of the taxon while others are seen as less typical of the category.

7. A substantial majority of ethnobiological taxa will correspond closely in content with taxa recognized independently by Western botany and zoology, with the highest degree of correspondence occurring with taxa of generic rank. Taxa of intermediate rank often correspond to portions of recognized biological families. Taxa of life-form and subgeneric rank exhibit the lowest correspondence with recognized biological taxa.

II. *Nomenclature*

1. Taxa of the ranks of kingdom and intermediate are generally not named. There is growing evidence that some covert life-form taxa may also be found. When such taxa are labeled, they often show polysemous relations with taxa of subordinate rank.

2. Names for plants and animals exhibit a lexical structure of one of two universal lexical types that can be called primary and secondary plant and animal names. These types can be recognized by recourse to linguistic, semantic, and taxonomic criteria. Primary names are of three subtypes: simple (e.g., *fish*), productive (e.g., *catfish*), and unproductive (e.g., *silverfish*). Secondary names (e.g., *red maple, silver maple*), with generally specifiable exceptions, occur only in contrast sets whose members share a constituent that refers to the taxon that immediately includes them (e.g., *maple*).

3. A specifiable relationship can be observed between the names of taxa and their rank. Life-form and generic taxa are labeled by primary names; subgeneric taxa are labeled, in general, with secondary names.

4. There are two well-understood conditions under which subgeneric taxa may be labeled by primary names, although these two conditions do not account for all of the empirically observed data. The first condition (4a) occurs when the name of the prototypical subgeneric is polysemous with its superordinate generic. Disambiguation of polysemy is accomplished by the optional occurrence of a modifier glossed as 'genuine' or 'ideal type'. The second condition (4b) occurs when nonprototypical subgenerics refer to subgeneric taxa of great cultural importance.

5. Ethnobiological nomenclature is semantically active in that the linguistic constituents of plant and animal names often metaphorically allude to morphological, behavioral, or ecological features that are nonarbitrarily associated with their biological referents.

1.8 THE CHANGING CONVENTIONS OF DATA PRESENTATION AS A REFLECTION OF CHANGING THEORY IN ETHNOBIOLOGICAL CLASSIFICATION

In their classic work on methods and principles in systematic zoology, Mayr, Linsley, and Usinger open their chapter on presentation of the results of one's research with the following understatement: "After [analysis of the data] there remains the important task of recording the findings and presenting them in a useful manner" (1953:155). In a sense, this statement seems almost trivial, even if one has abandoned the fallacious view that "the data speak for themselves." With minimal introspection, however, it is clear that decisions on how to present one's data in a useful fashion are neither obvious nor straightforward.

The conventions that one adopts will highlight certain aspects of the data and necessarily deemphasize others, leading the analyst to make decisions that relate directly to the overall impact of the report. One cannot expect one's readers, even the most careful and enthusiastic ones, to take the time to reanalyze one's materials in search of patterns that have been obscured by the particular form of presentation that one's descriptions have assumed.[8]

Nonetheless, while it is crucial to recognize how the modes of presentation adopted reflect (and influence) the ways in which one thinks about the data, many of the criticisms by Hunn (1976, 1977, 1982), Ellen (1986), Friedberg (1968, 1970), Healey (1978–1979), Randall (1976), and Sillitoe (1983), to mention the most vocal, to the effect that ethnobiologists who employ taxonomic conventions have "reified" (their term) their diagrams are, I think, far off the mark. If earlier conventions have been inadequate, as I now believe they have been, it is not because they suffered from the rigidity of reification

---

[8] This is not at all to say that ethnobiologists should begin at once to contemplate their dirty fingernails amid the smells of sweaty armpits, rotting plant specimens, formalin-filled collecting jars, and stuffed bird skins and begin the long but liberating journey of transformation that leads to the recognition that we are all, in the end, engaged in nothing but a literary game (cf. any issue of *Cultural Anthropology*; Clifford and Marcus 1986; Clifford 1988; and Marcus and Fischer 1986 for a sampling of what we have been missing). As proclaimed by Tyler, "[Postmodern anthropology] denies that 'I speak of the world by means of language' . . . and declares that 'The world is what we say it is' " (Tyler 1987:172). Ethnobiologists concerned with the nature of human categorization as it reflects in the complex world of plants and animals have not yet entered what Kay (1987) has characterized as the deconstructionists' hall of mirrors, where one's reflections of reflections of reflections can be viewed and reviewed in infinitely many-varied forms, and interpreted, of course, in infinitely varied ways.

so much as because our empirical and theoretical understanding of the complexity underlying the nature of ethnobiological classification was less than it is now as a result of the concerted efforts of many dedicated researchers. Conventions should change to reflect a more profound theoretical understanding of this richness. I have no doubt that more appropriate forms of representation will replace those offered here with future research and consequent theoretical development.

Historical Antecedents of Diagrammatic Conventions in Ethnobiology

The brief but lively history of the conventions used to display data about ethnobiological classification is interesting to survey in that it shows clearly how these conventions have changed as a reflection of advances in theoretical understanding of some of the principles underlying human categorization. More important, such a survey reveals something of the natural evolution of the subfield of ethnobiology itself. In most instances, new proposals have been put forth in a positive, constructive manner, building on the cumulative efforts and insights of previous investigators rather than, as in a number of other subfields of anthropology, by proclaiming ever new Kuhnian scientific revolutions.

At the beginning of the 1960s, Conklin (1962) and Frake (1961, 1962) published three influential articles that ushered in the tradition of cognitively focused ethnography and ethnobiology. In their description of certain semantic properties of hierarchically ordered categories (referred to in this early literature by the neutral term "segregates"), they offered a set of diagrammatic conventions that were to have considerable influence in the visualization of semantic field relations. The most important of these conventions were the box diagrams made famous in Conklin's description of the classification of Hanunóo peppers, and Frake's statement on Subanun disease categorization. The former is shown in figure 1.3.

Kay's work on the nature of the semantic structure underlying folk taxonomies quickly followed the papers by Conklin and Frake. Kay introduced a set of diagrammatic conventions that had already been used for many years in biology and certain branches of mathematics and linguistics and were well known in anthropology. These conventions are the "tree diagrams" described in Kay's first paper on the topic, written as a succinct response to Colby (1966).

It was not until several years later, however, that the theoretical importance of the diagrammatic conventions adopted in the presentation of hierarchical relations in ethnobiology was explicitly addressed. This was one of the themes of Kay's subsequent paper on taxonomy and semantic contrast (Kay 1971). In this paper, he compares and contrasts the use of tree diagram versus box diagram conventions in displaying the semantic structure of a domain, and argues

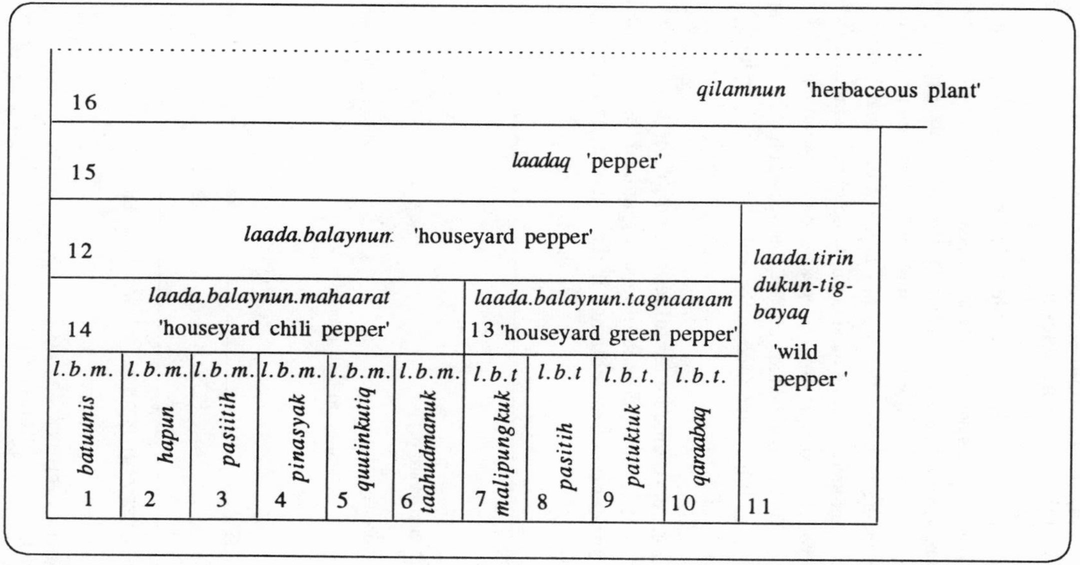

qilamnun 'herbaceous plant'

16

15

laadaq 'pepper'

12

laada.balaynun. 'houseyard pepper'

laada.tirin dukun-tig-bayaq 'wild pepper'

	laada.balaynun.mahaarat 'houseyard chili pepper'					laada.balaynun.tagnaanan 13 'houseyard green pepper'				
14										
l.b.m.	l.b.m.	l.b.m.	l.b.m.	l.b.m.	l.b.m.	l.b.t	l.b.t	l.b.t.	l.b.t.	
batuunis	hapun	pasitih	pinasyak	quutinkutiq	taahudmanuk	malipungkuk	pasitih	patuktuk	qaraabaq	
1	2	3	4	5	6	7	8	9	10	11

Figure. 1.3 A fragment of Hanunóo classification of peppers (*Capsicum* spp.), as shown by the use of conventional box diagram (After Conklin 1962:133). (Long vowels are presented here as double segments, e.g., *laada*.)

that the use of the latter is partially responsible for the confusion that existed in the early ethnographic semantic literature on notions related to the "level of contrast" of particular taxa. Analyzing a portion of Conklin's diagram for Hanunóo peppers, Kay produced the figures shown in figure 1.4. In regard to the notion of taxonomic level, Kay notes that

> It is true that, in the box diagram [of figure 1.4], the box containing WILD PEPPER is visually 'on a level,' so to speak, both with the box containing HOUSEYARD PEPPER and the one containing HOUSEYARD CHILI PEPPER. However, this is merely an observation on the visual properties of box diagrams, and reflects nothing about the taxonomic structure being pictured. Perhaps this accident of visual imagery has led people to imagine that there is some meaningful sense of taxonomic 'level' according to which a taxon (for example t3-WILD PEPPER) may be said to have two distinct levels. If so, I have found no indication of what that sense might be. The expression 'level of contrast,' as it has been used in the anthropological literature, is at best ambiguous. (Kay 1971:876)

Kay's formalization represented a useful refinement of the ways in which anthropologists and, particularly, ethnobiologists organized their data. His demonstration of the greater precision obtained in the use of tree diagrams over the

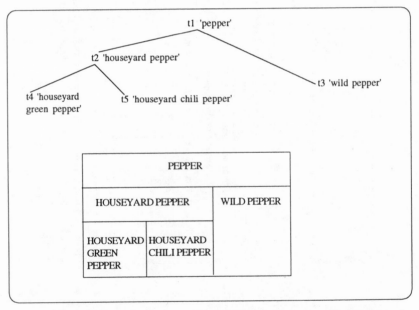

Figure 1.4 Comparison of diagrammatic representation of the semantic structure of a fragment of Hanunóo classification of peppers using a tree diagram (top part of figure) and box diagram (bottom part of figure). (After Kay 1971:876)

earlier box figures led to the general adoption of tree diagrams in many subsequent studies. This method of presentation has been the one used by me and coworkers on Tzeltal and Aguaruna ethnobiological classification as well as by many other researchers (e.g., Bulmer 1970; Hays 1974; Headland 1981; Hunn 1977; Ellen, Stimson, and Menzies 1976, 1977; Felger and Moser 1985; Waddy 1988).

At about the same time that Kay's work was published, and as modern research on ethnobiological classification was being initiated in many parts of the world, a number of inadequacies in the taxonomic model and, consequently, its form of presentation began to be discussed. Unfortunately, these inadequacies led a number of scholars to argue forcefully for the abandonment of notions of taxonomic hierarchy altogether.

The first and still perhaps the most influential paper to appear that questioned the strictly taxonomic presentations of ethnobiological material was that of Bright and Bright (1965). Curiously, this research was not specifically ethnobiological at all, but was directed toward an evaluation of the Sapir-Whorf hypothesis and the influence of language on thought among American Indians in California. Recognizing that the level of acculturation was extremely high among the surviving members of these groups, Bright and Bright nonetheless felt that much could yet be learned by focusing on the ethnobiological knowledge that they still retained, although this is perhaps debatable.[9]

The major research finding of their work is stated by the authors as follows:

> One fact emergent from a study of the Yurok and Smith River taxonomic systems is that they are less hierarchically organized than our own. We nearly exhaust the universe of living things with a multileveled hierarchical classification . . . 'animal, insect, louse, body louse.' The Indians, by contrast, have relatively few [higher order] generic terms*, and many terms which do not fall into any hierarchy. (Bright and Bright 1965:252) [*The use of *generic* here is not the sense proposed by Berlin and coworkers.]

Bright and Bright anticipate a number of the issues raised by Hunn (1976) and Randall (1976) a decade later, and a decade later yet by Ellen (1986)—

---

[9] The Brights encountered numerous problems in the conduct of their research that I believe are at least partially accounted for by the advanced age of many of their informants. A memorable example concerns some of the responses of the investigators' "most knowledgeable informant . . . a Yurok, Mrs. Alice Spott Taylor, aged 95 years . . . and the most 'Indian' informant who could be found" (Bright and Bright 1965:252). In one session, attempting to determine the life-form affiliations of certain animals, Bright and Bright recorded the following exchange with Mrs. Taylor:

Q: *nunepuy hes wi' k'i lo'co'm* "Is a toad a fish?"
A: *paa', nimi' nunepuy k'i lo'co'm* "No, a toad isn't a fish."
Q: *ti' ni sho. wi' k'i lo'co'm* "What *is* a toad?"
A: *lo'co'm kwel wencoks we'* "A toad is a woman."

issues that had already been generally resolved in Kay's (1975) modal logic and model-theoretic reformulation of his 1971 paper on the structure of folk taxonomies. The Brights make two significant observations concerning the appropriateness of the taxonomic model and its diagrammatic conventions for depicting relationships. The first deals with the semantic association between two taxa joined in a relation of immediate precedence where the two taxa are labeled by the same polysemous term. The second relates to the observation that their informants, when asked to identify a plant for which they had no name, would respond that the species in question was "like such-and-such" rather than assigning it to a named class. This leads Bright and Bright to conclude that

> a hierarchical model, which shows only the relationship of *domination* [i.e., class inclusion], cannot account adequately for the Indian taxonomies. In a hierarchy, an item either is or is not a member of the class named by the higher node. But there is no way of indicating in a hierarchical tree, the situation where a specific term like Yurok *tepo*: 'fir, [and] tree' . . . can also be used as a generic term, thus including other trees which resemble the fir by being coniferous. In addition, there is no way of indicating when an item is classified in a certain way because it is 'like' another item which is more central to the focus of the domain in question. Therefore, the aboriginal taxonomies . . . can be represented more faithfully by a kind of 'sphere of influence' model [as seen in figure 1.5]. (Ibid.:253)

The circle indicated by a faint gray line in the diagram on the left in figure 1.5 is meant to convey Bright and Bright's solution to the polysemous labeling of the life-form and generic taxa 'fir' and 'tree'. The partially overlapping

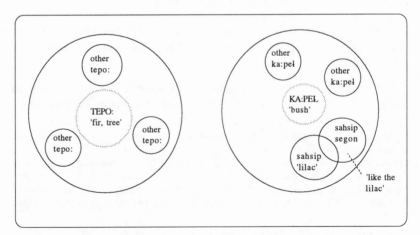

Figure 1.5 Schematic representation of Yurok classification of trees (TEPO:) and bushes (KA:PEŁ) as depicted in Bright and Bright's "sphere of influence model." (After Bright and Bright 1965:254)

circles in the figure on the right designating 'lilac' (*sahsip*) and 'like the lilac' (*sahsip segon*) are meant to convey the relationship of similarity of the latter unnamed taxon to the former labeled category.

Bright and Bright's treatment of polysemously labeled taxa is clearly less than satisfactory. While aware of both Conklin's and Frake's previous solutions to the treatment of this common phenomenon, they reject it with the following commentary:

> A center-oriented classification, such as proposed here, can be converted into a hierarchical classification by putting a single term on several hierarchical levels, as Frake (1961:119) has done. . . . We feel, however, that the investigator who follows this procedure runs the risk of imposing a scientific taxonomy . . . upon the folk-taxonomic data that he is studying. Where members of a culture use a single term to classify objects at different levels of generalization, it may be that the concept of levels and of hierarchy is irrelevant to their semantic structure. (Bright and Bright 1965:258)

It is difficult to understand how the authors could arrive at such a conclusion. If the Yurok term *tepo:* has both the senses of 'fir' and of '(coniferous) tree' (a widespread feature in many North American Indian languages), the most plausible semantic relation that characterizes the two senses is one of class inclusion. To make such a claim is not to impose a "scientific taxonomy" on that of the folk. Furthermore and as important, it is not at all clear *what* semantic relation is intended by Bright and Bright's diagrammatic convention for the two taxa in question. As with the ambiguity that box diagrams imply for the taxonomic level of taxa, the conventions adopted by Bright and Bright obscure rather than clarify the underlying semantic structure.

The second issue raised by Bright and Bright, however, is more fundamental. At the time their paper was published, there were no established conventions for dealing with descriptively named taxa ('like a lilac') that were conceptually treated as outliers of habitually labeled ethnobiological categories ('lilac'). Descriptions that were shortly to follow, however, indicated that semantic categories might more properly be characterized as having an *internal structure*, with some members being thought of as more central and others more peripheral (see Berlin and Kay 1969 and the structure of color categories). This development was to influence significantly future analysis of data on plant and animal classification.

Ethnobiological taxa were found typically to show *basic* and *extended* ranges in their referential meaning (Berlin, Breedlove, and Raven 1974:56–58), a property that Hunn was later to rename as *core* and *periphery* (Hunn 1976). Nonetheless, classical set theoretical notions disallowed such taxa as forming part of the taxonomic structure (see Gregg 1954). The Brights' intuitions in resorting to the use of Venn diagrammatic conventions anticipated the conceptual change that was imminent with the developing notions of prototypes and fuzzy set theory, ideas that were to set the stage for a more flexible treatment of semantic structure generally.

When Breedlove, Raven, and I began our work on Tzeltal ethnobotanical classification, we were also confronted with data comparable to those of the Brights. Our data showed clearly that

> informants will regularly classify a plant specimen as either (1) a legitimate member of a named class or (2) as related to some recognized category. . . . [Thus] categories [have] relatively *unambiguous foci* which shade into rather *ambiguous boundaries* . . . [that allow one to] speak of the *basic* and *extended* range of a plant class. The basic range of a class includes all of its genuine referents; the extended range includes all those plants which are habitually seen as being more closely related to it than any other category. Basic ranges of plant taxa sharing the same immediately superordinate taxon are always mutually exclusive. Extended ranges of terms, however, may overlap in some instances and, in fact, often do. Finally . . . [a plant] falling within the *extended* range of a particular . . . taxon may at the same time be within the *basic* range of that taxon's superordinate class. (Berlin, Breedlove, and Raven 1974:57)

We found that the use of the standard tree diagrams was less than satisfactory for depicting these facts about Tzeltal plant classification and briefly explored the use of Venn diagrams to visually display our findings, as seen in figure 1.6. This procedure, however, was not exploited in the remainder of the monograph and was finally dropped as a diagrammatic convention.

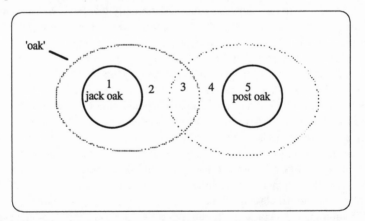

Figure 1.6 Diagrammatic representation of the basic and extended ranges of plant taxa proposed by Berlin, Breedlove, and Raven (1974). Numbers indicate individual plant species, where species 2 and 4 are conceptually within the extended range of the named taxa 'jack oak' and 'post oak', respectively. Species 3 falls within the extended range of both. Nonetheless, all species, 1–5, are part of the basic range of the superordinate taxon 'oak'. (Modified slightly from fig. 3.2 of Berlin, Breedlove, and Raven 1974:57)

Two years later, both Hunn (1976) and Gardner (1976) introduced the use of Venn diagrams as a major departure from the standard conventions used in earlier writings on ethnobiological classification, although the use of the diagrams for displaying category membership was well established in systematic biology, and had been for many years. Simpson's important book, *Principles of Animal Taxonomy* (1961), provides perhaps the earliest modern explicit statement on these conventions when used to depict biological relationships. Simpson's "group-in-group formalization" is

> readily visualized as a series of circles or boxes of different sizes and inclusiveness. . . . Circles, for instance, of the same size can be directly equated with taxa of the same rank, and inclusion in larger circles with inclusion in higher taxa. In typological terms, the circles represent archetypes of increasing generality or abstraction. . . . The number of shared characters is (approximately) *inversely* proportional to the sizes of the circles because they are additive: the individuals in a small circle share not only the characters represented by that circle but also those represented by the larger circles that include it [as can be seen in figure 1.7]. (Simpson 1961:60)

Hunn's major concern was to develop a perceptual model of ethnobiological classification, recognizing the inadequacies of the classical set-theoretic proposals of Gregg (1954) and Kay's first formalization (1971). However, the conventions Hunn introduced in his paper (1976:515–516, 521, figs. 6, 7, and 9) were not incorporated into his major monographic work on Tzeltal ethnozoology, where he continued to employ rooted tree diagrams as the preferred graphic form of data presentation.

Gardner is to be credited with building on the intuitions of Bright and Bright's highly informal 'sphere of influence' model, by proposing a set of diagramming conventions that were developed in explicit recognition that earlier forms of presentation fell short of capturing the properties of actual systems of ethnobiological classification. He plainly states that "the conventional ways in which taxonomies are represented do not permit representation of fo-

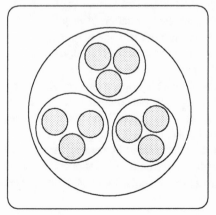

Figure 1.7 Simpson's diagrammatic convention for showing "groups-in-groups" (after Simpson 1961:59). Dots represent individuals. Circles of varying sizes represent taxa of different levels of inclusiveness.

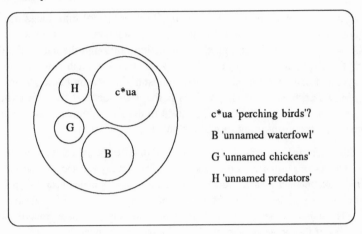

Figure 1.8 Major groupings of birds by a single Dene informant using the modified Venn diagrammatic conventions. (After Gardner 1976:455, fig. 3)

cus or class overlap [but such properties] can be readily portrayed in Venn diagrammatic form'' (Gardner 1976:453).

Gardner proposed two new conventions. Using circles to indicate taxa, the focal members of polytypic taxa are centered, allowing concentricity to indicate focus. Secondly, peripheral taxa (however this might be measured) are shown against the perimeter of the circle meant to depict the inclusive category. Figure 1.8 indicates the classification of birds by one of Gardner's Dene informants, showing only the major groupings without indication of the number of lower-level taxa included in each group. Unfortunately, Gardner did not continue to experiment with these conventions in subsequent monographic research on ethnobiology, and his analysis of Dene ethnoornithological classification as seen in the 1976 article is highly programmatic.

Ellen (1979b) was the next ethnobiologist to explore similar graphic forms of presentation in his description of Nuaulu categorization of lizards. As the numbers of species represented are relatively few, it is possible for Ellen to depict the variation in systems of classification of several informants in an explicit, concise, and easily understood manner, as seen in figure 1.9.

Jensen (1988), in his full-scale description of Wayampí bird classification, develops an ingenious set of graphic conventions that combines the use of tree diagrams with what might be called a ''rings of Saturn'' model. These conventions allow Jensen to depict the prototypical category of a group of related taxa as the central member, which is then surrounded by taxa of varying degrees of similarity to the focus, with those bird taxa on the periphery the least similar to the prototype and those closest to the center the most similar. The

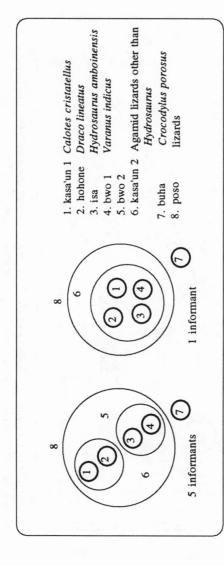

1. kasa'un 1 *Calotes cristatellus*
2. hohone *Draco lineatus*
3. isa *Hydrosaurus amboinensis*
4. bwo 1 *Varanus indicus*
5. bwo 2
6. kasa'un 2 Agamid lizards other than
   Hydrosaurus
7. buha *Crocodylus porosus*
8. poso lizards

Figure 1.9 Nuaulu classification of lizards presented in the form of Venn diagrams, indicating two variant systems of classification. (Modified after Ellen 1979b:344, fig. 1)

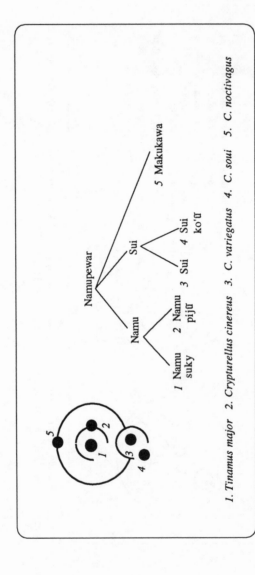

Figure 1.10 Diagrammatic representation of Wayampí classification of tinamous, combining branching tree diagram as well as "rings of Saturn" model of presentation. (After Jensen 1988)

Wayampí classification of the tinamous, using these conventions, is depicted in figure 1.10.

Conventions Used in the Present Work

All of the above graphic innovations represent, I think, creative ways of presenting the findings of moden research in ethnobiological classification in a useful manner, as Mayr, Linsley, and Usinger have pointed out. In the conventions used in the present work, I borrow freely from many of the proposals presented above, while making some additional ones. These can be best described by reference to a real example, as seen in figure 1.11.

Figure 1.11 shows one of the variant systems of the Aguaruna Jívaro classification of eight species of woodpeckers found in the rain forests of north-central Peru; the data are presented in the form of modified Venn diagrams. In addition to the standard assumptions associated with such figures (e.g., circles within circles indicating class inclusion, overlapping circles indicating class intersection), five other simple conventions are systematically employed here.

1. *Biological taxa* are outlined as small solid circles always of the same size. Unless otherwise stated, these taxa will represent biological species.
2. *Ethnobiological taxa* are indicated as faint gray circles that encompass one or more biological species. Ethnobiological taxa so represented may be of any rank, as will be clear from the context of the discussion. If not, their rank will be indicated in the relevant figure.
3. *Prototypical* members of ethnobiological taxa will be indicated by distinctive hatching of the relevant biological species.
4. The *relative perceived similarity* of ethnobiological taxa will be indicated by the relative distance by which they are separated from one another in each diagram. Since most of the data that I will discuss here are not numerically quantified, the gaps separating taxa are to be taken as suggestive only.
5. Names of *ethnobiological taxa* will be given in **bold italics** while names of *biological taxa* will be given in their standard *plain italics*.

These conventions allow one to read figure 1.11 in the following manner. One first notes the most inclusive taxon, 'woodpeckers', which is covert. The context of the description will indicate that it is a category of intermediate rank. Within the intermediate taxon 'woodpecker', one sees three major ethnobiological taxa referred to by the names ***dái, sawáke***, and ***tátasham***. The context of the discussion will indicate that these are folk generic taxa. One, ***dái***, has a biological range of four species, two of which are included in the range of another taxon, ***sawáke***. Of the two biological species uniquely associated with ***dái***, *Veniliornis affinis* and *V. passerinus*, *V. affinis* is the prototype of the folk genus and is so indicated by distinctive hatching. In like manner,

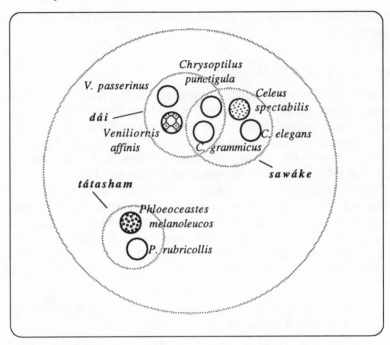

Figure 1.11 Classification of Aguaruna woodpeckers (this volume, chap. 5), indicating diagrammatic conventions used in the present monograph.

sawáke includes four species as well, two of which it shares with *dái*. Species unique to *sawáke* are *Celeus spectabilis*, the prototype, and *C. elegans*. The perceptual similarity of *dái* and *sawáke* is noted by their relative spacing. This similarity is great enough that the two folk genera partially overlap, their ranges (shown as overlapping intersection) being linked by *Chrysoptilus punctigula* and *Celeus grammicus*. Evidence for this claim, based on naming responses from many informants, will be presented in the text.

The remaining folk genus in the set is *tátasham*. This generic taxon ranges over two species of *Phloeoceastes*, *P. melanoleucos* and *P. rubricollis*. The prototypical species of *tátasham* is *P. melanoleucos*, often refered to as *shing tátasham* (lit. 'genuine tátasham,' a nomenclatural fact not shown in the figure). Members of this folk genus are separated in space from the other woodpeckers, indicating their greater relative distinctiveness. The naming responses to be discussed in the text justify this claim.

None of the data just described include taxa that represent the classification of species that are thought to be 'related' to some named taxon but are not properly included in it, examples of the sort described by Bright and Bright (1965) and Berlin, Breedlove, and Raven (1974). The conventions used for data of this sort are seen in figure 1.12. Here one notes that two Tzeltal generic taxa, *sabal tz'unun wamal* and *sak'al wamal*, are united in a covert taxon (rank will have been made clear from the context). The diagram also shows that each folk taxon is restricted in its basic range to a single species, *Salvia cinnabarina* and *S. coccinea*, respectively. Around *sabal tz'unun* float a number of species of *Salvia* which are treated as conceptual outliers. The several species of the genus nearest to *sabal tz'unun* were all named at the time of their collection with the expression *kol pajaluk sok sabal tz'unun*, 'like or related to *sabal tz'unun*'. Although these *Salvia* species are not legitimate members of *sabal tz'unun*, nor is *Simsia foetida* a legitimate member of *sak'al wamal*, they are unambiguously and conceptually related to the two central species of these taxa, and each is clearly included within the basic range of the the covert intermediate category. As we will see later, and building on an insight of P. M. Taylor (1990), it is more appropriate to treat these species as floating residue or conceptual outliers rather than as comprising "residual taxa," as they have been earlier analyzed by Hunn (1977) and Hays (1974).

Finally, the relative distance at which a particular species of *Salvia* is placed vis-à-vis the central species in the drawing is meant to convey the strength of affinity to that central species, as determined from the naming responses of our informants. Thus, *S. karwinskii* is shown to be closer to *sabal tz'unun* than *S. disjuncta*. The "perceptual distance" represented by the size of the gap separating the two named species in the set is large, indicating that they are the most distinct species in the group. This convention builds on the diagrammatic proposals of Simpson (1961:117, fig. 6) and is the one adopted by Hunn (1976). Again, it is important to reiterate that the width of the gap is to be interpreted loosely, inasmuch as no quantitative scale has been developed in terms of which perceptual distance can be given a numeric value.

The diagrammatic conventions suggested here could clearly be improved on. Nonetheless, they do allow for a number of properties relevant to the structure of ethnobiological categories to be visually displayed in a way that is not easily accomplished with the use of standard tree diagrams. First, the explicit indication of biological and ethnobiological taxa by means of circles drawn with contrasting boundaries makes it possible to discuss the biological ranges of folk taxa somewhat more clearly than when no distinction between the two classes is indicated. Second, attention is immediately drawn to the prototypical members of folk taxa by marking them with distinctive hatching. Third, overlapping membership of particular folk taxa is readily observed, leading to rapid inferences of affinity between taxa via the species that form the intersection of two or more categories. Fourth, the presentation of folk and scientific names in the figures themselves, adjacent to the (ethno)biological referents that they designate, is meant to provide the reader with a visual picture of the conceptual as well as the nomenclatural properties of the respective categories in an obvious and intuitively satisfying way.

Of course, three-dimensional figures would more appropriately capture a

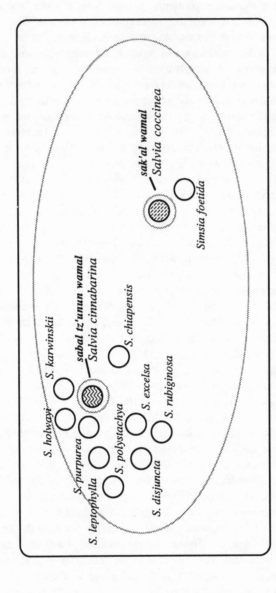

Figure 1.12 Schematic representation of the classification of locally occurring species of *Salvia* and one species of *Simsia* by the Tenejapa Tzeltal (Mexico) illustrating diagrammatic conventions used in present work. (Data from Berlin, Breedlove, and Raven 1974:331)

number of features of the classificatory space that are not possible to indicate in the present treatment, although the kinds of numerical data required for producing them are currently not available for most descriptions (see Ellen 1979b). Furthermore, we are close to the time when good drawings or photographs of the plant and animal species themselves can be produced in an economically feasible format, so that they can be used as part of any standard (ethno)biological description. Since much of ethnozoological nomenclature and major aspects of classification are associated with the sense of sound as well as sight, it will soon be possible to incorporate the calls of various creatures as well as their corresponding human vocalizations as part of the full presentation of one's analysis. And, as ethnobiological research develops more accurate measures of perceptual similarity and difference, the visual diagrams that are produced to intuitively depict such relations will begin to move away from metaphorical allusion to something closer to scientific accuracy.

CHAPTER TWO

The Primacy of Generic Taxa in Ethnobiological Classification

ONE OF THE ESSENTIAL questions of modern systematic biology is why species exist. For ethnobiological classification, one adds the equally essential questions, of those species that exist, *which* are recognized and *why*?

Picture an ethnographer in the field just beginning fieldwork with a group of Indians somewhere in the upper Amazon of South America. Building a vocabulary is high on her agenda, given the ethnographer's goal of wanting to start using the native language as quickly as possible. She sets off down a forest trail with an assistant who has agreed to help her in this difficult task. As they arrive at a clearing in the tropical forest, they sit down to rest on a fallen palm trunk and the ethnographer begins to inquire about the names of plants and animals. "*Umajú*" (male parallel classificatory sibling, female speaking), she says, pointing to a large tree, "*Husha, wajimpáya?*" 'That (over there), what's its name?' The assistant looks up from his task of methodically picking away at a thorn in the callus of his foot and responds, "*Numi dáajing*" '(It's named a) tree'. The ethnographer, puzzled, tries another tactic. Pointing to a second tree next to the one she has just queried about, she asks again, "*Husha, wajimpáya?*" to which the assistant quickly answers, "*Ha, numíshakam*" '(It's) also (called a) tree'. Trying to disguise a building sense of exasperation, she points to an inconspicuous broad-leafed plant at the trunk of the second tree and states, "*Wah! husha, numíkaik shakam?*" 'Well, is that (thing) also (a) tree?' Her assistant, pausing briefly, smiles and replies, "*Atsá, ha dupa*" 'No, that's an herb'.

What's wrong with this conversation? Why does it not only appear to be totally fictitious, but more important, improbable? In spite of the possible theory that our ethnographer's assistant is simply trying to be difficult, why does this vignette appear to any person who has done fieldwork as ludicrous? First of all, it is noteworthy that the interaction would not have appeared strange if the assistant had responded to the questions with a simple "*dékatsjai*" 'I don't know (its name)'. The biological world is complex, and there are many parts of it that do not get labeled. But this is not what we find strange about the scene.

2.1 THE SELECTED SUBSET OF PLANTS AND ANIMALS

The reason why we are left feeling uncomfortable partially lies in an implicit theory that we all share about how things in the world should be referred to in natural languages. Very loosely stated, and for the time being in the same spirit of the above example, the theory goes something like this, restating in a slightly different form the classic argument set forth by Roger Brown in his famous article, "How Shall a Thing Be Called?" more than thirty years ago (R. Brown 1958). The first part of the theory says that the world is divided up into a number of fundamental categories that can be referred to in a number of ways. While it is true that some of these categories may have several names, the second part of our intuitive theory tells us that some names are more common or important than others. These common labels of reference, the names of everyday speech, are even thought of at times as the *real* names of the corresponding categories. Furthermore, and here is the point relevant to our example, these names of common usage are neither too abstract nor, as we shall see, too concrete. Our ethnographer's assistant did not lie in his responses. Indeed, the first two plants referred to can be called 'trees' while the third is a member of a class called 'herbaceous plant'. Our intuitions about the dialog, however, tell us that the Indian's responses were clearly too abstract. What the ethnographer had hoped to elicit, of course, were the common plant names of "usual utility" (R. Brown 1958:16).

A major claim made here is that, in the categorization of plants and animals by peoples living in traditional societies, there exists a specifiable and partially predictable set of plant and animal taxa that represent the smallest fundamental biological discontinuities easily recognized in any particular habitat. This large but finite set of taxa is special in each system in that its members stand out as beacons on the landscape of biological reality, figuratively crying out to be named. These groupings are the generic taxa of all such systems of ethnobiological classification, and their names are precisely the names of common speech.

My goal in this chapter is to specify some of the most notable biological, nomenclatural, and, where I believe the data are adequate, psychological properties of these fundamental classes of plants and animals. I will present a brief historical sketch of the significance of these important groupings and provide my reasons for using the term "generic" as part of the analytic vocabulary of ethnobiology. I will also present evidence bearing on the claim that it is possible partially to predict what the subset of generic taxa in any system of ethnobiological classification will be, given relatively comprehensive biological inventories of the flora and fauna found in some particular habitat. This section is followed by a discussion of evidence that bears on the internal structure of generic taxa, evidence that shows them to be comprised of a prototypical species around which less typical exemplars are conceptually grouped. I will close with some empirical observations on the maximum numbers of generic taxa that are generally found in ethnobiological systems of classification, an upper limit that, while yet unexplained, most likely reflects the upper limit of fundamental named categories that can be maintained in nonliterate societies, building on an earlier speculation of Lévi-Strauss (1966).

2.2 THE CONCEPT OF THE GENUS: HISTORICAL ANTECEDENTS[1]

Harley Harris Bartlett, an unconventional University of Michigan botanist of the first half of the twentieth century, was a man of many talents, not the least of which was his intimate understanding of folk biological systematics.[2] His work in Sumatra, especially among the Batak of the island's eastern coast, provided him with more than a working knowledge of many of the principles of ethnobotanical categorization and nomenclature that are recognized in the current monograph and which I openly acknowledge, in a number of cases, as a modern elaboration of Bartlett's insights.

In a perceptive paper, Bartlett (1940) outlined the significance of the generic concept in folk botany as it relates to the history of botanical classification. He opens his article with an often-quoted phrase: the "concept of the genus must be as old as folk science itself" (Bartlett 1940:349). Furthermore, "the scientific concept of the genus is . . . not modern at all," being traced to the earliest times of human systematic reflection on the biological world. Quite literally, "the generic concept of folk botany [needs] little change to become essentially the generic concept of modern science" (ibid.:350).

---

[1] As the current monograph was being drafted, Scott Atran sent me a copy of the manuscript of his important new book, *Cognitive Foundations of Natural History* (1990). In it, he explores the transformation of natural history into what we know today as modern biology. Atran has outlined some of the more important ethnobiological foundations that historically underlie Western biological classification. It is not my goal to attempt to retrace his account of this fascinating period in the development of biological science. My more modest aim is to focus only on a number of remarkable observations that have been made by a handful of historians of biology as they relate directly to the early ideas about the genus as an analytic category, and to point to the antiquity and relevance of the concept as it will be developed here.

[2] In some ways, Bartlett might be considered the grandfather of modern ethnobotany in that it was he who encouraged H. C. Conklin to undertake his classic study of Hanunóo knowledge of the plant world.

Bartlett provides an intuitive linguistic definition of the genus when he notes that "wherever . . . we find naming and classification of plants [we observe] . . . a more or less well-defined idea of the genus as the smallest group that almost everyone might be expected to have the name for in his vocabulary. It might or might not be subdivided into species" (ibid.:351). And he reiterates:

> The important point is that it is quite as characteristic of folk botany as of modern systematic science to classify to the genus, which is more or less consciously thought of as the smallest grouping requiring a distinctive name. Within the genus, if the distinction of several kinds is necessary, a qualifying designation is used and the whole name becomes a binomial. If there is but one sort within a genus, no qualifying word is necessary, for the generic name is sufficient. (Ibid.:356)

Of course, the recognized generic taxa in any particular system do not among them exhaustively partition the domain of plants. Thus, in reference to his Batak materials, Bartlett says:

> Among the Batak the grouping of inconsequential [plants] is very inclusive. For instance, *"duhut"* will do for a wide range of weeds or herbaceous plants [interpreted here as one of the universal major life forms], but scores or hundreds of kinds of *duhut* that are important enough that they must be talked about have generic and specific names. . . . [Again, as] to plants in general, there is a partial classification, going to genera or species in hundreds of instances, but leaving many plants unclassified, regarding which all that the native botanist will say is that they are trees, herbs, vines, ferns, or mosses. (Ibid.:354)

For Bartlett, the biological scope of a folk genus might be unitary, making subdivisions of it unnecessary. However, should the internal diversity of the genus be perceptually distinctive enough, subgroupings will be recognized. The nomenclatural processes employed to note these distinctions, he claimed, were quite general:

> There is everywhere a tendency to group similar species under generic names, and to name the species by using some linguistic device not unlike the binomial nomenclature of Linnaeus. . . . [If one looks at the climbing palms one notes that] . . . they form, popularly, only a single genus, which may be called *[h]otang* (we get our English word 'rattan' from this). . . . Under the genus are arrayed the species, *hotang soga, hotang djorlang, hotang sumambu, hotang ahonir, hotang taritting, hotang pahoe*. (Ibid.:353)

Bartlett recognized that the generic taxa comprising the Batak system of plant classification were not arbitrarily organized but could be grouped as clumps of morphologically similar discontinuities of the plant world. Often, the conceptual affiliation of two or more generic taxa would be expressed linguistically. He writes:

Of all the plants called *hotang* . . . only one, *hotang da ursa*, is not a climbing palm, but it is *Flagellaria*, a climbing, monocotyledonous plant recognized by the natives as so different that *hotang da ursa* is treated as a genus. Whereas any of the climbing palms may be called simply *hotang*, the *Flagellaria* may not be. It must be called by its full name, *hotang da ursa*. Here we get an ink[l]ing of how generic designations of more than one word arose in other languages. (Ibid.: 353)

Bartlett's description, of course, points to the nomenclatural pattern described as generic name extension found widely in many scores of ethnobiological lexicons.

While Bartlett helped to clarify the concept of the folk genus as it relates to scientific botanical classification, a similar, if somewhat less explicit recognition of the nature of the folk genus was made several decades earlier by the University of California botanist Edward Lee Greene, founder of the Berkeley botany department. Greene provided an explicit and monographic evaluation of the chain of conceptual and nomenclatural similarities tying ancient folk science to the development of modern botany. In 1909 Greene published a detailed survey of what he was to call *Landmarks in Botanical History*.[3] Bartlett knew Greene's work well (Bartlett 1916), and it is possible that some of Greene's ideas on the significance of folk science played a part in the development of his own.

The aspect of Greene's writings that relates to the present chapter is the commentary he provides on the folk scientific foundations of botany as a science and the nature of taxa recognized at the rank of the genus. Focusing on the former first, he states:

Botany did not begin with the first books of botany, nor with the men who edited them. . . . The most remote and primitive of botanical writers, of whatever country or language, found a more or less extensive vocabulary of elementary botany in the colloquial speech of all [with words] . . . designating . . . different varieties or species that are evidently nearly akin, by two-fold names, one generic, the other specific or varietal. (1983:118)

It is impossible that men, even the most primeval and unlettered, manage their affairs with . . . the plant world without classifying them. Names of plants, generic and specific, and also other names more comprehensive, are part of the vernacular of every tribe of the uncivilized. . . . The very names attest the fact of classification; for no name is that of an individual plant. It is that of a group

[3] This work, long out of print, has recently been reissued (Greene 1983). The 1909 monograph appears now with a companion volume never before published and is carefully edited and annotated by the historian of science F. N. Egerton, with sketches of Greene the man by Robert McIntosh and Greene's botanical writings by Rogers McVaugh, both valuable contributions.

of plants, always; a group specific, generic or more comprehensive than either. (1983:115)

Greene continues his journey with the writings of Aristotle's student, Theophrastus, following the course of the development of botanical science through the Middle Ages, and ends up with Tournefort (1700), whose system of classification was not to be seriously modified until Linnaeus produced his own later synthesis. Theophrastus is important to Greene inasmuch as he sees the early botanist as a codifier of the first folk system of ethnobotanical classification. When Theophrastus "wrote of any tree or shrub or herb he used that name by which it was known in the everyday speech of the Greeks. It does not appear that it ever occurred to him that a living thing, or any group of living things, required to be named otherwise than as commonly designated in his mother tongue" (Greene 1983:189).

The system that Theophrastus describes is strikingly reminiscent of what is found in the ethnobotanical systems of peoples in traditional societies today. Theophrastus "mentioned about 550 kinds of plants" (Greene 1983:475), a number quite in line with the upper limits of generic taxa that one finds in typical modern folk botanical systems (see the last section of this chapter). Furthermore, these groupings "represented, in the great majority of cases, what we of today are accustomed to speak of as *monotypic genera*. Not any very considerable number of [these] genera are defined as consisting of two or more species, so that they had but one and small fraction species to each genus" (ibid.:330, emphasis added). This latter pattern, of course, is reflected as a common principle in contemporary systems of ethnobiological classification in horticultural societies, where approximately 80 percent of recognized folk genera are also monotypic.

The patterns of plant naming in early Greek ethnobotany as described by Theophrastus are also reflected in modern systems of ethnobotanical nomenclature. Greene is almost poetic in his description:

> The specific representative of a monotypic genus has . . . but one name, commonly a one-worded name; that is, the one species constituting such genus lacks a specific name. It really has not need of any. Where there is but one thing of a kind, there is never in ordinary speech a second and qualifying name. If neither men nor things existed but in monotypes, language would not need adjectives, and there would be none. . . . The Theophrastan nomenclature of plants is as simply natural as can be imagined. Not only are monotypic genera called by a single name; where the species are known to be several, the type species of the genus—that is, that which is most historic—is without a specific name . . . and only the others have each its specific adjective superadded to the generic appellation. (Greene 1983:191)

He then exemplifies this principle by providing a comparison of Theophrastan nomenclature with their modern equivalents, namely,

Theophrastus	Modern
Peuce	*Pinus picea*
Peuce Idaia	*P. maritima*
Peuce conophoros	*P. pinea*
Peuce paralios	*P. halepensis*
Mespilos	*Mespilus Cotoneaster*
Mespilos anthedon	*Cratageus tominalis*

The nomenclatural property described here, of course, is polysemous linguistic recognition of the prototype of a genus, as codified in nomenclatural principle 4a (chapter 1).

Not all of Theophrastus's genera, of course, were marked by "one-worded names." A large number were named by complex expressions representing terms that would be characterized in the present exposition as complex plant names. Greene is at pains to demonstrate that these "two-worded" names do not designate taxa of subgeneric rank but instead show the productive metaphorical capacity of language to form new generic names on the basis of analogy (our principle of generic name extension). Greene compares the following binary names from Theophrastus with their modern equivalents:

Theophrastus	Modern
Calamos Euosmos	*Acorus Calamus*
Dios Anthos	*Agrostemma Flos Jovis*
Dios Balanos	*Castanea vesca*
Carya Persica	*Juglans regia*
Syce Idaia	*Amelanchier vulgaris*
Ampelos Idaia	*Tamus communis*

Greene then describes, in what Lincoln Constance has characterized as his "self-consciously Victorian prose," the processes of the formation of new generic names by analogical reasoning, as these forms contrast with folk species designated by secondary names.

[The modern equivalents for Theophrastus's names] demonstrate beyond cavil that these particular binaries are not of the usual [specific] meaning of such two-fold names, but are purely generic. Theophrastus has a genus *Calamos*, the great reed-grass arundo its type, phragmites also being included in the genus. It is not imaginable that a botanist of Theophrastus' ripe experience . . . should think that those large grass plants [*Calamos Euosmos*] and the sweet-flag [*Acorus Calamus*] to be of the same genus. Beyond doubt, however, that name *Calamos Euosmos* did originate in the notion that arundo and acorus are next of kin; for, however unlike they are as to size, foliage, and other particulars, there is a remarkably close similarity in their rootstocks, these being of almost the same size, form, and color in the two. . . . [To the] gatherers of roots and herbs . . . it would be perfectly natural to place the sweet-flag alongside arundo . . . and then on account of the aromatic properties of the root to call the plant [*Calamos euosmos*]. (Greene 1983:193)

Then, chiding what he sees as the nomenclatural pedantry of present-day botanists, but specifying clearly the essential semantic properties of primary plant names, he asks:

[W]hat reasonable objection . . . can be raised against such binary generic names? . . . Outside the domain of our Latin-worded technicalities it makes not the least difference to any of us to-day how many words go to the making of a generic name. Ivy is a generic name, and as certainly such are Poison Ivy . . . Pine, Ground Pine, and Princes' Pine . . . names of . . . genera in no wise interrelated. (Ibid.:192)

If the fundamental unit focused on in the ethnobotanical system of the early Greeks was the genus, it was no less so in the system of classification devised by Linnaeus himself hundreds of years later. For Linnaeus, "the genus . . . becomes the real building block of the botanical system, and the ability to correctly gather species to form genera is considered the mark of the true botanist" (Lindroth 1983:28).

The zoologist A. J. Cain goes on to develop this idea as it relates to Linnaeus's whole theoretical system. Thus, an essential characteristic of Linnaean taxonomy

was that its primary category, as being most stable and memorable of all, was the genus not the species. All botanists (and by implication all zoologists and mineralogists) must know their genera, which must be separate, distinct entities with distinct names, and natural so that all would agree on their limits. . . . *The genus was the most useful practical unit.* (Cain 1959b:235, emphasis added)

Furthermore, to serve as an efficient mnemonic, the name of the genus must exhibit in the Linnaean system certain linguistic properties. It must be a "single word (and so most concise and memorable), diagnostic if possible . . . and therefore as stable as possible. To be memorable, it must also be distinct" (Cain 1959b:235). These characteristics capture much of the semantic properties recognized for primary plant and animal names.

In his early writings, Linnaeus continued to follow principles of ethnobotanical nomenclature in the treatment of monotypic genera. Thus, he fully "agreed that there are indeed genera containing only a single species each. . . . As a consequence, he maintained with perfect consistency that a species which is the only one in its genus cannot have a specific name" (Cain 1958:158). Polytypic genera, on the other hand, were appropriately designated with binomial terms that are clearly secondary names. Furthermore, the prototypical member of the genus is commonly given a specific epithet indicating 'usual', 'most common', or the like. From Linnaeus's early *Flora Suecica* one notes "*Pinguicula vulgaris*, in contrast to *P. alba* and *P. lapponica*, or *Utricularia major* in contrast to *U. minor*" (Stern 1959:11, emphasis added).

Only later, in 1751, when Linnaeus moved toward a "deliberate and systematic expansion of monomial [generics] into binomials" (Stern 1959:13), did he begin to artificially designate monotypic genera with secondary lexemes, the specific epithet representing in the acerbic words of Greene a "merely decorative or balancing appendage" (Greene 1888). The "decorative appendage" used in such cases was the application of the term *unicus*, hence, *Anthoxanthum unicus, Aphanes unicus, Hepatica unicus*, etc., "thereby indicating the then monotypic state of the genera concerned" (Stern 1959:13).

2.3 EVIDENCE FOR THE PERCEPTUAL SALIENCE OF GENERIC TAXA

Implicit in Bartlett's idea of the genus is its fundamental perceptual unity as a biological category readily recognizable at *first glance*, as a single gestalt or configuration. This is a powerful notion, intuitively understood by every field biologist and practicing taxonomist. The botanist Cronquist states it this way: "If circumstances permit, we try to define genera in such a way that one can recognize a genus from its *aspect*, without recourse to technical characters not readily visible to the naked eye" (Cronquist 1968:30, emphasis added). Greene made a similar claim nearly seventy-five years earlier about his own way of recognizing genera:

A genus is first *recognized* and afterwards *defined*; . . . its acceptability, as a genus, depends more upon the intuitions of . . . botanists, than upon the characters of flowers and fruit . . . in a word, that a genus bears some general features—presents some scarcely definable physiognomy [*sic*]—which, as a whole, signifies more . . . than does any technical peculiarity. (Greene 1894:12)

A. J. Cain would later make explicit this particular character of human beings' recognition of generic categories as they contrast with taxa of lesser rank. Citing Bartlett's 1940 article, Cain says:

The idea of the genus as the smallest 'kind' of plant or animal that can be recognized *without close study* was an extremely important one in the earlier periods of taxonomy. . . . The species was a subdivision of it, often requiring *expert examination* both before it could be recognized and before it could be named. (Cain 1956:97)

[The genus possesses] some characteristic peculiar to it . . . which will *instantly* serve to distinguish it from all others in the natural order. (Cain 1958:148, emphasis added in both quotations)

Cain thus added a significant psychological dimension to Bartlett's original intuition: it is *because* one can indentify a generic category without close study that humans are led to consider the category worthy of a distinctive simple name in the first place.[4]

Larson, in evaluating Linnaeus's actual method of recognizing genera (as opposed to *defining* them), states that an "appeal to general appearance was fundamental to Linné's establishment of genera. . . . Before [he] fixed upon the technical characters which defined plants as one genus, he involved a *coincidence of general appearance*" (Larson 1971:74, emphasis added). As Linnaeus was to state in *Philosophia Botanica*, the genus should furnish the character, not the character the genus. After all, "many people who can perceive a genus cannot define it" (Linnaeus 1751:119, quoted in Nelson and Platnick 1981:90).

It is clear, then, that the genus is seen as a configurational category, recognizable almost instantaneously, in contrast with that of subgeneric groupings whose differentiation often requires deliberate and conscious effort to distinguish. Hunn, elaborating on the ideas of the cognitive psychologists Bruner, Goodnow, and Austin (1956), has proposed that generic taxa be treated as inductively formed categories in ethnobiological systems of classification.[5] He asks us to consider the organism referred to by the term 'raccoon' (*Procyon lotor*) as an example of such an inductive taxon:

> [This category] does not exist by virtue of the fact that [organisms satisfying the conditions appropriate for use of the term possess] certain features such as hair, a banded tail, and a face mask. Rather, by observing . . . the things called raccoons an invariant perceptual pattern is *induced* that can only be labeled 'raccoonness'. This configuration is unique to those organisms that are called raccoons [and is] defined by the natural boundary that exists between the raccoon pattern and the pattern of each other category of organisms. (Hunn 1977:46, emphasis added)

The concepts represented by generic taxa are ones that elude linguistic definition. This point has long been recognized in the philosophy of language literature relating to natural kinds (cf. Atran 1987, 1990; Haiman 1980; Putnam 1975; Leech 1974). Until recently, this was also the position of Wierzbicka (cf. 1972, 1980), who states, "I must confess that I myself have claimed for many years that names of biological folk genera cannot be defined" (Wierzbicka 1985:163). In a remarkable recent book, however, she reconsiders this position and proposes that generic taxa can be verbally defined, even though the so-called definitions look very different from those normally ac-

---

[4] I am grateful to Paul Kay for pointing out Cain's conceptual advance over Bartlett's original observation.

[5] A critical evaluation of Hunn's use of "inductive" here, as it contrasts with his use of "deductive" for taxa of higher rank, has been made by Atran (1985). Hunn would also suggest that most subgeneric taxa are inductively formed. It now seems clear that configurational recoding of subgeneric taxa is at least in part a function of expertise, as work by Hunn himself on the identification of gulls by American birdwatchers demonstrates (Hunn 1975).

cepted as definitions in linguistics or philosophy. Wierzbicka's current position will be discussed in a later chapter, but it is important to report here a claim she makes about the semantic difference between the names of generic and subgeneric taxa.

> *Deer* and *horse* . . . are intended as positive identification terms for certain categories of animals, not as contrastive labels. *Siamese cat* [a folk species] is a contrastive label, but *cat* [a folk generic] isn't. *Polar bear is* intended to distinguish one type of bear from others, but *bear* is intended to identify, not to distinguish. . . . The claim that all concepts are contrastive or are 'delimited in terms of one another' is not only false; it also obscures the fact that *some* concepts indeed are contrastive. Folk genera are not but specific taxa are. (Wierzbicka 1985:231–232)

I will claim later that Wierzbicka is only partially right about the noncontrastive properties of generic terms and the taxa to which they refer, as can be seen in the direct semantic contrast relations that hold between *fir* and *spruce*, *wolf* and *coyote*, *butterfly* and *moth*, and *frog* and *toad* in American English folk biology. Nonetheless, Wierzbicka's intuitions on the essential 'indentificational' vs. 'contrastive' characteristics of generic taxa relate clearly to the unitary configurational properties of generic taxa as contrasted with the semantically complex and often verbalizable properties of subgeneric groupings.

The perceptual centrality of generic taxa can also be inferred from observations by ethnobiologists on the everyday use of generic names to talk about these groupings. Headland, in discussing his work among the Agta Negritos (Philippines), states that

> Psychologically, generic taxa are the most salient in the taxonomy; they were the *first terms our informants gave us in our early ethnobotanical inquiry.* . . . Generic taxa [encompass] plants which are readily perceived as different by any lay person (which is not the case with specific taxa). (Headland 1983:112, emphasis added)

> In our own period of language learning in Agta camps, we learned . . . generic terms of plants long before we ever learned the specific terms. (Headland 1981:97)

P. M. Taylor, in his comprehensive description of Tobelo (Indonesia) ethnobiology, provides a comparable characterization:

> In natural conversation and other contexts, the basic term [i.e., that which refers to a generic taxon] is the one most commonly used . . . to refer to plant and animal types . . . unless the basic type is unrecognized, or some lower-level term is specifically required. . . . Also, informants seem unperturbed by the fact that some basic classes . . . can ambiguously be considered either in the 'tree' or the 'herbaceous weed' superclass; nor do they seem to mind that they are unfamiliar with . . . other subclasses of so many local [plants]. Yet they can and do willingly argue about the 'name' (i.e., the basic term) which properly denotes any particular organism. *It is as if "the Elders" were especially careful to name all the organisms with basic*

terms, and now their less gifted descendants are expected to carefully learn those, but often to just fend for themselves at the higher and lower levels. (P. Taylor 1990:54, emphasis added)

Finally, the significance of fundamental groupings of plants and animals of generic rank can be inferred from studies on the acquisition of botanical terminology in traditional nonliterate societies. To my knowledge, only one such study has been carried out and that is the work of Stross (1973) among the Tzeltal (Mexico).[6] Stross's unique study involved the ingenious use of what he called a plant trail alongside of which some two hundred different plant species were spaced within easy viewing distance. Twenty-five children were led along the trail's course, each being systematically asked the names of the preselected plants in their natural state. The task would normally take about a day, with a long break in the middle. While Stross's study is cross-sectional rather than longitudinal, he was able to develop a number of suggestive hypotheses about how plant names might be acquired by Tzeltal Indian children. His results bear on a number of issues in developmental psychology, but those that are relevant here as regards my discussion of generic taxa are the following:

1. The first reaction of most children who can do so [i.e., who have reached the age of about four years] is to give a plant a generic name whether or not they know the specific or varietal name. That is, it looks as if the *generic name is by far the most salient for almost all plants*.

2. The number of plants that can be specified below the generic level increases with the age of the child. . . . This means that children generally learn the *generic name for a plant before they learn its specific and varietal names*. (Stross 1973:129, emphasis added)

Stross's data further show the importance of insights gained from analyzing the mistakes made by children to the understanding of the conceptual relations that hold between generic taxa, a methodological technique that was later to be used by Hays (1976) for the identification of taxa of intermediate rank in Ndumba (New Guinea) ethnobotany. For example, a child might designate

the *moen ch'o* specimen with the name *tumat* . . . (both of the genus *Physalis*). . . . [Both] quite similar morphologically, the major differences between them being leaf color and fruit size. The fruits of the *tumat*, however, are edible while those of *moen ch'o* are not. Thus, it could be inferred that the child was ignoring edibility, leaf color, and fruit size in making the identification. Nevertheless he must have been

---

[6] Two studies on the acquisition of botanical terminology by children in industrialized societies are Dougherty (1979) and Chambers (1972). In addition to methodological issues that make some aspects of their works difficult to interpret, it is questionable that generalizations drawn from the study of how American schoolchildren acquire plant names may be applied to children growing up in traditional societies who live close to nature on an everyday basis.

attending [to] the presence of fruit, leaf shape and texture, stem composition, and general plant outline in order to give the name *tumat* to the plant. (Ibid.:131)

As Berlin, Breedlove, and Raven were to show later (1974), these generics are conceptually related in two major intermediate taxa of the Solanum family in the Tzeltal system of ethnobotanical classification. They are brought together because of their striking morphological similarities that the inexperienced child learns to note first.

Stross's summary of his study is relevant here to the overall picture of the psychological significance of generic taxa:

It appears that in actual practice the child begins his acquisition of botanical nomenclature by learning generic names simultaneously with supra-generic names for other plants. Then, as he is learning specific names that differentiate the generics, he is also learning generic names that differentiate the supra-generics. It is in this light that we can state that the bulk of the child's first learned plant names are generic names, and that from this starting point he continues to differentiate nomenclaturally while cognitively he continues to differentiate and generalize plant [species] and attributes simultaneously. (Ibid.:140)

2.4 GENERIC TAXA, ETHNOBIOLOGICAL RANK, AND ANALYTIC TERMINOLOGY

Ethnobiologists will readily agree that in all systems of ethnobiological classification one can discover named groupings of plants and animals that represent Bartlett's "smallest groupings requiring a distinctive name" or, in Cain's rephrasing of Bartlett, "the smallest 'kind[s]' of plants or animals that can be recognized without close study." These fundamental taxa roughly correspond (as stated explicitly by Bartlett and Greene) to taxa known as 'genera' in modern biological systematics. The problem, of course, is the empirical observation that folk generic taxa do not in most cases correspond *perfectly* with taxa recognized as genera in the Western scientific system. Furthermore, subgeneric taxa that I refer to as 'folk species' or 'folk specifics' also do not generally correspond in a perfectly predictable way with taxa recognized as 'species' in Western taxonomy.

These observations are related to one major conceptual problem that has plagued ethnobiological theory for many years now. This is the confusion of two different but nonetheless intuitively related concepts, namely, the *level* of some particular taxon and its ethnobiological *rank*. In Western scientific biological classification, the level and rank of a particular taxon are always in perfect correspondence. While this may also be true for some portions of a folk taxonomic hierarchy, there are numerous exceptions leading to structural asymmetries where level and rank do not coincide perfectly. These asymmetries have often led to the development of terminologies that confound these analytically distinct concepts in a number of ways. As will be seen, "level" is trivially easy to define; "rank," on the other hand, is quite slippery.

The conceptual problems raised by these alternative analytical terminologies, while hardly of such proportions as to make cross-cultural comparisons between systems impossible, have nonetheless clouded interpretation of ethnobiological data on classification unnecessarily. As we will see, disagreement is only partially due to the similarity of the names chosen to refer to ethnobiological (vs. biological) taxa involved (e.g., *folk* generics versus *scientific* genera). At the core of the matter are confusions and disagreements about how best to characterize the differing taxonomic levels and ranks into which the plant and animal taxa comprising folk systems of biological classification are distributed.

In an effort to clarify these ambiguities, I contrast in the following pages my own views with the most prevalent alternative terminological proposals and the analytic positions that each entails, evaluate their strengths and shortcomings, and conclude with the reasons why I believe my current usage is preferable, at least for the time being. The goal is to develop a useful comparative analytic and typological framework that will allow for general comparisons to be naturally and easily drawn between ethnobiological systems anywhere in the world.

Bulmer: The Specieme and Taxonomic Level

As discussed in chapter 1, at about the same time that Breedlove, Raven, and I were developing our framework for discussing systems of ethnobiological classification, Ralph Bulmer was developing his own as he and his collaborators carried out their now classic work on Kalam ethnozoology. In a series of publications focusing on various vertebrate groups known to the Kalam, Bulmer describes zoological taxa in terms that indicate their structural position in the taxonomic hierarchy. There are five types:

1. *Primary taxa*: "those taxa not subsumable into any larger taxon other than *tap* 'thing' "
2. *Secondary taxa*: "immediate subdivisions of primary taxa"
3. *Tertiary taxa*: "immediate subdivisions of secondary taxa"
4. *Quaternary taxa*: "subdivisions of tertiary taxa"
5. *Terminal taxa*: "[taxa] regardless of their hierarchical status, if they are units with no standardly named subdivisions." (Bulmer 1970:1073–1074)

In an earlier article, Bulmer states the significance of these definitions as follows:

Ka[l]am zoological taxonomy is conveniently approached at two levels. . . . One can look at the broadest groupings, what I call the 'primary taxa', and try to see what sense these make as a set . . . [or] one can look at the smallest units which Ka[l]am discriminate, the 'terminal taxa', and with them the rather few intermediate taxa present in the system, to see what kinds of discriminations are being made. (Bulmer 1967:6)

In addition to classifying Kalam taxa in terms of their position in the taxonomic hierarchy, Bulmer introduces, in a paper written in collaboration with the herpetologist M. J. Tyler, the term "specieme" (Bulmer and Tyler 1968). There they define the specieme as "groups of creatures marked off from all other animals . . . by multiple distinctions of appearance, habitat, and behavior and not including recognized sub-groupings marked off from each other in a similar way" (ibid.:372–373). The word "specieme," of course, is a neologism, utilizing the suffix -eme to form a name analogous to the linguistic terms "phoneme" or "morpheme" as the smallest structurally significant units of sound and meaning in any language.

Bulmer is confronted with problems, however, when he tries to combine information about the *structural level* of a Kalam taxon and its status as a *specieme*. Thus, at the lowest level of the taxonomy the Kalam "show an enormous, detailed and on the whole highly accurate knowledge of natural history . . . [while at] the upper level . . . objective biological facts no longer dominate the scene. . . . This is the level at which culture takes over and determines the selection of taxonomically significant characters. It is not surprising that the result shows little correspondence . . . to the taxonomy of the professional zoologist" (Bulmer 1967:6).

When one looks at Bulmer's primary taxa, however, taxa "not subsumable under any larger taxon other than *tap* 'thing'," one discovers that the majority of these taxa show a great deal of correspondence with scientific taxa, e.g., **kayn** 'dog', **kaj** 'pig', **aypot** 'agamid lizard', **wowiy** 'small gecko', and many others. Of the ninety-four primary taxa reported by Bulmer, sixty-six, or 70 percent, are monotypic and satisfy his definition of specieme. Bulmer would not claim, I believe, that the primary taxon **wowiy** has the same cognitive status in Kalam ethnozoological classification as does the primary taxon **yakt** 'bird' with some 181 subordinate groupings.

Bulmer's scheme presents the unwieldy situation of talking about speciemes in a way that ties them to an arbitrary typology directly associated with their position in the hierarchy, when in fact level is only indirectly associated with cognitive status. Bulmer recognizes this, of course, by stressing the specieme status of the primary taxon **wowiy** while noting that the taxon **yakt** is a primary taxon of a "higher order" (cf. Bulmer and Tyler 1968:350). In the analytic framework outlined in the present book, while **wowiy** and **yakt** are taxonomically both "primary taxa" in Bulmer's formal sense, cognitively they are significantly distinct from each other because they are members of different ethnobiological ranks, *generic* and *life form*, respectively.

Further problems are introduced when Bulmer discusses Kalam ethnobiology by focusing on "terminal taxa." In his important paper, "Which Came First, the Chicken or the Egg-Head?", Bulmer presents a "number of generalisations concerning Ka[l]am terminal taxa" (Bulmer 1970:1076), the most important of which are their morphological distinctiveness, their assignment to characteristic habitats, and their being identified on the basis of song, calls, and other behavioral features. Most terminal taxa are "thus in a very real sense to be seen as 'natural' units" (ibid.:1077). But, as with the primary taxa of level 1 in the taxonomy, Bulmer is aware that not all terminal taxa are of the same status, some representing his so-called natural units that contrast on a large number of characters, while others represent groupings of organisms that are distinguished on but a few dimensions (e.g., *jejeg km* 'green *Hyla angiana*', *jejeg pkay* 'reddish *Hyla angiana*', *jejeg mlep* 'dull colored *Hyla angiana*', and *jejeg mosob* 'dark *Hyla angiana*').

Bulmer's proposal that terminal taxa as such are somehow special in ethnobiological classification is erroneous; however, he was not the first to make such a mistake. This is precisely the error that Berlin, Breedlove, and Raven made in 1966, when they treated all terminal taxa as "folk species." As we now know, the fact that a folk taxon is terminal has very little to say about its biological or cognitive status. (See Berlin, Breedlove, and Raven 1966 for their first unsuccessful analysis; Berlin 1973 for a reevaluation; and Gould 1979:209–210 for a recounting of this brief chapter in the history of false starts and rethinking of analytic concepts in ethnobiological classification.) In general, as Hays was to put it several years later, Bulmer's data clearly indicate that "not all taxa which appear at the same level are the same in terms of their biological content, and not all taxa with comparable content are found at the same structural level" (Hays 1979).

In a perceptive summary of his work in New Guinea up to the mid 1970s, Bulmer recognizes the differences between the terminology he proposes and the one suggested by my colleagues and me, although he never addresses the issue of the content of ethnobiological taxa (rank) and their structural position (level) directly. With characteristic understatement and good taste, he takes issue with my use of the term "generic" in spite of his general agreement about the nature of the taxa to which the term is meant to refer:

> While one can certainly accept Berlin's view that the uninomial categories [i.e., those labeled by primary names] which he distinguishes as 'generics' appear normally to be much the most numerous taxa in folk-classifications of plants and animals, and many of these taxa are psychologically and culturally very salient, I feel some hesitation about accepting his terminology. This is because I agree with Françoise Panoff (1972:101) that logically one cannot conceive of 'generic' categories without prior (or at least concurrent) conception of 'specifics', and that there are,

empirically, too many cases on record where uninomials in fact apply to logical (and often also biological) species. (Bulmer 1974a:22)

Unfortunately, both Bulmer and Panoff fail to understand my use of the term "generic" for two very different reasons. The first, as indicated by Bulmer's last sentence, is the belief that my colleagues and I propose a one-to-one correspondence of ethnobiological generic taxa and scientific genera. We have never argued for such a direct correspondence, any more than Bulmer has argued for a one-to-one relationship with his speciemes and scientific species. Bulmer's and Panoff's second confusion is the so-called logical impossibility of conceiving of "generic" taxa without prior conception of "specifics." As seen from my brief survey of early biological systematics at the beginning of this chapter, generic monotypy was no problem for early biologists, nor is it for present-day ones.

In all such cases, of course, the genus is identical in extension with the species. In any local habitat, large numbers of biological species, especially among the vertebrate animals and larger vascular plants, are often the sole representatives of their respective genera. While we commonly refer to these taxa as "species," the biological (and perceptual) gap that separates them from other organisms in the area is comparable to the gap that separates *genera*, not *species*, a point elaborated earlier in Berlin (1982). The issue of monotypy (in both ethnobiological and biological taxonomies) will be discussed further in chapter 4, which deals in part with the conceptual significance of unaffiliated generics vis-à-vis life-form taxa. It is sufficient to note here that there is no logical inconsistency in utilizing the term "generic" for taxa that are not further subdivided into named lower-order groupings.

Finally, it is worth pointing out that Bulmer may have been moving toward the use of the term "generic" for fundamental groupings of plants in his unfinished work on Kalam ethnobotany. In an appendix to his important work with Saem Majnep on Kalam birds, Bulmer writes the following:

A major problem in determining the content of Kalam plant taxa . . . is that a high proportion of these are 'generic' rather than 'specific' in nature; or, to be precise, the names for them are 'generic' as well as 'specific'. In this they contrast with the majority of frequently used taxa applied to vertebrate animals which may, in most contexts, be regarded as 'specifics'. Thus *jbl* . . . may apply either to a 'generic' group with some five named divisions and including certain, but not all *Syzygium* spp.; or *jbl* (*yb*), ('true') *jbl*, to a particular 'species', as yet undetermined. (Majnep and Bulmer 1977:193)

Conklin: The Specific Plant Type and Basic Plant Names

In his description of Hanunóo ethnobotany, Conklin provided a possible neutral terminology for referring to recognized ethnobiological plant (and, by implication, animal) taxa (Conklin 1954). Conklin recognizes 1,625 "specific plant types" which he defines as

> the smallest recognized plant segregate[s] all members of which exhibit similar and well known distinguishing characteristics. Finer division of such a plant type involves differentiation which is linguistically unrecognized or at least unsystematically describable, and which is based conceptually only on characteristics of individual plants, not on those of a specific plant category. (Conklin 1954:116)

Each of these plant types

> has a full specific name differing in at least one component from all others. Such a designation is comprised of either a single, full-word *basic plant name*, or a combination of a basic plant name and one or two full-word attributives. . . . All Hanunóo plant type names contain one basic plant name; 571 have only basic names. . . . Excluding . . . synonyms, there are 822 distinct . . . basic plant names in our inventory of Hanunóo plant type designations. (Ibid.:116–119, emphasis in original)

(Subsequent fieldwork by Conklin increased the inventory of "basic plant names" to more than 900. The number of terminal taxa is now reported to be 1,756 [Conklin, pers. comm.].)

Conklin does not explicitly recognize in his characterization of Hanunóo "specific" plant groupings those that would be referred to here as generics and subgroupings of these generic taxa. It is perfectly clear, however, that the 822 Hanunóo specific plant types given distinct basic plant names are not all of equal cognitive status or biological content. The majority of these taxa are monotypic (571, or 70 percent) and are named only by basic plant names. The remaining 251 taxa are further subdivided into contrast sets ranging from 2 to 92 taxa per set. These latter plant groupings are naturally treated in the current framework as *folk specifics* and take as their labels secondary plant names.

It would, of course, be possible to refer to the two groups of taxa using Conklin's terminology. In such a situation we would have categories of two types:

Type 1: "Specific plant taxa" labeled exclusively by basic plant names
Type 2: "Specific plant taxa" labeled by a basic plant name plus one or more attributives.

While technically accurate, such a characterization does not, in my view, point as concisely to the biological and cognitive distinctions that underlie these two fundamentally distinct kinds of taxa as does the contrast specified by the terms *generic* and *specific* used in the present framework.

Rosch: The Basic Level and Basic Level Objects

Eleanor Rosch, in a series of important papers, has generalized two of the findings made earlier in ethnobiological categorization (and, for that matter, in the categorization of color, see Berlin and Kay 1969) to more general psychological processes. The first finding deals with the internal structure of categories, particularly those natural categories that show what she was later to call "prototype effects." As will be seen in a number of places in the present work, prototypicality effects are of fundamental importance to understanding the nature of ethnobiological classification. Rosch's second contribution concerns what she calls "basic level categories" or "basic level objects." It is this latter concept that is relevant to a discussion of terminology for generic taxa in ethnobiological systems of classification.

On the basis of a series of ingenious experiments, Rosch was able to show that in a hierarchically organized set of categories one can isolate a single "level" comprised of categories that have greatest "cue validity" and "category resemblance." For Rosch, cue validity is a probabilistic concept: "The validity of a given cue x as a predictor of a given category y . . . increases as the frequency with which cue x is associated with category y increases and decreases as the frequency with which cue x is associated with categories other than y increases" (Rosch 1978:30). "Category resemblance," a concept she derives from Tversky and Gati (1978), is defined as "the weighted sum of the measures of all of the common features within a category minus the sum of the measures of all of the distinctive features" (ibid.:31). In a taxonomic hierarchy, some categories' total cue validity and overall category resemblance are "maximized at the level at which basic objects are categorized" (ibid.: 31).

In most instances, basic level objects fall somewhere in the middle of taxonomic hierarchies, and categories both superordinate and subordinate are psychologically less salient. In Rosch's words,

> Superordinate categories have lower total cue validity and lower category resemblance than do basic-level categories, because they have fewer common attributes; in fact, the category resemblance measure of items within the superordinate can even be negative due to the high ratio of distinctive to common features. Subordinate categories have lower total cue validity than do basic categories, because they also share most attributes with contrasting subordinate categories. . . . That basic objects are categories at the level of abstraction that maximizes cue validity and maximizes category resemblance is another way of asserting that basic objects are the categories that best mirror the correlational structure of the environment. (Ibid.:31)

The full range of Rosch's experiments need not be outlined here. However, I will briefly describe one of her experiments relating to the determination of the common attributes of categories in that it bears on the relationship of the level (read *rank*) of a taxon and its designation as one of Rosch's basic-level objects.

Rosch and her coworkers set out to determine the basic level of categories in several sets of hierarchically related classes. Terms of each taxonomy were selected on the basis of their frequency of occurrence using standard word frequency sources. An example of two such taxonomies is shown in table 2.1. The experimenters then gave subjects these sets of words and later showed them examples of the objects named in the taxonomies. Subjects were asked to

> list all of the attributes [they] could think of that were true of the items included in the class of things designated by each object name. . . . Very few attributes were listed for the superordinate categories, a significantly greater number were listed for the supposed basic level objects, and not significantly more attributes listed for sub-ordinate-level objects than for basic-level. . . . The single unpredicted result was that for the . . . biological taxonomies, the basic level, as defined by numbers of attributes in common, *did not occur at the level of the folk generic* but appeared at the level we had originally expected to be superordinate [e.g., *tree* rather than *oak*, *maple*, and *birch*]. (Ibid.:32–33, emphasis added)

Rosch's findings conflict with studies such as that of Stross (1973), in his work with Tzeltal children, and do not conform to accounts of other ethno-biologists in describing the central significance of generic taxa in the ethno-biological systems of classification of peoples in more traditional societies. They clearly do not support Berlin, Breedlove, and Raven's emphatic claim that "generic taxa mark the most salient conceptual groupings in any folk taxonomy" (Berlin, Breedlove, and Raven 1973:240).

Dougherty (1978) conducted a study that confirmed Rosch's results regarding the greater salience of taxa of life-form rank over generic taxa in the classification of plants by speakers of American English. This led Dougherty to

TABLE 2.1
Examples of the Terms for Kinds of Furniture and Trees Used in Rosch's Basic-Level Objects Experiments

Superordinate	Basic Level	Subordinate
Furniture	Chair	Kitchen chair Living-room chair
	Table	Kitchen table Dining-room table
Tree	Oak	White oak Red oak
	Maple	Silver maple Sugar maple
	Birch	River birch White birch

conclude that the rank at which the most psychologically salient taxa are found in ethnobiological taxonomies is variable. For her American subjects,

> there is a shift [upward] in the most salient taxonomic rank of a hierarchy toward increasingly more inclusive levels as the overall salience of the domain itself declines and the taxonomic structure devolves [e.g., American English folk botany]. The most basic or salient level [*sic*] will be shown to be a variable phenomenon shifting primarily as a function of general cultural significance and individual familiarity and expertise, and secondarily as a function of perceptual homogeneity, objective correlational structure, or, the degree of internal variation in the domain membership. (Dougherty 1978:67)

Boster (1980), in a detailed study of the classification of manioc (*Manihot esculenta*) among the Aguaruna (Peru), was later to make a similar claim, this time in relation to the *downward* movement of the so-called most salient rank. Boster used the frequency of choice of a term in reference as evidence of psychological salience and showed conclusively a significant difference in the way Aguaruna males and females referred to this important cultigen (as discussed later in chapter 5). Males, whose primary role in the Aguaruna economy is hunting and fishing, commonly chose to refer to manioc with its proper folk generic name, *máma*. Females, who have primary responsibility for Aguaruna horticultural activities, almost invariably referred to individual varieties of manioc using folk-specific terminology for these categories, e.g., *yakím máma, suhíknum, puyám*. As Boster puts it, "Appropriate level of reference [indicating salience] shifts according to the speaker's sexual social role" (Boster 1980:57).

These findings have the following interpretations for the current argument. First, none of the data summarized above lend support to Dougherty's claim that psychological salience is tied inextricably with rank, globally moving upward (as a system of folk classification devolves) or downward (with specialization) en masse. Even in American English ethnozoological classification, with its rapidly devolving ethnobiological taxonomy, many taxa of folk generic rank continue to have greatest saliency. It is curious that Rosch and her associates did not use as one of their biological hierarchies sequences of animal names comparable to *animal* (i.e., 'four-legged critter with hairy skin', technically *mammal*) > *rabbit* > *jackrabbit, cottontail rabbit; fox* > *gray fox, red fox*; and *peccary* > *collared peccary, white-lipped peccary*. Rosch recognizes that had she done so she would have found that folk generic mammal taxa would be shown to have higher salience than the superordinate taxon *mammal*. In anticipation of this result she notes:

> Indeed, differentiation of mammals (but not birds [and] fish) into basic level objects [*sic*] can be observed in our own culture which is more knowledgeable about mam-

mals than other animal classes . . . mammals are thought of as members of their basic level classes and are called by their basic names. The names of mammals are one level in the taxonomy lower than are the basic level classes and names for other major animal classifications (Rosch, Simpson, and Miller 1976:492).

Of course, Rosch does not mean that the folk generic taxa marking 'animal (mammal)' taxa (*fox, rabbit, peccary*) are *structurally* "one level in the taxonomy lower" than other generic taxa such as *robin, eagle*, and *cardinal*, or *trout, bass*, and *crappie*. (See comments on P. Taylor's use of "basic level category," below.) Although she unfortunately uses the term "level" quite loosely, what she is referring to is the *psychological salience* of these groupings.

Likewise, Boster, in noting the differences in the inferred psychological salience of manioc for Aguaruna males and females, does not necessarily imply that the salience of *all* taxa of subgeneric rank had increased for females simply on the basis of their specialized familiarity with the varieties of manioc. This is clearly a case of differential cognitive competence between men and women as concerns their knowledge of the domain of plants. Some portions of the domain are intimately known to members of one gender (wild plant species by men) while another portion (cultivated species, especially manioc) are more intimately known by women.

If psychological salience can be inferred from these kinds of data, one may make the following generalization and reformulation of an earlier principle of ethnobiological classification: *the psychological salience of individual taxa in ethnobiological systems of classification cannot unambiguously be inferred solely by reference to their taxonomic rank.*

The implications of this generalization and the use of the concept (or some variant of) "basic-level object" to characterize taxa of generic rank will be discussed in a moment. First, however, I describe briefly the use of Rosch's terminology by Paul Taylor and Darrell Posey.

Posey: The BOL

Posey (1979) provides a full-scale description of the ethnoentomological system of classification by the Kayapó (Brazil). In his analysis he adopts Rosch's terminology, noting that

> the term 'basic level object' has been used . . . to describe those natural forms most often recognized in folk systems. Basic object level (BOL) categories are encoded in a gestalt fashion, with gross morphological features being the prevailing criteria. The reference point of the folk entomological classification system is the basic object level (BOL) category. It is at this level that maximal psychological and cultural salience occurs [but see below]. (Posey 1979:93, 162)

His subsequent description shows clearly that these groupings are easily equated with generic taxa, *sensu* Berlin. Thus, Posey makes the following comparisons:

> If basic object level categories are equated with the concept of 'folk genus', then additional taxonomic concepts can be utilized. Subgroupings of BOL categories (folk genera) can be called 'folk species'. . . . The more refined (differentiated) the subdivisions, the more clearly or precisely defined the sets. . . . At higher levels . . . the sets are most vague. (Ibid.:163)

In spite of Posey's claim that his BOL categories are the most psychologically significant groupings for the Kayapó (see above quote), he makes the following contradictory statement:

> For bees, wasps, and ants, the sub-species [i.e., Berlin's subgeneric taxa] are of greater psychological and cultural salience than the more generalized BOL categories (*mehn* ['bees'], *amuh* ['wasps'] and *mrum* ['ants']). . . . There is a very fundamental difference in the basis of 'salience' between BOL and sub-specific categories. (Posey 1979:164–165)

What Posey is noting here is a phenomenon comparable to Boster's description for Aguaruna manioc: the psychological salience of a taxon varies with its cultural importance. Once again, Posey's data show that salience cannot unambiguously be associated with all taxa of a particular rank.

Taylor: The Basic B⁰ Level

Paul Taylor (1990) provides a comprehensive and cognitively oriented description of Tobelo (Moluccas, Indonesia) ethnobiology. Taylor recognizes the significance of taxa of generic rank in his analysis, but chooses to employ "basic term" and "basic level" for these groupings. He derives the term "basic" from Conklin, whom he cites, but his use of the concept of "basic level" is very close to that of Rosch, although there is no indication that he is aware of her work. In reference to the terminology of Berlin, Breedlove, and Raven, Taylor says:

> The frequently used terms 'generic' (basic or B^0) and 'specific' (B^{-1}) are avoided here because (1) this terminology invites confusion with the senses of these terms in biology; and (2) the normal everyday English meaning of a 'generic' word is simply a term at a higher level than other terms in question (e.g., 'furniture' is a generic word for tables, chairs, etc., just as 'tree' is a generic word for pine, oak, etc.). (Taylor 1990:183)

Both of Taylor's reasons have some merit inasmuch as any terminology that has some prior meaning associations can constitute grounds for confusion.

However, as seen in the opening section of this chapter, the genus has a long history in biology as constituting the fundamental and primitive building blocks of plant and animal classification. Folk generic taxa are logically comparable and often substantively similar in content to scientific genera. Furthermore, in the context of the study of ethnobiological classification, it should not be overly burdensome to distinguish the slightly more technical meaning of 'generic' used here from its more common everyday usage. To fully specify the meaning of "basic" in the sense required for discussion in ethnobiological systematics surely requires no less effort.

Taylor's own proposals, furthermore, do not provide the clarification that he seeks over the terminology employed by Berlin, Breedlove, and Raven. His unfortunate use of the convention of superscript numerals to designate the level of a taxon (and its associated term) in Tobelo ethnobiological classification leads to a number of problems in analysis. Superscript numerals, a common convention employed in kinship terminological analysis to designate generation in reference to ego, are used by Taylor to indicate the *number of levels* above or below his so-called basic level. The Tobelo taxon 'tree' *o gota*, for example, occurs at level B^{+1} while *o hulahi* (*Ocimum sanctum*), a particular kind of tree, is a basic level taxon labeled by a B^0 term. A particular subclass of this tree is *o hulahi ma doka-dokara* and is treated as a taxon of level B^{-1}.

The major ambiguity that this convention imposes on the analysis is that a number of taxa that I treat as generic, and Taylor as basic level, occur formally at the same hierarchic level as taxa that we would both wish to treat as conceptually distinct, e.g., life-form taxa for Berlin or B^{+1} taxa for Taylor. Thus, in Tobelo, as in perhaps most ethnobiological systems of classification, one finds the unlikely groupings of 'tree', 'vine', and 'herb' (life-form or B^{+1} taxa) at the same taxonomic level with such taxa as 'nipa palm', 'maize', '*Cycas* sp.', and many other unaffiliated generic or B^0 taxa. Taylor gets around this by defining a pair of contrast relations, *immediate contrast* and *disjunctive contrast*, that he thinks account for these asymmetries. In effect, however, his argument depends solely on assigning some special and unspecified meaning to the length of lines used in his diagrams which, on careful analysis, cannot obscure the empirical fact that 'tree' and 'maize', for example, are indeed at the same taxonomic level.

What Taylor is confronted with, of course, is the problem already mentioned for Bulmer's treatment of Kalam ethnozoology, namely, that taxa of differing ethnobiological ranks occur, at times, at the same taxonomic level in folk taxonomies, and conversely that taxa of the same rank may range over several structural levels in the hierarchy. In the complex but extremely interesting world that ethnobiologists are confronted with, the assignment of taxonomic rank must be based on an explicit evaluation of several biological, nomenclatural, and psychological criteria simultaneously.

Atran: The Generic-Specieme

Scott Atran (1988, 1990) has recently proposed yet another modification to the terminology for talking about the fundamental groupings that comprise ethnobiological systems of classification. Atran's framework corresponds fundamentally with that of my own (but see chapter 4 for several minor disagreements). However, he proposes an alternative terminology that represents a compromise between Bulmer's and mine, based in part on the observation that in locally circumscribed habitats one finds numerous monotypic genera. Building partly on an unpublished paper by Berlin (1982), Atran notes that

> within any given local community a principled distinction between genus and species is usually impossible perceptually because most genera are monospecific. The distinction is frequently also irrelevant conceptually inasmuch as the species of locally monogeneric or minimally polytypic families may have the same sorts of morphological, geographical and behavioral correlates as the genera of locally polygeneric families. In such cases, the perceptible morpho-ecological distance between species of the monogeneric or minimally polytypic family more or less correspond to that between genera of the polygeneric family (cf. Berlin 1982). Finally, the distinction is often inconsequential to anyone but a geneticist or micro-evolutionary theorist. . . . For the most part, then, local species are marked by 'generic gaps' in the local economy of nature, and have no rivals to compete with for generic status. That is why I label the basic level [*sic*] of folk taxonomy "generic-specieme." (Atran 1988:39)

In the main, I have no disagreements with Atran's suggestions here, although he is empirically off the mark when he states that most scientific genera in local circumscribed habitats are monospecific (i.e., monotypic) (Atran [pers. comm.] no longer holds this view). A substantial proportion of scientific genera are monotypic, to be sure, but these are restricted to selected groupings of vertebrate animals, for example, mammals, and some phylogenetically unique phanerogams, for example, the palms. Nonetheless, as I claimed earlier, the perceptual gap separating folk generics from one another appears to be comparable to that which generally separates biological genera, at least for many groupings of the larger vertebrates and higher vascular plants. This observation, of course, does not hold for most invertebrates or cryptogams.

As far as the hybrid term "generic-specieme" is concerned, and in spite of Atran's efforts to provide a useful compromise between the terminology used by Bulmer and mine, I find the terminological innovation less than satisfactory. Whatever terminology we decide to employ, it should, as Linnaeus advised us long ago, "be apt in meaning, easy to say and remember, and pleasant to hear" (as quoted in Stern 1959:8). If Bulmer's neologism "specieme" lacks a certain euphonic quality, I must confess that the second-degree coinage of "generic-specieme" sounds even less pleasing to the ear.

In summary, I have presented above several alternative analytic and terminological suggestions for discussing the primary taxa in folk systems of biological classification. In Bulmer's and Taylor's proposals, I have pointed out the problems that arise by confusing the taxonomic level of generic taxa, whether they be called *speciemes* or *basic B⁰ level taxa*, with their ethnobiological rank. Rosch's proposal of *basic-level objects* and *basic-object level* presents similar problems of confusion of rank with structural position, but its most serious weakness might be seen as its major strength. Rosch's goal was to demonstrate the special psychological salience of her so-called basic-object categories. As we have seen, Boster's and Posey's data show clearly that psychological salience may vary for individual taxa in any particular ethnobiological system of classification due to cultural and social factors. Thus, just as some taxa of generic rank vary in their taxonomic position, some likewise show differences in their psychological salience. If the notion of basic-level object is to serve a useful purpose in ethnobiological theory, then it should be used to point to the psychological properties of taxa and not be tied inextricably to considerations of their rank.

There is one additional aspect of Rosch's research that merits discussion here. It bears on Dougherty's (1978) claims about the relativity of the general salience of taxa of generic rank. Data from a number of studies of ethnobiological classification show that the salience of certain folk specific taxa is greater than that of taxa of generic rank. The data further allow one to conclude that the increased salience of these subgeneric taxa is due to the cultural significance of the organisms involved (e.g., important cultigens, insects important in the local economy and ritual, and so forth). The comparative materials on the overall structure of systems of ethnobiological classification also show, however, that the large majority (around 80 percent) of generic taxa are not further subdivided into groupings of lower rank. These terminal generic taxa also have high salience inasmuch as they represent the small subset of organisms singled out for linguistic recognition from the total inventory of species in any local environment. Berlin, Breedlove, and Raven were generally on the mark, as other ethnobiological studies have confirmed, in claiming that generic taxa are, *in the main*, also the most salient. But why are these groupings not further subdivided? Rosch addresses the issue as follows:

> We believe that for all taxonomies there is a level [rank] below which further differentiations cannot form basic level categories because, no matter how great the frequency of use of the objects or degree of expertise, there simply is not a sufficient number of attributes to differentiate objects below that level. Thus, for any taxonomy there should be a level [rank] at which the attributes common to objects which

are added by further distinctions will be outweighed by the attributes which the newly distinguished classes share with each other. (Rosch, Simpson, and Miller 1976:492)

The taxa disallowing "further differentiations [into] basic level categories" are, of course, most of the taxa of generic rank in folk biological taxonomies. While many of these taxa may be *potentially* subdivided on the basis of demonstrable morphological differences into distinct biological populations, this activity will be carried out for the most part by those specialists who have made this activity their professional occupation—systematic botanists and zoolologists employing the methods of Western science (for further discussion of this point, see chapter 3).

The empirical data suggest that no system of ethnobiological classification will divide all of its recognized generic taxa (i.e., the taxa most readily recognizable without close study) into taxa of lower rank, which might then assume greater saliency. As Lakoff has written, in summarizing my views, "Berlin's hypothesis . . . predicts that there will be no whole culture that will treat the level of the species or variety [i.e., taxa of subgeneric rank] as basic, but that individuals [with] expertise in a limited range of domains . . . may be able to treat a small number of more specific categories as basic" (Lakoff 1987:37).

2.5 ON PREDICTING THE SUBSET OF GENERIC TAXA

Twenty years ago, I sat with Eugene Hunn in the bar of the Hotel Bolívar in Lima, drinking pisco sours and listening to the melancholic sound of Peruvian *criollo* music. We had just returned from the field after having completed a short ethnobiological survey of the Aguaruna, a group of Jivaroan-speaking people residing in the rain forests of the Upper Marañón River valley and with whom I was ultimately to work for the next decade. I had just finished a long stint of ethnobotanical fieldwork among the Tzeltal of southern Mexico and Gene had just turned in the first draft of his dissertation on Tzeltal ethnozoology. The new work with the Aguaruna was to be aimed at testing some of the notions about the universal features of ethnobiological systems of classification that had begun to emerge from the work in Mexico.

As we continued to enjoy the Peruvian national beverage, we began to speculate about what form a unified theory of ethnobiological classification might take. We both agreed, along with Simpson, Mayr, and many orthodox biological systematists, on the reality of lower-level biological taxa—groupings of organisms "quite as obvious to [the] modern scientist as . . . to a Guaraní Indian" (Simpson 1961:57). The task was to determine how best to characterize the ethnobiological knowledge of the Guaraní Indian and, by implication, that of ethnobiological systems of classification in general.

Ultimately, we developed a fanciful research project. First, a group of biologists would carry out a detailed survey of the flora and fauna of some restricted region inhabited by a group of tropical-forest Indians. They would return to a home base where their specimens would be catalogued, identified, and given their proper place in the Western taxonomic system. For the purposes of our experiment, our botanists and zoologists would not talk to the Indians. (Our pisco sours suggested to us at this point that if this were a problem, we might temporarily remove the Indians by helicopter to another region while the biologists conducted their surveys, but this notion was quickly abandoned as unethical and, in any case, too expensive.)

Finally, a team of ethnobiologists would enter the scene. By this time, they would have read the biologists' faunal and floral surveys, which they would use, in combination with a number of other hunches about the nature of ethnobiological classification, to *predict which groupings of plants and animals would be named by the local human population*. Their predictions would be tested by standard ethnographic and ethnobiological data-collecting techniques and long hours of interviewing.

Hunn was later to codify these loosely organized notions into what he was to call an "ultimate test" of ethnobiological classification. This test would involve the prediction of the biological content of all ethnobiological categories nomenclaturally recognized in a particular folk system "and the subsequent and independent verification of the predictions by field investigations" (Hunn 1977:107).

I would now elaborate on the original proposal in the following way. An adequate theory of ethnobiological classification must provide general answers to at least the following fundamental questions:

1. Which groupings of organisms naturally occurring in some localized habitat will be recognized and which ones ignored in the local ethnobiological system of classification?
2. Of those groupings that are recognized, which are concordant with the natural system of classification of Western science, and what explains this concordance?
3. When the ethnobiological and scientific systems diverge, what factors best account for their divergence?

Hunn stated that the success of one's predictions would depend on several factors, the most important of which being a thorough knowledge of the "intergroup differences for all local groups of organisms. This [knowledge would] provide the basis for a rank ordering of the biological groups according to the degree to which they are distinctive" (ibid.:72). In general, he concludes, "the probability that a group of organisms will be recognized and named is directly proportional to the [distinctiveness] of [that group] as determined by taxonomic analysis" (ibid.:72).

No such "ultimate test" of the sort Hunn proposed has ever been undertaken in ethnobiology. Unfortunately, Hunn himself has significantly modified his view that the distinctiveness of organisms constitutes the primary platform on which all systems of ethnobiological classification are erected (see Hunn 1982; Randall and Hunn 1984). This change in perspective is motivated, in part, by the obvious empirical observation that only a small subset of the species diversity in any one local habitat is ever recognized linguistically by local human populations and that the absolute number of ethnobiological taxa is always much smaller than that recognized by Western science.

What, then, underlies the choice of individuals in traditonal societies to categorize those biological organisms that do indeed get named? For those who would take a strict utilitarian approach, there is but one simple answer. Since there are far too many distinctive pieces of biological reality to be dealt with conceptually and linguistically, then we have no alternative but "to impose a selective process based on *utility*. If we are to explain why a particular subset of the available natural discontinuities is selected for cultural recognition, we must model this selection process. This requires us to consider the *practical consequences* of knowing or not knowing some plant or animal" (Hunn 1982:834, emphasis added). Or, as Posey was to state later: "Description and analysis of classification . . . do not explain *why* certain natural domains are classified and named while others are not. This question is best investigated from the utilitarian/adaptionist approach" (Posey 1984:123).

There is a major problem with this a priori position. If the plant and animal species named in systems of ethnobiological classification were selected for linguistic recognition primarily on the basis of their utilitarian importance, then it should in theory be impossible to predict which classes of organisms will be named prior to conducting relatively complete ethnographic and ethnobiological investigations in any particular society. One of the major lessons of ethnography is that cultural knowledge is multifaceted and often unique to particular societies. The utilitarian would surely be the first to proclaim that the pragmatic and culturally defined significance of *particular* plants and animals must be *discovered*, not *deduced*. On the other hand, to the extent that one is able to predict which plants and animals in some society will be named without *prior knowledge of the cultural significance* of these organisms, the utilitarian argument loses much of its force.

How, then, might one test the predictability of which of the thousands of organisms in any particular local habitat might be singled out for naming? Let us imagine a day in the rain forests of the Amazon. A naturalist, someone with the scientific curiosity of a Bates or a Wallace, is actively engaged in systematic zoological collecting. His goal is to develop a local faunal inventory of the major vertebrates found to inhabit the forest and streams of an area circumscribed by, say, a 30-kilometer radius of his field site.

As he begins his collections, what does he see? He is not confronted by a vast continuum of animal species gradually and imperceptibly merging one into the other, species x gradually becoming species y. What he perceives is an array of discrete, discontinuous chunks of biological reality. As Ernst Mayr stated years ago, "At a given locality, a species of animal is . . . separated from other sympatric species by a complete gap. This is the [nondimensional] species of Ray and Linnaeus" (Mayr 1969:37; cf. also Mayr 1949, 1957; and Mayr, Linsley, and Usinger 1953). Furthermore, some of these species are seen to be more similar to one another than others, and some are so strikingly unique as to be thought of as unrelated to any other species at all.

Our naturalist now begins to classify the animals he has collected. He arranges them in groups based on their overall similarity or resemblance on the basis of "their outward appearance. . . . Such grouping 'by inspection' is the expressly stated or unspoken starting point of . . . all systems of classification" (Mayr 1981:510).

In addition, he begins to note that some organisms can be grouped into ever more inclusive groups, since he agrees with Darwin and many pre-Darwinian biologists, that "all organic beings are found to resemble each other in descending degrees, so that they can be classed in groups under groups" (Darwin 1859:431). He will observe that the differences between given pairs or groups of organisms are relatively small, leading to their being placed relatively close to one another in his growing taxonomy. Other creatures will appear to be perceptually very different, and he will place them rather far apart in his classification.

Imagine now another zoologist residing in the same area where our natural historian is presently collecting specimens. Unlike our Western-trained taxonomist, this person is illiterate and has no particular interest in producing a faunal inventory of the vertebrates in the region, although he could easily do so from memory. He has even worked as a collector on an occasional basis with our natural historian, who has found his knowledge of the local fauna to be rather extensive. As you will have guessed, this zoologist is an Indian.

Along with the visiting naturalist, our indigenous zoologist will have looked out upon the same forest and streams, will have regularly seen most of the same animals, and will have developed an implicit system of ethnozoological classification. And, along with the Western scientist, he will have used exactly the same kinds of perceptual cues of similarity and difference in the recognition and consequent naming of groupings of organisms. An obvious but necessary qualification is required here. If our Western zoologist was using special collecting equipment, such as fine-meshed bird nets, and if he worked systematically at night to collect bats, it is likely that he will have captured a number of these rapid-flying, nocturnal creatures that our indigenous ethnozoologist will never have seen. The behavior of these animals makes them essentially unobservable by native biologists. The relative size and prevalence of animals will also play a part, of course. In general, the smaller the organism, the less likely it is to be named. Likewise, if its prevalence in a region makes sighting of it highly unlikely, the probability of its getting named is reduced significantly.

Our example puts us in a position to address the question of which groups will be given names in the native system. The utilitarian position is quite clear. As Hunn has claimed, "[Ethnobiological] classification is *highly selective and* [knowledge of] *the practical significance of organisms is important in the selection process*" (Hunn 1982:835, emphasis added). If this were true, one would have to spend a good deal of time talking with our indigenous ethnozoologist prior to making any predictions on how he might classify the vertebrate creatures in the local environment.

The alternative view presented here leaves issues of utility aside as concerns the underlying bases of ethnobiological classification and makes a straightforward prediction. To the extent that the Western scientist and the native ethnozoologist see the *same organisms*, and to the extent that, without prior discussion of the local system of classification, the former's classification of the local fauna turns out to correspond closely to the latter's as regards which species are singled out for naming, then one may reasonably infer that in both systems grouping is based on the recognition of relative degrees of similarity and difference among species. Since the two naturalists are classifying exactly the same animals, the taxonomy of the Western scientist should be nearly identical to that of our indigenous ethnozoologist. This similarity could not be due to the cultural importance of the animals involved, since our naturalist lacks any information at all about these cultural facts. If this is true, a corollary is that one should be able to use a Western scientific description of a given local flora or fauna as a biological road map for predicting which organisms will be named in the corresponding folk system.

Western scientists have tried to make explicit their criteria for the erection of their taxonomic hierarchies on the basis of degrees of similarity and difference that can be observed among the organisms being classified. Determining what is meant by "similarity" has been one of the most controversial topics of modern evolutionary biology and continues to generate much debate, as can be observed from a brief perusal of almost any issue of *Systematic Zoology*, the journal where most of the recent debate has been carried out. Nonetheless, for my purposes here, it is sufficient to return to one of the most influential contributions to the debate made almost forty years ago by Mayr, Linsley, and Usinger (1953), elaborated by Simpson (1961), and later expanded further by Mayr (1969).

In discussing how the taxonomist groups species into genera, genera into families, and so on up the taxonomic hierarchy, Mayr, Linsley, and Usinger posit two primary considerations as fundamental. The first is the criterion of monophyly, or presumed descent from a common ancestor. Monophyly has very little to do with the actual nuts-and-bolts activities of classical taxonomists in developing their classifications of organisms, since the phylogenetic history of any group of plants or animals can only be inferred (Blackwelder 1967:351–372).

The second criterion mentioned by Mayr, Linsley, and Usinger is more critical to the discussion here. This is the notion of the perceived *distance* that separates two or more groups of organisms, a distance that they, and later Simpson, were to call "decided gaps." Gaps are perceptually recognized discontinuities of varying degrees within a series of contemporaneous organisms. The smaller the gap between two groups (i.e., the greater the similarity), the closer they will be placed in a system of classification; the larger the gap between two groups (i.e., the greater the difference), the further apart they will be placed. As a general rule, the practicing taxonomist will state that the differences between two species of the same genus represent a gap that is smaller than the gap separating two genera of the same family. Accordingly, two genera of the same family have more characters in common than either does with another genus in a separate family.

In addition, Mayr, Linsley, and Usinger suggest a third criterion relevant to the recognition of genera, which relates to their internal diversity. In general, they suggest that the distance separating genera in a family is inversely proportional to the number of taxa included in any particular genus. Thus, the greater the biological diversity of a set of genera as measured by the numbers of included species, the smaller the size of the perceptual gaps separating the respective genera.

Hunn has built on the insights of Mayr and Simpson in elaborating his own suggested perceptual model of ethnobiological classification. Thus, he notes that "the perceived size of gaps between sets of organisms and the heterogeneity of those sets account in large measure for the observed structure of folk biotaxonomies" (Hunn 1977:48). He furthermore develops a notational scheme that allows him to theoretically calculate several features relating to the observed structure of ethnobiological taxonomies where gap size and the diversity of individual taxa included in the same sets are defined as critical variables (see Hunn 1977:47–50). Unfortunately, as soon as the proposal has been made he feels obliged to remark that "the major difficulty with [the] formulation is the problem of measurement. If the quantities G [gap size] and H [heterogenity] cannot be measured in some valid and reliable manner, the analytical framework proposed will remain no more than a heuristic device" (Hunn 1977:53).

I am in overall agreement with Hunn that precise measurement eludes us. However, the structure of the scientific taxonomy itself can provide general guidelines in terms of the largely intuitive but perceptually valid and plausibly phylogenetically real characterization of distinctiveness. Before outlining the core of this argument in more detail, it is worthwhile to explore a bit further the analogy made earlier that the scientific classification of some local flora or fauna might serve as a biological road map to the ethnobiological landscape.

As is well known, on any good road map some of the lines will be highlighted, printed in darker or colored ink, being thicker and easier to read than others. These are the most important roads, the main highways, the significant freeways, the major routes of commerce and transport.

Likewise, in a scientific classification of local species, some groups of organisms will be highlighted in that they are more distinctive than others in the area. They gain their distinctiveness as a function of their relatively low level of internal biological diversity as well as their presumed phylogenetic divergence from other organisms in the area. In comparison with other species of the local fauna, these distinctive taxa are at once relatively homogeneous (in terms of their internal biological variation) as well as relatively isolated (in terms of the "size of gaps [separating them from] adjacent taxa" [Sneath and Sokal 1973:291]).

My colleague Paul Kay, in searching for an appropriate metaphor to characterize such taxa, says that they suffer from a high degree of "phylogenetic loneliness" (cf. also Hunn 1979). These phenetically (and, by implication, phylogenetically) distinctive organisms should be the best candidates for names in any ethnobiological system of classification. Ironically, Hunn was the first to make this observation in print. Other things being equal, he stated, "the probability that a group of organisms will be recognized and named is directly proportional to the [distinctiveness] of [that group] as determined by scientific taxonomic analysis" (Hunn 1977:72; cf. also Hunn 1979). Simply put, distinctiveness should be predictable from analysis *of the biological classification of the genera and species that comprise individual families in any local flora or fauna.*

This observation leads to the following speculations that focus on the internal structure of these higher-order taxa. At one extreme, one will note some families that are sparsely populated, being comprised of but a single genus that is itself monotypic. Monotypic genera of these families should be highly distinctive because the "decided gap" separating the species of such families from other groups is quite wide and each is homogeneous in extension. The likelihood of these groupings being named in a folk system of classification is high.

As the population density of families increases, one will note that some are comprised of several genera, but that these taxa are not further differentiated into biological species, at least as far as the local flora or fauna is concerned. The monotypic genera in families exhibiting this structure should be somewhat less distinctive than the monotypic family, since the perceptual gaps separating the monospecific taxa that comprise them is somewhat narrower. Nonetheless, these monotypic genera are homogeneous, compensating for the relatively more crowded perceptual space that they share with other genera in the family. One would expect the patterns of naming to still be fairly stable, although names would begin to show greater variation in their ranges of application.

At the extreme end of this continuum, families become increasingly dense in that there are large numbers of genera, some of which are monotypic but many of which are further subdivided and encompass several or many closely related species. Taxa comprising families with this structure will share many characters and will be the least distinctive because the gaps separating them have narrowed even further. The internally diversified polytypic genera complicate the perceptual scene even further. The likelihood of each individual species receiving a separate, "distinctive name," *sensu* Bartlett, in the folk system is lowest for these perceptually similar classes of organisms. More generally, one might argue that biologically recognized taxa of any rank showing low levels of polytypy should be more likely candidates for linguistic recognition in a system of ethnobiological classification than taxa showing high levels of polytypy.

The foregoing characterization of the perceptual distinctiveness of biological taxa and their relative potential for being linguistically recognized in a system of ethnobiological classification can be represented diagrammatically, as in figure 2.1.

Focusing solely on monotypic genera as the most likely candidates for linguistic recognition, the following hypothesis is suggested:

1. *If a scientific genus*, x, *is monotypic, it is highly likely to be given a distinct folk generic name.*

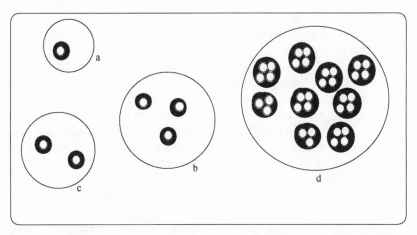

Figure 2.1 Schematic representation of taxonomic distinctiveness and the likelihood that species will be labeled by distinct folk generic names in ethnobiological systems of classification. Large circles represent biological families, dark, solid circles are genera, and small white dots represent biological species. *Left:* three sparsely populated families. Genera in monotypic families (a) or monotypic genera in small families (b, c) are likely to be named in folk systems. *Right:* a densely populated family (d) with numerous polytypic genera. These densely packed polytypic genera are less likely to be named in folk systems.

2. *The generic name will be restricted in its range of application to the single mono-typic genus, x.*

It is worth stressing the second part of the hypothesis. In addition to predicting that monotypic genera will be named, the hypothesis states that, in their range of meaning, the names will be constrained referentially. If some monotypic genus is perceptually distinctive, one should not expect its name to apply to any other groupings in the local flora or fauna.

To test the hypothesis fully, the data available must satisfy two rather stringent conditions. First, one must have at one's disposal comprehensive biological inventories for a local flora or fauna with complete determinations to the rank of species. The second condition requires systematic ethnobiological elicitation of the names applied to these general collections from a sizable number of knowledgeable informants. The methodological issues raised by these two requirements will be discussed in detail in chapter 5; no ethnobiological description has ever been carried out in which both conditions have been met fully. It must suffice for now to say that the data presented below from the Huambisa, Tzeltal, and Kalam are thought to satisfy the requirement of comprehensive biological coverage fairly well. The requirement of systematic ethnobiological elicitation with large numbers of informants is more problematic, but the data from each of the three studies are complete enough from this point of view to serve as an initial approximation. Of course, the hypothesis must be tested on a wide range of additional biological groups of both plants and animals taken from detailed ethnobiological descriptions in diverse parts of the world. My purpose here is to present findings that are suggestive rather than definitive.

The data I will focus on are drawn from monographic studies of three local avifaunas from three distinct regions of the world: Amazonian Peru, the southern highlands of Mexico, and the eastern highlands of New Guinea. The South American materials are taken from unpublished data on Huambisa bird classification collected in the early 1980s (Berlin, Boster, and O'Neill, in prep.). The Mexican materials are drawn from Hunn's comprehensive research on Tzeltal ethnozoology (Hunn 1977). The data from the New Guinea highlands are taken from the collaborative work of Bulmer and Majnep in their research on Kalam ethnoornithology (Majnep and Bulmer 1977, Bulmer 1979).

In each of the three studies, I first selected from the inventories of bird species all of those taxa that were scientifically classified as members of locally monotypic genera, along with the folk names, if any, that were applied to each monotypic genus. I subsequently divided the lists into two groups, the first comprising those monotypic genera that were named exclusively with a single folk generic name and those genera designated by generic names that ranged over two or more genera. The results of the tallies are shown in table

2.2, where the pattern revealed is clear-cut. None of the monotypic genera in any of the three avifaunas remains unnamed, or is referred to *exclusively* by the life-form names for 'bird/flying creature' (i.e., Tzeltal *mut*, Huambisa *pishak*, or Kalam *yakt*), although a minority of them share their names with two or more other genera. While data on the stability of the names applied to each of these monotypyic genera is not specifically given in Hunn's or Bulmer's reports, the data from Berlin, Boster, and O'Neill indicate general consensus among informants as to what a particular monotypic genus should be called. In two independent naming experiments, for example, *Daptrius americana*, the red-throated caracara, was called *yákakua* by nineteen of twenty-one informants on one test and by twenty of the twenty-three informants on the second (see chapter 5 for discussion).

The second part of the hypothesis concerns the range of application of individual names to monotypic genera. Table 2.2 also reveals marked similarities among the three groups. Folk generic names are highly restricted in their range of application to their respective monotypic genera. In all three languages, more than 70 percent of the folk generic names for such genera are limited in their designation to a single perceptually distinctive monotypic folk genus.

An examination of those taxa that disconfirm part 2 of the hypothesis reveals them to be exceptions that support the general principle of biological distinctiveness. In several cases in Tzeltal, Huambisa, and Kalam, a single folk generic name ranges over a diverse set of genera (e.g., Tzeltal *ulich* 'swallows' [five genera], Huambisa *ímia* 'American storks' [two genera], and Kalam *sjwewey* 'warblers' [two genera]), but all of these species are merged in the various folk systems precisely because of their strong perceptual affinities. The various mappings are shown in figure 2.2. In each of these cases, morphological and behavioral similarities mark the monogeneric taxa involved, and one might suppose that opportunities for direct observation of the birds is difficult. If they are merged, it is because they appear to be the same.

The Huambisa conceptual treatment of *ímia* supports this view. As seen in figure 2.2, this folk generic taxon lumps two storks, the American wood ibis

TABLE 2.2

Application of Folk Generic Names for Monotypic Bird Genera in Three Local Avifaunas

Group	Monotypic Genera	Folk Generic Names	Name Applied to a Single Genus	Name Applied to Two or More Genera
Tzeltal	142	82	59 (72%)	23 (28%)
Huambisa	137	119	94 (79%)	25 (21%)
Kalam	83	74	66 (89%)	8 (11%)

Note: p = ≤ .025, paired t-test

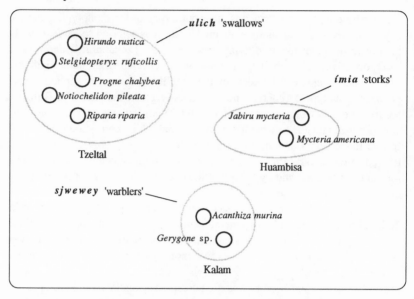

Figure 2.2 Schematic representation of the range of application of folk generic names over several monotypic bird genera of swallows (Tzeltal of Mexico), storks (Huambisa of Peru), and warblers (Kalam of New Guinea). (Data for Tzeltal are from Hunn 1977; Huambisa from Berlin, Boster, and O'Neill, in prep.; and Kalam from Majnep and Bulmer 1977)

(*Mytceria americana*) and the jabiru (*Jabiru mycteria*). Both of these birds are similar in appearance in their gross morphology. Each has white plumage, bare heads, slaty gray to black necks, and heavy black bills that from a distance make them difficult to distinguish. It is notable that this similarity is recognized, as well, in the scientific names for the two birds, where the generic name *Mycteria* comes to serve as the specific epithet for the genus *Jabiru mycteria*, literally, 'Mycteria-like Jabiru'.

More commonly, in Tzeltal and Huambisa bird classification, but less so for the Kalam, when the range of a folk generic name encompasses two or more scientific monotypic genera, the folk generic taxon itself is further divided into folk-specific taxa. The Tzeltal treatment of the Inca and ruddy ground doves, the Huambisa classification of the crested and harpy eagles, and the Kalam categorization of the pink-faced nuthatch and the Papuan sitella are illustrative of this situation, as seen in figure 2.3.

The foregoing data indicate that one can be guided with fair accuracy to those species most likely to be named in some ethnobiological system of classification by focusing first on those that are taxonomically most distinctive. The utilitarian might respond, of course, that the most distinctive creatures in any particular region are precisely those that will be found to be highly signif-

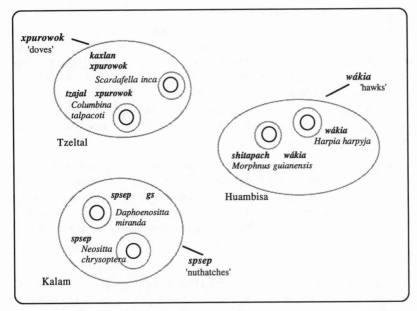

Figure 2.3 Schematic representation of range of application of folk generic names over two monotypic bird genera of doves (Tzeltal of Mexico), eagles (Huambisa of Peru), and nuthatches (Kalam of New Guinea) indicating recognition of included genera as folk species in each folk system. (Data for Tzeltal are from Hunn 1977; Huambisa from Berlin, Boster, and O'Neil, in prep.; and Kalam from Majnep and Bulmer 1977)

icant in terms of their cultural importance. From this point of view, "Biologically natural categories . . . will tend strongly to be categories *useful for many human purposes*" (Hunn 1982:834, emphasis added).

Such a position appears to be largely circular. More importantly, it is not supported empirically. More than half of the mammals given linguistic recognition by the Aguaruna and Huambisa of Peru have "no direct use either as food or for material goods" (Patton, Berlin, and Berlin 1982:124; see also Berlin and Berlin 1983).

Birds play an even less important role. Some thirty to forty bird species, mostly the larger game birds, contribute an average of 8 percent by weight to animal consumption, but none of these species contributes more than 3 percent. By far the most dietarily significant bird is the introduced chicken.

Fish are more important in the Jívaro diet than birds and mammals combined, contributing more than half of the animal biomass consumed. Nonetheless, very few scientific genera account for the majority of fish consumed. By far the largest contributors are a few genera of loricariid armored catfish, several large pimelodid and doradid catfish, and a handful of species of characids (see Berlin and Berlin 1983 for a detailed statement of the relative contribution of animals to diet among the Aguaruna and Huambisa).

The majority of vertebrate animals known to the Jívaro cannot be shown to have any immediate utilitarian importance, assuming that it might be possible to develop some direct measurement of utility. Such a measure, incidentally, is critically absent from the utilitarian program, and this represents one of its major weaknesses. Utilitarianists, however, are not daunted by problems of assessing direct importance. As Bulmer once argued, in a rare and uncharacteristic functionalist statement,

> If one sees individual plant and animal categories solely in their direct relationships to man, there are many which appear irrelevant, neither utilized nor noxious. However, if the relationships between different kinds of plants and animals are recognized as relevant, then a great range of additional forms will very usefully be identified and classified. . . . [Since] animals exist in significant relationships with other animals and plants, there is a considerable impetus to classify these forms also. (Bulmer 1974a:12–13)

However, if one is allowed to define utility in such an open-ended fashion, it seems that counterexamples are ruled out on a priori grounds. In this neo-Malinowskian world, plants and animals are classified, since, by definition, all of them are functionally related to one another in such ways as to make their linguistic recognition in the ethnobiological system adaptive. The circularity of this crude ecological argument makes it, in the final analysis, untestable, a position that Hays (1982) has cogently warned us about. Such a tautological view of utility reduces ethnobiological classification to something comparable to a classic Rube Goldberg cartoon, where a character finally gets a cup of coffee by indirectly manipulating a complex apparatus of levers, pullies, and toggle switches.

2.6 The Internal Structure of Folk Generic Taxa

Generic taxa do not constitute a uniform and homogeneous set of categories. Typically, many exhibit biological ranges that encompass one or more species of the same genus, but others will range over several distinct genera. In the case of smaller organisms, many correspond to biological taxa of even higher rank. A small but significant portion of generic taxa stand out from all others in that they themselves are further subdivided into named folk specific taxa. This unique set of folk generics and the taxa that they include will be discussed in detail in the following chapter.

A linguistically monotypic folk generic that ranges over several biological species is nonetheless characterized by its own internal structure. That is, it is generally the case that one or more closely related species that fall within the basic range of a folk generic are considered to be more representative of the folk generic than are others. From this perspective, a folk generic may be thought of as comprised of a central species (or small set of species) that comes psychologically to represent a prototypical image around which perceptually similar species are grouped. These images, of course, are the gestalten of generic categories.

An example of this common phenomenon is seen in the Aguaruna classification of lizards (Berlin and McDiarmid, in prep.). In the late 1970s, as part of an interdisciplinary project on Aguaruna ethnobiology to which I have already briefly referred, a number of naming and sorting experiments were carried out with prepared zoological specimens of birds, mammals, reptiles, and amphibians. In one experiment, eighteen informants (thirteen men and five women) were asked to sort a set of some fifty specimens of lizards, skinks, and geckos representing twenty-four species in seventeen genera. The only instructions given informants were to group the specimens into piles of those species that "go together" or are "companions." After the specimens were organized into groups, informants were asked to provide the name of each group. Subsequently, they were asked to point out the best example of each pile of specimens with the question, "*Tuwi̱ pujáwai shing X*," literally, 'Where is the genuine X seated?' With little hesitation, one (or more rarely, two) specimen(s) was/were immediately designated as the best exemplar of each named category.

Figure 2.4 indicates the biological range of the Aguaruna folk generic lizard taxon **súmpa**. As can be readily seen, this folk genus ranges over four species

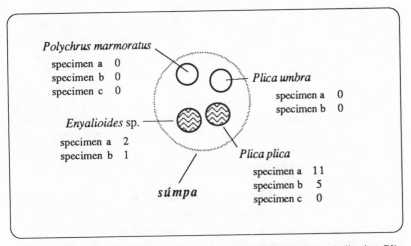

Figure 2.4 Biological range of the Aguaruna generic taxon **súmpa**, indicating *Plica plica* (16 informant responses) and *Enyalioides* sp. (3 informant responses) as prototypical of the folk genus. Specimen c of *Plica plica* was atypical in both size and general markings. (From Berlin and McDiarmid, in prep.)

in three distinct genera, *Plica*, *Enyalioides*, and *Polychrus*. The numbers of specimens for each species present in the sorting experiment are indicated directly beneath each species name. The number to the right of each specimen used in the task indicates the number of informants who selected that specimen as the genuine *súmpa*.

Earlier and subsequent interviewing with knowledgeable informants indicated that *súmpa* was linguistically monotypic and included no regularly named subdivisions. Nonetheless, data from the sorting experiment show clearly that *Plica plica* is seen as the focus of the folk genus (sixteen informant responses), followed next by *Enyalioides* sp. *P. plica* is a strongly marked iguanid lizard with distinctive bands along the tail and back and is perceptually the most distinctive of the four species represented in the set, likely reasons leading to its selection as focal. *Enyalioides* is morphologically quite similar in its gross morphology and markings. One highly knowledgeable male informant volunteered the ecological information that *P. plica* is commonly found on trees (*numínum pujau* lit. 'in trees it sits'), while *Enyalioides* sp. prefers a terrestrial habitat (*nugká pujau* lit. 'on the earth it sits').

The findings from the sorting experiments that indicate that *súmpa* is a folk generic category focused around prototypical species is given further support from data obtained from naming experiments. Thirty-six informants were asked to name a comparable series of reptiles, including the specimens used in the sorting tasks. Figure 2.5 shows the frequency distribution of the number of times two specimens of *Plica plica*, one specimen of *P. umbra*, and three specimens each of *Enyalioides* sp. and *Polychrus marmoratus* were given the name *súmpa*.

As with the sorting experiment, it is clear that *súmpa* ranges strongly over all of these species, with the large majority of thirty-six informants using this name for all specimens of these species. Nonetheless, the two species that receive the greatest number of *súmpa* responses are those that were identified as focal in the sorting tasks, *Plica plica* (thirty-two and thirty-one informants for the two specimens of *P. plica*) and *Enyalioides* sp. (thirty-one, thirty, and twenty-nine informants for the three specimens of *Enyalioides*). The other species in the set (*Plica umbra* and *Polychrus marmoratus*), while named *súmpa* in most instances, were also given the names of several other lizards (not indicated here), a fact indicative of their less salient status as members of the folk genus.

A further illustration of explicit internal structure of folk generic categories can be seen in the classification of curimatid fishes by the Huambisa, a Jivaroan-speaking population closely related to the Aguaruna who reside on the Santiago River in Amazonas, Peru. These data differ from those derived from sorting tasks or naming experiments described earlier in that they represent individual identifications of fish by native Huambisa speakers recorded at the time that the fish specimens were collected.

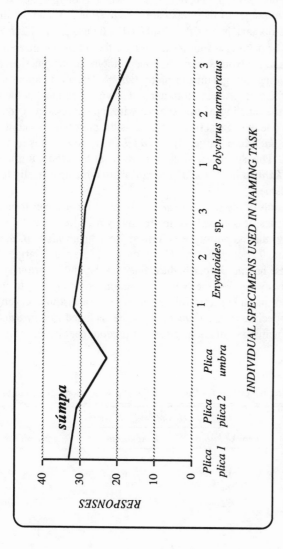

Figure 2.5 Frequency distribution of naming responses of thirty-six Aguaruna informants for specimens of *Plica* sp., *Enyalioides* sp., and *Polychrus marmoratus*, indicating greater number of *súmpa* responses for the inferred prototypical species, *Plica plica* and *Enyalioides* sp. (From Berlin and McDiarmid, in prep.)

The Curimatidae, a family of Upper Amazonian freshwater fishes, are represented in the Huambisa area of Peru by a single polytypic genus, *Curimata*, comprised of eight local species (all as yet undetermined). Data from systematic elicitation reveal that the Huambisa group these eight species in a covert taxon that includes but two folk generics, ***kúum***, which is bitypic, and ***yawarách***. The biological ranges of these taxa are seen in table 2.3, and the internal structure of the folk taxa involved is displayed in figures 2.6 and 2.7.

The distribution of naming responses allows for the following inferences. First, the bitypic generic taxon, ***kúum***, shows a prototypical subgeneric member, ***péngke kúum***, literally 'genuine or pretty ***kúum***'. The most common curimatid species in the area (as seen from our sixty-two collections) is the *Curimata* sp. 4, and the labeling of this species with the expression 'genuine/ pretty ***kúum***' leads one to suggest that it represents the prototype. Its contrasting subgeneric ***kángka kúum*** 'larger' (i.e., *kángka*-like *kúum*) finds its focus on *Curimata* sp. 5. This species is slightly larger than the others in the set, and the attributive ***kángka*** lit. '*Prochilodus* sp.' is used metaphorically to indicate relative robustness.

The other folk genus of the set is ***yawarách***. While it ranges over four species of curimatid fishes, it is clear from the relatively high frequency of naming responses (forty) that its prototype is formed around *Curimata* sp. 8. Curimatid species 6 and 7, but especially *Curimata* sp. 8, are much larger than the first five species, having deeper bodies, finer scales, and a variously developed fleshy or bony keel on the belly, distinctions great enough to merit their being grouped into a separate folk genus bearing a distinctive generic name. That three specimens of *Curimata* sp. 4 are included in ***yawarách*** is most likely due to naming confusion, given the predominant patterns for the

TABLE 2.3

Distribution of Naming Responses for Curimatid Fish Species among the Huambisa

| | Huambisa Fish Names | | |
| | --- | --- | --- |
Scientific Taxa	*péngke kúum*	*kángka kúum*	*yawarách*
Curimata sp. 1	3		
Curimata sp. 2	14	1	
Curimata sp. 3	24		
Curimata sp. 4	62	2	3
Curimata sp. 5		6	
Curimata sp. 6	2		13
Curimata sp. 7			2
Curimata sp. 8			40

Source: Berlin, Swift, and Stewart, in prep.

Note: Total number of individual specimens represented = 172. Responses are taken from individual specimens at the time of collection.

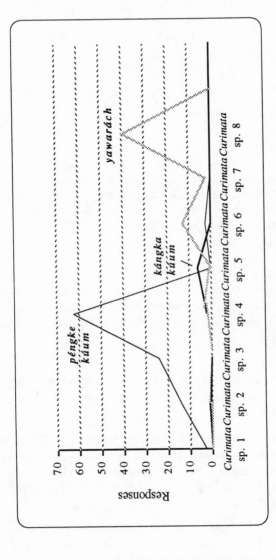

Figure 2.6 Graphic presentation of data from table 2.3 indicating distribution of Huambisa naming responses for 172 specimens of curimatid fishes. (After Berlin, Swift, and Stewart, in prep.)

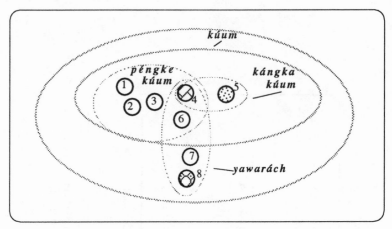

Figure 2.7 Diagrammatic representation of Huambisa classification of curimatid fishes indicating the internal structure of the respective taxa as focused around prototypical species of the genus *Curimata* (after Berlin, Swift, and Stewart, in prep.). The outer circle represents the covert intermediate category, which includes all Curimatid fishes. Numbers refer to distinct species of the genus *Curimata*.

set as a whole. Nonetheless, the naming confusions seen in the overlapping naming responses link the folk genera in the set in a patterned fashion and are indicative of the morphological features that all of these species share in common.

2.7 NATURE'S FORTUNE 500 + : EMPIRICAL GENERALIZATIONS ON THE UPPER NUMBERS OF GENERIC TAXA IN SYSTEMS OF ETHNOBIOLOGICAL CLASSIFICATION

In a brief passage in chapter 5 of *The Savage Mind*, Lévi-Strauss makes an observation, almost in passing, about the numbers of named categories of plants and animals in folk systems of ethnobiological classification, which I believe has important implications for a full understanding of such systems. Lévi-Strauss states that

> In going through ethnozoological and ethnobotanical works, one notices that, with rare exception, the species and varieties recorded seem to be in the order of several hundred, around three hundred to six hundred. No work of this kind is exhaustive, however . . . [and one] can therefore hardly go wrong in putting the real figure considerably higher. . . . In the present state of knowledge, the figure of two thousand appears to correspond well, in order of magnitude, to a sort of threshold cor-

responding roughly to the capacity of memory and power of definition of ethnozoologies or ethnobotanies reliant on oral tradition. (Lévi-Strauss 1966:153–154)

C. H. Brown's (1985:44, table 1) recent survey of the ethnobiological literature would lend support to Lévi-Strauss's upper threshold. According to his report on the numbers of labeled botanical taxa in twenty-nine languages, only one language (Ifugao, as reported in Conklin 1980) exceeds two thousand named plant categories; the mean is around five hundred. From a sample of seventeen ethnozoological systems, none appears to have more than eight hundred labeled animal taxa, and the mean is 435.

Furthermore, Brown notes a positive correlation in the total number of taxa and form of subsistence. The nineteen systems with more than three hundred named plant taxa are, with one exception (Gosiute), societies characterized by Brown as practicing "small-scale cultivation" (although it is difficult to imagine speaking of Ifugao terraced rice paddies as "small-scale"). Conversely, all but one (Mandarin Chinese, clearly an incompletely described system) of the twenty groups with less than three hundred named plant categories are classified as societies whose primary subsistence base is nonagricultural (foraging). (The Tasaday and Casiguran Dumagat are misclassified; see chapter 3 for discussion.) It is clear that named subgeneric taxa (folk species and varietals) contribute significantly to the total numbers of named categories for the cultivators, a fact leading Brown quite justifiably to conclude that with the onset of agriculture, ethnobiological systems of classification increase their inventories considerably.

While Brown's survey supports Lévi-Strauss's speculations on the upper limits of the number of plant and animal taxa found in folk systems of biological classification irrespective of rank, I have been stimulated by Lévi-Strauss's suggestions to collect data on the numbers of *generic* taxa found in systems of ethnobiological classification. On the basis of preliminary surveys of the systems available to me in the early 1970s, my intuitions were that folk systems would never approach two thousand in either the plant or animal kingdoms, but would more likely fall within the range of five hundred as the upper limit of named folk generic taxa in a single kingdom (see Berlin, Breedlove, and Raven 1973). Since then, I have pulled together what new data I could obtain from what I feel to be reliable sources.

The difficulties in collecting the necessary data that bear on this question are, of course, considerable. The number of relatively complete ethnobiological descriptions is lamentably small, and in those that are available one cannot escape problems of interpretation regarding the ethnobiological rank of the taxa described, a likely reason for which Brown's survey was restricted to reporting total inventories. Nonetheless, for those systems that I have been able to examine carefully, I conclude that, with few exceptions, both ethnobotanical and ethnozoological systems of classification have an upper threshold of generally five hundred or so named folk genera.

Table 2.4 shows the numbers of generic taxa for seventeen relatively complete systems of ethnobotanical classification where the supporting data include extensive botanical voucher collections, that is, not simply ethnobotanical vocabulary surveys or word lists. Furthermore, the descriptions cited here are presented in a form that allows one to make a relatively unambiguous assessment of the generic rank of the respective taxa enumerated. The data in the table support the general claim of an upper limit of five hundred generic taxa for ethnobotanical classification. Only two of the seventeen systems exceed 500: Tobelo with six hundred and eighty-nine taxa, and Hanunóo with

TABLE 2.4

Reported Numbers of Generic Plant Taxa in Seventeen Relatively Complete Ethnobotanical Descriptions

Group and Location	Numbers of Generic Taxa
Traditional noncultivators	
1. Lillooet (Canada)	137
2. Bella Coola (Canada)	152
3. Haida (Canada)	167
4. Anindilyakwa (Australia)	199
5. Navajo* (USA)	201
6. Sahaptin (USA)	213
7. Seri (Mexico)	310
	Mean = 197
Traditional Cultivators	
8. Quechua (Peru)	238
9. Mixe (Mexico)	383
10. Ndumba (New Guinea)	385
11. Chinantec (Mexico)	396
12. Tzeltal (Mexico)	471
13. Wayampí (French Guiana)	516
14. Aguaruna (Peru)	566
15. Taubuid (Philippines)	598
16. Tobelo (Indonesia)	689
17. Hanunóo (Philippines)	956
	Mean = 520

Sources: 1-3, Turner 1974; 4, Waddy 1988; 5, Wyman and Harris 1940; 6, Hunn 1980; 7, Brunel 1974; 8, Felger and Moser 1985; 9, Martin 1990; 10, Hays 1974; 11, Martin 1990; 12, Berlin, Breedlove, and Raven 1974; 13, Grenand 1980; 14, Berlin 1976a; 15, Pennoyer 1975; 16, P. Taylor 1990; 17, Conklin 1954, pers. comm.

* The Navajo acquired agriculture through their contact with farming populations in the southwestern United States after they migrated to this region from the north. They were in all likelihood nonagriculturalists traditionally.

over nine hundred folk generic categories. Furthermore, Brown's suggestions on the positive association of total numbers of ethnobotanical taxa and mode of subsistence appears to be borne out for the few systems reported here, with cultivators universally showing higher numbers of generic plant taxa than non-cultivators. However, this observation must be seriously qualified in that no complete ethnobotanical description has ever been carried out for a noncultivating population sharing the same tropical habitat with a group of cultivators. Furthermore, as Bulmer (1985) points out in discussing Brown's findings, it is highly likely that the relatively less rich biological habitats as well as social forces of acculturation leading to loss of ethnobiological knowledge account in large part for the lower numbers of generic taxa in the inventories of foraging groups for which we do have descriptions. (See chapter 7 for a more detailed discussion.)

If an upper figure of around five hundred generic taxa is found in ethnobotanical systems of classification, table 2.4 also suggests that the relative biological diversity of the habitat in which a particular society finds itself is a contributing factor in attaining this threshold. With the exception of the Ndumba of New Guinea, an exception that is likely explained on methodological grounds (see chapter 7), there is a general and quite expected increase in numbers of generic plant taxa recognized with presumed biological diversity of the environment. Systems with relatively fewer numbers of taxa are found in societies residing in biologically less rich regions (e.g., the Chancán Quechua of the Peruvian Puno and the Seri of the xerophytic coasts of the Mexican Gulf of California), while those with relatively greater numbers occupy regions of the humid tropics (Tobelo of the Moluccas of Indonesia and Hanunóo of Mindoro, with an average annual rainfall in excess of 3,000 mm).

Table 2.5 presents data from ten ethnozoological descriptions where zoological data are, in the main if not totally, supported by extensive collections or detailed elicitation and preliminary determinations with the use of published sources on the local fauna. Data on vertebrates, especially the birds, are likely to be the most reliable, and data on invertebrates are only suggestive.

Table 2.5 is similar in many respects to that found for folk generic plant taxa, with the exception that the range is less wide for animals. Aside from the Wayampí and the Aguaruna, all other systems show inventories of less than five hundred generic categories. The sample is too small to make any observations on the relationship of size of lexicon to mode of subsistence, but it is worth noting in passing that the historically noncultivating Anindilyakwa of Australia's Groote Eylandt rank sixth, with an inventory quite comparable to that of any cultivating peoples. Furthermore, again as expected, the greater the species diversity of the region that might be potentially classified, the greater the number of folk generic taxa reported. If this pattern holds as determined by new ethnozoological descriptions, it would appear that environmental factors take precedence over sociocultural factors (e.g., form of subsis-

TABLE 2.5
Reported Numbers of Generic Animal Taxa in Ten Relatively Complete Ethnozoological Descriptions

Group and Location	Numbers of Generic Taxa
1. Ndumba (New Guinea)	186
2. Sahaptin (USA)	236
3. Piaroa (Venezuela)	305
4. Tzeltal (Mexico)	335
5. Kalam (New Guinea)	345
6. Anindilyakwa (Australia)	417
7. Tobelo (Indonesia)	420
8. Hanunóo (Philippines)	461
9. Wayampí (French Guiana)	589
10. Aguaruna (Peru)	606
	Mean = 390

Sources: 1, Hays 1974; 2, Hunn 1980; 3, Zent 1989; 4, Hunn 1977; 5, Majnep and Bulmer 1977; 6, Waddy 1988; 7, P. Taylor 1990; 8, Conklin 1954; 9, Grenand 1980; 10, Berlin, in prep.

tence) as predictors of total numbers of generic taxa in systems of ethnozoological classification.

These data bearing on an upper limit for numbers of folk generic taxa in systems of plant and animal classification represent a general tendency rather than a clear principle, but an underlying pattern is fairly apparent. Furthermore, there is historical evidence to indicate that a threshold of around five hundred to six hundred taxa was also found in early systems of botanical classification prior to the rise of modern systematic botany. In this regard it is worth noting again the comment of Greene on early Greek botany: "Theophrastus . . . mentioned about 550 kinds of plants. Dioscorides mentioned 537 kinds of plants. One could swell the list by maintaining that some names refer to more than one species, but even with this qualification, the number of species would be close[r] [sic] to 550 than 600" (Greene 1983:475–476).

Finally, Tournefort, the French botanist credited with the scientific establishment of the genus as an analytical category, recognized 617 genera (Tournefort 1700). If the early efforts in Western botanical science were, as we know them to be, essentially codifications of existing folk systems present in common speech, that the numbers of fundamental genera should so closely approximate those documented for contemporary ethnobiological systems of classification cannot be without some cognitive foundation. At present, I have no notion just what this foundation might be and can do no better than second Lévi-Strauss's final comment on his own earlier observations about these patterns, namely, "It would be interesting to know if this threshold has any significant properties from the point of view of Information Theory" (Lévi-

Strauss 1966:154). If modern systematic botanists and zoologists, when required to list the distinct genera that they know from memory, fare no better
than nonliterate ethnobiologists in free-recall elicitation sessions, both approaching Nature's magic five hundred, then the threshold will merit even
further psychological examination.

CHAPTER THREE

The Nature of Specific Taxa

A FOLK GENERIC may be divided into two to several named subgroups. The categories that result from such splitting of folk genera will be referred to here as *folk specific taxa*. In accordance with standard usage, generic classes that are further divided into named subgroups are said to be *polytypic*, in contrast with the large majority of folk genera, that contain no further named subgroupings and are, accordingly, *monotypic*.

While some generics may be biologically polytypic and range over several species, as seen in the last section, this biological diversity may not necessarily be afforded linguistic recognition. When we speak of polytypic folk genera, it will be understood that the generic taxa in question include habitually recognized, linguistically labeled subclasses. As we shall see later, the degree of polytypy present, both for individual generic taxa and for the system as a whole, has important theoretical implications for the understanding of ethnobiological classification in general.

In chapter 1, I proposed that specific taxa comprise a distinctive ethnobiological rank. Members of this rank are characterized by a number of biological, nomenclatural, psychological, and cultural features that distinguish them from taxa of ranks superordinate to them. In addition, some specific groupings may themselves be further subdivided into yet smaller taxa (folk varietals). These more elaborate taxonomic distinctions occur exclusively with a small subset of species that have come under intensive human manipulation; many folk systems of classification lack varietal taxa altogether.

In the present chapter, I will first outline several of the semantic properties that distinguish folk specific categories. I will describe several general tendencies that can be noted about the internal differentiation of specific contrast sets as this relates to the cognitive process of linguistically recognizing prototypical specific taxa, and suggest at least some of the reasons why prototypical members of polytypic generic taxa should be recognized in the first place. This will lead to a discussion of general nomenclatural properties of subgeneric categories and earlier proposals on the nature of the linguistic structure of folk-specific names that, while widespread, are not universally applicable.

The importance of social factors in the recognition of folk specific categories will next be noted, leading to the conclusion that many folk species are culturally constructed, often as a result of direct human manipulation, that make them fundamentally distinct from taxa of higher rank. I will then move to the important topic of the patterns of distribution observed in the size of contrast sets comprised of specific taxa. This will involve a comparison of the similarities and differences found in the distribution of comparable taxa in the systems of biological classification of Western scientists.

3.1 DISTINCTIVE BIOLOGICAL PROPERTIES OF SPECIFIC TAXA

While a number of ethnobiologists have written a fair amount about the semantics of specific categories, the most cogent treatment to date is that of the linguist Anna Wierzbicka (1985:229–239).[1] In a few concise paragraphs she provides a succinct summary of most of the major distinguishing semantic properties of these categories. Consider the following:

> A *white gum* is a kind of gumtree which differs from other kinds of gumtrees in having white bark . . . a *blue spruce* is a kind of spruce which differs from other kinds of spruce in having bluish needles. Specific terms are seen as singling out something 'special', that is to say something 'different', 'not the same'. . . . Specific terms contain in their meaning negation: things of this kind are not like other kinds of things of this kind. . . . Roughly, white gumtree [is] . . . a kind of gumtree . . . which differs from other kinds of gumtrees . . . in having [white bark], white gum, [etc.]. A general semantic formula for the [subgeneric] rank would read: . . . a kind of X (one of the different kinds of X, not many different kinds) which differs from the other kinds of X in some ways, not many ways. (Wierzbicka 1985:219–230)

This characterization then leads Wierzbicka to propose what she calls the following "semantic analogues" that distinguish specific taxa from those of life-form and generic rank (ibid.:231):

---

[1] Wierzbicka's general writings (see references cited for most relevant publications) on the nature of ethnobiological classification, as part of her broader work on the nature of human categorization, have illuminated a number of important issues in ethnobiological theory, especially as they relate to the nature of natural kinds versus functional categories and the place that these categories play in natural taxonomy. She has recently finished an important paper on life forms that I have unfortunately not been able to discuss in the present work as it was received after the manuscript was completed.

Life form	A kind of X of which there are many different kinds (one couldn't say how many)
Folk generic	A kind of thing
Folk specific	A kind of X (one of the different kinds of X, not many different kinds) which differs in some ways, not in many ways.

Wierzbicka's commentary on specific taxa supports claims made earlier: "Specific taxa are quite similar except in a few distinctive characters" (Berlin 1976a:390), and "contrasting specific taxa differ on the basis of very few morphological characters, many of which are readily visible and sometimes verbalizable" (Berlin 1978a:21). Evidence for this generalization is readily available in the ethnobiological literature. Consider the Tzeltal folk species seen in figure 3.1.

The two mints, *Mentha spicata* (**skelemal tul pimil** lit. 'boy's tul pimil'), and *M. citratra* (**yach'ixal tul pimil** lit. 'girl's tul pimil'), are extremely similar in their overall morphology and habit. Close examination reveals that *M. citrata* is characterized by glabrous leaf surfaces while those of *M. spicata* are generally rugose. The two species are almost identical in all other easily observable features, making them nearly indistinguishable on casual inspection.

The pokeberries (*Phytolacca* spp.) reveal a similar pattern. Like the mints, the two specific taxa of the folk genus *j'ob* are morphologically quite similar. *P. rugosa* (**tzajal j'ob**) "usually occurs with pink flowers and reddish tinge to the stems and leaves . . . **sakil j'ob** [lit. 'white pokeberry'] (*P. octrandra*) [is] similar to **tzajal j'ob** [lit. 'red pokeberry'] in all respects except [that] the flowers are white, and the stems and leaves are green" (Berlin, Breedlove, and Raven 1974:349).

Similarly, among the Aguaruna Jívaro, the four kinds of achiote that constitute divisions of the generic **ípak** (*Bixa orellana*) are readily distinguished by the shape of the seed capsule as well as by the relative abundance and distribution of the flexible spinelike protuberances that cover the capsule surface of all but one specific class. The two kinds of cotton, **ujúshnum** (*Gossypium barbadense*), are distinguishable only in terms of the relative compactness of the seeds within the fruit, one relatively dispersed (**shing ujúshnum** lit. 'genuine cotton'), the other relatively compact (**káki ujúshnum** lit. 'pressed/squeezed cotton').

Comparable observations on the nature of subgeneric semantic contrast have been made by Hays in his treatment of Ndumba ethobotanical as well as ethnozoological classification. In an example from his ethnobotanical observations, Hays notes:

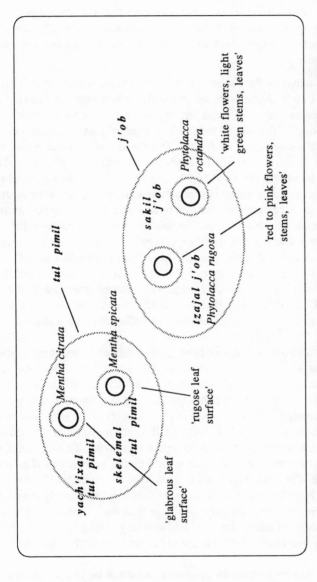

Figure 3.1 Schematic representation of the Tzeltal classification of the polytypic folk generics **tul pimil** (*Mentha* spp.) and **j'ob** (*Phytolacca* spp.), indicating the few contrastive morphological characters that distinguish the pair of folk species of each folk genus.

As expected from Berlin's characterization, members of any particular contrast set are distinguished on the basis of very few morphological characters. For example, the eight folk specifics of the generic *faa'nresa* (various Zingiberaceae) are apparently distinguished simply on the basis of leaf size and stem length; the two subdivisions of *kem'bora* (both . . . *Ficus dammaropsis*) differ only in fruit color; and the 23 *kaamma* (*Ipomoea batatas*, sweet potato) specifics are contrasted primarily by leaf shape and size, with the inside color of the tuber important in a few cases. (Hays 1979:262–263)

These observations on the nature of specific taxa make it appropriate to once again recall Cain's characterization of the distinction between the classical notions of genera and species and the two distinctive processes involved in their recognition: "[A genus is] the smallest 'kind' of plant or animal that can be recognized *without close study*. . . . The species was a subdivision of it, often requiring *expert examination* both before it could be recognized and before it could be named" (Cain 1956:97, emphasis added). The empirical evidence indicates that folk generic taxa conform closely to this characterization in that they are recognized as undifferentiated gestalten. However, as seen from the examples cited above, specific taxa are recognized on quite different grounds. Rather than instantaneously appreciating the genus from its general aspect, folk specific categories split the genus into groups that can often be known only by detailed inspection. Relative expertise, of course, will be a factor in the rapidity with which a subgeneric determination can be accomplished (see Hunn 1975). Nonetheless, it is accurate to claim that recognition is first to the genus, then, with more conscious effort, to those categories that subdivide it.

With cultivated plants that have been highly modified under domestication, folk specific taxa may finely subdivide a single biological species (cf. the more than one hundred folk specific taxa in the Hanunóo classification of rice, *Oryza sativa*). It is also common that specific taxa range over several species of the same biological genus, as seen in the examples of the mints and pokeberries discussed in figure 3.1. Finally, a folk genus may also be divided into two or more folk species that map to biological species of different genera, for example, the two canelike grasses recognized by the Tzeltal, *batz'il jalal* lit. 'genuine cane' *Phragmites australis* and *ton jalal* lit. 'stone cane', *Chusquea angustifolia*. Nonetheless, in these cases, the different but closely related biological species involved are quite similar in their most obvious and readily perceived features of morphology and lead naturally to their being considered, to paraphrase Wierzbicka (1985), as closely contrasting kinds of the same natural kind.

If specific taxa are contrastive categories, what can be said about their semantic dimensions of contrast? Analysis of many distinct systems reveals that the most common semantic dimensions comprise a small number of perceptually based parameters. The most commonly found include color, relative size, shape, habitat, habit (of growth), taste, 'sex', smell, and analogy with some object (e.g., Tzeltal **bakbak** 'bonelike') (cf. Conklin 1954:131–159; Berlin, Breedlove, and Raven 1974:37–45; Berlin, in prep.; Hunn 1977:82–99; Taylor 1990; Brunel 1974; Martin 1990; Laughlin and Breedlove, in press; Grenand 1980). One cannot escape the observation that most of these dimensions correspond to some of the most readily and immediately apprehended sense impressions that human beings have as they interact with the physical and natural world.

Furthermore, as might also be surmised from the above examples, it is commonly found that the principal differentiating dimensions used to contrast many (but not all) subgeneric taxa will be encoded in the names of the taxa themselves. This is usually accomplished linguistically by the use of an attributive that modifies the generic name and points to some value of the distinguishing semantic dimension (e.g., color [dark, light], size [large, small]; see nomenclatural principle 5). Metaphorical reference is highly productive (Walsh 1979). The following sets of expressions contrasting two or more specific taxa in the same contrast set are illustrative of this principle:

Tzeltal ethnobotany
> **sakil borbox** (*Govenia liliacea*) lit. 'white borbox'
> **tzajal borbox** (*G. superba*) lit. 'red borbox'
> Two folk species distinguished on the basis of the relative color differences seen in the flowers, white in *G. liliacea* and red to purple in *G. superba*. (Berlin, Breedlove, and Raven 1974:502)

Tzeltal ethnozoology:
> **tz'ibal sit tz'unun** (*Hylocharis leucotis*) lit. 'stripe-faced hummingbird'
> **texerex ne tz'unun** (*Doricha enicura*) lit. 'scissor-tailed hummingbird'
> Two of several hummingbirds distinguished by distinctive morphology. For *Hylocharis leucotis* Hunn states that "the name adequately characterizes this species" (Hunn 1977:164) due to the distinctive white stripe extending from the eye along the side of the head. *Doricha enicura* has an unmistakable forked tail, hence the attributive **texerex** 'scissor' (< OSp *texeras*).

Hanunóo ethnobotany:
> **'aligbangun malagti'** [lit.'white 'aligbangum'] **'aligbangun mabiru** [lit. 'red 'aligbangum'] two forms of the wild plant genus *Aneilem*, distinguished by their pale cream-colored and violet flowers, respectively. . . .
> **'anapla malagti'** [lit. 'white 'anapla'], **'anapla kilala** [lit. 'pinkish 'anapla'], two forms of the common second-growth forest leguminous tree *Albizzia procera* . . . distinguished by their almost white and pinkish inner bark layers, respectively. (Conklin 1954:147)

Cantonese ethnoichthyology:

tshat1 sing2 laap2 'seven-star sea bream' (from the bright spots on the body) [and] *uong5 kök2 laap2* 'yellow-foot sea bream'. So named from its yellow anal fins. (Anderson 1972:119–120)

Siona/Secoya ethnobotany:

weke yahé (Siona, 'tapir *Banisteriopsis*'; the tapir designation refers to the large size which this variety attains . . . *nea yahé* (Siona, 'black *Banisteriopsis*'; name said to refer to the dark coloration of the vine in this variety . . . [and] *tara yahé* (Siona, 'bone *Banisteriopsis*'; the vine of this variety is knobby and said to be 'hard like a bone'. (Vickers and Plowman 1984:18–19)

Palauan ethnoichthyology:

Two kinds of *maml* are distinguished: *didmecheilmaml*, which is almost entirely blue-green, and *triidlmaml*, which is darker than *didmecheilmaml* and has more black in the bars on its scales. *Triid* is also the name for the white-browed rail, *Poliolimnas cinereus*. (Helfman and Randall 1973:148)

Malay ethnobotany:

The following general rules may be safely accepted [in discussing the principles of Malay plant names]: Reduplication implies resemblance; animal names used qualitatively generally refer to size, e.g., *gajah* large, and *tikus* small; woody consistency is described by such words as *tulang* (bone), *besi* (iron), *tandok* (horn), *pasir* (sandy) . . . *jatan* (male), and *betina* (female) are not entirely obvious, but there are indications that they suggest smaller and larger forms respectively. (Watson 1928:21)

Aguaruna ethnozoology:

The Aguaruna recognize at least five subgeneric classes of *kujáncham* 'opossum' . . . *inítia kujáncham* [lit. 'creek opossum'] is, as its name indicates, the water opossum, *Chironectes minimus* . . . *nántu kujáncham* [lit. 'moon opossum'] . . . [and] . . . *súa kujáncham* [lit. 'dark opossum'] designate the light and black phases of *Didelphis marsupialis*. (Berlin and Patton 1979:76–77, translated)

3.2 THE INTERNAL STRUCTURE OF SPECIFIC CONTRAST SETS

Evidence from all systems of ethnobiological classification about which I have knowledge indicates that folk specific taxa are not afforded equal cognitive status. In the large majority of systems studied, it appears that a single taxon in each specific contrast set stands out as representing the prototype of the folk genus. Consider the following examples from Huambisa ethnoornithological nomenclature given in figure 3.2. Here one notes that *áuju* (*Nyctibius aethereus*), the greater potoo, and *cháje* (*Chloroceryle amazona*), the Amazon kingfisher, are the prototypical folk species of the folk genera *áuju* 'potoos'

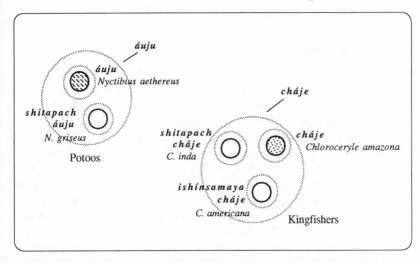

Figure 3.2 Diagrammatic representation of Huambisa classification of potoos and king-fishers, indicating polysemous marking of generic and prototypical folk specific taxa. (Data from Berlin, Boster, and O'Neill, in prep.)

and *cháje* 'kingfishers', respectively. In each case the prototype is polyse-mously labeled with the name of the more inclusive generic.[2]

Felger and Moser's recent work among the Seri along the Gulf of California in Mexico presents data on this particular nomenclatural convention. In forty-two of the fifty-four specific contrast sets found in Seri plant classification ("ethnospecies" in Felger and Moser's terminology), the prototypical mem-ber is polysemous with the folk genus, as the following examples show clearly (Felger and Moser 1985:65–67):

xtoozp	'native tomatoes'	
	xtoozp	*Physalis crassifolia* [prototype]
	xtoozp hapéc	*Lycopersicon esculentum* lit. 'cultivated xtoozp'
hamíp		
		'closely related genera in the Nyctaginaceae'
	hamíp	*Boerhavia coulteri* [prototype]
	hamíp caacöl	*B. erecta* lit. 'large hamíp'
	hamíp cmaam	*Allionia incarnata* lit. 'female hamíp'

---

[2] An analogous principle is currently in use in formal scientific nomenclature in naming sub-species and subgenera. Simpson states the rule as follows: "When a genus is divided into subgen-era, one subgenus . . . must have the same name as the genus, e.g., *Sciurus* (*Sciurus*) *vulgaris* belongs to one subgenus of *Sciurus*, *Sciurus* (*Parasciurus*) *niger* to another. Similarly, when a species is divided into subspecies, one (with the same [proto]type as the species) repeats the same name; e.g., *Sciurus niger niger* and *Sciurus niger neglectus* are subspecies of *Sciurus niger*" (Simpson 1945:25).

xoop		'elephant trees'
xoop		*Bursera microphylla* [prototype]
xoop	*ccacöl*	*B. laxiflora* lit. 'large xoop'
xoop	*inl*	*B. hindsiana* lit. 'fingers xoop'

Paso y Troncoso, in his description of classical Nahuatl ethnobotany, describes an almost identical situation. In the Nahuatl classification of sedges, the generic term *tollin* included "a *type*-species that carried simply the name *Tollin* and that [also] referred to the sedge family, various other related species of it having been grouped under the same name, each with a different determination" (Paso y Troncoso 1886:218, translated, emphasis added).

The biologists Wyman and Harris, noting this process to be widespread in Navajo ethnobotanical classification and nomenclature, describe the principle exemplified in the foregoing examples in an elegant fashion that has a decidedly modern ring to it: "The situation is as if in our binomial system the generic name were used alone for the best known species of a genus [the prototype], while binomial terms were used for all other members of the genus" (Wyman and Harris 1941:120). Of course, many situations will arise where it is necessary to distinguish a prototypical folk specific taxon from its contrasting neighbors. Disambiguation of polysemy with the superordinate generic is commonly accomplished by the application of a marking attributive that could easily be glossed as 'prototypical', but is often rendered as 'real', 'original', 'genuine', 'best looking', or 'ideal type'.

This linguistic feature, truly remarkable for its extensive distribution in many unrelated languages of the world, is exemplified in figures 3.3 and 3.4.

In each of the specific contrast sets pictured in figures 3.3 and 3.4, one taxon merits special cognitive recognition. Focusing on just a few examples, in the case of Tzeltal doves, it is *batz'il stzumut* lit. 'true dove' (*Leptotila verreauxi*), the white-tipped dove. For the three species of Huambisa pikelike fishes, the prototypical taxon is seen as *pengké champerám* lit. 'pretty, beautiful pikelike fish'. Finally, among the four armadillos recognized by the Wayampí, the nine-banded species, *Dasypus novemcinctus*, *tutu e'e* lit. 'armadillo true', is thought of as prototypical.

All of the examples provided above show the prototypical folk species to be highly visible, widely prevalent in the environment, and frequently observed. For the Tzeltal, Hunn writes, "The White-tipped Dove is a common and conspicuous resident to at least 2100 m . . . [and] it is larger than either of the two [contrasting] species" (Hunn 1977:154–157). Grenand states about the nine-banded armadillo: "C'est l'espèce la plus commune de toute la Guyane [It is the most common species in all of Guyana]" (1980:118). And among the Huambisa, of the three species of voracious, pikelike fish in the region, one, *Rhaphiodon vulpinus*, is the species most commonly caught and seen.

As suggested by Hunn's description, selection of one specific member of a

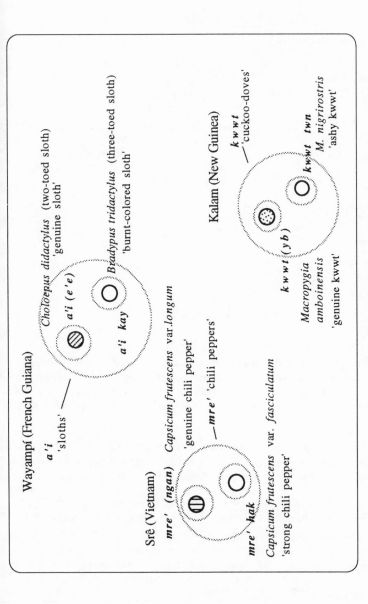

Figure 3.3 Examples from Wayampí, Srê, and Kalam ethnobiological nomenclature indicating optional linguistic marking of prototypical specific taxa where the linguistic modifier is glossed as 'genuine' or 'ideal type'. (Data from Wayampí are from Grenand 1980:109; Srê terms are from Dournes 1973:76–77; the Kalam materials are taken from Bulmer 1979:75 and Majnep and Bulmer 1977:79)

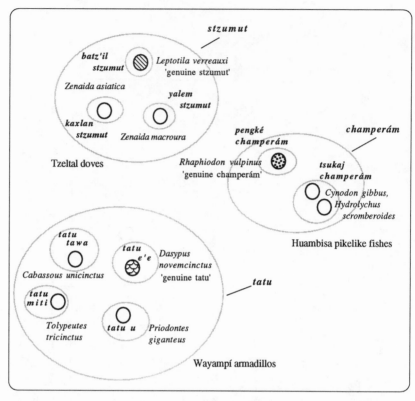

Figure 3.4 Diagrammatic representation of specific contrast sets of Tzeltal doves, Huambisa pikelike fishes, and Wayampí armadillos. The prototypical member of each set is indicated with distinctive hatching. (Data are taken from Hunn 1977:156–157, Grenand 1980:118–119, and Berlin, Swift, and Stewart, in prep.; see text for explanation)

polytypic generic as prototypical may involve considerations of the size of the organism as well as its abundance. Dentan made a similar observation several years ago as part of his work among the Semai of the Malay Peninsula:

> There is some evidence . . . supporting the idea that the largest species is the 'type species' of the taxon to which it belongs. . . . *ka' tapah* is generic for various kinds of catfish, of which one (*Wallago* sp.) grows to great size. To distinguish smaller sorts of *ka' tapah* from the giant one, informants would specify . . . that the small species is *ka' tapah i tane'*, "*ka' tapah*'s elder sibling." (Elder siblings are supposedly smaller than younger ones.) The giant species is the "real" (*batul*) *ka' tapah*. (Dentan 1970:21)

Conklin was the first modern writer to note this general feature as a regular ethnobiological principle of nomenclature in his work with the Hanunóo:

The single attributive *'urungan* 'original' . . . [denotes] that in each case the plant type referred to is considered the archetype of the specific plant segregate with which it shares the same basic plant name. [The use of this attributive is obligatorily] required where the designated plant name is distinguished from others in the same set. (Conklin 1954:130–131, 259)

Hays provides a concise and useful description of this same principle, and the problems that are superficially raised because of it, in his research among the Ndumba:

In many contrast sets, a subordinate taxon would be labeled with an expression identical to that which labeled the superordinate taxon. For example, the contrast set labeled by *nrauhi* consists of two members, one of which is labeled *nrauhi* and the other *pi'tu*. In some eliciting sessions, this was a source of confusion, since the informant could not be certain which of the categories was being discussed. However, such type specifics may be marked with an attributive-like expression *tuana'nraana*, which is best glossed as 'genuine' or 'real' (cf. Berlin 1972:60–62). Thus, if one wished to distinguish between the two kinds of *nrauhi*, one could refer to *pi'tu* and *nrauhi tuana'nraana*. Once this was discovered, I was able to avoid this kind of confusion by marking such polysemous expressions when appropriate. (Hays 1974:175)

Of course, the recognition of prototypical species in polytypic genera is common, as well, in Western biological systematics. The same ethnobiological principles noted earlier in Theophrastus's writings were carried directly into modern Linnaean nomenclature. Greene, in his perceptive treatment of early botanical nomenclature, shows how Brunfels follows in the footsteps of Pliny to disambiguate prototypical species from their contrasting congeners:

[The] early practice of leaving the one original representative of a genus without any cognomen, even after said genus has ceased to be monotypic, is a practice doubly suggestive in relation to the philosophy of nomenclature; for, in the first place it plainly reveals the antiquity of the idea of generic types, and emphasizes it. In the second place, the failing to assign a cognomen to the type species entails a difficulty . . . [of distinguishing the type from its contrasting neighbors, and demands] that the type species have also its particular cognomen. That botanists of fifteen centuries anterior to Brunfels had seen this to be desirable, one may infer from the nomenclature of *Plantago*. Two species of this genus were known to Pliny; and he had a specific cognomen for the type species as well as for the other. They were *Plantago major* and *Plantago minor*; and Brunfels follows Pliny in this. (Greene 1983:266–267)

Brown (1987) has argued that prototypical folk species such as those described above merit recognition as members of a new ethnobiological rank that he calls the "folk subgenus." The logical extension of this view would lead to the establishment of a new ethnobiological rank of "sublife forms" since one often finds prototypical generic taxa of particular life forms. The cottonwood is the prototypical tree for many Numic languages and the term for cottonwood is polysemous with tree (Trager 1939; Berlin 1972). A similar polysemous situation is found in a number of American Indian languages of the Northwest Coast where the prototypical trees are both firs and certain cedars (see Hunn 1980; Hunn and French 1984; Turner 1987).

Brown was led to make his proposal as a response to my comments on his earlier suggestion (Brown 1986) that folk species (*not* folk genera) represent the first ethnobiological taxa to be encoded in the growth of ethnobiological nomenclature. Although Brown has now abandoned this position because of its logical as well as empirical shortcomings (as outlined in Berlin 1986), his argument that prototypical species be afforded a new rank of "subgenus" is, as his earlier proposal, apparently motivated primarily by formalistic concerns. It has already been shown (see chapter 2) that biologically polytypic but nonetheless linguistically monotypic folk generics often, if not universally, show an internal structure where one or more closely related species are conceptualized as prototypical. If and when such monotypic folk genera subdivide into folk species, it is precisely these conceptual prototypical species that become the prototypical members of the emerging specific contrast set. Declaring these prototypical categories a new ethnobiological rank appears unwarranted.

3.3 RESIDUAL CATEGORIES?

As will be seen in the discussion of life-form taxa (see chapter 4), the generic and intermediate taxa included in a particular life form category do not always constitute a complete partition of the life form that includes them. Often, when questioned about a particular plant specimen, informants will state: "I don't know, it doesn't have a name, it's just an herb."

A similar situation may arise in the subdivision of generic taxa, where it is common that a particular species may be conceptualized as a clear member of a folk genus, but not be assigned to any of that generic's folk specific taxa. While this feature of ethnobiological classification had earlier been noted for Tzeltal ethnobotanical systematics by Berlin, Breedlove, and Raven (1974), Hays (1974:276, 1979:263), and Hunn (1976:511, 1977:57) were the first two ethnobiologists to formally (and independently) recognize species so designated as forming what they were to call "residual categories." Their proposal to treat unassigned organisms as members of residual taxa, however, is not uncontestable.

Both Hunn and Hays have described residual categories in their respective treatments of subgeneric taxa in Tzeltal ethnozoology and Ndumba ethnobotany. In both monographic treatments, residual taxa are reported for approximately 30 percent of subgeneric contrast sets (Tzeltal animals: sixteen of fifty-five sets [Hunn 1977:80]; Ndumba plants: fifteen of fifty-two sets [Hays 1974, 1979:124]).

The classic case described by Hunn is the Tzeltal treatment of 'butterfly'. He states that this Tzeltal generic taxon includes

> [five] consistently recognized specific taxa. . . . After these particularly noteworthy types (from the Tzeltal point of view) have been delineated, the remainder are treated as undifferentiated *pehpen*, 'just butterfly', or are dealt with by applying a descriptive phrase. . . . In strictly taxonomic terms, residual taxa must be treated as specific taxa. But the residual subdivision of *pehpen* is logically quite different from most taxa, i.e., it is defined *by the absence of any distinctive perceptual unity.* (Hunn 1976:511, emphasis added)

I adopted Hunn's and Hays's characterization of residual subgeneric taxa in my own earlier description of Aguaruna ethnobotanical classification (Berlin 1976a:391), but P. Taylor (1990) has suggested that such an interpretation is less than adequate. As an example, he asks that one consider the case of the Tobelo classification of *o arára* 'spider'. For the Tobelo, the taxon spider is divided into two named subgeneric taxa, *o oanga* 'wolf spider', and *o quhurua ma dadagoko* 'jumping spider'. However, the "vast majority of Arachnids are simply called by the higher-level 'spider' term" (Taylor 1990:64). The classificatory structure in this case might be indicated as seen in figure 3.5.

Taylor points out that the classification on the left of the diagram shown in figure 3.5 would indicate that the taxon spider is incompletely partitioned by A and B. Spiders not included in A or B are simply "residue." The diagram on the right of figure 3.5 suggests, in Taylor's view, that

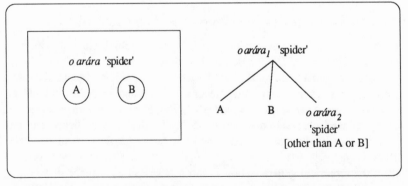

Figure 3.5 Two alternative classifications of Tobelo 'spiders'. (After P. Taylor 1990:64)

the spiders which are neither [A] nor [B] form an unmarked taxon *o arára2* 'spider (other than wolf or jumping spiders)'. . . . To posit a . . . 'residual class' (as at right) implies that this is in fact a semantic class having distinctive features. [However], a residual class so defined would be "logically quite different from most taxa" (Hunn 1976:511). . . . If our 'strictly taxonomic' structure requires that every class be completely subdivided, then we are forced to posit residual taxa [rather] than just note the residue; but when we also admit (as Hunn has) that no distinctive feature can be found . . . it seems simpler . . . to consider such cases residue rather than as a residual class . . . and to consider . . . that the higher-level term denotes 'residual' organisms . . . *not* because the higher-level term is polysemous with a lower-level 'residual' semantic class. (Taylor 1990:65)

Independently, Waddy has made a similar observation in her work on Groote Eylandt ethnobiology. "Residual categories may not necessarily be a single category . . . but a whole series of categories which can be distinguished by phrases such as 'a friend of X' and yet are formally named only by the name of the superordinate taxon" (Waddy 1988:88).

Taylor's and Waddy's insights are important observations and represent a more fruitful way of thinking about incompletely partitioned ethnobiological taxa of any rank. It is a position I adopt in the present theoretical framework. In this view, organisms not assigned to the named subdivisions of some particular polytypic taxon do not, by this fact alone, form an amorphous although legitimate category. Rather, these species float as a linguistically undifferentiated "residue," to use Taylor's term, as part of the superordinate generic that includes them. Thus, the classification of Tzeltal butterflies, given figure 3.6A in Hunn's characterization, might be more appropriately represented as in figure 3.6B. Given Hunn's recent writings on the subject, I think it likely that he would agree with this more flexible, although less elegant, characterization.

3.4 GENERAL NOMENCLATURAL PROPERTIES OF SPECIFIC TAXA

In the first statements of general principles of ethnobiological classification (Berlin 1972, 1973, 1976a; Berlin, Breedlove, and Raven 1973, 1974), I claimed that subgeneric taxa would be labeled by complex binomial expressions, referred to in chapter 2 as "secondary plant and animal names" (e.g., *white oak, scrub jay, large-mouthed bass*). That there are patterned exceptions to this general observation—exceptions that I will deal with below and that have been pointed out several times by a number of scholars (Headland 1981, 1983; Hays 1979, 1983; C. Brown 1986; P. Taylor 1987)—in no way detracts from the empirical generalization of the widespread occurrence of binomial specific nomenclature for many scores of languages throughout the world.

When the names of specific taxa deviate from their usually binomial struc-

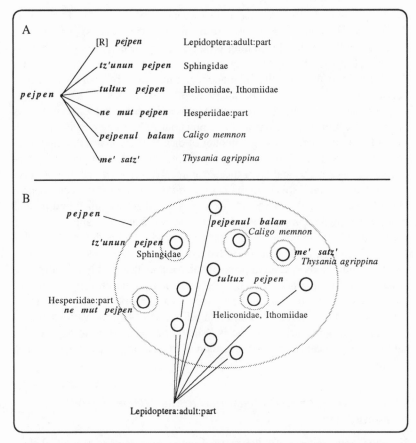

Figure 3.6 Two alternative treatments of unassigned species to the partially partitioned polytypic generic taxon **pejpen** 'butterfly' in Tzeltal ethnozoological classification (after Hunn 1977:xxxix, 280–282). (A) Categorization of Tzeltal 'butterfly' with unassigned species treated as residual taxon. (B) Categorization of Tzeltal 'butterfly' with unassigned species treated as "floating residue." Tzeltal orthography is slightly modified from the original. Hunn's earlier (1976:517, fig. 7) diagrammatic depiction of the set is logically equivalent to that shown by the tree diagram in (A), where all unnamed butterflies are assigned to a single residual taxon. Conventions of this diagram differ from earlier figures in that small solid circles represent biological taxa of any Western scientific rank.

ture, taking instead a monomial expression, I proposed that such taxa would either (a) represent the prototypical member of the contrast set, whose name would be polysemous with the superordinate generic (as discussed above), or (b) would constitute members of a residual taxon, a position that I no longer hold, witness the preceding section. A third condition leading to monomiality was also proposed: "It now appears that where a generic taxon is further partitioned into specific classes, and one or more of the included specifics are monomially designated [excluding prototypical members], *the monomial(s) will invariably refer to a taxon of major cultural importance*. One will not find, in light of this hypothesis, monomial names for organisms which lack major cultural significance" (Berlin 1976a:391–392).

The strongest hypotheses are ones expressed in terms that make instances of their disconfirmation clear and unambiguous. The foregoing is one such example. While there is a large amount of data to show that monomially labeled folk specifics often correspond to culturally important species, especially cultivated plants and domesticated animals (e.g., *terrier* but not usually, if ever, **terrier dog*), this is surely not *invariably* the case. Data recently provided by Hays and Taylor include examples of subgeneric plant and animal taxa labeled by monomial expressions that do not in any way appear to be of particular cultural importance (cf. Hays 1979:264, 1983:604–605; P. Taylor 1990). These data alone disconfirm the hypothesis as earlier stated. It is now clear that the proposed general principle on the prevalence of binomialization of subgeneric taxa is not an exceptionless nomenclatural universal. I was in error to have originally framed the principle in a categorical rather than statistical fashion. Nonetheless, as Hays himself has observed, the various exceptions to the original strict hypothesis "should not be allowed to obscure the nature and significance of binomialization as a commonly occurring pattern of folk [biological] nomenclature" (Hays 1979:265).

3.5 CULTURAL FACTORS CONTRIBUTING TO THE RECOGNITION OF SPECIFIC TAXA

Since the large majority of folk generic taxa in folk systems of biological classification are monotypic (around 80 percent in most systems, a point that will be examined in detail in the following section), what motivates the cognitive subdivision of those generic taxa that are polytypic? One of the first and most likely factors that suggests itself is that if a particular generic taxon ranges over several biological species or genera, the inherent perceptual differences of these several biological taxa might also be recognized linguistically. While plausible, this observation is only partially correct. An examination of the monotypic generics in folk systems of biological classification reveals that many of them are biologically diverse, corresponding in their denotative ranges to several Western biological species, genera, or even families or orders. (In earlier treatments [Berlin, Breedlove, and Raven 1966, 1973, 1974] such groupings have been said to be ethnobiologically "underdifferentiated," inasmuch as the folk systems failed to discriminate linguistically the actual biological diversity present in them.)

Furthermore, a significant number of polytypic folk genera are found to have biological ranges of a single species, often dividing the biological taxon into fragments that have no counterparts in the scientific biological system of classification. (Groupings of this sort were said to be "overdifferentiated" in my earlier writings.) Thus, the biological diversity of a particular folk genus, as determined by its biological range, is not a sufficient factor for leading to its split into smaller subgroupings.

An equally plausible explanation is one that relates to the cultural value attributed to the particular generic taxon in any given folk system. If most ethnobiological genera are recognized primarily because of their raw perceptual distinctiveness, it now appears likely that many specific taxa gain their conceptual and linguistic recognition at least in part because they have become imbued with properties of cultural significance. Data from many different systems appear to support this claim for ethnobotanical classification, although they are somewhat less clear-cut for ethnozoological classification.

A number of ethnobotanists have attempted to develop a rough index of the cultural significance of plant species as might be determined by the degree of human interaction or management that these species receive (cf. Conklin 1954:260–270; Berlin, Breedlove, and Raven 1966, 1974:99–100; Berlin, Breedlove, Raven, and Laughlin 1973; Brunel 1974; Baleé 1986; Turner 1988). If the recognition of subgeneric taxa is motivated, at least partially, by the degree of cultural attention that they receive, then this association should be revealed by some measure of the relative intensity of human management.

Table 3.1 provides the raw data on the complete inventories of folk generic

TABLE 3.1

Monotypic and Polytypic Generic Plant Taxa Grouped by Degree of Human Management in Four Relatively Complete Systems of Ethnobotanical Classification

	(a)				
Group	Cultivated	Protected	Significant	No Use Reported	
Tzeltal					
Monotypic	32	32	167	167	
Polytypic	31	9	28	5	(p≤.001)
Aguaruna					
Monotypic	37	31	215	177	
Polytypic	24	14	53	12	(p≤.001)
Quechua					
Monotypic	80	18	61	46	
Polytypic	22	2	4	5	(p≤.05)

	(b)				
Group	Cultivated	Planted/Cultivated	Planted/Watched	Protected	Not Treated
Hanunóo					
Monotypic	29	4	14	4	519
Polytypic	53	6	9	2	276 (p≤.001)

taxa from four relatively well-studied ethnobotanical systems. In each case, the compilations of generic plant taxa are divided into those taxa that are monotypic, incorporating no further named subdivisions, and those that are polytypic and include categories of folk specific rank.

The data from Tzeltal (Berlin, Breedlove, and Raven 1974), Aguaruna (Berlin 1976a), and Chancán Quechua (Brunel 1974) presented in table 3.1a are roughly comparable. Cultivated species are understood as forms that are deliberately planted and managed by constant and direct human intervention. Protected forms represent plant species that are not consciously destroyed in normal horticultural activities. Significant plant species are those that yield useful products but are not systematically protected. The fourth category includes species for which there is no reported cultural utility.

Conklin's data from the Hanunóo given in table 3.1b (Conklin 1954) are not directly comparable with those of the former three groups in that a slightly different index was employed. In Conklin's analysis, cultivated plant species include those forms that are known only from cultivation and are "fully dependent on man" (Conklin 1954:263). "Planted and cultivated" is a category for those plants that are cultivated but require no special care. "Planted and watched" refers to species that are planted and harvested but do not receive special cultivation. Conklin's categories "not treated" and "protected" "include only undomesticated plant types, though plants in the second category are saved from destruction in clearing and burning activities" (Conklin 1954:263). The degree of polytypic differentiation within each category of cultural plant management is seen to be highly significant statistically in each of the four groups. Figure 3.7 presents a proportional graphic representation of the same data in table 3.1.

Hays, who has voiced well-reasoned concerns about the clearly arbitrary assignment of plant species to rigid, nongraded categories that are meant to reflect cultural importance, has not organized his data from the Ndumba in a form comparable with those given in table 3.1 and figure 3.7. Nonetheless, he is led to state that "35 of the 43 (81.4 per cent) folk specific sets with more than two members include plants of 'high' or 'medium' cultural importance, while 31 of the 35 (88.6 per cent) sets with more than three members do. The three largest sets, with 19, 22, and 23 members, include the three principal Ndumba root crops: yams, taro, and sweet potatoes, respectively" (Hays 1979:263). These data, and others like them from distinct systems (cf. Baleé 1986), indicate that the polytypy observed in folk generic plant taxa is driven by cultural concerns: in general, polytypy increases directly with the intensity of direct human management.

A more detailed examination of these and additional ethnobotanical data reveals that the highest levels of polytypy occur within the most intensely managed generic taxa, lending support to the claim that subgeneric contrast sets of three or more members "tend to refer to organisms of major cultural

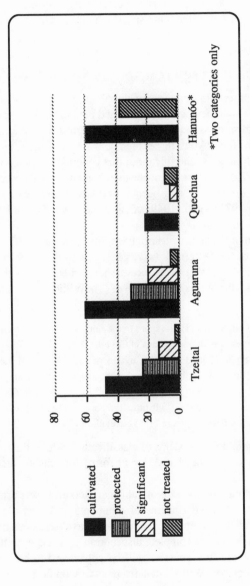

Figure 3.7 Relationship of intensity of cultural management to degree of polytypy in four systems of ethnobotanical classification. (Tzeltal data are from Berlin, Breedlove, and Raven 1974; Aguaruna from Berlin 1976a; Quechua from Brunel 1974; and Hanunóo from Conklin 1954)

importance and larger sets of twenty or more taxa invariably do" (Berlin, Breedlove, and Raven 1973:216). Table 3.2 presents data from eleven ethnobotanical systems that indicate the biological ranges of all polytypic generic taxa of ten or more members. The large majority of the contrast sets shown in table 3.2 include major cultivated plant species, and the pattern is remarkably strong.

3.6 PATTERNS IN THE DISTRIBUTION AND SIZE OF SPECIFIC CONTRAST SETS

Specific taxa show interesting patterns of distribution in terms of the size of the contrast sets in which they occur. As outlined in chapter 1, a general principle of ethnobiological classification is that folk species most commonly occur in contrast sets of few (two to three) members. I believe that, in reference to systems of ethnobiological classification, this general observation was first made in Berlin (1972). Unknown to me then, however, its counterpart in Western biological systematics had been formulated many years earlier by J. C. Willis (1907, 1922, 1940, 1949; cf. also Yule and Willis 1922; Yule 1924; and Guppy 1906).

Willis observed that there is a strikingly regular pattern in the frequency distribution of taxa of the same rank (say, genera) with differing numbers of members (say, species). Because of its special shape when plotted, this pattern came to be known as "the Willis hollow curve." As Willis was to characterize it in 1940,

> The curve was first noticed in 1912 in regard to the flora of Ceylon, which consisted of 573/1 (573 genera each with one species in Ceylon), 176/2 [i.e., 176 genera each with two species], 85/3, 49/4, 36/5, 20/6 and so on. If one take[s] the first few numbers, one finds that the numbers to [the] right and left of any single number (e.g., of 176/2) add up to more than twice as many (573/1 + 85/3 = 658) as itself, so that the curve must be hollow. . . . It turns the corner between 3 and 5 , and as the numbers get small it becomes more or less irregular (Willis 1940:33).

The data from ethnobiological systems of classification exhibit this same kind of pattern, although in a somewhat different form, for reasons that will be discussed shortly.

Table 3.3 presents data on the size of subgeneric contrast sets drawn from several linguistically unrelated systems of ethnobotanical classification for which relatively complete inventories of subgeneric taxa have been compiled. For the purpose of showing the complete distribution as it relates to the Willis hollow curve, monotypic folk generics will be considered to be subgeneric contrast sets of one member. Willis's data from his Ceylon flora are shown for comparison.

As can be seen in figure 3.8a, each system, with the exception of Ndumba (3.8b), exhibits a distributional pattern that approximates fairly closely that observed by Willis in his classification of the flora of Ceylon (figure 3.8c). This point is made even clearer when comparing Willis's botanical classification with that of the Hanunóo in figure 3.8c, the ethnobotanical system with numbers of taxa most closely approximating those of Willis. Ndumba (figure 3.8b) is notable in its aberrance from the general principles of numbers of taxa per group, with an exceptionally low number of subgeneric contrast sets of two and three members, but considerable numbers of taxa of greater size. The possible reasons for this variation from the norm, first raised by Geoghegan (1976), will be discussed in chapter 7.

Comparison of several systems of ethnozoological classification bears out this general structural trend in the distribution of subgeneric taxa by size of contrast set, as can be seen in table 3.4. Figure 3.9 presents the frequency distributions for the three relatively complete systems of Tobelo, Wayampí, and Tzeltal. As we can see from all these data, the distribution of folk specific taxa conforms in many respects to that observed in the distribution of biological taxa as represented by the Willis hollow curve. One major difference, yet unexplained, concerns a general observation on the regularity in the *proportion* of monotypic to polytypic generic taxa in any particular system of ethnobiological classification. In 1976, when I first noted this phenomenon, I wrote, in relation to Aguaruna Jívaro ethnobotanical classification, that

> the ratio of monotypic to polytypic taxa found for Aguaruna folk generic taxa is curiously close to that discovered in other systems of folk biological classification which have been recently described. . . . It is worthwhile considering the possibility that a specifiable constant of polytypy—somewhere in the range of 15 percent—may be characteristic of many ongoing systems of folk [biological] classification and might possibly be explained as a function of a subtle but specifiable interplay of biological and cultural constraints. (Berlin 1976a:389)

This observation has been strengthened by additional data from a number of other systems of ethnobotanical as well as ethnozoological classification, although the polytypy constant now appears to be in the range of 18–20 percent, as can be seen in tables 3.5 and 3.6, which reveal a rough ratio of approximately 80:20 percent of monotypic to polytypic generic taxa in these several systems of ethnobiological classification. This proportion is approximately the same for both major kingdoms of plants and animals. The distinct social, cultural, and ecological conditions prevailing in the various parts of the world represented by these individual systems do not, it seems, influence in any major way this apparently constant ratio of polytypy.

In this regard, it is instructive to determine whether some such comparable constant, which for this purpose can be referred to as the Proportional Polytypy Index, P (in contrast to alpha, the Index of Diversity used by Williams 1964 in his discussion of the logarithmic series), might be observed in the classification of plants and animals by systematic biologists. Clayton, in a

TABLE 3.2
Subgeneric Contrast Sets ≥ Ten Members from Eleven Systems of Ethnobotanical Classification

Group	Polytypic Generic	N Subgenerics	Cultivated?	Botanical Range
Tzeltal				
	chenek' 'bean'	17	yes	*Phaseolus* spp.
	lo'bal 'banana'	12	yes	*Musa acuminata* × *balbisiana*
	ech' 'epiphyte'	10	no	Various bromeliads
Hanunóo				
	labasa 'squash'	10	yes	*Cucurbita maxima*
	talung 'eggplant'	10	yes	*Solanum melongena*
	lada 'chili pepper'	11	yes	*Capsicum* sp.
	ma'is 'maize'	15	yes	*Zea mays*
	tubu 'sugarcane'	17	yes	*Saccharum officinari*
	gabi 'taro'	24	yes	*Colocasia esculenta*
	ubi 'yam'	28	yes	*Dioscorea alata*
	saging 'banana/plantain'	31	yes	*Musa* sp.
	kamuti 'sweet potato'	34	yes	*Ipomoea batatas*
	paray 'rice'	100+	yes	*Oryza sativa*
Wayampí				
	pako 'banana/plantain'	10	yes	*Musa* sp.
	kala 'yam'	11	yes	*Dioscorea trifida*
	ke'ey 'chili pepper'	11	yes	*Capsicum frutescens*
	ynga' 'inga tree'	12	some	*Inga* spp.
	mani' 'manioc'	13	yes	*Manihot esculenta*
Aguaruna				
	ajéng 'ginger'	10	yes	*Zingiber officinale*
	sámpi 'inga tree'	10	no	*Inga* spp.
	páantam 'banana/plan-tain'	17	yes	*Musa* sp.
	máma 'manioc'	30+	yes	*Manihot esculenta*
Chancán Quechua				
	papa 'potato'	15	yes	*Solanum tuberosum*
	sara 'maize'	12	yes	*Zea mays*
Siona/Secoya				
	bia 'chili pepper'	13	yes	*Capsicum* spp.
	ã'só 'manioc'	15	yes	*Manihot esculenta*
	bené 'inga tree'	18	some	*Inga* spp.
	noka 'banana/plantain'	26	yes	*Musa* × *paradisiaca*
Raga				
	bua 'bamboo'	20	no	'bamboo species'
	kumara 'sweet potato'	20	yes	*Ipomoea batatas*
	batai 'breadfruit'	20	yes	*Artocarpus altilis?*
	mologu 'kava'	25	?	*Piper methysticum?*

TABLE 3.2 (*Cont.*)

Group	Polytypic Generic	N Subgenerics	Cultivated?	Botanical Range
	toi 'sugarcane'	35	yes	*Saccharam officinarum*
	ihi 'banana/plantain'	40	yes	*Musa* sp.
	damu 'yam'	75	yes	*Dioscorea alata*
	bweta 'taro'	80	yes	*Colocasia esculenta*
Taubuid				
	amle 'taro'	11	yes	*Colocasia esculenta*
	ubi 'yam'	15	yes	*Dioscorea alata*
	saging? 'banana/plantain'	16	yes	*Musa* spp.
	amunti 'sweet potato'	20	yes	*Ipomoea batatas*
Casiguran Agta				
	biget 'banana/plantain'	18	yes	*Musa* sp.
	uway 'rattan'	22	no	'Rattans'
	pahay 'rice'	31	yes	*Oryza sativa*
Tobelo				
	o kahitela-tonaka 'sweet potato'	13	yes	*Ipomoea batatas*
	o peda 'sago palm'	13	yes?	*Metroxylon* sp. or spp.
	o pine 'rice'	17	yes	*Oryza sativa*
	o tahubí 'manioc'	18	yes	*Manihot esculenta*
	o bole 'banana/plantain'	50 + ?	yes	*Musa* spp.
Ndumba				
	kwaza'kwaza 'wild orchids'	10	no	Various Orchidaceae
	ho'hondí 'beans'	10	yes	Various Leguminosae
	hora'vaira 'composites'	10	no	Various Compositae
	saivu 'pandanus'	11	yes	*Pandanus* sp.
	taaqu 'bamboos'	12	yes	Various Gramineae
	heng'gunru 'gingers'	14	no	Various Zingiberaceae
	qeta 'bananas/plantains'	17	yes	*Musa* sp.
	saaqaa 'sugarcane'	20	yes	*Saccharum officinarum*
	saara 'cordyline'	21	yes	*Cordyline* sp.
	sara 'taro'	23	yes	*Colocasia esculenta*
	kaamma 'sweet potato'	24	yes	*Ipomoea batatas*
	taana 'yam'	26	yes	*Dioscorea alata*

Sources: Tzeltal: Berlin, Breedlove, and Raven 1974; Hanunóo: Conklin 1954; Wayampí: Grenand 1980; Guaruna: Berlin 1976a, personal data files; Chancán Quechua: Brunel 1974; Siona/Secoya: Vickers and Plowman 1984; Raga: Walsh 1979; Taubuid: Pennoyer 1975; Casiguran Agta: Headland 1981, 1983; Tobelo: Taylor 1990; Ndumba: Hays 1974.

Notes: Minor changes in original orthographies for native terms have been made for typographic consistency. Several cultigens for Ndumba show figures higher than those given in original source and are obtained from Hays (pers. comm.). Data from Walsh 1979 do not include botanical determinations, and numbers of subgenerics are given as round numbers. I have provided scientific names on the basis of the English glosses.

TABLE 3.3
Size of Specific Contrast Sets as Attested in Seven Systems of Ethnobotanical Classification Compared with Willis's Taxonomic Diversity Distribution of Genera/Species
for the Flora of Ceylon

System	1	2	3	4	5	6	≥7	Polytypic Sets (N)
	Number of Generic Taxa per Group							
Tzeltal plants	398	41	16	2	5	5	5	73
Aguaruna plants	463	68	12	9	2	3	9	103
Ndumba plants	333	9	8	6	7	5	17	52
Wayampí plants	438	47	13	4	2	3	7	76
Hanunóo plants	621	224	53	15	9	5	16	327
Tobelo plants	490	142	13	22	7	3	12	199
Seri plants	255	32	7	8	3	3	1	54
Flora of Ceylon	573	176	85	49	36	20	NA	NA

Sources: Tzeltal: Berlin, Breedlove, and Raven 1974; Aguaruna: Berlin 1976a; Ndumba: Hays 1974; Wayampí: Grenand 1980; Hanunóo: Conklin 1954, pers. comm.; Tobelo: P. Taylor 1990; Seri: Felger and Moser 1985. Flora of Ceylon figures are from Willis 1940:23.

series of papers evaluating the nature of the genus concept in biology (Clayton 1972, 1974, 1982), has compiled a useful set of data on the numbers of species per genus for several of the most important families of flowering plants, as well as that for the Gramineae (Clayton's specialty). Clayton's data were taken from Airy Shaw's seventh edition of J. C. Willis's *Dictionary of Flowering Plants and Ferns* (1966).

In table 3.7, I present the P index for Clayton's nineteen families, as well as for Steudel's (1855) and Bentham and Hooker's (1885) classification of the Gramineae. The table reveals a constant proportion of polytypy for these several families of flowering plants, as well as for the grasses, with a value of P at 64 percent. It is higher than the 80:20 percent ratio found in folk systems, but it appears to be as stable. In spite of this proportional difference, folk and Western scientific systems show similar curves for polytypy because the Western systems are comprised of many more sets of polytypic taxa in the tail of the curve (i.e., in sets of about seven or more members).

The P value of 64 percent seen in Clayton's analysis of botanical families is very near the proportion given by Willis (1922) in describing the so-called hollow curve of distribution that he first noticed in 1912 in his work on the flora of Ceylon (see figure 3.8c). Casting the proportions in terms of the percentage of monotypic forms, Willis writes:

No less than 4853 out of the 12,571 genera of flowering plants in my *Dictionary* (4th ed.) are monotypic. . . . A number [of them] will doubtless prove to have more than one species when we finally know the flora of the world . . . [but] there is little likelihood that the percentage will fall much below its present figure of 38.6 per cent

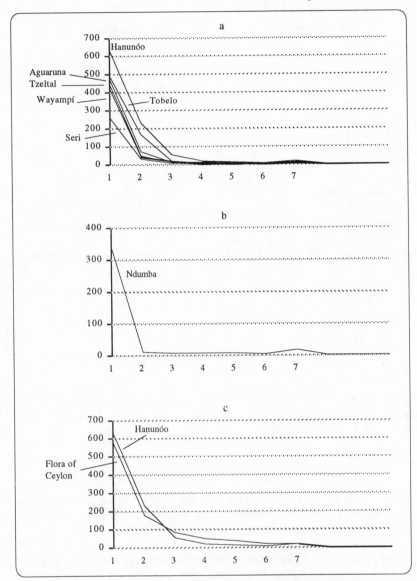

Figure 3.8 Frequency distribution of generic taxa in seven systems of ethnobotanical classification in terms of numbers of taxa included in sets with 1 (monotypic genera) to ≥7 members. (Numbers of taxa per set for (a) and (b) taken from table 3.3; numbers for (c) taken from Willis 1940:33)

TABLE 3.4

Size of Specific Contrast Sets as Attested in Eight Systems of Ethnozoological Classification

System	1	2	3	4	5	6	≥7	Polytypic Sets (N)
			Number of Generic Taxa per Group					
Tobelo animals	342	46	20	9	2	1	4	82
Ndumba animals	156	17		2	3	1	7	30
Tzeltal animals	280	25	18	5	3	2	1	54
Wayampí animals	489	55	22	14	5	1	3	100
Huambisa birds	202	36	9	2	0	0	0	47
Huambisa fish	52	8	4	1	2	2	1	18
Aguaruna mammals	38	9	3	4	1	0	0	17
Cantonese fish	160	6	7	5	3	1	9	31

Sources: Tobelo: P. Taylor 1990; Ndumba: Hays 1983; Tzeltal: Hunn 1977; Wayampí: Grenand 1980; Huambisa birds: Berlin, Boster, and O'Neill, in prep.; Huambisa fish: Berlin, Swift, and Stewart, in prep.; Aguaruna mammals: Berlin and Patton 1979; Cantonese fish: Anderson 1972.

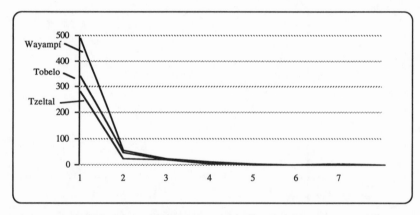

Figure 3.9 Frequency distribution of generic taxa in three systems of ethnozoological classification in terms of numbers of taxa included in sets with 1 (monotypic genera) to ≥7 members. (Numbers taken from table 3.4)

of the total [or that the proportion of polytypic forms will rise much above the present figure of 61.4 percent]. (Willis 1922:185)

Given the biological diversity inherent in these groups, it is highly unlikely, as Willis stoutly maintained, that this result is due to something other than the regular processes of random evolution (although Willis differed from most evolutionists in placing a much greater significance on mutation as a causal factor). It appears that the Willis curve expresses an important natural law (see Holman 1985; Yule 1924; Mandelbrot 1956; Williams 1964; but for a contrary

TABLE 3.5
Relative Proportions of Monotypic/Polytypic Generic Taxa in Twelve Relatively
Complete Systems of Ethnobotanical Classification

Group and Location	Monotypic	Polytypic	Total	% Polytypic
Quechua (Peru)	205	33	238	14
Ndumba (New Guinea)	333	52	385	14
Wayampí (French Guiana)	438	78	516	15
Taubuid (Philippines)	507	91	598	15
Tzeltal (Mexico)	398	73	471	17
Aguaruna (Peru)	463	103	566	18
Seri (Mexico)	255	55	310	18
Navajo (USA)	162	39	201	19
Mixe (Mexico)	321	62	383	19
Chinantec (Mexico)	313	83	396	21
Tobelo (Indonesia)	490	199	689	29
Hanunóo (Philippines)	621	335	956	35
				Mean = 20%

Sources: Quechua: Brunel 1974; Ndumba: Hays 1974; Wayampí: Grenand 1980; Taubuid: Pennoyer 1975; Tzeltal: Berlin, Breedlove, and Raven 1974; Aguaruna: Berlin 1976a; Seri: Felger and Moser 1985; Navajo: Wyman and Harris 1941; Mixe: Martin 1990; Chinantec: Martin 1990; Tobelo: P. Taylor 1987; Hanunóo: Conklin 1954, pers. comm.

TABLE 3.6
Relative Proportions of Monotypic/Polytypic Generic Taxa in Eight Relatively Complete Systems of Ethnozoological Classification

Group	Monotypic	Polytypic	Total	% Polytypic
Tzeltal	280	55	335	16
Ndumba	156	30	186	16
Wayampí	489	100	589	17
Tobelo	342	78	420	19
				Mean = 17%
Systems with Relatively Complete Data on a Single Major Life Form				
Cantonese fish	160	31	191	16
Huambisa birds	202	47	249	19
Huambisa fish	52	18	70	25
Aguaruna mammals	38	17	55	30
				Mean = 22%

Sources: Tzeltal: Hunn 1977; Ndumba: Hays 1983; Wayampí: Grenand 1980; Tobelo: P. Taylor 1990; Huambisa birds: Berlin, Boster, and O'Neill, in prep.; Huambisa fish: Berlin, Swift, and Stewart, in prep.; Aguaruna mammals: Berlin and Patton 1979; Cantonese fish: Anderson 1972.

TABLE 3.7
Relative Proportion of Monotypic/Polytypic Genera in Nineteen Families of Angiosperms and in the Gramineae (after Clayton 1972:286, from Airy Shaw 1966)

Bontanical Family	Monotypic	Polytypic	Total Genera	% Polytypic
1. Compositae	451	842	1,293	65
2. Leguminosae	265	410	775	66
3. Orchidaceae	192	500	692	72
4. Rubiaceae	237	388	625	62
5. Gramineae	243	418	418	65
6. Euphorbiaceae	316	(figures missing in source)		65
7. Labitae	70	163	233	70
8. Scrophulariaceae	109	178	287	62
9. Melastomataceae	76	149	276	66
10. Acanthaceae	142	229	371	62
11. Aizoaceae	142	229	371	64
12. Rosaceae	34	93	127	73
13. Umbelliferae	172	210	382	55
14. Cruciferae	157	231	388	60
15. Palmae	108	176	284	72
16. Asclepiadaceae	132	141	141	52
17. Apocynaceae	89	178	267	67
18. Araceae	51	76	127	60
19. Cucurbitaceae	54	63	117	54
Gramineae (Steudel)	140	300	440	66
Bentham & Hooker	104	188	292	64
				Mean = 64%

view see Walters 1986). Williams, who has applied the logarithmic series to the distribution of biological taxa perhaps more productively than any other biologist (cf. Williams [1946, 1947, 1949, 1951]), observes that the regular mathematical form of the curve "expresses some real biological relationships in the evolutionary history of species and higher groups" (Williams 1964:297).

Williams also notes that the striking regularities in the distribution do not appear to be influenced by the classificatory propensity of particular biologists to be either "lumpers" or "splitters":

It appears that different taxonomists, with their different basic ideas on what differences should justify a 'genus' or other group, produce classifications with different [biological] diversities. The diversity is low for 'lumpers' and high for 'splitters', but the pattern behind [their classification] is the same for all. Thus . . . good taxonomists may be splitters or lumpers, each interpreting equally correctly the fundamental pattern of evolutionary relationships. (Ibid.:297)

In what ways do these observations, and others implicit in Williams's remarks, relate to the constant P indexes for ethnobiological and biological genera? I can offer no good ideas as to the reasons underlying the stability of P in either Western biological or ethnobiological classification. However, the differences between P in folk and Western systems of biological classification might plausibly be interpreted in light of the relationship of generic polytypy to cultural significance discussed earlier. If the recognition of biological generic polytypy is the result of close, detailed inspection of the biological diversity of some region (or group, family, or whatever rank), then it seems likely that polytypy will begin to develop when the social and cultural conditions of a society particularly favor this cognitive activity and that it will increase with the emergence of modern biosystematics. This generalization is suggested by the following observations.

First, there is some evidence that generic polytypy is quite low or absent in the ethnobiological systems of classification of foraging populations. (See chapter 7 for a discussion of the noncultivating Seri, who are a clear exception to this hypothesis.) If additional new data should continue to support this generalization, then the appearance of polytypic generic taxa in the systems of horticulturalists might be interpreted as one of the resulting changes in the patterns of ethnobiological classification associated with the emergence of domestication, as recently argued by Whistler (1976), Waddy (1983), Hunn and French (1984), and C. H. Brown (1985). Domestication leads, of course, to the direct manipulation of biological species culminating ultimately with the literal creation and linguistic recognition of subgeneric taxa in a variety of distinct forms.

Second, with the emergence of systematic biology and the development of specialties comprised of individuals who could enjoy the luxury of studying the diversity of nature as part of paid professions, the further subdivision of recognized genera was continued leading to the high values of P (in the range of 64 percent for the several values of P in table 3.7) for the well studied groups of flowering plants. That many such groups have been studied systematically for several hundred years (e.g., the Gramineae) and yet show relatively stable P values is perhaps indicative that a point of stability has been reached. One would not expect, given this view, that the proportion of polytypic grasses recognized by Western systematists will increase significantly in the future, no matter the number of new species described, as Willis observed earlier.

If the families of flowering plants cited by Clayton show remarkable stability in the recognition of proportionally few monotypic genera, this may not be the case with other groups of organisms, of which birds and fish come to mind, and which, for different although related reasons, may still be in the process of achieving their maximal P values. Williams provides data on the classification of the birds of Great Britain and Ireland, where this group of vertebrates is "probably as well known as those of any similar area in the world" (Williams 1964:133). Using the British Ornithological Union checklist of 1952, Williams reports that of the 191 genera, 115 are monotypic (P = .40). I calculated the P value for the local avifauna reported in Hunn's study of Tzeltal ethnozoology (Hunn 1977) and arrived at a somewhat lower figure for this area of Mexico (163 monotypic genera from a total number of 237, P = .31). These figures depart significantly from the .64 values derived for flowering plants. Clearly, ornithologists recognize a much larger proportion of monotypic bird genera than do their botanical colleagues. Has evolution worked in differing ways with the birds?

Mayr's views on the relatively high proportion of monotypic bird genera leads to a different conclusion:

> Generic 'splitters' [among bird taxonomists] compared every species of a genus with the type species and found in this manner that most of these species had slight structural differences, even though they consisted only in the presence of an extra bristle or in slightly different body proportions. . . . They considered these often infinitesimal differences as sufficient excuse for the creation of additional generic names. [I]t happened not infrequently that they placed different races of the same polytypic species in different genera. (Mayr 1942:286)

Cain echoes Mayr's analysis. In one of his more cynical pieces devoted to proclaiming the need for a nomenclatural revolution in biological systematics, Cain lambastes his ornithological colleagues in the following way:

> I should judge that . . . in the birds, the group with the most refined systematic arrangement . . . at least one-quarter of the genera used in the classification of passerine birds are worthless. . . . Genera are . . . great temptations to show off specialist knowledge. In consequence many groups have been grossly oversplit. The so-called order *Psittaciformes* (the parrots) would be a *single genus* in almost any other group of animals. (Cain 1959b, emphasis added; cf. also Cain 1959a:315)

In some respects, the modern classification of fishes shows similarities to that of the birds in the recognition of a large proportion of monotypic genera. Again, drawing on data reported in Williams, the fishes of Britain, as published in Jenkins (1936), comprise 232 genera, 169 of which are monotypic. The value of P here is .27, comparable to that found for birds (say in the range of .30 to .40) and considerably lower than that observed for flowering plants (.64). There is some evidence that ichthyological classification recognizes a larger number of monotypic genera than might be expected in more well-studied groups. As with the birds, this might possibly be due to generic oversplitting.

Two examples from Huambisa ethnoichthyology will illustrate this claim. In Huambisa fish classification, the several species of *Leporinus* and the genus

Abramites are united in a single folk generic taxon, **katísh**. Until the early 1900s the Western scientific classification recognized but a single genus, as well, and *Leporinus* and *Abramites* were united. In 1906 Fowler established *Abramites* as a separate genus (Fowler 1906). Fowler's justification for the new taxon was based on a single feature, that of a larger anal fin. Recently, body shape has also played a part in the recognition of the two taxa. However, Gerí, in a modern consideration of the Characidae, states that "the genus *Abramites* has the *same characteristics* of the genus *Leporinus* with the exception of a higher body, a post ventral keel, and a larger anal fin" (Gery 1977:175, emphasis added). Here we see the establishment of a genus not by the recognition of what Mayr and Simpson refer to as a "decided gap," but by a few characters that most biologists would consider to be more appropriate to the definition of species.

A second example concerns the classification of some of the armored cat-fishes, a group that has been severely oversplit in recent years by the creation of numerous monotypic genera (the most extreme example can be seen in Isbrücker 1980). In the flat-bodied armored catfishes, the genus *Sturisoma* has been broken off from *Loricaria* on account of small features of dentition— small to moderate numbers and not setiform in *Loricaria*, numerous and setiform in *Sturisoma*. Otherwise, the two are almost indistinguishable.

One finds a similar situation among the deep-bodied armored catfishes. Historically, the three genera to which the Huambisa folk generic name **pútu** refers were all united in the genus *Hypostomus*. The current classification has split the original taxon into three genera, adding *Cochliodon* and *Pseudancistrus*. As a group, these creatures are quite similar, so much so that the great South American ichthyologist Eigenmann was led to state that "the genus *Cochliodon* is a *Hypostomus* with large, unipointed teeth" (Eigenmann 1922:225). It would appear that Cain's views on the modern classification of birds could equally well be applied to the current taxonomy of freshwater fishes, at least in these cases.

If the views of systematists of birds and fish are at variance with those in other branches of vertebrate zoology on the nature of genera, in that a few minute characters can be used to justify the formation of new taxa of generic rank, it should not be surprising that the number of monotypic forms would be so much higher in these subfields. The foregoing discussion shows that systematic biology is not that different from folk biology, that is, its principles are flexible and not fixed and may vary in interesting ways by particular subfield.

CHAPTER FOUR

Natural and Not So Natural Higher-Order Categories

> Every animal has a something in common with all of its fellows:
> much, with many of them, more, with a few; and, usually, so much
> with several that it differs but little from them.
> —Thomas Huxley, *The Classification of Animals*, 1869

TOWARD THE MIDDLE of chapter 2, I provided a hypothetical example of the biological collecting efforts of a naturalist somewhere in the rain forests of South America. The reader will recall that the naturalist was involved in carrying out a survey of the major vertebrate fauna found in the area. Briefly, let me take up the story from where we left off.

After considerable effort, the naturalist will have assembled a sizable collection of mammals, birds, reptiles, amphibians, and fish, all having been carefully prepared and preserved. The reader will also remember that the Western biologist had, from time to time, been aided by an Indian whose "knowledge of the local fauna [he found] to be rather extensive," especially in that many of the creatures that made their way into his traps and nets were often readily named by his native companion.

Late one morning, under a cloudless sky suggesting not the faintest sign of rain until late afternoon, the naturalist is struck by the desire to carry out a fanciful experiment. He spreads a large tarpaulin on the ground in front of his provisional laboratory and begins to draw out various preserved fish specimens from their tin storage cans—armored and pimelodid catfishes, stingrays, characids, hatchet fishes, eels, curimatids, and many others. Being careful to include several examples of each kind, he dumps them in a growing heap in the middle of the tarp.

His native assistant, who had been working in a nearby shack, is called over and observes with some curiosity the pile of preserved fish specimens.

Shortly, the naturalist, motioning toward the tarpaulin, makes a simple request: *"Yatsujú, apustá kumparí"* 'Brother, classify (them)' (literally, 'put each together with its close companions').

The assistant squats patiently near the edge of the assortment of creatures, gingerly picks up a specimen, examines it briefly and places it decisively in a clear area of the tarpaulin. He repeats the process with each specimen until the random conglomeration of fish species is exhaustively divided and grouped into a series of smaller assemblages.

When his assistant signals that he is finished, the naturalist begins to examine the resultant groupings. He notes that the various armored catfishes have been divided into two groups, the long-bodied and deep-bodied forms, but are nonetheless placed side by side next to one another, that the three specimens of stingrays (representing but a single monotypic genus) are neatly stacked together, that all of the curimatids are grouped in a single class, that the several genera of pimelodid catfishes are arranged in their own respective group, that the electric eel is placed in a small pile with the nonelectric eels, and so on for the remainder of the specimens. Our naturalist thanks his assistant, walks to his makeshift desk of river cane, opens a battered volume, and writes "further support for the claim" next to the following passage: "From the most remote period in the history of the world organic beings have been found to resemble each other in descending degrees, so that they can be classed in groups under groups. This classification is not arbitrary like the grouping of the stars in constellations" (Darwin 1859:431).

There is, of course, nothing particularly remarkable about our scientist's experiment, nor the results he obtained. Naturalists long before Darwin had claimed that biologists organize the perceptual resemblances they observe between plant and animal taxa into a taxonomic hierarchy. Likewise, in ethnobiology, the significance of the hierarchical structure of folk systems of biological classification has been recognized since the beginnings of cognitively founded studies in the United States, as seen in the seminal ethnobotanical and lexicographic research of Conklin (1954, 1962) and the formalization of ethnobiological taxonomic principles by Kay (1971, 1975). The centrality of hierarchic conceptual organization was given even wider recognition in Lévi-Strauss's important work on primitive classification (Lévi-Strauss 1966). Virtually every major field study on ethnobiological classification confirms the hierarchic ordering of plant and animal taxa into a unified conceptual system, lending support to Frake's claim that taxonomic organization of concepts "is a fundamental principle of human thinking" (Frake 1962:81).

In recent years, however, this view has come under attack from two quarters in anthropology. The first set of criticisms unfortunately (and remarkably) revives what one might have thought to be the fully refuted ethnocentric nineteenth century notions of primitive mentality and cognitive deficiency of peoples of traditional societies. Hallpike is the primary proponent of such a position, which is most stridently argued in his *Foundations of Primitive Thought* (1979; cf. also Hallpike 1976). His stance on folk classification is a curious mixture of neo-Malinowskian functionalism and orthodox Piagetian developmental psychology (for an insightful review, see Lave 1981). For Hallpike, "primitives tend to classify their universe into 'realms' such as 'things of the forest', 'things of the village', 'things of the sea', and so on, which are not ordered hierarchically. . . . Theorists such as Lévi-Strauss have greatly exaggerated the well-ordered nature of taxonomic hierarchies in primitive societies" (1979:203). In briefly reviewing one of Bulmer's papers on the Kalam (Bulmer 1967), Hallpike makes the unsupportable claim that "it is not surprising that their [the Kalam's] taxonomic system is not reducible to any consistent logical principles" (ibid.:206).

Hallpike is surprisingly unaware of, or has ignored (cf. Waddy 1988:44), the large amount of published ethnobiological research which contradicts these naive, extreme claims. This is especially disconcerting in that, while Hallpike may not have had access to the published materials of obscure American investigators, his knowledge of Bulmer's work must be assumed given his citation of Bulmer's 1967 research. Bulmer's views on the importance of taxonomic structure in Kalam are well known and had been published in numerous journals and monographs prior to 1979 (e.g., Bulmer 1968, 1970, 1974a, 1974b, 1978; Bulmer and Menzies 1972–73; Bulmer and Tyler 1968; Bulmer, Menzies and Parker 1975; Majnep and Bulmer 1977). Given that Hallpike does not confront the considerable ethnobiological data available on the topic of the taxonomic underpinnings of ethnobiological classification, his position does not bear on the present discussion.

A more serious, although curiously equally strident, attack on the significance of taxonomic hierarchy in ethnobiological classification comes from within ethnobiology itself (Ellen 1979a, 1979b, but especially 1986). Unlike Hallpike, Ellen does not raise explicitly the discredited argument that primitives are incapable of logical, and by implication, hierarchical thinking. Well aware of the numerous studies that have been published, even outside the Commonwealth, in support of the natural taxonomic organization of plant and animal classification, Ellen prefers to interpret the resulting taxonomic structures not so much as a reflection of the nature of folk systems of classification, but as a figment of some ethnobiologists' imagination:

> I am particularly troubled that some scholars should believe so readily that taxonomies are incontrovertibly 'in the data', that they emerge from the data as a consequence of their *natural properties* [citing Lakaatos and Musgrave 1970:98]. The taxonomic view of classification is . . . like Lévi-Straussian structuralism, in that if you try hard enough it is possible to discern the kind of order you are seeking wherever you wish. . . . There is nothing *in* [my] data . . . which would suggest that . . . there exists something called 'the Nuaulu classification of animals', which is some kind of structured totality. . . . This is a construction which I have placed on the

data. Certainly, one of the properties of the Nuaulu data (as I have presented them) is that many permit a taxonomic construction; but they may permit others as well. The 'natural' properties referred to are ambiguous and the term contentious [*sic*]. I . . . strongly resist the kind of empiricism which uncritically sees taxonomies as simply facts out there waiting to be collected, like so many herbarium specimens. (Ellen 1986:89)

However, if folk taxonomic structures have been widely reported in the published descriptions of ethnobiological systems of classification, Ellen goes on to state, there must be a reason. The most obvious is that the ethnobiologists who have posited taxonomic relationships of inclusion and exclusion are simply aping their biological and linguistic colleagues in an explicit

> mimicry of natural historical taxonomy and linguistics. This latter influence is evident both in terms of how the enterprise is phrased [*sic*], the ways in which data are conceived, in the technical procedures for elicitation, in the formal precision of analysis, and in the formulation of the problematic. In some [unnamed] cases, I would suggest that individuals with a grounding in natural history have a hidden bias towards finding 'natural' categories, and towards an under-emphasis of variation, with a corresponding stress on the taxonomic approach. (Ibid.:87)

Later on, Ellen does name at least one of the contentious ethnobiologists who has reified the notion of taxonomic structure, having invented the hierarchic relations described in his ethnobiological comparisons and descriptions, an automaton ready to check "yes" or "no" on his clipboard of preconceived questions, concerned more with "style" than substance, and anxious to ignore issues of cognitive variation. As Ellen clearly put it,

> The restricted check-list approach exemplified by the work of Berlin and his associates cannot, then, cope with the wider dimensions of variation between systems. [Their work] not only tends to reify a particular kind of classification (that which we call taxonomic) but seems to claim [*sic*] that a large number of semantic fields are at all times similarly organized. It [taxonomy] is compelling because it is a stylish representation of relationships among natural elements. . . . (Ibid.:90)

This criticism is voiced by Ellen's associate, Kesby, who is even more straightforward than his teacher in suggesting that the data reported by my colleagues and me is a deliberate invention, this time as part of a conspiracy with our Mayan consultants:

> Many naturalists and ethnographers will ask whether these results [of Berlin, Breedlove, and Raven] do not represent a refinement [of what people actually know]: have not ethnographers and local people between them produced an artefact, an elaborated classification which the local people would never have spelt out for themselves, if they had not been questioned, or led to re-examine their own earlier identifications and observations? (Kesby 1986:93)

In the following sections, I will present evidence that shows such views to be widely at variance with the results of a range of field studies of ethnobiological classification much broader than those presented by an American anthropologist, a botanist, and a small band of Maya Indians. While it may be claimed that in each instance the investigator is simply forcing the data into a preconceived taxonomic mold, I believe the data will show that such an interpretation is highly unlikely.

4.1 HIGHER-ORDER CATEGORIES IN ETHNOBIOLOGICAL CLASSIFICATION

Generic taxa, as the smallest fundamental units of ethnobiological taxonomies that can be recognized without much effort, are treated conceptually as mutually exclusive categories. As we have seen, while the biological ranges of many of these taxa may encompass several species or genera and will often overlap at their edges, one is generally able to identify a biological species or closely related set of species from which humans conceptually form or abstract a prototypical image. It has also been seen that folk generic categories comprise a large portion of the recognized taxa in any system of ethnobiological classification, numbering in the hundreds of classes. A major goal of ethnobiological research is to discover in what ways these fundamental generic groupings are conceptually related to one another—to understand the cognitive structure that links them in a unified conceptual system.

Numerous field studies in ethnobiology have shown that these groupings are generally organized in a shallow taxonomic hierarchy.[1] The hierarchy, of course, is not one best characterized in terms of the early formalized set-theoretic proposals of Gregg (1954, 1967), or the special application of some features of these proposals by Kay (1971). Instead, folk hierarchic structures are more appropriately seen in terms of Kay's model-theoretic formulation (Kay 1975), as a special extension of modal and model-theoretic logic (cf. Hughes and Cresswell 1968). Kay's new suggestions allow one to formalize many of the empirical observations about folk taxonomic structure that were not captured by the standard set-theoretic treatment, especially notions of prototypical taxa, the presence of superordinate taxa that contain members that are not themselves contained in recognized subtaxa (as the floating residue mentioned in chapter 3), and problems associated with logical transitivity.

It is disconcerting that those who continue to point out the inadequacies of Kay's 1971 paper on folk taxonomic structure consistently ignore his second

---

[1] The empirical observation that the hierarchy is shallow has led Ellen to imply that it is improper to use the term "hierarchical" in characterizing such relations, e.g., "although, used in a *loose metaphorical* way all folk classifications are 'hierarchic', none are of great depth in any absolute sense" (Ellen 1986:84, emphasis added). To my knowledge, Ellen never states why the number of links between the most encompassing category and any particular terminal taxon in some chain of taxa should in any way be relevant to the empirical fact of the type of logical relation (in this case, class inclusion) that unites them.

formulation (cf. Atran 1985; Hunn 1976, 1977, 1982; Hunn and French 1984; Ellen 1979a, 1986; Randall 1976), preferring to employ the rhetoric of strawman argumentation in suggesting that one abandon hierarchical structure in folk taxonomies in any form.

One can discern three types of suprageneric taxa, each with particular although not mutually exclusive biological, taxonomic, and nomenclatural properties. In the present chapter, I will focus first on those groupings that represent taxa of intermediate and life-form rank, and close with a discussion of some of the more salient features of the most inclusive taxa that respectively mark the kingdoms of plants and animals.

4.2 TAXA OF INTERMEDIATE RANK

The suprageneric higher-order categories of lesser scope than those of life-form taxa (e.g., tree, vine, bird, or fish) have been called "intermediate" or "midlevel" taxa (Berlin, Breedlove, and Raven 1973, 1974). While I readily admit that these terms are somewhat clumsy and inelegant, they are descriptive of the empirical fact of their typical structural position in between taxa of life-form and generic ethnobiological rank.

Taxa of intermediate rank have been attested (if not recognized as forming an integral part of the folk taxonomic structure) in most if not all ethnobiological systems of classification that have been subjected to intensive study. Taxa of this rank typically unite from two to a dozen or so perceptually related folk generics. Figure 4.1 illustrates intermediate taxa attested in the ethnoornithological classification of the Kalam (New Guinea), the Wayampí (Brazil), and the Huambisa (Peru). The three intermediate groupings of birds shown in the figure—'doves' (Huambisa), 'jacamars' (Wayampí), and 'owlet nightjars and forest nightjar' (Kalam)—are all immediately included in the broad life-form taxa marking 'birds and flying things', namely *píshak*, *wyra*, and *yakt* in Huambisa, Wayampí, and Kalam, respectively. (These higher-order taxa are not shown in figure 4.1.) We can see that each intermediate taxon includes several named folk generics, five taxa in Huambisa (*yámpits, yápangkam, shímpa, pupuí,* and *páum*), four generic taxa in Wayampí (*karamama, maratito, jawaimi'a,* and *tamagu*), and two generic taxa in Kalam (*pow* and *kwlep*).

In addition to their importance as evidence for the existence of taxa of intermediate rank, the groupings further illustrate several other general principles of ethnobiological categorization and nomenclature. The nomenclatural patterns observed in each of the three cases allows one to discern a prototypical generic taxon in each set—*yámpits* in Huambisa, *karamama* in Wayampí, and *pow* in Kalam, inasmuch as these names are used polysemously to label the three respective intermediate taxa. Furthermore, figure 4.1 shows that, although each of the three prototypical generics is polytypic, nomenclatural patterns point to one species (or in the case of Kalam, a distinctive color phase

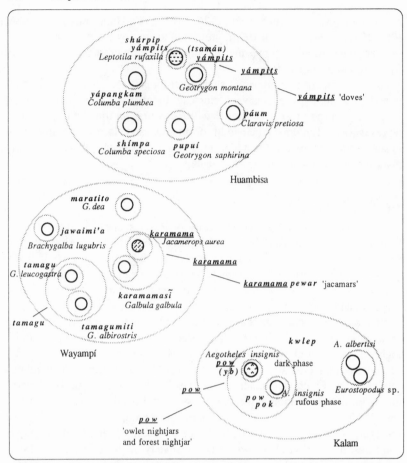

Figure 4.1 Schematic representation indicating taxa of intermediate rank in three systems of ethnoornithological classification: 'doves' (Huambisa of Peru), 'jacamars' (Wayampí of Brazil), and 'owlet nightjars and forest nightjar' (Kalam of New Guinea). Underlined names (**_yámpits_**, **_karamama_**, and **_pow_**) in Huambisa, Wayampí, and Kalam, respectively, demonstrate chains of polysemously labeled taxa. The Wayampí term **_karamamapewar_** is complex, meaning literally 'family of karamama'. (Huambisa data are from Berlin, Boster, and O'Neill, in prep.; Wayampí from Jensen 1988:36; Kalam from Bulmer 1969:78; see text for explanation)

of a single species) in each generic taxon as prototypical, namely *Geotrygon montana*, the ruddy quail-dove, for Huambisa doves; *Jacamerops aurea*, the great jacamar, for Wayampí jacamars; and the ruddy phase of *Aegotheles insignis*, the large owlet nightjar, for Kalam nightjars. Here we see a chain of prototypicality over three ethnobiological ranks (cf. also Berlin 1972 for comparable data from Apache; and Ellen, Stimson, and Menzies 1977 for an essentially similar treatment of data on the Nuaulu classification of reptiles).

In the case of the Wayampí materials, the prototypical member is recognized explicitly as the 'chief' or 'head' of the group, a feature analogous to Wayampí notions of social organization where a single individual, one who has usually formed a group of consanguineal and affinal relatives, is seen as the primary authority. Thus, Jensen states that "in the same manner, each group of birds (or group of birds considered to be related) also has their chief. In this case, the chief serves as the model or typical species of the group" (translated from Jensen 1988:22). An identical structure, both conceptually and nomenclaturally, is described by Turner (1986 ms.) for the ethnobotanical system of classification of the Thompson and Lillooet Interior Salish (British Columbia):

> Included within the . . . broad [life-form] classes, but still more general than the hundreds of basic 'generic-level' taxa in these languages, are a multitude of categories corresponding with, at least in level of generality, the intermediate taxa of Berlin *et al.* (1973). . . . Altogether, 79 midlevel plant taxa are identified from Thompson and 38 for Lillooet. (Turner 1986:9)

> Names for many Thompson and Lillooet midlevel categories are derived through expansion of reference of a name for a particularly salient folk genus and are polysemous with the generic level name. . . . Here a primary species, usually of high cultural significance and having a generic level name, is a focal taxon ('type') for a group of species in some way identified with it, usually either by appearance or function, or both. AY [one of Turner's informants] calls this primary plant the 'boss' or 'chief' of the group [cf. Jensen's comments on the Wayampí]. This is the usual situation when the name for the midlevel taxon is polysemous with a generic-level name. Hence, *qʷlála'* in Lillooet and *qʷléwe(')* in Thompson is both the generic level name for nodding onion (often called *qʷlála(')-'úl* 'real/original onion') and a general name for the various types of onions. (Ibid.:11)

Covert Taxa of Intermediate Rank

While taxa of intermediate rank might be commonly named in some systems, such as the Wayampí, this is not generally the case in many other systems of folk biological classification. Thus in the Huambisa and Aguaruna classification of birds one finds named intermediate taxa for such groups as doves, hawks, puffbirds, ant shrikes, and toucans, but many other recognized groupings such as woodpeckers, rails and crakes, quails and partridges, trogons, and parrots lack habitual linguistic designations altogether. These taxa, which have been referred to as "covert categories" (Berlin, Breedlove, and Raven 1968) or "covert complexes" (Berlin, Breedlove, and Raven 1974), nonetheless form a highly significant part of the total organizational structure of ethnobiological systems of classification.

Covert taxa are well documented for Tzeltal ethnobotany, for which Berlin, Breedlove, and Raven (1974) describe some seventy taxa of this rank. In his detailed treatment of Tzeltal ethnozoological classification, Hunn defines forty-five covert groupings of animals. Hunn states that "though these horizontal relationships [among the generic members of covert taxa] may fail to generate discretely bounded higher-order taxa, they constitute an integral aspect of the texture of the fabric of folk classification. I try to describe this aspect of Tzeltal folk-zoological classification by defining covert 'complexes' " (Hunn 1977:37).

The recognition of intermediate covert taxa is not simply a Mayan, or, as Ellen might suggest, an American formalist, bias. According to Bulmer, the Kalam of highland New Guinea

> are well aware of certain groupings higher than the species (which are in fact in most cases related in zoological 'genera' or 'families') that share a complex of morphological and behavioural characters. Notable examples, where the Kalam appreciate the association of four or more related species are: hawks and falcons; parrots; and within the parrots, lories, or lorikeets, i.e., 'nectar-feeding smaller parrots'; pigeons; 'typical' nectar-feeding, long-beaked honey-eaters; and medium sized birds of paradise and bower birds. I must stress that they do not have standard names for these 'natural' groups—they are what Berlin calls 'covert categories' or 'complexes' . . . —but their reality in Kalam thinking is unquestionable. (Bulmer 1979:62; cf. Majnep and Bulmer 1977)

The importance of such covert groupings among the Kalam is further evidenced by the groupings in which bird species are discussed in the book on Kalam folk ornithology jointly authored by Bulmer and his Kalam assistant, Saem Majnep (Majnep and Bulmer 1977). Here, a substantial portion of the major chapters bring together covert groupings of folk generics (Bulmer's speciemes) that represent well-formed biologically natural taxa, for example,

> We may note . . . that Saem keeps the widely recognized covert categories together as groups, for example loris in Chapter 4, typical honey-eaters in Chapter 6, pigeons in Chapter 8 and diurnal raptors in Chapter 20. . . . Within the seven chapters devoted mainly to forest birds, 4, 5, 6, and 8 are devoted largely to natural taxonomic groups, though in 4, 5, and 8 arboreality and feeding habits are also stressed (Bulmer 1979:68).

In spite of these and other findings (see Hays 1976, particularly), the nature of covert taxa in folk biological systems of classification continues to be a topic of considerable debate in ethnobiology. Since 1968, when my colleagues and I first proposed the hypothesis that covert taxa be considered as an integral part of folk taxonomic systems, some ethnobiologists have argued that, while covert taxa may indeed form an integral part of ethnobiological classification, the methods used to establish their existence have been inadequate (see Atran 1985 and P. Taylor 1984). In addition, C. H. Brown (1974), who was the first to object to the validity of such taxa, argues not only against the methodological procedures employed to recognize covert midlevel groupings, but also that they are artificial, or special-purpose, culturally motivated categories based on function or utility. Brown feels so strongly that intermediate taxa are a Berlinian invention that he recently wrote: "[Berlin's proposed] . . . ethnobiological rank 'intermediate' is not represented [in a schematic diagram of the taxa of various ranks] because [intermediate] classes are rarely found in [ethno]biological taxonomies. . . . For reasons that I outlined 12 years ago (Brown 1974), I do not believe in the psychological reality of covert categories" (Brown 1986:1, 17).

Finally, Ellen seizes on taxa of this rank to again call into question hierarchical structuring in ethnobiological classification altogether: "Covert categories, in so far as they can be demonstrated to exist at all, seem to contradict the very idea of taxonomy" (Ellen 1986:86).

Most of the earlier methodological suggestions put forth by Berlin, Breedlove, and Raven should more appropriately be viewed as heuristic procedures aimed at establishing the *internal structure* of contrast sets of folk genera (or, for that matter, sets of subgeneric taxa). The methods of triads testing (Romney and D'Andrade 1964; Romney and Weller 1988), comparison of all possible pairs of taxa in some proposed set, and construction of folk keys (Berlin, Breedlove, and Raven 1968), cannot be used as the principal means by which one comes to recognize the contrast sets themselves. More indirect, although no less formal, methods have since been employed to establish the existence of covert taxa that are independent of those that can be used to explore their internal structure.

My major aim in the following sections is to present evidence to substantiate the claims that covert taxa are, in the main, perceptually recognized on the basis of their shared morphological (and in the case of animals, morphological and behavioral) characteristics (Berlin 1974). Special purpose considerations, such as the importance of the plant or animal for some cultural application such as medicine or ornamentation, can be found to form the bases of a small portion of intermediate taxa, more commonly in the classification of plants than animals, but these classes represent a minority of such groupings.

More commonly, as the reader will already have inferred from the examples cited in figure 4.1, taxa of intermediate rank correspond closely to portions of recognized biological families, lending support to Atran's (1983, 1985) suggestion that they be treated as (covert) family fragments. However, he is in error to suggest that such groupings are generally "extrataxonomic" in that they typically exhibit nontransitive relationships with their immediate superordinate life-form taxon (see below). A number of such taxa do include some members that are themselves included in distinct life forms, but these are the exception and in any case are easily accounted for in Kay's model-theoretic treatment (see Kay 1975:156–158).

The substance of Atran's arguments, however, represents an important insight, and I am convinced by his suggestion that such fragments, perhaps in their earliest form as covert taxa that only later come to be labeled linguistically, can be seen as the origin of the biological family as recognized in modern systematics. As such, intermediate taxa have much in common with the folk generics they encompass, in that they form natural, biologically well-founded groupings whose recognition is based on obvious patterns of similarity that reflect what can best be interpreted as affinity due to evolutionary propinquity.

Evidence on the Reality of Covert Taxa

The presence of covert groupings of contrasting generic taxa in folk biological classification may be informally suggested to field investigators in the process of their learning to use the names of plants and animals correctly. Just as ethnographers hope eventually to develop linguistic skills in a local native language as a means of conducting in-depth ethnographic research, ethnobiologists hope ultimately to recognize and identify at least the most common plant and animal taxa with something approaching the accuracy of one's native collaborators. In addition to the personal satisfaction that this knowledge confers, one's informants are more likely to maintain an active interest in the often tedious daily tasks of ethnobiological collecting when they are aware that the investigator not only knows how to *ask* questions about the names of things being collected, but eventually has learned the correct answers for at least some significant portion of them (cf. Bulmer 1969 on the importance of this point).

Testing one's knowledge of the appropriate biological referent of some native plant or animal name is comparable to a child's natural acquisition of an ethnobiological vocabulary as part of the normal process of socialization—the novice, in the presence of an expert, examines and names a particular plant or animal and the expert either approves or corrects the assertion.

Like most other field ethnobiologists, I have had many opportunities to become involved in just this kind of self-testing. Most commonly, when the name that I recalled was incorrect, my native collaborators would patiently repeat, as they had done on numerous other trials, the plant's or animal's correct generic name. On just as many other occasions, however, as I would identify a particular plant, say, a species of Cecropia in Amazonian Peru, my Aguaruna assistants might respond, "No, brother, that is not a *tséke* [*Cecropia engleriana*], it is a *satík* [*C. tessmanii*]. Both *tséke* and *satík* are companions, along with *súu* [*C. sciadophylla*], as you can easily tell from their appearance." These comments were identical in content to many made earlier in my work among the Tzeltal of Mexico. Commonly, during botanical collecting, Breedlove's and my Maya Indian informants would volunteer the observation that such and such a plant was similar to some other plant that we had not yet collected. Just as often, indigenous collectors would state that species x and species y belonged together in that they were "companions," "brothers," or "members of the same family": e.g., "*Te sune, ya sjoy sba sok ch'ajkil, sok soj, sok k'uxban tz'antz'an, sok bajk'al te', sok pom te'; melel lom pajal sok spisil ta yilel*" 'The *sun* plant (*Tithonia scaberrima*) joins itself as a companion with *ch'ajkil* (*T. diversifolia*), *soj* (*Lagascea helianthifolia*), *k'uxban tz'antz'an* (*Brickellia guatemalensis*), *bajk'al te'* (*Coreopsis mutica, Bidens squarrosa*), and *pom te'* (*Zexmenia frutescens*); in truth they are all very similar in the way they look'.

A number of ethnobiologists have described quite similar situations. Turner's tape-recorded transcription of the remarks of her Salish Indian informant, Annie York, is typical: "The *sxʷusum* [soapberry] is a relative of *la'áse* [squaw currant]—sticky, red berries. It's got the same kind of woolly leaves. I don't know if it has any other relatives. That's the only one I know that's similar to it, and the old people always say, 'That's *sxʷusum*'s relative.' You see, all berries have relations" (Turner 1986:3).

Hays, in describing his work on covert intermediate taxa among the Ndumba of New Guinea notes that

> in Ndumba, informants often volunteered statements, as they reportedly do in Tzeltal, that plants A, B, and C 'go together' or 'are brothers' . . . but lack any inclusive name except at the very highest taxonomic rank of life form (e.g., *sa'tari* 'trees and shrubs'). (Hays 1976:495)

> Informants volunteered statements to the effect that certain named plant classes 'are brothers' or otherwise discussed plants with me in such ways that I have no reason to doubt that unnamed categories in fact exist. (Ibid.:505)

Bulmer found the use of the kinship metaphor to be so significant in describing relationships of this sort in ethnobiological classification, that he proposed it as one of his five general principles, namely, "The language used in discussion of the relationship of taxa of similar order (i.e., within the same contrast set) is the language of kinship and descent—'brothers', 'one father', 'one lineage' " (Bulmer 1974b:95).

In addition to informal discussions about the relationships that generic taxa are thought to have with one another, relationships that lead the investigator to propose their membership in more inclusive midlevel taxa, standard ethnographic elicitation is also suggestive. In both the Tzeltal and Jívaro research, I have found it profitable to ask informants to write out the names of plants and animals that they considered to "go together," as members of the same family. The limitations of this method in situations where informants are nonliterate have been amply discussed by Hays (1976), who offers useful and positive alternatives, some of which are discussed below.

One alternative that Hays does not mention, and one that I have used suc-

cessfully with nonliterate Aguaruna and Huambisa informants, is to systematically work through a relatively complete inventory of generic plant (or animal) names, or better yet, relatively complete sets of prepared specimens,
when informants are simply asked, "Does X [name of plant, animal] have any
relatives?" The results to be obtained from such a seemingly simple method
are quite rewarding.

In one instance, I interviewed a knowledgeable Aguaruna male informant
over several days of lengthy, tape-recorded sessions. The interviews consisted
of working through an alphabetically arranged field slip file of all of the al-
leged bird names that had been collected from earlier interviews, as well as
the names associated with any specimens that had been collected up to that
time. The inventory, although far from complete, included approximately 250
bird names. As each slip was pulled from the arbitrarily organized file, I would
read the term aloud and ask my informant to give me the names of its relatives,
if any. As the eliciting sessions progressed, I found it impossible to remember
which expressions I had already recorded as the relative of some particular
category because of the large number of bird names involved. When we came
upon a bird name that had already been mentioned, my informant would state
emphatically, "*Husha, pujáwai*" 'We have already done that one!' (lit. 'that
one is already present here').

The stability of my instructor's groupings became evident when, on beginning an analysis of the results, I discovered that he had provided some fifty
mutually exclusive complexes of generic bird names with the exception of two
names which had been assigned to more than a single group. This is a frankly
remarkable finding. However, I have carried out the same procedure with
other Aguaruna, as well as Huambisa, informants and obtained similar results.
Rather than as suggesting that these individuals tend to have unusually good
memories, the results are more readily interpreted as reflecting something
about the nature of each individual's ethnobiological system of classification.

Covert groupings of generic taxa are also suggested by the patterns that
emerge from informants' variable naming responses when they are asked to
name plants and animals in semiformal experimental contexts. The discussion
of the Aguaruna Jivaro's classification of curimatid fishes in chapter 2 showed
that the biological ranges of names for generic taxa systematically overlap in
such a way as to suggest close perceptual similarity of the categories to which
these names are applied. When the generic categories of a covert taxon elicited
from knowledgeable informants correspond to those generic taxa tied together
in terms of the naming response patterns derived from systematic independent
naming trials, there is good reason to propose that the covert taxon represents
a salient, stable grouping of organisms that must be recognized in a cognitively revealing description of the given ethnobiological system of classification.

Hays (1976) has also used patterns of variation in naming in the study of ethnobiological classification as evidence to posit covert taxa. To my knowledge, he was the first to explicitly interpret patterned variation as evidence for such groupings. In his research on Ndumba ethnobotanical classification, Hays asked ten Ndumba informants to independently name prepared herbarium vouchers of 517 botanical collections of the local flora. After eliminating variation due to the use of synonymous names, Hays noted striking patterns underlying superficial differences in naming responses for many of the plant species. As he puts it, when informants were asked to name a particular plant, it seemed that "the pertinent question was not, 'Which of all possible 1,100 or so names [in the Ndumba plant lexicon] applies to this?' but rather, 'Which of a small subset of plant names applies to this?' In other words, having decided initially that it was one of the relatively few possible plants, which *of these* was it?'' (Hays 1976:497). An example of this kind of patterned variation can be seen in the responses of Hays's informants to the five collections of distinct species of *Saurauia* that he included in his experimental herbarium, as seen in table 4.1. For the five species of *Saurauia* used as stimuli in Hays's naming experiments, only four Ndumba plant names were elicited as appropriate responses. An examination of table 4.1 allows for the straightforward inference that each of the four names finds its focus on one of four of the five botanical species, namely, **hori'ori** on *Saurauia* sp. 1, **tondaam'bu** on *Saurauia* sp. 2, **tu'raatura** on *Saurauia* sp. 3, and **fo'vasra** on *Saurauia* sp. 5. The fourth *Saurauia* species is not well defined, falling within the extended ranges of at least three of the Ndumba generics.

As with the Huambisa materials discussed earlier, the variable naming responses allow for the inference that the four categories are linked to one another as members of a closely knit set of contrasting generic taxa. As Hays sees it,

> It seems reasonable to postulate that *fo'vasara* and the other folk genera [that refer to species of *Saurauia*] do constitute a legitimate conceptual grouping that does not happen to be named. . . . Multiple instances of such co-occurrences, I propose, may

TABLE 4.1

Distribution of Naming Responses for Five Species of *Saurauia* among the Ndumba of Highland New Guinea (after Hays 1976:501)

	Ndumba Folk Genera			
Scientific Name	*hori'ori*	*tondaam'bu*	*tu'raatura*	*fo'vasara*
Saurauia sp. 1	10			
Saurauia sp. 2	1	9		
Saurauia sp. 3		1	8	
Saurauia sp. 4	4	4	2	
Saurauia sp. 5			1	9

be taken as evidence of conceived similarity among the categories designated by the names such that their tokens were readily 'confused' with each other, whether by several informants when presented with a particular plant to identify or by the same informant when presented with the same . . . plant on different occasions. The categories designated by these co-occurring names, then, may be considered as conceptually grouped, whether the grouping itself is habitually named or not; when it is not, it may be referred to as a covert category or complex. (Hays 1976:503)

The Biological Bases of Intermediate Taxa

If taxa of intermediate rank can be demonstrated to form an integral part of ethnobiological classification, it is appropriate to ask what underlies their recognition. The data available indicate that such taxa are formed on the basis of readily perceived morphological similarities among the contrasting generics of which they are comprised. As a consequence, intermediate taxa often make good biological sense.

Partial justification for this claim can be seen in table 4.2. This table presents a comparison of the intermediate taxa found in the classification of birds among the Tzeltal, as described by Hunn (1977) and the Wayampí, as described by Jensen (1988). In addition to the careful documentation that these authors provide for taxa of this rank, their materials are noteworthy for two other reasons. First, while the Tzeltal taxa described by Hunn are covert, those documented for the Wayampí are habitually labeled. Second, in spite of the great ecological differences that separate the two societies, one from the highlands of southern Mexico and the other from the rain forests of northern Brazil, the careful reader will note remarkable similarities in the content of the intermediate taxa described for each of the two systems.

While the information indicated in table 4.2 cannot be easily appreciated at a glance, it is worthy of detailed study. Comparison of the two systems allows for at least the following inferences as concerns the biological underpinnings of taxa of intermediate rank in the folk classification of birds. First, the data show that the intermediate taxa in both systems are best interpreted as groupings of birds that are, in the main, closely related phylogenetically, in that each grouping brings together members of the same or closely related biological families. Second, some taxa include folk generic classes that range over species of a single biological family (e.g., vultures, doves, parrots) or two or three closely related biological families (e.g., guans, quails and tinamous, owls, nightjars and potoos, trogons and motmots, woodpeckers and woodcreepers, sparrows, blackbirds and crows). In those groupings that range over three or more biological families, strong perceptual factors can be surmised as to why they would be seen by the Tzeltal or Wayampí as similar.

The species included in the Tzeltal grouping of waterbirds show both behavioral and morphological features in common that reflect, in part, their ecological adaptation to riverine food sources. The three intermediate taxa of waterbirds among the Wayampí show even greater similarities in terms of the overall morphology and dietary preferences of the species that comprise them (e.g., members of the Ardeidae, Threskiornithidae, Anhingidae, Phalacrocoracidae, and Cochleriidae).

Groupings of the smaller birds, especially among the Wayampí, bring together species of similar size that are also often marked by striking plumage. Classes of this type, especially that of the cotingas and relatives that encompass members of six diverse families, are clearly less biologically well founded than the smaller groupings referred to earlier. It seems likely that these taxa are explicable partly by cultural reasons, in that the plumage of many species in these families is sought for decorative purposes (Jensen 1988:40). Overall, however, intermediate groupings of this type form a minority of those recognized.

That distinct societies such as the Wayampí and the Tzeltal should group birds as similar as the parrots, or vultures, or toucans into midlevel intermediate taxa should not be surprising to anyone but the most recalcitrant cultural relativist. In general, higher-order taxa of animals, especially at the rank of family, have evolved in such a way as to provide the human classifier with a number of maximally distinctive clusters of species that are readily recognizable on the basis of their overall structural characteristics. The species encompassed in these groupings have developed quite distinctive adaptive strategies that are peculiar to a particular ecological niche or to what Mayr has called an "adaptive zone" (Mayr 1969:95). In the world of plants, however, the higher-order groupings, especially among taxa of intermediate rank, are of a somewhat different character. Few families of the higher vascular plants are as unitarily distinctive in their morphological appearance as are the intermediate groupings of animals. The grasses and the palms come to mind as striking exceptions, but even here one is confronted with atypical examples, for example, the giant bamboos (among the grasses) or the vinelike or essentially trunkless forms of palms.

Nonetheless, when one examines the midlevel categories of plant taxa in systems of ethnobotanical classification, one observes that, as with the classification of animals, groupings of intermediate rank appear to be comprised primarily of folk generics that range over species of the same biological family or closely related families. When the familial affiliation of species of some intermediate taxon differ, it can usually be shown that the species nevertheless exhibit similar morphological features that lead them to be grouped as perceptually related. A much smaller residue of categories remains that is clearly formed on the basis of cultural considerations and that relates to the economic significance of the respective species.

The above claims are supported in part by an examination of the 108 generic plant taxa, forming fifty covert intermediate categories, reported for Huambisa

TABLE 4.2

Comparison of Tzeltal (Mexico) and Wayampí (Brazil) Ethnoornithological Classification of Taxa of Intermediate Rank

Intermediate Taxa		Composition of Group
Vultures	T	3 generics, Cathartidae
	W	2 generics, Cathartidae
Birds of prey	T	5 generics, Accipitridae, Falconidae
	W	13 generics, Accipitridae, Falconidae {part}, Pandionidae, Ramphastidae
Guans	T	5 generics, Cracidae, Meleagridae
	W	5 generics, Cracidae, Opisthocomidae
Quails and tinamous	T	2 generics, Tinamidae, Phasianidae
	W	3 generics, Tinamidae
Doves	T	5 generics, Columbidae
	W	3 generics, Columbidae
Owls	T	6 generics, Tytonidae, Strigidae
	W	3 generics, Tytonidae, Strigidae
Nightjars and potoos	T	2 generics, Caprimulgidae {part}
	W	2 generics, Caprimulgidae, Nyctibiidae
Swift-swallows	T	3 generics, Apodidae
	W	Grouped with flycatchers (see below)
Parrots	T	4 generics, Psittacidae
	W	13 generics, Psittacidae
Trogons/motmots	T	2 generics, Trogonidae, Momotidae
	W	3 generics, Trogonidae, Momotidae
Woodpeckers	T	5 generics, Picidae
	W	3 generics, Picidae, Dendrocolaptidae, Furnariidae {part}
Flycatchers	T	3 generics, Tyrannidae
	W	13 generics, Tyrannidae {part}, Hirundinidae, Bucconidae {part}
Wrens	T	2 generics, Troglodytidae
	W	Grouped with antbirds (see below)
Mockingbirds	T	2 generics, Mimidae {part}
	W	Grouped with cuckoos (see below)
Thrushes	T	4 generics, Turdidae {part}, Parulidae {part}
	W	Grouped with barbets (see below)
Wood warblers	T	6 generics, Vireonidae, Coerebidae, Parulidae {part}
	W	Grouped with tanagers (see below)

TABLE 4.2 *(Cont.)*

Intermediate Taxa		*Composition of Group*
Sparrows	T	4 generics, Fringillidae {part}, Ploceidae {part}
	W	5 generics, Fringillidae, Parulidae {part}
Siskin-seedeaters	T	2 generics, Fringillidae {part}
	W	See sparrow
Blackbirds	T	7 generics, Icteridae, Corvidae, Cuculidae {parts}
	W	5 generics, Icteridae, Corvidae
Waterbirds	T	5 generics, birds that frequent wet areas, poorly known in highlands of Chiapas, including members of Anatidae, Podicipedidae, Rallidae, Charadriidae, Scolopacidae, Laridae, and Ardeidae
	W	Three intermediate taxa
		2 generics, Anatidae, Anhimidae, Heliornithidae
		9 generics, Phalacrocoracidae, Cochleariidae, Anhingidae, Ardeidae, Threskiornithidae
		6 generics, Rallidae, Charadriidae, Rynchopidae, Eurypygidae, Aramidae, Scolopacidae

The remaining intermediate taxa reported only among the Wayampí

Toucans	2 generics, Ramphastidae, Falconidae {part}
Jacamars	4 generics, Galbulidae
Contingas and relatives	14 generics, Cotingidae {part}, Turdidae, Rupicolidae, Capitonidae, Thraupidadae
Antbirds (part)	11 generics, Formicariidae, Troglodytidae, Furnariidae
Antbirds (part)	12 generics, Formicariidae, Pipridae {part}, Tyrannidae {part}
Tanagers (part)	13 generics, Thraupidae {part}, Cotingidae {part}, Vireonidae {part}, Parulidae {part}
Puffbirds	3 generics, Bucconidae {part}
Cuckoos	3 generics, Cuculidae {part}, Mimidae, Tyrannidae {part}

Sources: Tzeltal: Hunn 1977; Wayampí: Jensen 1988.

Note: T = Tzeltal intermediate taxon; W = Wayampí intermediate taxon.

ethnobotanical classification (Berlin, in prep.). Table 4.3 presents the full inventory of all such groupings for which relatively complete botanical data are available. A number of documented groupings, most notably among the palms, are not included for lack of final botanical determinations. Although it is likely that the resulting picture will be modified slightly by the addition of these forms, the overall pattern revealed is likely to be strengthened rather than weakened with the inclusion of these new data.

The fifty intermediate categories from Huambisa ethnobotanical classification shown in table 4.3 strongly support the claim that taxa of this rank are biologically well-founded groupings. Three-quarters of the complete inventory encompass folk generic classes whose botanical ranges are either closely related members of the same botanical family (sometimes even of the same genus) or species from different families that nonetheless exhibit general similarities in stem habit or gross morphology. The smaller minority of remaining groupings appear to be formed on the basis of functional, special purpose considerations. Given the broader picture that has emerged of the nature of intermediate taxa for both the plant and the animal kingdoms, it is debatable whether these special purpose groupings should be considered as part of the general system of ethnobotanical classification at all. It is reasonable to suggest that they might better be described as part of a cross-cutting system of classification based on considerations of their economic or cultural significance, for example, trees useful as fuel, medicinal plants, and so forth.

The Internal Structure of Intermediate Taxa

If taxa of generic and specific rank show an internal structure, where a single species or group of closely related species assumes a central and prototypical status around which other contrasting taxa are arranged in terms of their similarity to the prototype, it now appears that intermediate taxa are no different in this respect. Here, too, a perceptually salient generic assumes a central role and becomes the prototype. As with the recognition of prototypical folk species, the primary factor underlying the selection of these prototypical taxa relates directly to greater size and/or prevalence in the local environment.

This principle is most strongly supported by materials in the ethnoornithological literature, but data from other major groups appear to exhibit the same properties. Bulmer was the first, I believe, to describe these facts in reference to his work on Kalam bird classification. In discussing covert groupings of Kalam birds and their relationship to the symbolic associations the Kalam assign to these species, Bulmer notes:

> These 'natural' taxonomic groups and covert categories [intermediate taxa] above the level of the species are important to my argument, as when the Kalam are discussing and defining such groups, they tend to do so by taking the *largest typical species* as the reference point for comparison. . . . The same pattern appears when the Kalam discuss other groups of fauna—mammals, reptiles, frogs, grasshoppers. Thus I feel confident in asserting the following proposition: 'In Kalam animal classification, within any formally recognized taxon or covert category, size, other things being equal, implies salience [i.e., prototypicality]. (Bulmer 1979:62–63)

The identical principle holds true for Wayampí bird classification as described by Jensen. Of the twenty-nine intermediate groupings of birds recognized by the Wayampí of Amapá, Brazil, each grouping exhibits a "chief" (*chefe*) that is considered to be prototypical. Among the various tinamous, the prototype is the great tinamou, *namu* (*Tinamus major*) (for a diagrammatic representation, see again figure 1.12 and Jensen 1988:27). Among the three generic taxa that make up the intermediate taxon of vultures, the great Amazon vulture *uruvu* (*Sarcoramphus papa*) is selected as representative of the category. For the more than twenty species of eagles and hawks, the harpy eagle, *wyrau* (*Harpia harpyja*), stands out as the largest and most spectacular, assuming the status of prototype (cf. Jensen 1988:27–32). Nomenclaturally, among the Wayampí each prototypical form shares a polysemous name with its superordinate intermediate, following linguistic principles identical to those already observed in the naming of prototypical species in polytypic generic taxa, as described in the preceding chapter. Comparable patterns are described by K. I. Taylor in his treatment of Sanuma ethnozoology (K. I. Taylor 1972) and by Posey (1979, 1984) for Kayapó ethnoentomology.

Ancillary Evidence on the Reality of Intermediate Taxa from Oral Literature

The evidence that I have presented thus far on the reality and significance of intermediate taxa in ethnobiological systems of classification has been drawn from the standard kinds of data that ethnobiologists collect as part of general ethnobiological research. I want to close this section by reporting on less common sorts of ethnographic data that can, at times, serve as corroborative evidence to that which can be inferred from these more standard materials. Here I refer to inferences that can be drawn from mythological accounts about plant and animal relationships as part of the oral literature of traditional societies.

A widespread myth that plays a significant part in Jivaroan mythology is that of *Núngkui*, the earth mother (Harner 1972; Berlin 1978b). The myth can be recounted in the following fashion, focusing only on an aspect of the story that bears directly on the nature of intermediate taxa. The version provided below is drawn from the Aguaruna and differs in minor details from versions among other Jivaroan populations.

> In the beginning, the Aguaruna were hungry for they possessed no cultivated plants. The people ate the fruits of the balsa tree and the leaves of other wild plants that they found in the forest. One day, an Aguaruna woman came upon a powerful (female) spirit called Núngkui washing manioc tubers in a stream with her small daughter. The woman approached the two spirits and asked for a small piece of manioc but Núngkui replied, "No, but take the child with you and she will provide you with all the food you need. However, you must not mistreat the child, for if you do, you will be punished."

TABLE 4.3
Covert Intermediate Plant Taxa in Huambisa Ethnobotanical Classification

Group	Generic Taxa	Botanical Determination	Botanical Family
1.	*yaís*	*Unonopsis* sp., *Oxandra* sp., *Guatteria* sp., *Cymbopetalum* sp.	Annonaceae
	chuáchua	*Xylopia cuspita, Duguetia* spp., *Cymbopetalum* sp.	
	achuán	*Anaxagorea dolichocarpa*	

Comment: Species of trees with similar overall aspect in the annona family.

| 2. | **wakám** | *Theobroma subincanum* | Sterculiaceae |
| | **akágnum** | *Theobroma* sp. | |

Comment: Closely related tree species of cacao.

| 3. | **úntuntup** | *Piper tenue, P. macrotrichon, P. amazonicum* | Piperaceae |
| | **ámpar** | *Piper* sp. | |

Comment: Similar species of pipers with edible leaves.

4.	**áti**	*Ficus maxima*	Moraceae
	yántu	*F. trigona*	
	wámpu	*F. insipida*	

Comment: Similar-appearing trees of the same family, only one of which (*F. insipida*) has a reported cultural use as an anthelminthic.

| 5. | **timúna** | *Pterocarpus amazonum* | Leguminosae |
| | **charapáyu** | *Platymiscium stipulare, Lonchocarpus* sp. | |

Comment: Trees of the bean family, similar in overall aspect.

| 6.* | **manchúngnum** | *Tabebuia capitata* | Bignoniaceae |
| | **chikáina** | *Myroxylon balsamum* | Leguminosae |

Comment: Two tree species in distinct families whose trunks are important for their use in house construction.

| 7. | **tséek** | *Miconia splendens, M. longifolia, Blakea rosea* | Melastomataceae |
| | **chinchák** | *Miconia* spp. (many), *Clidemia* spp. | |

Comment: All trees and shrubs of the melastome family, of no cultural value.

8.*	**murúshinim**	*Cordia* spp.	Boraginaceae
	yuwích	*Heisteria acuminata*	Oleaceae
		Ocotea sp., *Endlicheira* spp., *Aniba* spp.	Lauraceae
	chínchi	*Nectandra* spp.	Lauraceae

Comment: Similar tree species of three distinct families; *Cordia* useful as a firewood, remaining species of no known cultural importance.

TABLE 4.3 (*Cont.*)

Group	Generic Taxa	Botanical Determination	Botanical Family
9.	*sungkách*	*Perebea guianensis*	Moraceae
	chími	*P. vanrochmya, Pseudolmedia laevis*	

Comment: Trees of the Moraceae with edible fruits.

10.	*chunchukía*	*Tetragastris panamensis*	Burseraceae
	chípa	*Protium glabrescens, P. finbriatum*	
	chunchuína	*P. trifoliatum, P. ferrugineum, P. decandrum*	

Comment: Tree species of the Burseraceae, all similar in appearance; sap useful as a glaze for pottery, wood as firewood.

| 11. | *yurángmis* | *Physalis lagascae* | Solanaceae |
| | *chuángmis* | *P. ixocupa, P. angulata* | |

Comment: Morphologically similar but culturally unimportant herbaceous solanums.

| 12. | *yantána jángki* | *Acacia polyphylla, A. macbridei* | Leguminosae |
| | *íjach jángki* | *Smilax insignis, S. febrifuga, S. cumanensis* | Lilliaceae |

Comment: Perceptually similar, strongly armed vines.

| 13. | *inák* | *Gustavia macarenensis* | Lecythidaceae |
| | *inakuám* | *G. inakuama* sp. nov. | |

Comment: Two closely related species of *Gustavia*, one cultivated, one wild and recently described, with edible fruits.

14.	*ipiák*	*Bixa orellana*	Bixaceae
	ipiáknum	*Vismia* sp.	Guttiferae
	yámpia	*Vismia* sp.	

Comment: Although members of distinct families, *Bixa* and *Vismia* show similar features in superficial gross morphology of their leaves and many-seeded fruits.

| 15. | *tsémpu* | *Virola loretensis, V. elongata, Otoba parvifolia, Iryanthera* spp. | Myristicaceae |
| | *irísh* | *Iryanthera ulei, I. juruensis* | |

Comment: Several species of trees in the Myristicaceae. The species of *Iryanthera* that fall within the range of *irísh* are said to be good firewood, but no cultural importance is attributed to those recognized as *tsémpu*.

| 16.* | *wáyu* | *Allophyllus punctatus* | Sapindaceae |
| | *jimajmánim* | *Trichilia* sp. | Meliaceae |

Comment: Two tree species of distinct families important as firewood.

| 17. | *yáas* | *Neoxythea elegans* | Sapotaceae |
| | *kaimítu* | *Pouteria caimito* | |

Comment: Perceptually similar trees in the Sapotaceae with edible fruits.

TABLE 4.3 (*Cont.*)

Group	Generic Taxa	Botanical Determination	Botanical Family
18.*	*tsápa*	*Crescentia cujete*	Bignoniaceae
	kansúnit	*Posadaea sphaerocarpa*	Cucurbitaceae

Comment: Two distinctive plant species, one a tree, the other a vine, that produce fruits whose rinds are employed as drinking vessels.

| 19.* | *kawaíkum* | *Hasseltia floribunda* | Flacourtiaceae |
| | *papárnum* | *Tapirira guianensis, Spondias* sp. | Anacardiaceae |

Comment: Tree species; *Tapirira* said to be a useful firewood.

| 20. | *sugkách* | *Perebea guianensis* | Moraceae |
| | *kawít* | *Perebea* sp. | |

Comment: Closely related trees in the Moraceae, useful as a firewood.

| 21. | *múnchi* | *Passiflora* spp. | Passifloraceae |
| | *kemúntsu* | *Passiflora candollei* (*Melothria* sp.) | Cucurbitaceae |

Comment: Similar passifloras with edible fruits; *Melothria* is superficially similar.

| 22. | *kúpat* | *Socratea exorrhiza* | Palmae |
| | *kuúntas* | *Catoblustus drundei* | |

Comment: Similar palms whose trunks are useful in house construction.

| 23. | *surík* | *Mendoncia glabra* | Acanthaceae |
| | *mákish* | *Mendoncia spruceii, M. pedunculata, M. smithii* | |

Comment: Closely related vines, seeds are used in necklaces.

| 24. | *kúwai* | ? | Meliaceae |
| | *mancharék* | *Guarea pterorhachis* | |

Comment: Two trees in the Meliaceae, one yet to be determined; one useful as firewood, the other with no known importance.

| 25. | *másur* | *Clibadium* sp. | Compositae |
| | *masúrnum* | *Clibadium* sp., *Schistocarpha* sp. | |

Comment: Two or three closely related composites; *Clibadium* is sometimes used as a fish poison.

| 26. | *yantsáu* | *Guarea guidonia* | Meliaceae |
| | *míchar* | *G. macrophylla* | |

Comment: Two treelike species of *Guarea*, neither of which is said to have cultural utility.

| 27. | *yuánts* | *Olyra latifolia* | Gramineae |
| | *nángkuchip* | *Lasiacis ligulata* | |

Comment: Conspicuous grasses with no cultural importance.

TABLE 4.3 (*Cont.*)

Group	Generic Taxa	Botanical Determination	Botanical Family
28.	*súwa*	*Genipa americana*	Rubiaceae
	siwánim	*G. spruceana, Randia* sp., *Alibertia edulis, Borojoa* sp.	
	namukáinim	*Tocoyena willianosii, A. stenentha*	

Comment: Closely related members of the Rubiaceae. *Genipa americana* is an important facial dye, but the related species are not used by the Huambisa.

29.	*náum*	*Couma macrocarpa*	Apocynaceae
	táuch	*Lacmellea* spp., *Lacmellea* sp. nov.	
	yumí	*Brosimum utile*	Moraceae
	shiríng	*Hevea* sp., *Aparisthmium cordatum*	Euphorbiaceae

Comment: All three families represented in this covert intermediate taxon are remarkable for their whitish latexlike sap.

30.	*shuwát*	*Eschweilera gigantea*	Lecythidaceae
	pinúsh	*E. coriacea*	

Comment: Two similar trees of the same genus; no cultural use reported.

31.	*waté*	*Macrolobium* sp.	Leguminosae
	samíknum	*Pithecellobium basijugum, Calliandra decrescens*	

Comment: Trees of the bean family; no reported use.

32.	*tapákea*	*Guarea purusana, G. macrophylla, G. kunthiana, G. grandifolia*	Meliaceae
	sanchínakash	*G. pubescens, G. corrugata*	

Comment: Several related species of *Guarea*, those within the range of **sanchínakash** producing seeds used in necklace production.

33.	*tsáke*	*Cecropia ficifolia*	Moraceae
	yanát	*Cecropia* sp.	
	<u>*suu*</u>	*Cecropia* sp.	

Comment: Several distinctive species of *Cecropia*. The bark of *C. ficifolia* is sometimes used to tie native dogs to beds at night. All species are inhabited by stinging ants.

34.	*turúji*	*Geonoma laxiflora*	Palmae
	yungkúp	*G. trailii, G. pycnostachys*	
	súpap	*G. camana, Bactris amoena*	

Comment: Several species of palms, primarily of the genus *Geonoma*. Sometimes used as house thatch.

35.	*yapáu*	*Verbena litoralis*	Verbenaceae
	shámpijuk	*Verbena* sp.	

Comment: *V. litoralis* is used medicinally for headaches.

TABLE 4.3 (*Cont.*)

Group	Generic Taxa	Botanical Determination	Botanical Family
36.*	**tsái**	*Sapium martii, S. marmieri*	Euphorbiaceae
	shapítna	*Himatanthus* sp.	Apocynaceae

Comment: Trees with milky latex, useful as glaze for blowguns.

37.	**wampúsh**	?	Bombacaceae
	ménte	*Chorisa* sp.?	

Comment: Two similar trees in the bombax family, both with kapok-enveloped seeds.

38.*	**shingkát**	*Bauhinia tarapotensis*	Leguminosae
	shingkátnum	*Neosprucea grandiflora*	Flacourteaceae

Comment: Trees with no known cultural importance; basis of grouping unknown.

39.	**tungkápna**	*Coussapoa* sp.	Moraceae
	shuíya	*Pourouma tomentosa,*	
		P. mollis	

Comment: Similar genera of trees in the Moraceae with edible fruits.

40.*	**temáshnum**	*Mayna odorata*	Flacourteaceae
	sawáu	*Tetrameranthus* sp.	Annonaceae

Comment: Trees with no known cultural importance; basis of grouping unknown.

41.*	**yungkumái**	*Anthodiscus peruanus*	Caryophyllaceae
	tampúch	*Senna silvestris, Cassia* sp.	Leguminosae

Comment: Several species of trees; basis of grouping unknown.

42.*	**tsángki**	*Xylosma tessmannii*	Flacourteaceae
	waijá	*Celtis iguanaea*	Ulmaceae
	tsáchik	*Randia* spp.	Rubiaceae
		Strychnos tarapotensis	Laganaceae

Comment: Heterogeneous grouping of trees and vines from several families that are thought to have medicinal qualities in the treatment of stomach pains.

43.	**tsápatar**	*Fevillea cordifolia, F. pedati-folia*	Cucurbitaceae
	yápam	*Cayaponia* spp.	

Comment: Similar wild cucurbits.

44.	**wayáp**	*Psidium guajava*	Myrtaceae
	wapúk	*P. acutangulum*	

Comment: Closely related species of guava, one cultivated.

45.	**yúgkua**	*Rollina* sp.	Annonaceae
	yugkuánim	*Rollina* sp., *Fusaea peru-viana, Annona duckei, A. ambotay*	

Comment: Related genera of trees in the annona family.

46.*	**kapirúna**	*Calycophyllum* sp.	Rubiaceae
	yumpíng	*Picramnia* sp.	Simaroubaceae

TABLE 4.3 (*Cont.*)

Group	Generic Taxa	Botanical Determination	Botanical Family
		Talisia peruviana	Sapindaceae
		Trichilia sp.	Meliaceae
		Drypetes amazonica	Euphorbiaceae
		Tapura peruviana	Dichapetalaceae
		Terminalia sp.	Combretaceae

Comment: Highly heterogeneous grouping of tree species valued as firewood.

47.	**kúnapik**	*Bonafousia sanajo*	Apocynaceae
	yawã kúnapik	*Tabernaemontana undulata,*	
		T. markgrafiana	

Comment: Similar trees in the Apocynaceae.

48.	**shushuí inái**	*Serania rubicaulis*	Sapindaceae
	pángki náek	*Paullinia* sp. nov.	
	tangkitíng	*Gouania tomentosa, G. lupu-*	Rhamnaceae
		loides, G. mollis	

Comment: Superficially similiar climbing lianas, all three of which exhibit distinctive watch-spring tendrils.

49. *sámpi* (named intermediate)			Leguminosae
	sámpi	*Inga* spp., especially, *I.*	
		punctata, I. macrocephala, I.	
		selva, I. thibaudiana	
	wámpa	*I. oerstediana, I. stenopoda*	
	wampukásh	*I. ruiziana*	

Comment: Strikingly similar trees of the genus *Inga* characterized by long linear fruits, seeds covered in some species by an edible, sweet, pulpy mesocarp.

50. *nára* (named intermediate)			Urticaceae
	nára	*Urera baccifera*	
	sukú	*U. caracasana*	

Comment: Closely related small trees and shrubs whose stems and leaves are covered with small stinging hairs, sometimes used in the treatment of rheumatism.

Note: I have judged groupings marked with an * as formed primarily on the basis of utilitarian considerations.

And so it came to pass. The Núngkui child provided rich gardens filled with manioc, bananas, plantains, yams, sweet potatoes, and many other plants. [At this point, some twenty-two plants are mentioned in the myth by name.]

One day, the Núngkui child was left in the woman's house accompanied by the woman's son. The young boy wanted the Núngkui child to perform magical, dangerous tricks, such as making devils and jaguars appear, in spite of the Núngkui child's admonitions that once such creatures were brought into existence they could not be made to go away.

When he insisted, the demons were made to manifest themselves, and the young boy became frightened. He asked again and again that the Núngkui child make the demons go away, with no success. Finally, in frustration, the boy threw ashes into the eyes of the Núngkui child, who at once began to cry. At the same moment, all of the cultivated plants that had been given the Aguaruna were transformed into nondomesticated species. [Each of these nondomesticated species is mentioned by name.]

The Núngkui child took refuge in a node of bamboo. When the Aguaruna woman returned, she opened the node of bamboo and asked that the Núngkui child bring back the cultivated plants. This time, the cultivated plants returned, but deformed and smaller in size. In this form, they remained forever.

The myth is of particular relevance to the subject at hand in that the pairs of cultivated and nondomesticated plants mentioned in the story show precisely the kinds of systematic botanical relationships that are found as the basis of the generally covert taxa of intermediate rank discussed earlier. The dyads of cultivated and wild plants species mentioned in the myth are listed in table 4.4. The pairs of plants shown represent the most important cultigens for the Aguaruna, including one species that is semicultivated as a fish poison (*Lonchocarpus* sp.). The pattern of similarity observed between each pair is unmistakable—82 percent represent pairs of species linked as members of the same botanical family. In six pairs, the relationship is as close as that of the same genus.

In all of these cases, there is a striking parallelism in the overall morphological aspect of the species involved, for example, the herbaceous habit of *Arachis hypogea* and the culturally useless *Desmodium silvestre*, the various bananalike species of the genus *Heliconia* as they are compared with the cultivated bananas. When distinct families are involved, as with the yam bean *Pachyrhizus tuberosus* (Leguminosae) and its wild counterpart *Stigmaphyllon kuhlmanii* (Malpighiaceae), there are notable similarities in general appearance—in this case, two similar vines with tuberous roots.

One need not make mighty interpretive leaps to observe that the conceptual affinities pointed out explicitly in the story of Núngkui are based on the empirical recognition of the scientifically valid botanical relationships that hold for most of the pairs, or for the obvious perceptual factors of similar morphology that unites the remainder. In a number of instances, the very linguistic structure of the generic names attests to these conceptual relationships (i.e., *kéngke-kengkéngke, ínchin-inchínchi, dúse-dusenés, yuwí-yusímas, basú-basúmsu, papái-papaínim, sháwi-shawín*). Furthermore, it is reasonable to suppose that these are the same kinds of perceptual facts that lead to the formation of taxa of intermediate rank. The myth of Núngkui provides cosmological validation of the perceptual facts of nature, reinforcing the Aguarunas' instinctive recognition of nature's basic plan.

4.3 Taxa of Life-Form Rank

Taxa of life-form rank have received more attention in the recent literature on ethnobiological classification than perhaps any other topic in the field (for some of the central articles, see Atran 1985, 1987, 1990; C. Brown 1984a, and his earlier works leading up to that publication, especially 1977, 1979a, 1979b, 1981a, 1981b, 1982a, 1982b; C. Brown and Witkowski 1982; Hunn 1982, 1987; Randall and Hunn 1984; Randall 1976, 1987; Turner 1987; Bulmer 1967, 1974a; Hage and Miller 1976). The major questions that have arisen in this literature range from the character of life-form taxa as natural or artificial categories and the bases of their formation, to their purported universality and evolutionary development, and to the precise types of relationships that they share with taxa of generic and intermediate rank, to mention some of the most central issues.

I will not attempt to review all of these arguments directly but rather first outline what, in my view, are the issues about the nature of life-form taxa that most, if not all, ethnobiologists would likely agree on. From this platform of general consensus, I will then discuss those areas where debate continues to be carried out. In this discussion, I will also provide some new data and offer several additional interpretations and needed reinterpretations on the topic as a result of recent investigations by other scholars in the field.

Life-Form Taxa: Areas of General Agreement

In the elicitation of names for plants and animals in any study of ethnobiological classification, field investigators typically, but not universally, record not only the terms for the most common generic taxa, but also a small number of highly general terms that have come to be referred to as "life-form" names.[2] These large, comprehensive groupings are exemplified by taxa labeled by terms that could be glossed as 'tree', 'vine', and 'herbaceous plant' in ethnobotanical classification and 'bird', 'fish', and 'snake' in ethnozoological classification.

As glosses, terms such as 'tree' or 'bird' are not, of course, to be considered as totally equivalent in meaning to these terms as they are ordinarily used in vernacular English. Nonetheless, that such general terms are attested in most systems of ethnobiological classification would not, I think, be generally denied, in spite of the remarkable commentary that one finds in Randall and Hunn (1984) and Randall (1987).

[2] Dennis Breedlove introduced me to the term "life form" as part of our Tzeltal work. The expression was borrowed directly from botanical systematics, where it first gained widespread acceptance as a result of the work of Christen Raunkiaer in his *The Life Forms of Plants and Statistical Plant Geography* (1934). I am grateful to Peter H. Raven for providing this historical citation.

TABLE 4.4
Cultivated and Noncultivated Plants Found in the Aguaruna Myth of Núngkui

Cultivated Species	Transformed into Noncultivated Form	Similarities
1. 'manioc'		
máma Manihot esculenta	*tsanímtsanim* Manihot sp.	Same genus, Euphorbiaceae
2. 'yam'		
kéngke Dioscorea trifida	*kengkéngkeng* Dioscorea sp.	Same genus, Dioscoreace.
3. 'yantia'		
sángku Xanthosoma spp.	*sungkíp* (various aroids)	Same genus, Araceae
4. 'sweet potato'		
ínchin Ipomoea batatas	*inchínchi* Ipomoea spp.	Same genus, Convolvulaceae
5. 'yam bean' (vines with quite similar roots in the Leguminosae and Malpighiaceae, respectively		
nambáu Pachyrhizus tuberosus	*nambáunum* Stigmaphyllon kuhlmannii	
6. 'peanut'		
dúse Arachis hypogea	*dusenés* Desmodium adscendens	Similar herbaceous legume
7. 'cooking plantain'		
páantam Musa spp.	*winchú* Heliconia spp.	Same family, Musaceae
8. 'eating banana'		
sétash Musa spp.	*tumpéa* Heliconia spp.	Same family, Musaceae
9. 'edible solanum'		
kukúsh Solanum coconillo	*untukáng* S. siparunoides	Same genus, Solanaceae
10. 'edible solanum' (different families, Solanaceae and Caricaceae, respectively, but similar-looking fruits and leaves)		
shiwánkúsh Solanum tromanifollium	*iwánchi shiwankúsh* Carica macrocarpa	
11. 'pineapple'		
pínya Ananas comosus	*kuísh* (all epiphytic bromeliads)	Same family, Bromeliaceae
12. 'anona'		
anúna Rollinia microcarpa	*yúngkua* Rollina sp.	Same family, Annonaceae
13. 'squash'		
yuwí Cucurbita sp.	*yuwísh* (various species of wild cucurbits)	Same family, Cucurbitaceae

TABLE 4.4 (*Cont.*)

Cultivated Species	Transformed into Noncultivated Form	Similarities
'peach palm' **uyái** Bactris (Guilielma) gasipaes	**chuchúk** Syagrus tessmannii	Same family, Palmae
'sugarcane' **pangaát** Saccharum officinarum	**tangkán** Gynerium sagittatum	Canelike grasses in same family, Gramineae
'maize' **sháa** Zea mays	**saák** Setaria vulpiseta, Paspalum virgatum	Similar grasses, Gramineae
'huaca' **basú** Clibadium strigillosum	**basúmsu** C. asperum, C. sylvestre	Similar composites, Compositae
'barbasco' **tímu** Lonchocarpus sp.	**máyu, shimpiyú** ?	Similar legumes used as fish poison, Leguminosae
'achiote' **ipák** Bixa orellana	**yámpia** B. platycarpa	Same genus, Bixacaceae
'achira' **kúmpia** Renealmia alpina	**chíang** R. breviscarpa, R. nicolaioides, R. thyrsoidea	Same genus, Zingiberaceae
'papaya' **papái** Carica papaya	**papaínim** C. microcarpa	Same genus, Caricaceae
'guava' **sháwi** Psidium guajava	**shawín** P. acutangulum	Same genus, Myrtaceae

A large body of evidence supporting the claim that general higher-order groupings of this rank are commonly found in systems of ethnobiological classification has been assembled by C. H. Brown (1984a). While the evolutionary interpretation that Brown has given these data has been the target of much of the controversy in the recent literature on life forms, the compendium of materials that he has amassed constitutes a major contribution to the field.

In addition to the data cited in Brown's monograph, it is worthwhile to set the stage for the discussion that follows by providing here a short inventory of ethnobiologists' own straightforward characterizations of taxa of life-form rank, focusing first on descriptions of ethnobotanical systems of classification and then going on to systems of ethnozoological classification.

PLANTS

Hanunóo (Philippines):

The Hanunóo classify almost all plants as belonging to one of three major groups (designated by what Chao calls 'class names'), distinguished by the apparent habit of stem growth: *kayu* 'wood', *'ilamnun* 'herb', or *wakat* 'vine'. Each of these terms covers a wide semantic range, but their generalized meanings as occur in this triad are quite definable: *kayu*: includes all plants whose stems are typically woody, but not vinelike . . . *'ilamnun*: includes all herbaceous (non-woody), or very small plants, whose stems are not vinelike . . . *wakat*: includes all plants whose basic habit of growth results in twining, vinelike stems. (Conklin 1954:92–93)

Ndumba (New Guinea):

[In Ndumba ethnobotanical classification] taxa of the life-form rank are the most-inclusive, wide-ranging named categories. . . . They include the majority of all other taxa [of lesser rank], they are biologically diverse in content; and they are . . . defined by a small number of biological characters, most of which in folk botany refer to stem habit. . . . There are five [life-form taxa which] include 552 out of 761 taxa of lesser rank. . . . These taxa and glosses of their respective names are: *foringa*—mosses, lichens, and some fungi; *mauna*—herbaceous plants and some ferns; *muso*—grasses, sedges, and rushes; *sana* —vines and lianas (herbaceous or woody); *sa'tari*—trees, shrubs, and tree ferns. (Hays 1983:260)

Agta (Philippines):

All Agta categorize their plant world into three major life form categories . . . *lamon* 'grasses and herbaceous plants', *lanot* 'climbing and trailing plants, or vines', [and] *kayo* 'woody plants and trees'. (Headland 1981:24)

Ka'apor (Brazil):

The Ka'apor subdivide the domain of vascular plants into three major morphological discontinuities, i.e., life forms. These are labeled by words for 'tree' (*myra*) . . . 'herb' (*ka'a*) . . . and 'vine' (*sypo*). Below the ethnobotanical rank of life form are folk generics—names for individual taxa of trees, vines, and herbs, as well as plant taxa which are unaffiliated with any of the life forms (such as manioc and other cultigens). (Baleé and Daly ms. 1987)

Amuzgo (Mexico):

Eight life forms have been identified [in Amuzgo] which include all plants . . . : *tz'on* 'tree', *tz'ö* 'vine', *jndë* 'grass', *tzko jndë* 'herb', *tzko ndoen* 'wide-leafed plant', *ndoa* 'maguey', *tzkwa* 'fern' and *ndy'ein* 'mushroom'. In general terms, the life form 'tree' includes all plants with woody trunks, 'vine' includes all plants with a twining habit, 'grass' includes plants with certain leaf characteristics, 'herb' includes herbaceous plants without woody stems and certain leaf types, 'wide-leafed plants' includes bananas, elephant ear and similar plants, 'maguey' includes agaves and cacti (as well as bromeliads), and 'fern' and 'mushrooms' include ferns and mushrooms. . . . The first four life forms may be considered to be the major life forms, in terms of the number of generics and specifics they include. (Hopkins 1980)

Hill Pandaram (South India):

The plant world . . . comprises three main classes. . . . The first of these, **maram** [in one of its polysemous senses] refers to woody plants, and includes trees and shrubs. Lianas . . . together with climbers and creepers and even the rattan plant . . . are placed under the taxon **valli**. The remainder of the plant kingdom, consisting of epiphytes, ferns and herbaceous plants, is included under the term **chedi** or small plant. All the plants I collected and questioned the Hill Pandaram about were categorized under [one of] these three primary taxa. (Morris 1976:547)

Wayampí (French Guiana):

[In addition to an ecological] categorization of the plant kingdom, there exists a categorization relevant to the morphology of plants. Thus, the Wayãpi distinguish:
-*wyla* 'tree' {"arbre"}
-*ka'a* 'herbaceous plant/shrub' {"herbe, arbuste"}
-*ypo* 'liana' {"liane"}. (Grenand 1980:34–35, translated)

ANIMALS

Hanunóo (Philippines):

[In the Hanunóo classification of animals] seven general categories—*hayup*, *manuk*, *'ulay*, *'isda'*, *biyuku*, *pakinhasun*, *'iyay*—refer, respectively, to the following animal groups: domestic and wild mammals, domestic fowl and wild birds, snakes, fish, land snails, salt water shellfish, insects [also arachnids and most other very small forms of animal life]. (Conklin 1954:92)

Tobelo (Halmahera Island, Moluccas):

The following tallies will summarize data on each of the five subclasses of FAUNAL FORM: *o totaleo* 'bird' [86], *o dodihna* 'snake' [11], *o nawoko* 'fish' [159], *o bianga* 'mollusk' [73], and finally all 'unaffiliated' animals ('other') [91]. (P. Taylor 1990:119)

Ndumba (New Guinea):

Ndumba animal taxonomy . . . includes 4 life form taxa: *fai* ('marsupials and monotremes'), **kaapa'raara** ('reptiles, eels, centipedes, and worms'), **kuri** ('bats and birds'), and *tovendi* ('insects and arachnids'). . . . The 4 taxa that I have assigned to the rank of life form include 283 (88.7%) of the 319 named taxa of lesser rank. (Hays 1983:602)

Seri (Mexico):

The classification of plants and animals was generally similar although there were a few more higher categories for animals. . . . The general term for fish was *zixcám*, which derives from the overall term for animal. . . . The generic word for bird was *ziic*. . . . Various small lizards could collectively be called **haquímet**, although each species also had a distinct name. . . . Non-poisonous snakes . . . were sometimes referred to as *ziix coimaj hant cöquiih* 'thing non-rattlesnake land what-is-on'. . . . *Xica ccam heecot cocoom* 'things with-life-desert what-is-lying on' was a seldom used life-form category. It was said to include animals which are fairly large, with fur, four legged, and stand off the ground. (Felger and Moser 1985:59)

Rofaifo and Etolo (New Guinea):

Rofaifo . . . grouped all vertebrate animals except tadpoles within five or six primary taxa, two of which included most invertebrates as well. . . . Etolo named seven primary taxa that included most, though not all, vertebrates. . . . [These taxa are, respectively] (Dwyer 1984:323):

Etolo	Rofaifo
oheo Larger species of monotreme marsupial and rodent	*hefa* Eel, cassowary, larger species of monotreme, marsupial, and rodent plus pig, dog, and the larger mammalian species introduced by the Europeans
ebele Smaller species of marsupial and rodent	*hunembe* Smaller species of marsupial and rodent
haia All birds except cassowaries	*nema* Bats and all birds except cassowaries
gomaio Lizards with possible exception of semiaquatic agamids	*hoiafa* Lizards, snakes, fish other than eels, molluscs, earthworms, leeches, planaria, centipedes, millipedes, *Peripatus*
nupa All snakes	*hera* Frogs other than those of the genera *Asterophrys, Xenobatrachus*, and *Barygenys*
sai All frogs	
seme All fish	

A number of inferences can be drawn from the descriptions just cited, and many more illustrative cases like them (cf. C. H. Brown 1984a). First, in terms of the developing structure of ethnobiological systems of classification, it is apparent that taxa of life-form rank mark groupings that are biologically diverse in their respective ranges, for example, "all plants whose stems are typically woody, but not vinelike" (Conklin 1954:92); "herbaceous plants and some ferns" (Hays 1983:260); "all snakes" (Dwyer 1984: 323).

Second, such broadly inclusive classes generally occur as the first major groupings within each ethnobiological kingdom, forming a contrastive group of a small number of taxa of plants and animals. In some systems, the set of life-form taxa serves to partition the kingdom rather completely, as do the categories glossed 'tree'–'vine'–'herbaceous plant' among the Hill Pandaram or the Hanunóo. Much more commonly, however, while plant and animal life forms include a large proportion of the lower-order taxa, there remains a considerable residue of unincorporated forms, for example, "For Etolo there were more than 70 primary [first level] taxa . . . that could not be assigned to any labeled [higher order] category" (Dwyer 1984:323). The implications of this partial or incomplete conceptual subdivision of the kingdom by life-form categories will be addressed shortly.

Finally, as is clear from the glosses that have been used by ethnobiologists to characterize the meanings of life-form taxa, and recalling what has already been said on the nature of taxa of intermediate rank, it is obvious that while some groupings generally correspond rather closely to recognized scientific higher-order taxa (e.g., Aguaruna *shíngki* 'palm' or Tobelo *o dodihna* 'snake'), most life form taxa do not reflect biologically natural classes of organisms. Recall, for example, the Ndumba zoological life-form *kaapa'raara* 'reptiles, eels, centipedes, and worms', or the Rofaifo category *nema* 'bats and all birds except cassowaries'.

Likewise, in the plant world, the focus on major differences based on stem habit, probably one of the primary perceptual features leading to the recognition of the most common major life-form taxa found in folk systems of ethnobotanical classification (e.g., 'tree', 'vine', 'herbaceous plant') leads to groupings that often violate natural biological taxa at the family level. As Cronquist put it,

> The thoroughgoing structural differences which mark the higher taxa of vertebrates have no real parallel among the higher taxa of angiosperms. Differences in growth habit, which might perhaps be roughly compared to the evident differences among the higher taxa of vertebrates, occur repeatedly *within* the higher taxa of angiosperms, especially among the dicotyledons. . . . The ancient folk classification of land plants into trees, shrubs, and herbs, cuts squarely across the natural taxonomic arrangement. (Cronquist 1968:22)

In summary, most ethnobiologists would likely agree that major life-form taxa, whether they are called "primary taxa" (Bulmer 1974a; Dwyer 1976), "major classes" (P. Taylor 1987), or "major groups" (Morris 1976), are commonly found in most systems of ethnobiological classification. Secondly, it is empirically demonstrable that such groupings typically have a broad biological basis, incorporating a large majority of the taxa of lesser rank. Third, life-form categories constitute contrastive sets at the first level of the taxonomic hierarchy, representing the first partition of those taxa marking 'plant' and 'animal', respectively. Finally, life-form groupings do not generally represent biologically natural categories in the same sense that taxa of intermediate or generic rank do, in that they often cross-cut biologically natural groupings of organisms.

Life-Form Taxa: Areas of Continuing Debate

There are two primary areas of controversy relating to a detailed understanding of life-form taxa which continue to attract the analytic interest of ethnobiologists. The first concerns the criteria that one might propose for the recognition of life-form taxa as such. How do you know a life-form when you see one? While there might be some general consensus on the obvious cases, as seen in the preceding section, there remain a number of ambiguous taxa that might also merit life-form status, depending on the kinds of evidence one is willing to accept in any particular instance. Much of the debate surrounding this particular facet of life-form taxa is underlain by issues that relate to the notion of ethnobiological rank.

The second area of major contention concerns the psychological motivational bases of life-form taxa. Why are such groupings recognized at all in systems of ethnobiological classification? As will be seen in the discussion that follows, one set of arguments suggests that life-form taxa are primarily perceptually based, placing secondary emphasis on cultural significance as part of the basis of their formation. The second position favors a more functional/utilitarian interpretation. In this latter view, while admitting that perceptual factors play some small part in the recognition of such major groupings, the primary reason for their existence derives from a pragmatic appreciation of their direct economic importance in human life.

Ethnobiological Rank and the Recognition of Life-Form Taxa

Although some writers have claimed that life-form taxa "represent an exhaustive partitioning of the local flora" (Atran 1985:308) and some descriptions, such as the Hill Pandaram classification of plants, seem to support such a view (Morris 1976), the data now available indicate that these claims are not generally true for the large majority of systems of ethnobotanical classification. It is almost certainly not the case that the life-form taxa of systems of ethnozoological classification in any sense exhaustively subdivide the recognized animal kingdom into mutually contrastive groups. As pointed out earlier, however, the validity of such a position depends entirely on what kinds of evidence one will accept for the recognition of taxa that merit the designation "life form"; furthermore, to address this issue, we must consider once again the notion of ethnobiological rank.

One of the major contributions of Kay's explication of folk taxonomic structure was the clear definition of formal semantic contrast (Kay 1971). This notion is maintained in his later, more flexible model-theoretic treatment (Kay 1975), where taxa are defined intensionally rather than extensionally.

Of the four types of semantic contrast that Kay defines as a consequence of relations of immediate precedence, one, that of *direct contrast*, is relevant to the present discussion of life-form taxa. Recall that two taxa are in direct contrast if they are immediately preceded by the same taxon. Thus, *scrub jay* and *Steller's jay*, two common birds of the U.S. Pacific Coast, are in direct contrast in that they are both immediately included in a taxon generally called *jay*. Likewise, most speakers of American English would agree that *elm* and *hickory* are in direct contrast in that they are both immediately preceded by the life-form taxon named *tree*. Finally, *tree* and *vine* directly contrast in that they are both included in the taxon labeled by the term *plant*.

The direct contrast seen for each of these pairs led Kay to define for the first time the notion of *contrast set*, a concept, like *taxonomic level*, that had been used quite loosely in the ethnographic semantic literature prior to his formal definition (cf. chapter 1). Formally, a contrast set is comprised of just those taxa that are immediately preceded by the same taxon.

On introspective grounds, the notion of contrast sets makes good intuitive sense. The taxa in the pairs {Steller's jay, scrub jay . . .}, {elm, hickory . . .} and {tree, vine . . .} are psychologically similar to one another in that, loosely speaking, each pair contains taxa that mark the *same kinds of natural kinds*. The categories in each set are not only structurally similar in terms of their taxonomic relationships; they are thought of as psychologically similar in that they represent taxa that people sense as comparable in their biological content.

Focusing specifically on the differences between generic and life-form taxa, Wierzbicka crisply captures the notion of contrast between the same kinds of natural kinds as follows:

> The basic categorization contained in the concept of a folk genus is 'a kind of'; the basic categorization contained in the concept of a life form is: 'a kind of . . . [many different kinds]'. . . . This means that a life form is conceptualized as a supercategory, a category including many different categories, whereas a folk genus is conceptualized simply as a category . . . i.e., 'a kind'. . . . This means that while concepts such as *animal, bird, tree,* or *flower* are thought of as having many different kinds, concepts such as *cat, lion, parrot, swallow* or *spruce* are not. When they give the matter some thought, native speakers of English will no doubt agree that there are different kinds of cats, parrots or spruces, and that there might even be different kinds of lions and swallows. But this differentiation is not essential to their understanding of the concept *lion, swallow, parrot* or *cat*. On the other hand, if someone doesn't know that there are different kinds of . . . birds or flowers then I think he doesn't really understand the full meaning of the words *bird* or *flower*. (Wierzbicka 1985:189, 192, 228–229)

Unfortunately, for the supporters of the formal notion of contrast set, the taxa that almost any ethnobiologist would agree to recognize as life-form groupings (e.g., 'tree', 'vine', 'herbaceous plant', or 'bird', 'snake', 'fish') often formally occur as members of a contrast set including taxa that differ radically in their biological and, I will claim, psychological status in precisely the sense that Wierzbicka describes. This particular situation was first noted explicitly in an infrequently cited paper by Glick, who studied the ethnobotany of the Gimi of Highland New Guinea. Glick remarks that "there are more than twenty [level 1] botanical categories, ranging in size from *da* 'tree' with at least 200 members, through *koi* 'ginger', with four, and on down to several problematical sets containing only two or three members. . . . Do these have the same taxonomic rank, as say, *da* in Gimi thought? My answer is, probably not" (Glick 1964:274). This situation is comparable to that observed among numerous other systems of ethnobotanical classification (Hays 1976; Berlin, Breedlove, and Raven 1974; Brunel 1974; Hunn 1977; Bulmer 1974a; and many others). In Aguaruna ethnobotany, for example, there are at least fifty plant taxa that are immediately included in the covert taxon 'plant'. One, *númi* 'tree', is polytypic and includes more than fifty intermediate taxa and 265 folk generic classes ranging over four hundred botanical species. Others, such as the common river bank cane, *tangkán* (*Gynerium sagittatum*), are monotypic and refer to but a single species. In the current treatment, these latter solitary taxa are not best considered as life forms but represent what I shall refer to as *unaffiliated generics*.

The data from ethnozoological classification are quite comparable. Conklin observed that, while the Hanunóo recognize seven general life-form taxa, "Even when the few general animal group categories are combined, many faunistic forms remain unaccounted for except by specific terminology [i.e., are not included in any of the major life forms]" (1954:92). The descriptions of Cantonese ethnoichthyology (Anderson 1972), Kalam frog classification (Bulmer and Tyler 1968), and Tzeltal animal classification (Hunn 1977) all report similar findings. As Hunn describes the Tzeltal case,

One would like to say that *sotz'* 'bat' (level 1 [and an unaffiliated generic]) *contrasts with* categories such as *hex* 'jay' (level 2) rather than with *mut* ['bird', level 1 and a life-form] which by Kay's definition belongs to the same 'contrast set'. . . . [T]axonomic structures defined solely in terms of the relation of set inclusion cannot adequately account for the notion of contrast, which relates taxa to one another by reference to the degree of differentiation they exhibit, a notion relevant to folk as well as to scientific classification. Taxonomic ranks must be defined to account for this relation. (Hunn 1977:43–44)

While Kay's 1971 formal treatment did not incorporate a notion of rank, that given in 1975 does, but this is of little consequence to the matter at hand. As I have stated earlier (Berlin 1976) assignment of a taxon to a rank, in any system of biological classification, scientific or folk, is never totally determinable by structural considerations alone. This is not so much a problem with otherwise helpful formalisms as it is a reflection of the real world. As Kay rightly advises the ethnobiological fieldworker: "Ranks must be stipulated on the basis of empirical considerations. *They are not in general deducible from knowledge of the relations of immediate precedence''* (Kay 1975:161, emphasis added).

Just what empirical considerations are involved is a matter on which ethnobiologists' views vary considerably. Bulmer, arguing strongly that one consider only taxonomically defined direct contrast relations among first-level taxa, asks for criteria on how to ''distinguish clearly between unaffiliated generics [such as Aguaruna 'river cane', Tzeltal 'bat', and Gimi 'ginger'] and life-forms'' (Bulmer 1974a:23). Hunn, in spite of his awareness of the need to recognize ethnobiological rank in some form, has concluded that since formal considerations are not conclusive, the ''boundaries between adjacent ranks of taxa are arbitrary . . . due to the continuous variation of taxonomic heterogeneity'' (1977:54). Later, Hunn rejected ethnobiological rank altogether, suggesting that ''the notion of taxonomic rank is [nothing but] a purely formal distinction imposed by the analyst'' (Hunn 1982:836). As will be seen, I (along with Wierzbicka 1985) believe that this claim is wrong. However, to appreciate fully the complexity of the argument here, it is necessary to discuss in some detail the properties of unaffiliated generic taxa.

Brent Berlin, from *Folk Classification Bulletin*, 1978.

4.4 The Nature of Unaffiliated Generic Taxa and the Life-Form Debate

Berlin, Breedlove, and Raven recognized explicitly two general classes of unaffiliated generic taxa in their work among the Tzeltal: *unaffiliated* generics and *ambiguously affiliated* generics (Berlin, Breedlove, and Raven 1973:216, 1974:415–513; cf. also Berlin 1976a:387–389). In this Mayan system of folk botanical classification, an unaffiliated generic is a class not thought to be included in any of the four life-form taxa; that is, the Tzeltal do not consider such taxa to be a kind of a *te'* 'tree', *ak'* 'vine', *ak* 'grass', or *wamal* 'herb'. The ambiguously affiliated forms are generic taxa about which informants disagree as to their class assignment to one of the four life-form taxa, or, in some cases, to the group of unaffiliated plants.

Berlin, Breedlove, and Raven found a rather large number of such forms among the Tzeltal—at least ninety-one unaffiliated taxa were described, and some eighteen generics were found to be ambiguously assigned to two (rarely, three) of the life forms, or seen by some as a member of a particular life form and by others as simply unaffiliated.

We suggested that two primary factors best accounted for the classificatory treatment of unaffiliated forms: morphological aberrance, vis-à-vis the most general defining characteristics of the recognized major life forms, cultural significance (e.g., domestication), and, in some cases, a combination of both factors.

An example of morphological aberrancy can be seen in the Tzeltal classification of the ground bromeliad *tanib* (*Gynerium sagittatum*). When questioned about the life-form affiliation of such taxa, for example, "*Binti te tanibe, te' bal, wamal bal, binti*"? 'What is a *tanib*, is it a kind of tree, a kind of herb, just what is it?' our informants would respond, often impatiently, "*Kere . . . ja' nax tanib . . . tanib stukel*" 'Well, brother, [pause] it's just *tanib* [pause] *tanib* by itself!' I often felt that, for our Mayan collaborators, our even asking such questions was something of a mystery.

On the other hand, several folk generics that were sometimes variously classified as members of competing life forms referred to plant species that showed the general stem habits characteristic of two life forms. An example is *balam k'in* (*Polymnia maculata*), ambiguously classified as either a tree or an herb in that it is a semiherbaceous shrub that can attain three meters in height but really does not exhibit truly woody stems. Likewise, some generic taxa, such as *borbox* (*Govenia* spp.), ranging over two common ground orchids, are herbaceous in overall aspect (leading them to be classified by some as an herb), but their non-net veined, basal lanceolate leaves and curious scape set them apart from the typical dicotyledonous plants that make up the majority of the life form *wamal* 'herbaceous plant'.

Many cultivated species and some semicultivated forms are not considered to be members of the four major life-form groupings in Tzeltal ethnobotanical classification. In a number of cases, some cultigens have also developed a strikingly distinctive aspect, for example, *ixim* (*Zea mays*) 'corn', *wale'* (*Saccharum officinarum*) 'sugarcane', certainly not trees, herbs, or vines and, if kinds of grasses, clearly aberrant examples of the life form in their mature states from the folk-botanical point of view. In these cases, it might be argued that they are comparable to the other morphologically aberrant forms mentioned earlier (see Atran 1985:310, and discussion below). Other species, however, would appear to be good examples of one or another life form in all respects except for their being cultivated, for example, the two introduced grains, *kaxlan ixim* (*Triticum aestivum*) 'wheat' and *móro ixim* (*Sorghum vulgare*) 'sorghum', grasses in most respects. Similarly, the two herbaceous solanaceous species, *tumat* (*Physalis philadelphica*) 'husk tomato' and *ichil ok* (*Lycopersicon esculentum*) 'cherry tomato', are good candidates for membership in the *wamal* class but, so it appears, due to their semiprotected status, are seen as unaffiliated. The implications of these groupings for the utilitarian argument on life-form taxa will be discussed shortly.

A situation quite similar to the Tzeltal case has been observed in Aguaruna Jívaro ethnobotanical classification. In addition to the four major life-form groupings of *númi* 'tree', *dáek* 'liana/vine', *dúpa* 'herbaceous plants', and *shíngki* 'palms', the Aguaruna recognize additional taxa that also occur at the first level of the taxonomic structure and which are not incorporated in any of the four larger groupings. Of these, some fifty are clearly unaffiliated, in that informants will fervently deny that they could be considered as a kind of one of the major groupings. The remaining forty-five are variously assigned to one or another of the four groups, or are considered by some informants as also unaffiliated.

As in the Tzeltal materials, clearly unaffiliated taxa are either morphologically aberrant vis-à-vis the perceived dimensions that define the four life-form groups, or are cultivated forms, or else are both cultivated and aberrant in some way. Examples include *santaník* (*Dracontium* sp.), a terrestrial, tuberous aroid that sends up a single broad leaf with a foul smelling flower (Croat 1978:200); *idáuk* (*Ipomoea batatas*), the cultivated sweet potato; and *chíki* (*Maranta ruiziana*), a cultivated maranth similar to arrowroot.

Taxa that are ambiguous in their life-form assignment are exemplified by *baikuánim* (*Acnistus arborescens*), a semiherbaceous, treelike solanaceous shrub; *dáshiship*, most ferns that are variously given unaffiliated status or seen as kinds of the herbaceous life form *dúpa*; or *bakangá* (*Desmonchus longifolius*), a spreading, climbing palm with vinelike habit that is seen by some as a palm and by others as a vine.

The asymmetries of ethnobiological taxonomies, leading to the occurrence of taxa of vastly differing types at the first level of the hierarchic structure, have long perplexed ethnobiologists, and various solutions to the paradox have been proposed. One solution, suggested by Taylor, is to develop a formal set of definitions that will remove what I have treated as unaffiliated generics from the contrast set that includes the major life forms, such as tree, vine, and herb, and put them at the second level of the hierarchy. This is partially accomplished by Taylor's notion of *immediate contrast*, which he defines as follows:

> If T is a set of two or more taxa $\{t_1, t_2, t_3, \ldots t_n\}$, all of which are subclasses of a higher-level taxon t_a; and if no other taxon t_z can be found which is both a subclass of t_a and a superclass of any of the taxa in set T, then that set T of taxa is in immediate contrast. (For purposes of this and the following definition we exclude considering a class as subclass or superclass of itself.)
>
> From this definition it can be seen that, in a symmetric taxonomy, immediately contrasting taxa will be at the same level: but in a non-symmetric taxonomy they might not be. Thus, in both diagrams . . . t_b, t_c, and t_d *immediately contrast*. (P. Taylor 1990:66)

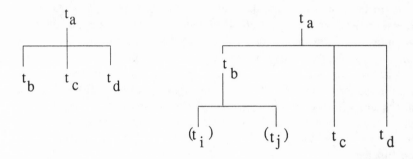

The question, of course, is: How does one determine the levels in a nonsymmetrical hierarchy? Clearly, Taylor would have us believe that the taxa $\{t_b, t_c, t_d\}$ are at different taxonomic levels in his two taxonomic diagrams. Such a conclusion could only be arrived at if one were to assign some special meaning to the different lengths of the lines connecting taxa t_c and t_d on the left side of his diagram with those connecting taxa t_c and t_d on the right side. But as Kay has pointed out, if it is to be employed in any useful analytic way in ethnobiological theory, the taxonomic concept of level cannot be posited from the "visual properties . . . of [our] diagrams" (Kay 1971:876, and chapter 1). Rather, the level of a taxon is determined by counting the number of inclusion relations that connect some taxon, x, with the most inclusive taxon in the hierarchy, which is, by convention, assigned to level 0.

But, then, if what I have been calling unaffiliated generics cannot be easily removed from the contrast set they share with full-blown life-form taxa, perhaps their assignment to generic rank is in error. This is the view of Bulmer (1974a), who simply chooses to treat all level 1 classes as "primary taxa," regardless of the vast differences that separate them in their biological content.

A similar but more carefully considered view that leads to this same conclusion is that of Atran (1985, 1990). In analyzing my own treatment of unaffiliated generic taxa in Aguaruna, Atran reformulates the conceptual status of the monotypic folk genus *ikamánch* (*Wittinia amazonica*), a climbing, vine-like tropical forest cactus. Since this is the only cactus in the region, Atran reasons that "The Aguaruna may thus judge the cactus to be conceptually equivalent to other life forms in view of its distinct morphology relative to the overall habits of the surrounding floral (and faunal) life. In that case, the cactus would not be so much an unaffiliated generic as a monogeneric life form" (Atran 1985:309). Atran then suggests that, since Lamarck and Candolle made cactus a monogeneric family, predicting that "one day cacti will probably be divided into many very distinct genera on the basis of habitus" (Atran 1985:309, quoting Lamarck and Candolle 1815, iv:404), the Aguaruna might do the same: "There is some evidence for, but no direct evidence against, supposing that the Aguaruna consider the cactus peculiar enough . . . to merit life-form status" (ibid.:309).

The only evidence that can be adduced to support the claim that the Aguaruna consider *ikamánch* a life form is that it occurs at the first level of the taxonomic hierarchy. I do not know what other kinds of evidence Atran might consider as direct evidence that the Aguaruna do not treat it as a taxon of life-form rank. Nonetheless, when asked to provide the names of *dúkap áidau* 'all plants' lit. 'all leaves', a question that I eventually found useful for obtaining free-recall inventories of plant names in Aguaruna, *ikamánch* appeared spontaneously in the resulting listings along with the hundreds of other names of generic taxa, those that were included in recognized life-form groupings as well as terms for taxa that were ultimately shown to be unaffiliated. Life-form taxa such as *númi* or *daék* never occurred in these lists (recall the opening passages of chapter 2). I know of no contexts where these unaffiliated forms were talked about as if they were conceptually equivalent to the major life forms such as tree or vine.

In the same paper, in the attempt to solve the dilemma of unaffiliated generics, Atran weakens his ingenious if empirically unfounded proposal of monogeneric life forms by next suggesting that unaffiliated generics be treated as having *both* life-form *and* generic status. He justifies this have-your-cake-and-eat-it-too compromise in the following fashion:

> Monogeneric life forms . . . [are peculiar in] that they appear to have intuited aspects of both generics and life forms. Like generics, their facies are readily perceptible at a glance. Like life forms, they occupy a distinctive role in the economy of nature. . . . If one considers taxonomy to operate as a logically convenient system for accessing the intuitional structure of the living world, then the most obvious way to access a grouping that has the intuitional characteristics of both the life form and the generic would be to index it twice, once as a life form and once as a generic. . . . Double indexing with respect to rank—by divisional [life-form] and relational [generic] contrast—thus marks the truly weird and isolated groupings . . . while perfectly integrating them into our overall picture of living nature. (Atran 1985:309–310)

While Atran's solution to the conceptual treatment of aberrant generics is surely more appealing than either Taylor's or Bulmer's, it appears to be motivated at base by similar formalistic concerns—since such taxa occur in direct contrast with taxa of life-form rank, they *must* be assigned to the same rank as well. On the other hand, since they also look suspiciously like the remaining generics in the system, they should have generic rank at the same time. If this is so, it would seem that taxa labeled by terms such as *ikamánch* must have two polysemous senses, *ikamánch*$_1$, cactus as a life form, and *ikamánch*$_2$, cactus as a generic (cf. Kay 1975:164). The evidence for positing such polysemous senses, not only for the example in question but for the many scores of other solitary generic taxa like it, is decidedly lacking.

Remarkably, Waddy (1988) has come upon—it would seem independently—a solution almost identical to that of Atran. In her important new monograph on Anindilyakwa ethnobiological classification, she notes that some of the stranger sea creatures such as *dingarrkwa* 'sea urchin' (*Diadema setosum*), *yininya* 'bristleworm' (Amphinamidae), and *arrkwara* 'beachworm' are "considered as isolates" (Waddy 1988:78) in the folk system of classification. However, since these taxa are "the only isolated unaffiliated generic taxa, from an Anindilyakwa speaker's perspective" (ibid.:80), they merit special status:

> To my mind, unaffiliated generics such as *yininya* and *dingarrkwa* are in fact monotypic generic taxa in monotypic covert life form taxa. Even though they are not formally labeled at the life form level, they are recognized as distinct groups in contrast to other life form taxa, while at the same time maintaining the generic rank of the named taxa on the basis of apparently equivalent psychological salience. (Waddy 1988:82)

The result of Waddy's reasoning is identical to Atran's in that two distinct intensional senses are required for the monotypic taxa in question. She differs from Atran in retaining the lexical realization of one of these senses at generic rank only, while positing what might be called a covert "position holder" at life-form rank. In the end, however, both solutions are ad hoc and flow from formalistic notions of maintaining taxonomic symmetry where, in fact, there is none.

Waddy makes an additional proposal, however, that has far-reaching implications for the treatment of unaffiliated generics that among themselves form groups of conceptually related taxa. This is dealt with in the following section.

4.5 Covert Groupings of Unaffiliated Generics = Covert Life Forms?

While many unaffiliated generic taxa appear as isolates in ethnobiological systems of classification, a considerable number combine to form groupings of

TABLE 4.5
Examples of Covert Groupings of Unaffiliated Generic Taxa in Tzeltal Ethnobotanical
Classification (after Berlin, Breedlove, and Raven 1974:415–417)

1. 'mosses'

tzon te'	'tree mosses', e.g., *Schlotheimia rugifolia, Racopilum tomentosum*
tzon lumilal	'ground mosses', e.g., *Macrolejeunea lancifolia*
tzon ch'en	'cave mosses', e.g., *Bryum* sp., *Lepidozia* sp.

2. 'agaves and palms' (Agavaceae, Palmae)

chi	*Agave* spp., *Furcraea* sp.
met	*Furcraea guatemalensis, Agave* sp.
met chij	*Agave* sp.
tim	*Yucca elephantipes*
nap	*Acrocomia mexicana*
xan	*Brahea prominens*
ch'ib	*Chamaedorea cataractarum*

3. 'bananas and relatives' (Musaceae, Zingiberaceae, Cannaceae)

lo'bal	*Musa acuminata*
yal chitam jaben	*Hedychium coronarium*
xch'uch'i jaben	*Canna edulis*
jajtal tzek	*Heliconia schiedeana*

4. 'large leafed aroid' (Araceae)

xch'ox	*Philodendron polytomum*
yixim ajaw	*Anthurium* spp.
noromax chi'in	*Xanthosoma violaceum*
pajal matz' chi'in	*X. violaceum*
pijtz chitam	*X. robustum*

5. 'bamboos and bamboolike grasses' (Gramineae)

jalal	*Phragmites australis*
chanib	*Merostachys* sp., *Lasiacis sloanei*
tzu'um	*Lasiacis divaricata*

conceptually higher-order taxa that are reminiscent of the covert taxa of intermediate rank. Berlin, Breedlove, and Raven described ''17 covert groupings
of morphologically similar taxa . . . which include 59 of the 91 unaffiliated
forms'' (Berlin, Breedlove, and Raven 1974:415). The biological nature of
groupings of this sort can be seen from the examples given in table 4.5. Comparable covert groupings of unaffiliated (and, in some cases, ambiguously affiliated) generic taxa are found in the Aguaruna materials, as well. Table 4.6
provides a listing of several typical examples of such taxa. These small groupings of few to several unaffiliated generic taxa fall clearly outside the ranges
of the recognized major life forms. Nonetheless, they form tightly meshed sets
of species that have many perceptual features in common. In the main, the

TABLE 4.6

Examples of Covert Groupings of Unaffiliated Generic Taxa in Aguaruna Ethnobotanical Classification

1. 'strangler figs' (Moraceae, Guttiferae)	
apaíyujang	*Ficus parensis*
yapít	*F. pertusa*
kuásua	*F. trigona*
bijukú	*Helicostylis tomentosa*
kangkúm	(undetermined strangler)
pée	*Clusia* spp., *Clusia* aff. *decussata*
úwe	*Clusia decussata, Havetiopsis flavida*
2. 'canna lily' (Cannaceae)	
túju	*Canna indica*
wayampái	*C. paniculata, C. jaegeriana*
3. 'large-leafed native gingers' (Zingiberaceae)	
chiáng	*Renealmia nicolaiodes, R. thyrsoidea*
kúmpia	*R. alpina*
4. 'anthuriums' (Araceae)	
chinumás	*Anthurium alienatum*
ináimas	*A. cenepanum*
jíncham eep	*A. clavigerum*
jíncham nánchik	*A. eminens*
5. 'philodendrons and relatives' (Araceae)	
mangkamák	*Monstera* spp.
shíng dáek	*Philodendron* spp.
chuju dáek	*Philodendron paxianum*
katípas	*Rhodospatha* sp., *Spathiphyllum* sp.

groups bring together similar species of the same family, often of the same genus. When two or more families are involved, such as the Aguaruna strangler figs, which draw on genera from the Moraceae and the Guttiferae, the stem habit similarities of the species involved make them unmistakably perceptually related. All show hemiepiphytic or epiphytic growth patterns, in that they seek the support of other trees in the early stages of development, some (especially *Ficus*) ultimately becoming free-standing.

Similarly, the Tzeltal grouping of bananas and their relatives (Musaceae, Cannaceae, and Zingiberaceae) brings together perennial large-leafed herbaceous monocots placed by some botanists in the same order (Hutchinson 1959, vol. 2:522). Even the Tzeltal category of palms and agaves is explicable in terms of their botanical relationships since both families of plants are considered to be phylogenetically quite closely related.

It is possible to reconsider Conklin's evaluation of the small proportion of unaffiliated taxa in Hanunóo in light of the foregoing discussion. As Conklin states,

> About three per cent of the Hanunóo plant types are recognized as consituting separate groups, not easily classed as *kayu*, *'ilamnun*, or *wakat* ['tree', 'herbaceous plant', 'liana'], and yet lacking any single-word general designation. The bamboos are an outstanding example. Eleven specific bamboo types [folk genera in the present framework] are named for which no single general term exists. It is commonly stated, however, that they are similar in having hollow centers, hard and similarly-structured exteriors, similar culm sheaths, very small flowers, etc. In reference to several kinds of bamboo, one informant stated . . . 'if they have hollow centers one can call them neither *kayu* nor *wakat*'. In reference to a kind of *Dinochloa* [a genus of bamboo] another said 'not really *kayu* nor *wakat*'. (Conklin 1954:94)

This characterization is a clear description of a covert grouping of closely related unaffiliated folk genera that has considerable cognitive and biological reality. I believe it would not represent an inappropriate interpretation of the facts to treat Hanunóo bamboos in precisely the same fashion as those similar groupings described for Tzeltal and Aguaruna.

How might one best consider these sets of plant taxa, as relates to our discussion of life-form taxa? Are they best treated as comparable to taxa of intermediate rank which bring together closely related kinds of trees, vines, and herbs? Berlin, Breedlove, and Raven are curiously silent on this issue. Waddy, instead, makes a striking proposal. On the basis of intensive, long-term research with two knowledgeable Anindilyakwa informants, she derived the classificatory structure for the animal kingdom seen in figure 4.2. Building to her major point on covert groupings, Waddy states that

> The taxon *yimenda* 'marine turtles' is interesting because of its apparent status as a life form taxon but one which includes only five, or at the most, six generic taxa [in contrast to life-form taxa in other systems that] tend to include a large number of generic taxa. . . . In addition to the labeled taxon . . . 'marine turtles', there are three significant but covert taxa which can be glossed as crustaceans, marine mammals and coelenterates. Scientific categories such as these are very distinctive and yet are limited in species diversity. . . . The existence of generic taxa, of apparently equivalent cognitive status to other generic taxa within the total system, within each of these more inclusive categories suggests that these higher level categories might be considered as life form taxa, whether named or covert. These higher level taxa would be in contrast to other labeled life form taxa. (Waddy 1988:78)

This observation appears to have much merit. I believe the evidence presented in the first part of this chapter has shown that covert groupings of generic taxa are widespread and empirically demonstrable in many systems of ethnobiological classification. These groupings have been treated as intermediate or midlevel taxa inasmuch as they are most prevalent as subdivisions of recog-

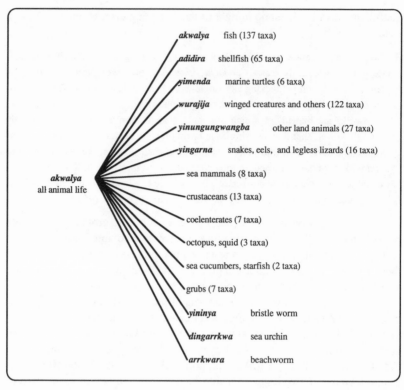

Figure 4.2 Ethnozoological classification of the animal kingdom as seen from an Anindilyakwa (Groote Eylandt, Australia) point of view. Numbers indicate generic taxa. (After Waddy 1988:76)

nized, and linguistically labeled, broad-ranging taxa that most ethnobiologists would treat as life forms.

On the other hand, my work and that of other researchers has failed to deal directly with comparably well-established groupings of generic taxa that fall outside the intensional scope of the well-established life-form groupings. Waddy's proposal corrects this inadequacy, leading her to propose the following principle of ethnobiological classification: "Covert groups of labeled generic taxa, which are not included in a labeled life form taxon but which nevertheless form a highly distinctive category, should best be considered as covert life form taxa rather than each generic taxon being regarded as an unaffiliated generic" (1988:88). Waddy's principle maintains the intuitive validity of Wierzbicka's insight on one of the distinctive differences between generics and life-form taxa, namely, the generic as "a kind of," versus the life form as "a kind including many different kinds" (Wierzbicka 1985:192). Although the generic categories that comprise such covert life-form taxa are generally fewer than those included in the standard named taxa of this rank, their distinctiveness compensates for their small numbers.

Furthermore, the intuitively satisfying notion of direct contrast between taxa that represent kinds of similar kinds is also maintained by Waddy's proposal. Fish (named) and crustaceans (covert) represent highly distinctive first-order groupings of organisms that play what Atran would call "similar roles in the economy of nature" (Atran 1985:87). Likewise, the covert groupings of Aguaruna taxa strangler figs and Tzeltal large-leafed monocots are similarly distinctive and contrastive with the recognized, more inclusive labeled life-form taxa. Finally, in none of these cases is the assignment of generic rank problematical nor does one need to posit unfounded and probably indemonstrable polysemous intensional senses by proposing different ranks for taxa that are extensionally identical in their ranges. The resulting picture, of course, is considerably more complex, but as Harnad has stated in this regard, "God never promised a parsimonious universe" (Harnad 1987:542).

4.6 THE BASES OF LIFE-FORM TAXA: UTILITARIAN VS. PERCEPTUAL MOTIVATIONS

One of the most controversial areas of debate surrounding life-form taxa concerns the psychological bases of their recognition in ethnobiological systems of classification. It has already been shown that the major life-form groupings glossed by expressions such as 'tree' and 'vine' or 'bird' and 'snake' do not always correspond in their intensional meaning to biologically natural groupings of organisms. The pervasive distinguishing feature of stem habit that typically contrasts the life forms 'tree', 'vine', and 'herb' cross-cuts many phylogenetically valid natural taxa. Likewise, many obvious life-form taxa in ethnozoological classification bring together organisms that do not correspond to evolutionarily sound higher-order taxa, for example, the Samal category *manuk-manuk*, which is said to include all birds, bats, and most flying insects (Randall 1976; Randall and Hunn 1984).

This incontestable observation has led a number of ethnobiologists, most notably Randall and Hunn (1984), and Hunn (1982) to make two remarkable claims. The first is that since most life-form taxa are not phylogenetically natural groupings, such classes must be "biologically arbitrary," "residual," and "artificial" in their overall composition (see Hunn 1982:837–838). As Hunn starkly puts it: "There is no perceptual . . . discontinuity motivating the recognition of 'tree' " (ibid.:837).

The second claim relates to the underlying factors motivating the recognition of life forms as part of folk biological systems of classification in the first place. Again, referring to the life form 'tree' (but, as we will see, for all life-form taxa in general), Hunn rhetorically asks: "How then are we to explain the near universal labeling of a concept [glossed 'tree']? . . . Perhaps the answer lies in the universal *practical value* of 'trees' rather than in the *perceptual salience* of 'tree' '' (ibid.:837, emphasis added). I will first examine the claim that life-form taxa lack perceptual motivation and then turn to the more serious suggestion concerning the utilitarian bases of these major groupings.

The Perceptual Validity of Life-Form Taxa

What is the evidence to support the first claim of the utilitarian argument that life-form taxa lack "perceptual motivation"? Hunn develops an unusual line of argumentation to support this view. First, and most important, since most life-form taxa are not natural taxa in the biological sense, the characters that usually define them vary continuously—'' 'trees' shade imperceptibly into 'bushes' and 'bushes' into 'herbs' '' (Hunn 1982:837). Unlike generic taxa that are often separated by natural gaps as observed in the covariation of large numbers of characters, life-form groupings are much more variable: ''The more encompassing the biological taxon—as in the case of life forms—the less likely the taxon will be bounded by such a [natural] gap'' (ibid.).

Second, in Hunn's formulation, life-form taxa are examples of *monothetic* concepts, erected on the basis of a few features, while generic taxa are *polythetic*, formed on the basis of many cooccurring different characters: ''But more essential, the monothetic [life-form] concept is *imposed* on reality by logical fiat, the polythetic concept is *recognized* by virtue of a family resemblance shared by instances of the concept'' (Hunn 1984:836). Hunn's argument as it relates to the perceptual reality of life-form taxa appears deficient logically and, most crucially, empirically. First, the perceptual significance of a life form is in no way related to the number of features that might be found to define it, nor to the observation that such features might be imposed by logical fiat. Consider, for example, the possible definition of Etolo *haia*, a life form (''primary taxon'' in Dwyer's terminology) that includes ''all birds except cassowaries'' (Dywer 1984–85:323) as *birds whose typical mode of locomotion is flight*. Or, making the category less biologically natural still, consider as a definition of the Kalam life-form taxon *yakt*—a category that includes bats and all birds except the cassowary—something like *vertebrates whose typical mode of locomotion is flight*. Are these culturally defined taxa perceptually less striking than, say, the more biologically natural Etolo *nupa* 'snakes' or Kalam *yn* 'skinks'?

More importantly, the suggestion that life-form taxa are poorly defined in that they ''shade imperceptibly'' into one another and as a consequence lack ''perceptual motivation'' is simply not supported by the empirical evidence available from detailed descriptions of ethnobiological classification. Consider the major life-forms 'tree', 'herb', and 'vine', three major superordinate taxa found to be the most common set of ethnobotanical life forms in Brown's worldwide survey, constituting more than a quarter of his inventory of 188 languages. For Hunn (and Randall in their collaborative 1984 article) these groupings are exemplars par excellence of monothetic, biologically arbitrary groupings. Yet none of the ethnobotanical descriptions of such systems provide statements that indicate that the classification of lower-level taxa into one of the recognized life forms is generally problematic because of the latter categories' arbitrary boundaries. On the contrary, most statements sound almost prescriptive in tone, for example:

> The Hanunóo classify almost all plants as belonging to one of three major groups. (Conklin 1954:92)
>
> All [of] the plants I collected [among] the Hill Pandaram . . . were categorized under . . . three primary taxa. (Morris 1976:547)
>
> The three major or most inclusive named Tobelorese groupings of FLORAL FORM are . . . 'tree', . . . 'vine', and . . . 'herbaceous weed'. (P. Taylor 1990:43)
>
> The plant taxonomy of the Easter Subanun . . . has three segregates which together include almost all of the more than 1,400 segregates at the most specific level of contrast within the taxonomy . . . 'woody plants', 'herbaceous plants', [and] . . . 'vines'. (Frake 1962:83)
>
> The three major groups of plants in the Taubuid classificatory system are distinguished by the criterion of the habit of stem growth . . . trees and woody shrubs, . . . [h]erbs, herbaceous shrubs, weeds, grasses, and terrestrial ferns [and] [p]lants whose stems are vinelike. (Pennoyer 1975: 210)

For those systems that do include a sizable number of folk generics that are not easily assigned to a major life form, such as the Tzeltal, Ndumba, or Aguaruna, the ambiguity is not due to the lack of perceptual definition of the life-form groupings themselves but rather to the distinctive characteristics of the particular generic taxa that exclude them from the intensional scope of the higher-order taxa. As we have seen, this may be due to morphological aberrancy, measured against the major defining characters of the recognized life-form groupings, or to features relating to the cultural importance of the particular plant species involved.

In sum, while the biological discontinuities marked by most life-form taxa do not designate biologically natural taxa in the sense that most generic and intermediate groupings do, their perceptual salience is no less real. That they are often defined by a small number of characters does in no way impinge on their perceptual recognition. Finally, in spite of their wide-ranging intensional scope, the boundaries of life-form taxa are not arbitrary nor do they intergrade in an imperceptible fashion.

On the Utilitarian Bases of Life-Form Taxa

While the utilitarian position finds part of its justification in the observation that most life-form taxa represent not-so-natural higher-order groupings, the

most crucial aspect of the argument relates to the proposed pragmatic significance of these groupings. This view, in turn, is directly motivated by the
emerging critique in ethnobiological theory that research to the present has
discredited the practical implications of ethnobiological knowledge (cf. Randall 1987; Hunn 1982; Morris 1983). In Hunn's view, "the fact that cultural
knowledge of the natural world might also be of use practically has been
treated as beside the point, almost as an embarrassment. . . . We have unduly
stressed the disinterested intellectualism of our informants. Pragmatism is no
sin" (Hunn 1982:831). An analysis of the implications of this neo-Malinowskian position as concerns the naming of generic taxa in folk systems of ethnobiological classification has been presented in chapter 3. What is the form
that the utilitarian view takes in relation to life-form taxa?[3]

First, it is argued that in many languages the terms that label life-form categories are often polysemous with concepts that have explicit functional value
for some particular society. Thus an important comparative survey by Brown
and his colleagues (Witkowski, Brown, and Chase 1981) demonstrates that
the term for 'tree' often has two polysemous senses, one meaning roughly
'large erect woody stemmed plant with nontwining habit' and the other meaning 'wood, timber'. Hunn interprets this polysemy in such a way as to claim
that "it is . . . likely that an aspect of the meaning of 'tree' in many languages
is the organism's practical value as a source of burnable wood" (Hunn
1982:837). This suggestion is then given questionable empirical support when
he notes that "Samal 'tree' (kayu) is more accurately glossed 'burnables' [cit-
ing Randall 1976]" (ibid.:837). Comparative linguistic and ethnobotanical research in many other Philippine languages indicates that such a gloss as the
primary meaning of kayu is highly unlikely (see the sources cited for the meaning of kayu 'tree', and its variants, for Hanunóo, Dumagat, Cagayan, Ibataan,
Iloko, Ilongot, Itawis, Manobo Blit, Sambal, Taubuid, Subanun, Pagan Gad-
day, and Tasaday given in C. H. Brown 1984a).

In a similar vein, Hunn states that the life-form 'vine', which in some languages has a second polysemous sense meaning 'binding material, lashing',
"may more faithfully reflect the utility of vinelike plants for bindings than the
perception of any purely morphological discontinuity" (ibid.:837). In its most
bold outlines, this line of argument makes the recognition of the functional
attributes of plants and animals an a priori condition to their recognition as
perceptual discontinuities. A more likely explanation would see the direction-
ality as just the other way around. Trees and vines are first of all known by
their immediate phenomenological properties (Berlin 1973; Lévi-Strauss

---

[3] Recent and as yet unpublished work by Alejandro de Avila among the Mixtec of Oaxaca,
Mexico, suggests a similar utilitarian motivation for the life forms found in this Otomanguean
language. If de Avila's materials are borne out by further studies, the Otomanguean languages
will be shown to differ in a major respect from other Mesoamerican systems of ethnobotanical
classification, as well as most other well-described systems from other parts of the world.

1966; Atran 1985:307) to which secondary functional attributes are attached as part of the ethnobotanical socialization process of learning their uses, a point that Stross has carefully documented in his study of the acquisition of ethnobotanical knowledge by Tzeltal children (Stross 1973). As Atran concisely puts it: "Certainly children don't *learn* 'wood-use' when they learn *'tree'* " (1987:150–151).

Randall and Hunn, in their concern to correct "the marked bias against [the acceptance of] evidence for the intrusion of practical inference into folk-biological thought" (Randall 1987:146), move to abandon the distinction between perceptually based and functionally constructed higher-order groupings, leading to the remarkable neo-functionalist conclusion that in ethnobiological classification " 'Vegetables' and 'farm animals' may yet turn out to be more psychologically salient and evolutionarily important than 'bushes' and 'snakes' " (Randall and Hunn 1984:346). This position is seen clearly in their summary description of Sahaptin higher-order plant classes. They list five such groupings: *pátat* 'tree', *c'ic'k* 'grass', *latít* 'flower', *xnit* 'edible root', and *tmaanít* 'edible fruit'. They note that the latter two taxa are "highly salient categories for Sahaptin speakers. These are functionally defined, however, and thus are not what have been considered 'taxonomic categories' in standard ethnobiology" (Randall and Hunn 1984:340; cf. Turner 1987, who also recognizes a taxon 'edible berries/fruits' as part of Thompson and Lillooet Salish botanical classification).

Randall and Hunn are only partially correct in this latter assertion. It may well be the case that 'edible root' and 'edible fruit' are taxonomic categories, but if they are, they form part of the Sahaptin classification of 'edible things', not part of the general-purpose classification of plants (cf. also Wierzbicka 1984, 1985).

This point is dealt with in detail by Waddy (1988) in her discussion and reanalysis of Fowler and Leland's early treatment of Northern Paiute (U.S. Great Basin) ethnobiology (see Fowler and Leland 1967). It is clear from Fowler and Leland's description that at least three different organizing principles are represented as a single system, two of which are functionally based. As Waddy states,

> [Fowler and Leland's analysis] represent[s] three different systems of classification, viz. (i) the classification of edible plants . . . (ii) the classification of useful plants which is logically based on the various uses to which the plants are put, and (iii) the classification of plants which are not used, which appears to be linked to what I would term biological classification. The more commonly used systems may be those based on utilitarian features *but that does not mean that the various systems must be interpreted as one*. (Waddy 1988:6, emphasis added)

That several alternative systems of classification make up the total system of ethnobiological knowledge of any particular society has never been a theoretical point of contention, in spite of efforts by some critics to raise the topic as a strawman issue (especially Sillitoe 1983; Hunn 1982; Randall 1987). One may note, as typical examples of such alternative systems, Waddy's (1988:97–107) treatment of Anindilyakwa food classification or Berlin, Breedlove, and Raven's (1974:112–113) description of the categories of edible things among the Tzeltal. This latter system of classification can be seen in figure 4.3.

As Randall and Hunn have done for the Sahaptin food classes 'edible fruits' and 'edible roots', one could claim that the Tzeltal system is highly salient as well. This is really not the issue. The point is that two systems of classification are present here—the classification of food, which cuts squarely across a second morphologically based general purpose classification of plants and animals. Surely, in contexts where the classification of food is important, as in weekly markets, the former may take precedence in normal conversation. However, it does not form part of the broader, general-purpose ethnozoological and ethnobotanical systems of classification that organize the plant and animal worlds in terms of overall perceptual features of similarity.

One of the most curious and contradictory aspects of Randall and Hunn's functionalist argument is their analysis of the role that unaffiliated generic taxa play in supporting their utilitarian interpretation of the bases of life-form taxa. They select Berlin, Breedlove, and Raven's 1974 description of Tzeltal eth-

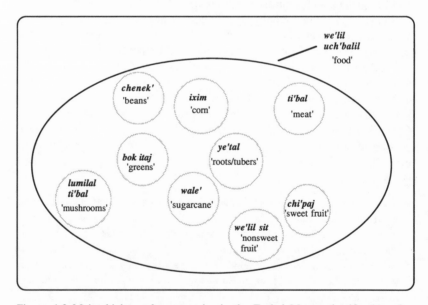

Figure 4.3 Major higher-order categories in the Tzeltal Mayan classification of 'food'. (After Berlin, Breedlove, and Raven 1974:112–113, and Berlin, personal data files)

nobotanical classification to demonstrate—quite contrary to their earlier line of argumentation—that three of the four Tzeltal life-form taxa are recognized not because of their practical significance but rather because of their lack of cultural importance: "Life forms are often residual with respect to practical significance" (Hunn 1982:838). They begin this line of argumentation as follows:

> It is ironic that the very case study that inspired Berlin, Breedlove, and Raven's . . . initial statement on the nature and role of life-form taxa in ethnobiological classification systems should, on closer inspection, illustrate a serious defect in that formulation. . . . [W]e find a clear . . . utilitarian factor in the denotative meaning of Tzeltal botanical life-forms. If terms that incorporate notions of utility in their definitions are excluded from the life-form inventory . . . Tzeltal would have but a single botanical life-form rather than . . . four. (Randall and Hunn 1984:344)

How do Randall and Hunn arrive at the conclusion that Tzeltal life forms are defined by "notions of utility"? They do not come to this view by reading the definitions proposed by Berlin, Breedlove, and Raven, who suggest the following glosses for the four major suprageneric taxa (1974:30):

te' 'plants exhibiting erect to ascending woody stem habit and arborescent stems, generally more than 2 m tall at maturity'

ak' 'plants exhibiting twining stem habit and lianous stems'

ak 'plants exhibiting grass-like leaves and herbaceous stems'

wamal 'plants exhibiting net-veined leaves and herbaceous to infrutescent stems generally less than 2 m tall at maturity'

For Randall and Hunn, these glosses are inaccurate, as can be inferred from the exclusion of some ninety-seven unaffiliated generic taxa from membership in one of these four life forms. This fact leads them to draw the following extraordinary conclusion:

> Taxa are left unaffiliated by the Tzeltal on the basis of morphological aberrance and/or *cultural significance.* . . . *Cultural utility* is thus an important Tzeltal criterion for excluding a plant from life-form membership, and examples cited by Berlin, Breedlove, and Raven make it clear that at least three of the four Tenejapa Tzeltal botanical life-forms (*wamal, 'ak'*, and *ak*) are defined by uselessness [*sic*]. (Randall and Hunn 1984:344)

C. H. Brown (1984c) has provided a concise and lucid rebuttal to Randall and Hunn's logically inappropriate conclusions and empirically inaccurate assertions as regards the Tzeltal data. The important point to summarize here is that while some highly significant cultivated plant species such as corn and squash may be *excluded* from membership in one of the life-form taxa, this in no way implies that all those generic taxa which are *included* in recognized life forms are culturally insignificant. In an earlier publication, Hunn acknowledges this very fact. Chiding Berlin for not being sufficiently concerned with Tzeltal ethnobotanical pragmatics, he states:

A careful examination of Berlin's own data discloses some explicit or likely practical relevance for nearly all of the Tzeltal folk botanical categories he has labeled 'culturally insignificant'. . . . Some are poisonous, others invasive weeds, other[s] inedible 'twins' closely resembling edible forms, others useful 'just' as firewood, and so forth. (Hunn 1982:831)

In spite of Hunn's and Randall's faulty analysis on the nature of life-form taxa, a significant question raised by their work remains unanswered: Why are plant species of high cultural importance, predominantly cultivated and protected forms, the ones commonly excluded from life-form membership? This particular feature of ethnobotanical classification has been observed not only among the Tzeltal, but also among the Ndumba (Hays 1974), the highland Quechua (Brunel 1974), the Aguaruna and Huambisa (Berlin 1976a, personal data files), and the Taubuid (Pennoyer 1975). As already observed, it is not difficult to comprehend why a species such as corn (*Zea mays*), which, while unambiguouly a grass in its early stages of growth, comes to manifest an aberrant habit at maturity, might be removed from the scope of the life-form 'grass'. Atran has speculated that "in this case cultural significance *would* affect taxonomic status, but only to the extent that cultural meddling has actually altered perception of relative distinctiveness in the economy of nature" (1985:310).

Unfortunately, such an argument does not hold in other instances, such as that of the Tzeltal unaffiliated generic *k'ajk'an* (*Chenopodium ambrosiodes* var. *ambrosiodes*) 'epazote', a protected plant among the Tzeltal who widely use it as a potherb as well as vermifuge. On purely perceptual bases, *k'ajk'an* would most certainly be included in the herbaceous life-form category, *wamal*.

Likewise, several perceptually similar herbaceous solanums are afforded quite different conceptual treatment on the basis of the intensity of human management that they receive. Thus, *moen* (*Solanum nodiflorum*), the juicy fruits of which are used as one of the most important treatments for eye infections, and *paypay eal* (*Saracha procumbens*), significant for its edible berries, are both considered to be kinds of *wamal*. On the other hand, two species closely related to *moen* and *paypay eal*, that is, *tumat* (*Physalis philadelphica*) and *ichil ok* (*Lycopersicon esculentum* var. *cerasiforme*), protected and highly prized for their edible fruits, are treated conceptually as unaffiliated generics. In these instances, it is not the case that one pair is useful and the other culturally insignificant, since all four species are relevant parts of Tzeltal economic botany. The distinction here is that two species are protected (not destroyed in the normal cultivation of Tzeltal swiddens) while the other two, perhaps because of their abundance or somewhat less importance, receive no such special care.

At this time, I must say that I have no adequate explanation for these facts and others like them, although the data clearly show that these differential conceptual treatments do not directly or indirectly relate to the utilitarian significance of the life-form categories themselves. A tentative and inadequate [critics read ad hoc] observation builds on a comment made by Conklin:

> Crosscutting [the Hanunóo] three-way classification of plants [i.e, 'trees', 'herbaceous plants', and 'vines'] is the recognized practical categorization of those [plant] types which are artificially propagated as distinct from the wild flora. The domesticated plants are known as *halaman*. Since most of these are well-known cultigens, *there is seldom any call for differentiation except at levels far below—and more minute than—the three-way categorization just outlined.* Maize and rice are still *'ilamnum,* ['herbaceous plant'] but the fact is seldom commented on. By contrast, untreated wild plants are in general less well-known to most Hanunóo and thus the three-way distinction is of very frequent use. (Conklin 1954:94–95, emphasis added)

In discussing the life-form affiliation of cultivated plants that are otherwise nonaberrant when compared to the recognized major life forms, Tzeltal speakers (and perhaps other groups as well), may find it strange, or even unlikely, to think of well-known cultigens or important protected species in terms of their potential perceptually valid life-form affiliations, since they are rarely if ever discussed in this way (or, as Conklin would say, represent a "fact seldom commented on"). In my own fieldwork experience, I have not systematically and consistently queried informants with such questions as, for example, "O.K., so you don't normally consider *x* an herb, but if *y* (some biologically and perceptually closely related form) is an herb, might not *x* be one also?"

In effect, data are not available that would clarify this important puzzle about the life-form membership of such classes. There is no doubt in my mind that species such as the extraordinary ground bromeliads and epiphytic Spanish mosses will continue to resist life-form affiliation in taxa glossed as 'tree', 'herb', and 'vine'. While I am not now so confident about the conceptual treatment of beans, coriander, and wild mustard, I do feel the data necessary to clarify my doubts can, and eventually will, be collected along the lines of the preceding discussion.

What we do know about taxa of life-form rank can be summarized as follows. Life-form taxa form rather large *groupings of perceptually similar* folk genera. Such taxa appear to be based on a *small number of biological characters*. In general, life forms represent folk biological taxa that *cut across recognized scientific natural categories*. In the main, life-form taxa are recognized linguistically. However, new interpretations of a growing body of empirical evidence now suggest that some small number of these taxa is unmarked or covert. In spite of the strong perceptual phenomenological bases of life-form taxa, in numerous systems of ethnobiological classification some, but not all, culturally important folk genera are excluded from particular life-form groupings. No convincing explanation has yet been proposed for this curious fact.

4.7 THE PLANT AND ANIMAL KINGDOMS

Paul Taylor opens a section of his important description of Tobelo ethnobiology with the following passage: "Undoubtedly one of the most vexing problems for an ethnographer attempting to study folk classification of fauna and flora occurs when he discovers that, for speakers of many languages, no 'unique beginner' or highest-level term exists (such as 'animal', 'plant' or 'living thing') which can define the domain of his investigation" (Taylor 1990:42). This observation has been made, in one form or another, by many ethnobiologists for various parts of the world (Berlin, Breedlove, and Raven 1974; Berlin 1976a; Berlin, Boster, and O'Neill 1981; Turner 1974, 1987; Bulmer 1970; Diamond 1966; Hays 1974; Hunn 1977; Brunel 1974; Lefebvre 1972; Walsh 1979; Thompson 1972). Indeed, a general principle of ethnobiological classification seems to be that, in most systems, the taxa marking the domains of 'plants' and 'animals' lack habitual linguistic designation (see chapter 1, as well as Berlin 1972; Berlin, Breedlove, and Raven 1973). This empirical generalization has led to some consternation among ethnobiologists, as Taylor has suggested. How can one justify an analysis of a semantic domain that is not named?

Ethnobiologists have taken one of two positions on this general topic. One, first taken by C. H. Brown (1974), admits nothing other than lexical evidence as supporting the presence of a concept—lack of a linguistic designation is considered to be prima facie evidence for the absence of the concept. A more cognitive, rather than formal, position adopted by myself and numerous other colleagues takes the view that, while a habitual lexical expression may be an unambiguous indicator of the existence of a category, absence of a name does not necessarily imply absence of a category. From this latter point of view, the crucial question is: If one observes that the domains of plants and animals are named in some languages and not in others, as is the case empirically, are there data that would support the cognitive recognition of these categories in those languages where the kingdoms are not named?

The kind of evidence assembled by ethnobiologists in support of the covert cognitive recognition of the plant and animal kingdoms is of three primary sorts. The first is the recognition and documentation of a diversified vocabulary that can be shown to be associated only with organisms of the plant and animal kingdoms, respectively, as defined by Western biological science. The second is indirect linguistic and behavioral evidence of one kind or another indicating that native speakers recognize and systematically treat plants and animals as distinctive groupings. The third kind of evidence is the presence of syntactic or morphological linguistic markers that obligatorily occur with the names of plants and animals (of any rank) and which unambiguously assign them to mutually exclusive semantic classes. I briefly present examples of each of these three types of evidence.

Specialized Vocabulary as Evidence for the Covert Kingdom

In Tzeltal, Huambisa, and Aguaruna, the three groups from which I have collected firsthand field data, there exists an extensive phytographic vocabulary that applies exclusively to organisms that Western biologists would unambiguously recognize as plants in contrast to animals. A partial listing from Aguaruna will provide the flavor of this extensive vocabulary:

dúka 'leaf'
kángkap 'buttress root'
susují 'underground root'
saép 'bark'
jii 'bud'
titíji 'main stem above first branching'
kuijí 'terminal growing tip'
néje 'tuber'
numíji 'erect stem'
sakúti 'inner node'
yangkují 'flower'
hingkayí 'seed'

Turner, in her study of the ethnobotanical systems of several American Indian groups in the U.S. and Canadian Northwest Pacific Coasts, makes a similar observation: "There are numerous morphological terms for different parts of plants that are exclusive to the domain. These include words for 'leaf', 'root', 'branch', 'stem', 'shoot', and 'seed' " (Turner 1987:60). Comparable data could be cited for the Hanunóo (Conklin 1954), the Ndumba (Hays 1974), and many other groups.

Linguistic and Behavioral Evidence

The domains of plants and animals are often distinguished by linguistic circumlocutions or descriptive phrases. Among the Hanunóo, for example, "All living elements which are observed to grow upward but which lack the power of self-locomotion are grouped together as *ti (manga) tumubu'* 'those (elements) which germinate and grow in place' " (Conklin 1954:91).

In Tzeltal, plants 'don't move' (*ma xnijkik*), whereas animals do. The transitive verb *-ti'*, 'eat meat', occurs, with two exceptions, only in reference to organisms that would be classified by biologists as 'animals'. The two exceptions are *ich* 'chili pepper' and *lumilal ti'bal* 'mushrooms' lit. 'flesh of the earth'. The Tzeltal explain this obvious anomaly by reference to a mythological time in the distant past when chili peppers were 'birds'. The folk explanation for the use of the verb 'to eat meat' with mushrooms is that the texture of these fungi is rather like 'meat'. However, it is certainly unexpected that chili peppers and mushrooms should be grouped with snakes, flies, or horses because the former 'don't move' while the latter clearly do.

In sorting tasks with sets of animal and plants, or slips of paper onto which the names of plants and animals have been written, a number of ethnobiologists have demonstrated that informants have no problems separating the specimens or names of plants from those of animals, forming groups that would attest to the cognitive recognition of the two separate domains (cf. Berlin, Breedlove, and Raven 1968; Hays 1974:150–151).

Finally, and as importantly, the day-to-day interaction with native assistants in the normal activities of ethnobiological data collection supports the cognitive recognition of the plant and animal kingdoms. Among the Aguaruna and Huambisa, where informants were directly or indirectly involved in collecting more than twenty thousand botanical specimens, my assistants never selected organisms *other* than plants in actual field-collecting situations (the Aguaruna, as the Tzeltal, do not consider mushrooms and other fungi to fall within the domain). This experience is identical to that of Hays in his work among the Ndumba:

> In the course of discovering over one thousand lexemes which were subsequently validated as plant names, I never encountered uses of these expressions as labels for anything which I would not consider to be plants. . . . By the same token, nothing I considered to be plants, except for 'mushrooms' and 'bracket fungi' was ever labeled with a lexeme which could not be meaningfully inserted in the elicitation frames in the same ways as could plant names. . . . Aside from the exclusion of most fungi . . . the domain of 'plants' in Ndumba corresponds quite closely with what Westerners usually mean by that term. (Hays 1974:148–152)

Again, as with data on specialized vocabulary contrasting plants and animals, the above kinds of indirect linguistic and informal behavioral observations could be multiplied many times by a review of the ethnobiological literature.

Formal Morphosyntactic Evidence

Perhaps the strongest evidence to support the conceptual recognition of the domains of plants and animals when they are not overtly labeled is the obligatory occurrence of morphosyntactic linguistic markers that occur with plant and animal names and which, by implication, assign them to semantic classes. In Tzeltal and many Mayan languages, for example, names of organisms that biologists would classify as "plants" and "animals" obligatorily occur with numeral classifiers that indicate explicitly their respective semantic categories.

In these languages, in order to enumerate a particular object, action, or event, the speaker is obliged to specify the semantic class of the object, action, or event being counted by means of an appropriate numeral classifier. Examples of these particular constructions, contrasting plants with animals, are as follows:

cha'-tejk taj 'two (members of the plant class) pine', i.e., 'two pine trees'
ox-tejk jalal 'three (members of the plant class) bamboo', i.e., 'three bamboos'
juk-tejk chi 'seven (members of the plant class) agave', i.e, 'seven agave plants'
cha'-kojt tz'i' 'two (members of the animal class) dog', i.e., 'two dogs'
ox-kojt xulem 'three (members of the animal class) buzzard', i.e., 'three buzzards'
juk-kojt k'intun 'seven (members of the animal class) lizard', i.e., 'seven lizards'

Human beings receive their own special numeral classifier, *tul*, for example, *bajtik ta lum jo'-tul kerem sok chan-tul ach'ix* 'five boys and four girls went to town'. A comparable system of classification is described by Thompson for Yucatec Maya: "The [plant] domain is an unnamed lexical set . . . *all* and *only* the members of which must take the genus [*sic*] classifier *kúul*. As this is the Yucatec classifier for plants only, then it is appropriate to gloss the domain as 'plants' " (Thompson 1972:2). Similarly, in Thompson and Lillooet Salish, Turner reports suffixes (*-az'*, *-lp*, *-lap*, or *-alp*) which obligatorily occur with most plant names in these languages and "which may be variously translated as 'plant', 'bush' or 'tree'." Examples from Lillooet (Turner 1987:59) include the following:

pún-lap 'Rocky Mountain juniper'
malín-lap 'subalpine fir, grand fir'
c'k-az' 'whitebark pine'
káwkw-az 'big sagebrush'

Turner notes that "[in Lillooet] . . . about 50 percent of all plant names of generic rank include the 'plant' suffix . . . [and in] Thompson, about 20 percent of the plant names incorporate the 'plant' suffix . . . either optionally or mandatorily. It is notable that the names including this suffix pertain to a broad range of plants—mostly trees and shrubs, but also denoting some low herbaceous plants such as pine grass and wild strawberry" (Turner 1987:60).

Brown would see the kind of formal linguistic evidence cited above as not only "gratuitous" (C. H. Brown 1974:326) but also motivated by a culturally prescribed bias. In reference to the obligatory Maya numeral classifiers described by Berlin, he states: "Does this syntactic [actually, *semantic*] feature have anything to do with *taxonomy* . . . ? Berlin et al. are simply being ethnocentric [in their positing the covert recognition of the domain 'plant'], i.e., they make the taxonomic distinction, so hence everyone else must too" (ibid.:

326). Recognizing once again that the data do not speak for themselves, the evidence already available in 1973, when Brown first raised this criticism, as well as the large amount of new data that has been collected over the last fifteen years, indicate that Brown's claims are simply not supported. It would now seem appropriate to return the question to Brown in the following fashion: When Tzeltal speakers enumerate plants or animals, they must make an explicit decision to choose the appropriate classifier, *tejk* or *kojt*. All evidence available indicates that these expressions do not represent a frozen grammatical feature, such as gender in the Romance languages, but that their use is semantically productive. If the obligatory and productive occurrence of *tejk* with species of the plant world and *kojt* with species of the animal world does not indicate an implicit cognitive recognition of the domain called 'plants' and 'animals', then what does it indicate? In scientific dialogue, counterproposals must be supported by evidence. Brown provides none.

Nomenclatural Features of the Kingdoms in Languages in Which These Taxa Are Named

In Berlin (1972:78) it was noted that, in those languages in which the plant and animal kingdoms are given habitual, overt linguistic recognition, one commonly finds the use of an expression that is polysemous, either totally or partially, with one or another of the major life-form terms in the languages in question. This observation has been confirmed by subsequent investigations on numerous other languages. A good example of this principle is seen in Waddy's description of Groote Eylandt ethnobiological classification.

> Unlike most languages, Anindilyakwa has terms which are used as unique beginners both for the plant kingdom, viz. *amarda*, and for the animal kingdom, viz. *akwalya*. Both these terms are used polysemously. Thus, the term *amarda* is also used to refer to one of the two life form taxa, viz. non-woody plants. . . . [Likewise] . . . the term *akwalya* is used at a number of successive levels, viz., i) animal kingdom, ii) animals in the sea, iii) all fish, and iv) bony fish. (Waddy 1988:70)

A comparable situation is found in Seri (Mexico). Felger and Moser report:

> The . . . term for any animal, *ziix ccam* 'thing that is alive', would have been used until one knew what the specific animal was. The general term for fish was *zixcám*, which derives from the . . . term for animal. Another general term for fish was *zixcamáa* 'fish true' [perhaps more appropriately glossed as 'true animal']. *Hehe* . . . was the general term for any plant, regardless of size. This term could also signify wood, log, stick, branch, tree, pole. (Felger and Moser 1985:59–60)

Brunel's and Lefebvre's work on highland Quechua ethnobotanical classification reveals a similar pattern:

Unlike many non-literate cultures, where the unique beginner [kingdom] lacks an habitual linguistic label, in Quechua this taxon is known by many informants by the term *sach'a* 'plant'. However, there is good evidence to suggest that *sach'a* is a recent acquisition inasmuch as *sach'a* is also the name of the life-form 'tree' (Brunel 1974:71). In the Cochabamba taxonomy, the [kingdom] is polysemous with the word for tree, *sach'a*. [In contexts of ambiguity the latter] becomes optionally marked: *sach'a (puru)* 'true *sach'a*. (Lefebvre 1972:50) [cf. the Seri case just cited]

It might be argued that in English folk biology, the terms *animal* and *plant* are also employed in the same polysemous fashion as found in the preceding examples. The latter term is often claimed to mark a life form that indicates 'herbaceous plants' (cf. Spanish *planta*) while the former is said to be used to label the life form 'mammals' (four-legged, warm-blooded creatures with hair or fur). Wierzbicka has recently argued that the terms "plant" and "animal" are more restricted in their meaning, each having but a single sense: "In ordinary English *plant* has only one meaning, and this meaning doesn't extend to all *plants* in the scientific sense of the word. [Likewise] in ordinary English one would not call a snake, a turtle, or even a bat, an *animal* (Wierzbicka 1985:156–157). These observations, I believe, could likely be challenged empirically. However, were they accepted as correct, then ordinary English should be considered a language where the plant and animal kingdoms remain as yet covert, providing yet another instance of the general ethnobiological principle discussed earlier.

A nomenclatural pattern alternative to that of polysemous usage of a single life-form category to mark the kingdom is represented by lexical compounding. This occurs in Tzeltal, where the terms *te'* 'tree' and *ak'* 'vine' are sometimes joined in the coordinate nominal compound *te'ak'* to refer to the domain of plants as a whole. Likewise, Hunn notes an analogous pattern in Tzeltal ethnozoology: "The name *chanbalam* is morphologically complex, *balam* is the name applied to the jaguar (*Felis onca*) while *chan* . . . may mean [alternatively] 'snake' or 'bug' " (Hunn 1977:124).

Comparable coordinate compounding has been attested for Sumerian, where the concept 'plant' was designated by the joining of three lower-order terms translated as 'tree', 'grass', and 'vegetable' (McC. Adams, pers. comm.). This, in turn, is supported by what we know of ancient Latin, where the words for 'tree' and 'herb' were used in conjunction (*arbor et herba*) as an idiom to designate the more general concept of 'plant' (Ullman 1963).

PART TWO

Process

p'ilich

bung

CHAPTER FIVE

Patterned Variation in Ethnobiological Knowledge

EVER SINCE SAPIR (1938),[1] anthropologists have recognized the truism that cultural knowledge is distributed throughout a population in ways related to a number of factors, associated at least with a person's sex and age, social status and role, kinship affiliation, personal experience, and basic intelligence. The manifestation of this knowledge in action is strongly constrained by social context.[2] Ethnobiological knowledge is no different in this regard, and researchers working on ethnobiological classification have made some efforts to deal with the differences observed in the variable ways native speakers conceptually organize the world of plants and animals. Although I cannot provide firm evidence, my overall feeling is that ethnobiologists are perhaps more aware of issues relating to problems of intracultural variation than are most ethnographers in other subfields. Ellen is essentially correct, however, when he notes that "little quantitative information has been presented on the distribution of response variability in interpretations between informants according to such normally important variables as geography, age, gender, kinship affiliation, ideology, degree of literacy, and so on" (Ellen 1979b:338). The major exceptions to this comment are the monographic works of Hays (1974) and

---

[1] Sapir's discussion of Dorsey's (1884) encounter with variation has made his "Two Crows denies this" comment so well known as to have become an anthropological cliché.

[2] How to deal positively with the subject of intracultural variation has received a good deal of attention in the general social anthropological literature in the last several years. Excluding research on ethnobiology, the work of Cancian (1963), Berlin and Berlin (1975), Berlin, Kay, and Merrifield (1985; in prep.), Dougherty (1975), Hage and Hawkes (1975), Garro (1986), Mathews (1983), Pelto and Pelto (1975), Sankoff (1971), Burton and Kirk (1979), Foster (1979), Furbee and Benfer (1983), Kempton (1981), Weller (1983, 1984, 1987), and Young and Garro (1982) offer useful proposals with substantive examples.

Boster (1980) and the various developments of their work (e.g., Hays 1976; Boster 1986). The useful general guidelines suggested by Ellen (1975, 1979b), his careful descriptive treatment of the Nuaulu classification of amphibians and reptiles (Ellen, Stimson, and Menzies 1976, 1977), as well as the more pessimistic views of Gardner (1976), all point to several of the most important issues relating to describing intracultural variation as it relates to ethnobiological knowledge specifically.

An unstated assumption of work in ethnobiological classification is that, while informants will differ in their responses to the stimuli presented to them in natural or artificial ethnographic contexts, their responses will show a patterned distribution that will allow the investigator to infer some underlying structure(s). If this were not so, no description would be possible. If patterned distributions can be discerned in the ways plants and animals are classified and named, then efforts can be made at providing tentative explanations for these patterns.

My major goal in this chapter is to outline some of the ways in which the search for patterned distribution in ethnobiological knowledge illustrates how variation can be the key to the discovery of the underlying system(s) of a people's classification of plants and animals. I will touch briefly on methodological issues, since the procedures one employs and the kinds of data one collects play a major role in the kinds of variation that emerges from the data. A comprehensive manual on field methods in ethnobiology is sorely needed (cf. Bulmer's 1969 unpublished manuscript for New Guinea).

5.1 Werner's Gray-haired Omniscient Native Speaker-Hearer

In beginning to describe ethnobiologial knowledge, one might take one of two positions. An ethnobiological description might theoretically consist only of that knowledge unanimously agreed upon by all informants consulted, or it might aim to represent the knowledge of all. Werner characterized these two extremes in an important paper some twenty years ago: "Culture may be viewed as the common element which all members share, or the set theoretical INTERSECTION of individual competences. In ethnographic ethnoscience, as in traditional lexicography, the complementary view is taken: the description is an attempt to characterize the set theoretical UNION of all individual competences" (Werner 1969:333). Most ethnobiologists would probably not argue strongly in favor of solely describing Werner's intersection of cultural knowledge, rather opting for the more encyclopedic description of all individual competences. Gardner (1976), however, has suggested that such a view is not possible, at least for his ethnoornithological work among the northern Dene of Canada. What is missing from Werner's account is how best to characterize the set theoretic union of the knowledge of all. Some knowledge is more important, in that it is more salient and widely shared, while some is idiosyncratic and unique to single individuals. An adequate description, it would seem, must distinguish between these extremes, on the one hand, and the gradation that necessarily unites the two ends of the scale, on the other.

5.2 THE BASIC DATA OF ETHNOBIOLOGICAL DESCRIPTION AND THE SEARCH FOR PATTERNS

Patterned variation emerges from data and it is therefore appropriate to touch briefly on just what kinds of basic data ethnobiologists take as fundamental to any adequate ethnobiological description that claims to deal with the ways humans categorize the world of plants and animals. Most ethnobiologists would agree that the initial steps of any description are, first, to determine the intensional meanings of a set of concepts, most of which are realized by names in a given language, as can be inferred from the ways these terms are applied to a set of living organisms; secondly, to discover the structure(s) that unite these concepts into a classificatory system. The first step is largely possible because of the assumption among most ethnobiologists that one can closely approximate, although never match perfectly, the primary denotative meaning of native plant and animal names by comparing the mappings one detects in the folk system with the scientific classification of the biological taxa to which they refer. Thus, from the earliest stages of research, one uses the Western scientific system as the metalanguage in terms of which the folk system can be understood. As Bulmer characteristically understates it,

> If folk-taxonomy bore no relation to scientific taxonomy, but was entirely based on biologically arbitrary but culturally relevant discriminations, there would be no point in obtaining [biological] identifications for the creatures [and plants] concerned, no way of relating biological information about them to ethnographic information about the uses to which they were put or the manner in which men conceptualized them. (Bulmer 1969:4)

It is to this scientific classification of the organisms in some local habitat, expressed in the language of systematic biology, that the parallel ethnobotanical and ethnozoological systems of classification can be compared and contrasted. (I do not use the phrase ''parallel (ethno)botany'' in the same sense as Leo Lionni 1977.) One of the major tasks of ethnobiological description is to determine the several types of mapping relationships that hold between the two systems of classification, the folk and the scientific.

Although the scientific system of classification is not fixed and is constantly being revised as more information becomes available on poorly known groups of organisms, it can serve as a relatively solid constant in terms of which data on ethnobiological classification can be productively organized and analyzed. If ethnobiological data collection has been carried out so as to approximate as much as possible exhaustive floral and faunal inventories, then, as Hunn has claimed, "The scientific system . . . may serve as an etic grid, rather than as simply a convenient language for glossing exotic [names for plants and animals]" (1977:62).

5.3 COLLECTING THE BASIC DATA FROM WHICH PATTERNS MIGHT EMERGE

There is no substitute for spending hours each day with one's native collaborators, walking slowly down a forest trail on the lookout for any and all plant species in flower or fruit, be they majestic palms or humble "shitty little herbs," as my collaborator Breedlove likes to speak of the pepperomias, collecting them, talking about them, spreading them out in an appropriately dry spot and pressing them, all the while attempting to record essential botanical and ethnobotanical notes on a multitude of topics that will later become part of the full description. During the course of the day, when you also make the chance discovery of a blue-throated piping-guan through a broken clearing, anxiously watch it drawn into shotgun range by your assistant's deceptively plaintive calls over a folded leaf, see it shot, and then, while examining it, engage in animated discussions about its habits and closest relatives, then, that's a good day's ethnobiological fieldwork.

The problem is, of course, as those readers who have conducted ethnobiological fieldwork will readily acknowledge, the work would never get finished under such movie-set conditions, real as they may be. Unfortunately, until funds are made available for the establishment of ethnobotanical gardens and ethnozoological preserves in natural settings through which one can accompany native collaborators on guided ethnobiological excursions, in most cases one must be grudgingly satisfied with the use of data-collection methods that are considerably less than ideal, leading our results to be infected with what Ellen (1979b) calls a "methodological indeterminacy" that contributes in large part to the variable results that one ultimately obtains.

In addition to the many kinds of informal methods that any competent field worker will employ, there are at least two well-established systematic ways of gathering the basic data on which the ethnobiological description is based, from which the patterns of variation in our informants' differing classificatory structures may emerge. The two procedures are quite distinct, each having major disadvantages that are offset to some degree by other positive properties.

The first method entails the use of prepared specimens, either recently collected or fully dried plant voucher specimens, as well as prepared zoological specimens or skins, which multiple informants are requested to view and name, preferably independent of one another. A second method implies the use of several different informants who identify multiple plant or animal species in their natural state at the time of collection but none of whom see the full set of collections.

The first method is superior to the second in that it is quasi-experimental, and it guarantees that a large sample of informants will view and respond to the same stimuli, while the experiment can be controlled to some degree by the researcher. The disadvantages are that the biological specimens observed often distort the organisms to such an extent as to radically change their natural appearance, especially with the colors of fish, reptiles, and amphibians, as well as stuffed museum skins of certain mammals. The most serious disadvantage is that it is difficult if not impossible to have any subject, let alone a full set of subjects, view a complete set of specimens approaching the total species diversity present in the area.

The second method, that of collecting extensively with multiple informants where no single informant views the full collection, has been widely used in ethnobiological research. It has the advantage that large numbers of species can be collected in a reasonable amount of time, given the constraints of fieldwork budgets, by several teams of collectors and their assistants. More importantly, all species collected are viewed in their natural state prior to their being prepared as voucher specimens. A particular collector, either the field ethnobiologist or a native assistant, might work with several scores of informants over a year's time using this method. The disadvantage that numbers of informants cannot view the identical stimulus is balanced somewhat, inasmuch as several collections of the same species will be collected multiple times and that each will be named by multiple informants over the course of a season's work. If several collecting teams are at work simultaneously, thousands of informant identifications can be obtained for the full set of collections. Both of these methods have been used in the collection of the kinds of data that will discussed below. They are not mutually exclusive, and ideally some combination of the two should be employed.

5.4 SOME SIGNIFICANT TYPES OF VARIATION IN ETHNOBIOLOGICAL KNOWLEDGE

It is important to be clear about what kinds of variation one is confronted with in work on ethnobiological classification before discussing how variation might be used to discover pattern(s) in a given classification system. Two of the most immediately apparent ways in which people differ can be found in what may be called, on the one hand, *lexical* variation and, on the other, *cognitive* (or categorical) variation. The two may coincide, of course, but they are usefully discussed as separate topics.

Lexical Variation

Boster (1986:179) has pointed out that among the reasons that led Gardner (1976) to treat the Dene classification of birds as highly variable is that Gardner attributes excessive importance to what appears to be simple phonological variation in the names applied to particular species. While the Dene may call the ruffed grouse (*Bonasa umbellus*) *etsetsue̲*, *etsets*ue̲*, *ets*ets*esa*, *O*ets*ue̲*, *ets*ue̲ts*ue̲*, informants apparently nonetheless seem agree on the referential ethnobiological range of these various expressions.

Straightforward phonological variation of this sort is quite common in the nomenclatural systems of most languages. Consider, as a further example, the following terms for the cardinal flower, *Lobelia laxiflora*, in the dialect of Tzeltal from which the materials found in Berlin, Breedlove, and Raven (1974) were derived.

Generic Name	Number of Informants Using Expression
príma najk	11
príma najk'	3
prímo najk	2
príwa najk	1
primajk'	1
prinajk	2
pírma najk	3
piríma najk	4
pririm najk	1
pirinajk	1

In addition to differences in simple phonological form (see Stross 1975 for an ingenious and stimulating discussion on this phenomenon in Tzeltal), one frequently notes great lexical variation in ethnobiological nomenclature where distinct or partially distinct lexical expressions are employed to designate the same ethnobiological category. As Hays states for the Ndumba, "Synonyms [lexical variants] account for almost exactly one-half of the lexicon variability" (Hays 1974:234), and such synonymy is rampant in Tzeltal.

Lobelia laxiflora, in addition to its phonological variants listed above, is also known as *we'el t'ul* lit. 'rabbit's food' and *tulesnail wamal* lit. 'peachlike herb'. Likewise, two similar species of the common white milkweed, *Asclepias similis* and *A. curassavica* (the prototype), are widely recognized by expressions such as *panyat* lit. 'penis's handkerchief' (*panyo* < Spanish *pañuelo* 'handkerchief', *at* 'penis'), *yu' ahaw* lit. 'snake's mushroom', *pojowil wamal* lit. 'pus herb', *yax akan te'* lit. 'green-legged tree', *tzu at pojow wamal* lit. 'bottle gourd penis pus herb', among several others. All of these expressions are restricted in their semantic ranges, however, to the species in question.

The underlying factors leading to lexical variation, either strictly phonological or lexical, have not been fully explored. The detailed study of this topic would have considerable importance for understanding the nature of historical change in systems of ethnobiological classification. As we will see from the brief discussion of semantically opaque and transparent generic names (chapter 6), it now appears likely that factors relating to the attributed cultural importance of particular plant and animal species will work toward the reduction of linguistic variation for highly important organisms and propel variation forward in the case of less important species.[3]

The evidence for this claim is found in a comparative historical study of the ethnobotany of the Tenejapa Tzeltal and Zinacantán Tzotzil, two Mayan-speaking peoples of southern Mexico that separated about twelve hundred years ago. In comparing a relatively complete inventory of the plant species found in common between these two communities, Berlin, Breedlove, Raven, and Laughlin (1973), demonstrated that as much as 87 percent of the names for cultivated plants are shown to be cognates (e.g., Tzeltal *may*, Tzotzil *moy* 'tobacco', *Nicotiana tabacum*). The number of cognate forms drops to 80 percent for protected plants, then to 45 percent for wild-useful forms, and finally to just 17 percent for plant species that are only sporadically treated, or managed, to use Balée's terminology. Noncognate forms vary greatly between the two languages for these culturally less important plant species.

Balée independently came to similar conclusions in his research on comparative Tupian ethnobotany. His data show that "for 151 plant species known to exist among three or more of the five [Tupian] groups [with whom the study was conducted], there is a distinct gradient of lexical similarity [i.e., lexical variation] from unmanaged plants to intensively managed plants. Specifically, the proportions of lexical similarity are .29 for unmanaged plants, .60 for semi-managed plants, and .77 for intensively managed plants" (Balée 1986).

Cognitive Variation

While people may have different names for the same things, a more significant aspect of intracultural variation deals with the differential distribution of ethnobiological knowledge as it relates to different ways of classifying the same things. To what extent do people agree on the referential meaning of the terms they do share? What does it mean when, in an ethnobiological description, one finds statements indicating that "X is the name of species Y in society Z"?[4]

[3] Hays (1974:320–350) found no such association in his work in Ndumba ethnobotany. However, Hays's calculations were based on naming experiments that did not include specimens of cultivated plants, the species that are most likely to have the greatest cultural importance if one accepts the assumption that intensity of human interaction with a particular plant species is an indication of its cultural value.

[4] Since all ethnobiological research takes for granted the obvious fact that people differ in the ways they categorize plants and animals, the crucial issue is how best to discover this variation, describe it, and account for it given the constraints of time, human resources, and financial support. The problems associated with such a research agenda are enormous if one takes as the primary goal the production of an initial description of some complete system, making an effort to elicit relatively comprehensive inventories of names for plants and animals that are documented by extensive voucher specimens. When this is accompanied, as should be the case in any complete study, by detailed descriptions of the cultural significance of plants and animals in everyday life, the work rapidly becomes monumental.

The only certain way to discover what an ethnobiological term means denotatively is to ask numbers of informants the same questions about the same stimuli. Since people in traditional societies will likely vary in what they know about plants and animals as a function of their sex, age, or social status, a primary goal in any general field-research program is to include as many subjects as possible who vary in one or more of these major categories. However, as anyone who has ever tried to do the work will readily admit, our informants are usually those who appear on a voluntary basis, and it is often impossible to attain representativeness in our samples.

The applicability of these totally obvious statements will, of course, depend a great deal on the nature of the specific investigation. It would have done Boster (1980) little good to spend a lot of time interviewing Aguaruna males about the scores of varieties of manioc, since this is an area of ethnobiological reality about which men know essentially nothing (see below). Likewise, Bulmer's work on Kalam ethnozoology (e.g., Bulmer 1970; Bulmer and Tyler 1968; and the numerous other references cited earlier) focused on the classification of the world of animals as seen through the eyes of a few highly knowledgeable Kalam men, given the role of males as hunters in Kalam society. The research that Breedlove, Raven, and I carried out among the Tzeltal of southern Mexico is also biased with respect to gender, in this case for quite serious reasons related to maintaining good rapport with the community. On numerous occasions we were cautioned "not to go into the woods with women" to collect plants, because everyone knows the *real* reason men go into the woods with women.

Nonetheless, statements to the effect that "men know more about the forest than do women" or that "the old guys are the wisest," with no subsequent documentation, is little better than journalistic reporting. In this regard, part of the goal of a general description is to show where cognitive variation exists and, having done so, to provide some explanation for it. In the following sections, I want to focus primarily on the variation in ethnobiological knowledge as it relates to the differences in categorization between men and women in Aguaruna Jívaro society. In the process, I also hope to show how inter-informant variability may allow one to draw inferences about the denotational meaning of ethnobiological categories that would be impossible without querying sizable numbers of informants with multiple and fairly complete sets of biological collections.

5.5 DISCOVERING THE PATTERNS UNDERLYING THE BIOLOGICAL RANGES OF FOLK TAXA

The primary datum of all serious studies of ethnobiological classification consists of an *exemplar of some biological species* accompanied by its *linguistic designation*, if any, obtained from a *native speaker*. The degree of sophistication of one's ethnobiological elicitation methods, however, even if the investigation is carried out with numerous subjects and with living species, has little consequence in determining the biological ranges of the names of ethnobiological taxa *unless* the collections of the plants and animals to which these names are applied are general and extensive, comprised of a number of specimens that approximates the total species diversity of the given local flora and fauna. Even then, adequate biological surveys are likely to approach comprehensiveness for only the higher vertebrates and the larger vascular plants.

Given these considerations, establishing *which species are included* in the biological range of some generic taxon, X, is not a sufficient condition; one must also satisfy the further condition of establishing *which potentially contrastive species are not included* in its range. As Bulmer reminds us, "one cannot say of *any* taxon that it corresponds to species 'X' unless one knows of all other locally occurring species which could conceivably be identified or confused with 'X' " (Bulmer 1970:1075).

The Bird-Naming Experiments

In the late 1970s, as part of an ethnobiological expedition to the Upper Marañón River region of Amazonian Peru, the ornithologist John O'Neill and I conducted several experiments aimed at providing evidence on how the Aguaruna Jívaro classify birds. Part of this work directly relevant to the present context has been reported in Berlin, Boster, and O'Neill (1981), but it is important to mention some of the practical aspects of the conduct of the research to place the examples to be discussed in the appropriate perspective.

After several months of ethnobiological data collection in the region, prepared specimens of some 157 species of commonly occurring birds were used as stimuli in three naming experiments. This set of specimens does not nearly represent the total species diversity of the region, which may range as high as five hundred species, but it is beyond question that it includes the most common species present and surely represents those birds most usually encountered by the Aguaruna in their daily lives.

When possible, species showing sexual dimorphism were represented by both male and female specimens. A total of 260 specimens were employed in three separate naming trials. Bird skins were spread out on long cane worktables (whose primary function was the sunning of mammal and bird specimens) against backgrounds of cardboard corrugates standardly employed in botanical collecting.

The tables were located along a high bank parallel to the Cenepa River in a clearing about 15 meters directly in front of our field laboratories and living quarters. Prior to each experiment, specimens were laid out in a specified order, care being taken not to place exemplars of the same species immediately adjacent to one another. Informants who agreed to participate did so on a voluntary basis but were paid a nominal sum for their cooperation. The experimenter on one side and an informant on the other passed slowly down the tables looking at each specimen in turn, each informant being asked the question, "*Husha, wajímpaya?*" 'That, what is its name?'

Twenty-eight informants (eighteen males, ten females) participated in the first test, twenty-five (twenty-one males, four females) in the second, and twenty-seven (twenty-one males, six females) in the last. The sample is biased toward males because women were hesitant to participate. Each experiment took about twenty minutes and subjects were allowed (if not encouraged) to pick up, handle, and often smell the specimens if they chose to do so (and many did) prior to giving an answer. All responses were recorded in a notebook for later analysis.

Efforts were made to keep the area clear of curious onlookers, who might overhear the names provided by our experimental subjects. In spite of this, we cannot claim with certainty that informant responses were totally independent from one another. However, given the large numbers of specimens, it is unlikely that informants were influenced by others' partially overheard responses.

These experiments represented something totally novel for the Aguaruna and, at least for the women, were slightly intimidating. Nonetheless, the types of stimuli used in the study were nothing new—prepared bird skins, especially those of the smaller species, are commonly found among this group, as well as among the related Huambisa. Once a bird is killed, usually with the use of a blowgun, many brightly colored species are skinned and stuffed with native cotton for use in decorating traditional head crowns and in some cases to serve as flashy earrings (along with the iridescent wings of certain beetles). The recognition of the extent of native skills in bird skinning ultimately led us to use Aguaruna assistants in the preparation of standard ornithological museum specimens.

I have selected as examples for discussion here sets of naming data of varying degrees of complexity that illustrate several different problems in the interpretation of informant variation, as it relates to the establishment of the biological ranges of recognized folk generic names. The first and least problematical case is seen in table 5.1. This table presents the naming results from the experiments described above for the two species of barbets found in the Aguaruna region, the lemon-throated barbet (*Eubucco richardsoni*) and the black-spotted barbet (*Capito niger*). These brightly, perhaps even "gaudily colored" (de Schauensee 1970:175) creatures are the only two local representatives of the Capitonidae, a small family of birds of three genera in South America. They are conceptually related to one another in Aguaruna bird classification and form a well-established covert intermediate taxon of two folk generic taxa. It is clear from table 5.1 that there is considerable agreement among the eighty informants participating in the three experiments, but the

TABLE 5.1

Distribution of Aguaruna Naming Responses[a] for Two Species of Barbets[b] from Three Naming Experiments, Presented by Number of Responses by Sex of Informant (see text for explanation)

Scientific Name	Aguaruna Name	Sex of Informant	Responses
Capito niger (f)	?	m	2
	?	m	2
	?	f	1
	púu	f	2
	púu	m	1
	púu	m	2
	sawáke	f	1
	takáikit	f	2
	takáikit	f	3
	takáikit	m	16
	takáikit	m	18
	ukúshkit	m	1
	úntunch	f	1
Capito niger (m)	?	f	1
	jijím	m	1
	púu	f	1
	shíik	f	1
	takáikit	f	5
	takáikit	m	16
	ukúshkit	f	1
	wisuí	f	1
	?	f	2
Eubucco richardsoni (f)	?	m	2
	?	m	2
	kuíntam	f	1
	púu	f	1
	púu	f	2
	púu	m	14
	púu	m	17
	shíik	m	1
	takáikit	f	1
	takáikit	f	2
	taláikit	m	1
	takáikit	m	1
	tángki píshak	f	1
	tíwa	m	1
	ukúshkit	f	1
	úushap	f	2
	wampangkít	f	1
	?	f	3

TABLE 5.1 (*Cont.*)

Scientific Name	Aguaruna Name	Sex of Informant	Responses
	?	m	2
	?	m	3
	bakakít	f	1
	chángke	m	1
	dái	f	1
Eubucco richardsoni (m)	chángke	f	1
	isúmchik	f	1
	púu	f	1
	púu	f	3
	púu	m	15
	púu	m	18
	semanchúk	f	1
	takáikit	f	2
	tátse	m	1
	tíwa	m	1

ᵃ Terms other than *púu* and *takáikit*, in this table and subsequent tables, refer to ethnozoological genera whose biological denotata are, on the basis of general consensus, neither *Eubucco* nor *Capito*.

ᵇ Represents the combined naming responses for seven specimens—four *Eubucco* specimens and three *Capito* specimens. Total number of informant responses for all specimens = 187.

agreement is far less than universal. The underlying pattern of consensus is seen more clearly in table 5.2. For the genera in question, the sex of the bird specimen obviously has minimal influence on informants' identifications and has been ignored here. The table shows that one would not be far off the mark to claim that just two generic names, *takáikit* and *púu*, each applied in strongly patterned ways, have as their referential meanings *Capito niger* and *Eubucco richardsoni*, respectively. About 10 percent of the male informants and 15 percent of the female informants indicated that they did not know the name of either barbet species, but none of the competing alternative names occurs with a frequency that would indicate them to be anything other than guesses. Furthermore, the close perceptual similarity between the two barbet species is seen in the reverse application of the folk generic names *púu* and *takáikit* in a few instances, mostly by females.

If one may draw inferences about classification from such data, it is clear that women's knowledge of these extremely common birds is less developed than that of men, in spite of the fact that the women's combined knowledge indicates that their categories are most likely equivalent in meaning to those of the men. This can be seen more clearly in table 5.3, which presents the summary naming responses for females alone.

TABLE 5.2
Summary of Aguaruna Naming Responses for Two Species of Barbets Used in the
Naming Experiments (see text for explanation)

| Aguaruna Name | Scientific Name | | Total |
	Capito niger	Eubucco richardsoni	
?	6	14	20
bakakít	1		1
chánge		2	2
dái		1	1
jijím	1		1
kuíntam		1	1
pisúmchik		1	1
púu	6	71	77
sawáke	1		1
semanchúk		1	1
shíik	1	1	2
takáikit	60	7	67
tangkí píshak		1	1
tátse		1	1
tíwa		2	2
ukúshkit	2	1	3
untúnch	1		1
úushap		2	2
wampangkít		1	1
wisuí	1		1
Total	80	107	187

Note: ? = informants "don't know."

If one wished to behave in a culturally appropriate way in Aguaruna Jívaro
society (à la Goodenough 1957), one would get high marks by selecting the
generic name *takáikit* for *Capito niger*. In fact, 96 percent of men do just this.
Women, however, while having a generally appropriate idea about which
creature this term should be correctly applied to, get it right only about two
thirds of the time. For the first two specimens of this species, only one woman
in ten and one in six, respectively, applied the culturally appropriate name.
Here one sees how patterned variation allows one to infer imperfect knowledge of a culturally shared category.

A more complex picture is revealed in the classification of the several species of woodpeckers found in the region. Here, one finds differential knowledge associated not only with sex, but also with age. Table 5.4 displays the
naming responses of adult males and females for eight of the perhaps ten spe-

TABLE 5.3

Summary of Naming Responses of Aguaruna Females for Two Species of Barbets
Used in the Naming Experiments (see text for explanation)

| | Scientific Name | | |
Aguaruna Name	Capito niger	Eubucco richardsoni	Total
?	2	5	7
bakakít		1	1
chángke		1	1
dái		1	1
kuíntam		1	1
pisúmchik		1	1
púu	3	7	10
sawáke	1		1
semanchúk		1	1
shíik	1		1
takaíkit	10	5	15
tangkí píshak		1	1
ukúshkit	1	1	2
untúnch	1		1
úushap		2	2
wampangkít		1	1
wisui	1		1
Total	20	28	48

Note: ? = informants "don't know."

cies of tropical forest woodpeckers present in the area. As it is the case with
the barbets, the woodpeckers are grouped as a covert intermediate taxon in
Aguaruna bird classification. Our collections of the full species diversity
found in the region are fairly complete, although, as mentioned above, there
are perhaps at least two additional species present for which we do not have
collections and which are not represented in the naming experiments. Table
5.4 shows that the more than 260 naming responses for this group manifest a
consistent, underlying pattern, one made more apparent in table 5.5.

The distribution of individual responses seen in table 5.5 leads to the following inferences:

1. Most informants group the eight species into three folk generic taxa, *tátasham*,
   sawáke, and *dái*.
2. For speakers using only these three terms, each of the generic taxa formed by
   them is biologically, although not linguistically, polytypic, including two or
   more species.
3. Each of these three linguistically undifferentiated taxa, however, is characterized
   by a single species that can be interpreted as prototypical in that they are the most

TABLE 5.4

Distribution of Aguaruna Naming Responses for Specimens Representing Eight Species of Woodpeckers, by Sex of Informant (see text for explanation)

Scientific Name	Aguaruna Name	Sex of Informant	No. of Responses
Phloeoceastes melanoleucos	tátasham	m	43
	tátasham	f	8
Phloeoceastes rubricollis	tátasham	m	17
	tátasham	f	6
	samamú	m	4
	?	f	1
Celeus elegans	sawáke	m	18
	dái	f	1
	egátinu	f	1
	sawáke	f	5
	tátasham	f	1
	?	f	2
	?	m	2
Celeus grammicus	sawáke	m	10
	dái	f	4
	dái	m	6
	kuíntam	f	1
	sawáke	f	2
	shíik	f	1
	?	f	1
Celeus spectabilis	sawáke	m	33
	dái	m	2
	jíip	m	4
	sawáke	f	7
	tátasham	f	5
	tátasham	m	2
	?	f	2
	?	m	1
Chrysoptilus punctigula	dái	m	10
	dái	f	5
	sawáke	f	2
	sawáke	m	4
Veniliornis affinis	tejashá	f	1
	?	f	3
	?	m	1
	dái	f	6
	mujáya píshak	f	1
	sawáke	m	2

TABLE 5.4 (*Cont.*)

Scientific Name	Aguaruna Name	Sex of Informant	No. of Responses
	dái	m	15
Veniliornis passerinus	?	m	2
	dái	f	2
	sawáke	f	1
	sawáke	m	5
	tingkísh	f	1
	tushím	m	1
	dái	m	13
Total			264

TABLE 5.5
Summary of Aguaruna Naming Responses for Eight Species of Woodpeckers in Amazonian Peru (modified and corrected from Berlin, Boster, and O'Neill 1981)

Scientific Name	Aguaruna Naming Responses						
	tátasham	*samamú*	*sawáke*	*jíip*	*dái*	*tejashá*	?
Phloeoceastes melanoleucos	51						
P. rubricollis	23	4					1
C. spectabilis	7		40	4	2		3
Celeus elegans	1		23		1		4
C. grammicus			12		10		1
Chrysoptilus punctigula			6		15		3
Veniliornis affinis			2		21	1	4
V. passerinus			6		15		2

Note: Six terms—*egaátinu, tingkísh, kuíntam, mujáya píshak, shíik,* and *tushím*—occurred once each as responses and are not shown in the table. On the basis of in-depth interviews, the term **tejashá**, while occurring but a single time, is nonetheless thought to be the name of a woodpecker species not yet represented in our collections.

commonly recognized and widely named. While *Celeus elegans* and *C. spectabilis* vie as the prototype for **sawáke**, additional evidence presented shortly will clarify why one, *C. spectabilis*, is the likely prototype.

The internal structure of each of the three most widely recognized folk generics is shown diagrammatically in figure 5.1. Males and females have roughly the same conceptual structure for these three major generic categories, although women have broader categories for both **dái** and **sawáke**, as we can see in figure 5.2.

While the number of responses is clearly too low to make any general definitive statement, it would appear that females who do not know either *Celeus elegans* or *C. spectabilis* prefer to apply the word *tátasham* as a general term that might be interpreted as meaning 'general woodpecker'. In fact, there is some evidence from other interviews that the woodpeckers, like the doves, puffbirds, hawks, and some other few intermediate taxa in Huambisa, represent a named intermediate in Aguaruna, its label being taken from the largest and most conspicuous species, namely, *Phloeoceastes* (cf. Bulmer 1969 for a similar observation about Kalam bird classification).

Two additional terms, *júip* and *samamú*, occur as responses from four mature Aguaruna males as the names for *Celeus spectabilis* and *Phloeoceastes rubricollis* (see table 5.4). In addition to having been elicited in the naming experiments, these two terms were elicited in in-depth interviews with older male informants as folk specific taxa. These interviews show that the expression *júip* is a synonym for the binomial form *apu sawáke* lit. 'leader/father sawáke'. Likewise, *samamú* is an abbreviated form of the full name *samamú tátasham*. Thus, for knowledgeable adult males, the generics *tátasham* and *sawáke* are bitypic. This would lead to the tentative conclusion that there are at least two congruent although cognitively distinct classifications at work in Aguaruna ethnoornithology for this group of birds. The two systems might be represented visually as in figure 5.3.

The distribution of naming responses is understandable in terms of the biological characteristics of the species involved. Of the four genera represented in the set, *Phloeoceastes* is the largest and most vividly marked. Members of this genus could hardly be confused with any other woodpecker in the area. As a consequence, the genus is linked with *Celeus* only three times. The remaining three genera, *Celeus*, *Veniliornis*, and *Chrysoptilus*, are smaller and more similar to one another in size and plumage, leading to their being confused in naming tests.

For each of the three polytypic genera (*Phloeoceastes*, *Celeus*, and *Veniliornis*), the data suggest a single prototypical member. *P. melanoleucos*, the crimson-crested woodpecker, occurs as the focal member of *tátasham*. It is marked by black and white bars on its belly and lower breast, in contrast to the somewhat smaller *P. rubricollis*, the red-necked woodpecker, which is more uniformly chestnut-colored. In addition, *P. melanoleucos* is more likely to be observed due to its habits of frequenting tree falls, the forest edge, and clearings. Its prototypicality is further supported by the fact that it is known as *shing tátasham* lit. 'genuine tatasham' by those males that treat the folk genus as polytypic. *P. rubricollis* prefers denser forest, often the upper canopy, and is not easily observed; it is treated as a named category only by those individuals who have intimate knowledge of the forest, that is, older males.

The prototype of the generic taxon called *sawáke* appears to be *Celeus spectabilis*, the rufous-headed woodpecker, although it is followed closely by *C*.

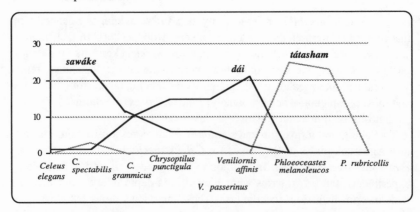

Figure 5.1 Graphic presentation of data from table 5.5 indicating the biological ranges of the three most commonly known Aguaruna folk generic woodpecker taxa, *sawáke* (*Celeus* spp.), *dái* (*Veniliornis* spp.), and *tátasham* (*Phloeoceastes* spp.). (Modified and corrected from Berlin, Boster, and O'Neill 1981)

elegans. All species of the genus are fairly similar in appearance. *C. spectabilis* is the most visually striking of the three species with a back covered profusely with small, black, heart-shaped spots. One of the synonymous names used to refer to it by splitters, *apu sawáke* 'leader sawáke', is indicative of its perceptual salience.

The generic name *dái* refers to two similar species of *Veniliornis*, with *V. affinis*, the red-stained woodpecker, selected as prototypical. As with the larger *Phloeoceastes* woodpecker, *V. affinis* frequents the edges of clearings and is more commonly observed than is *V. passerinus*, a species of the deep forest.

As can be seen from figures 5.1 and 5.2, *Crysoptilus punctigula*, the spot-breasted woodpecker, is sometimes thought of as *dái*, but is also placed with *sawáke*. That it should be ambiguous is perceptually founded. *C. punctigula* is about the same size as the typical *Celeus* species, but its drab colors make it also similar to *Veniliornis*, leading it to be confused with both competing genera.

The preceding examples show differential knowledge of folk taxa that nonetheless constitute recognized categories in the ethnobiological repertoires of adult males and females. On the other hand, there are clearly substantial portions of this domain that are exclusively the knowledge of Aguaruna men because of their more complete understanding of the species diversity of the region, gained in great part in their capacity as hunters. As a single example out of many that could be cited, I will mention that of *b~urchik* (*Ramphocaenus melanurus*), the long-billed gnatwren, a small, secretive bird of the Sylviidae. Although two collections were present in the naming tasks, not a

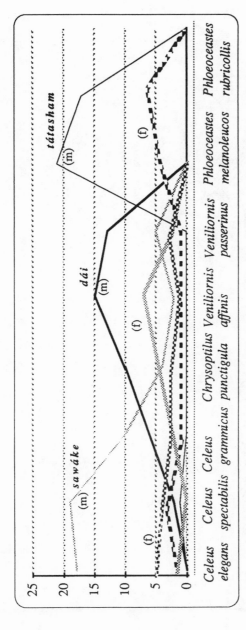

Figure 5.2 Graphic presentation indicating the biological ranges of the three most commonly known Aguaruna folk generic woodpecker taxa, *sawáke* (*Celeus* spp.), *dái* (*Veniliornis* spp.), and *tátasham* (*Phloeoceastes* spp.) by Aguaruna
males (top three graphs) and females (bottom three graphs).

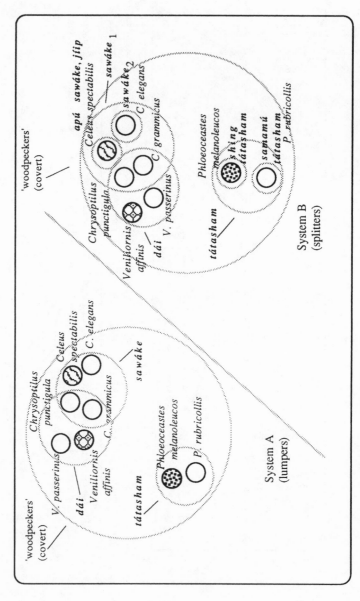

Figure 5.3 Two congruent classifications of the Aguaruna classification of woodpeckers. System B, where *sawáke* and *tátasham* are split into two folk species, is attested only for older, knowledgeable males. (Data modified and corrected from Berlin, Boster, and O'Neill 1981)

single woman used this term,[5] confusing the species totally with *tiíngkish* (*Microcerculus marginatus*), the nightingale wren, probably because of its rather similar long bill. Here is a likely example of distinct categorization as a reflection of one's sex.

Up to this point, the major kinds of data that have been used to determine the patterns underlying the variation in the biological ranges of particular categories have been those that reflect the ways in which particular species, as recognized in the scientific system, are named in the folk system. In this respect, one can state that "the most appropriate name for *Veniliornis* spp. is *dái*" (with some qualifications because of the differential knowledge of informants as a function of their sex, age, and so on). For the inverse claim to be valid, however ("*dái* is the name of *Veniliornis* spp."), one must be able to show that of all the species of birds that an informant might name with *dái*, the biological taxa to which this name is attributed are basically restricted to *Veniliornis* spp.

Table 5.6 presents the data for all the species to which the term *dái* was applied from the complete sample of 176 species and 260 specimens of birds used in the three naming experiments described above, along with the number of times a particular species was so designated. As the figures show, the primary range of *dái* is clearly on the two *Veniliornis* species, with an extended range covering the very similar *Chrysoptilus*. Our inference that the former species represent the primary foci of the folk generic is confirmed. Further-

---

[5] The expression b~*urchik* is unique in Aguaruna bird nomenclature in that the first segment of the word represents the distinctive voiced bilabial trill (comparable although not identical to the famous "Bronx cheer"). This segment is not a phoneme in Aguaruna Jívaro and, to my knowledge, is attested lexically in this one form. When I first heard the name, I thought that my informants were providing me with a vocalization of the bird's call. However, none of the vocalizations that I have recorded for this bird's sounds include the bilabial trill as an initial consonant, nor anything phonetically similar to it. Taken by the uniqueness of the name for this poorly known creature, in a moment of frivolity I was led to characterize the bird in the following verse (the bilabial trill is represented by the repeated letter "b"):

Oh, little *bbbbchik*, inconspicuous among eight in a family of doubtful affinities.
At one time, you and your first cousins placed with the tawdry antbirds,
Your next of kin with the warblers of far-off Africa, or worse.
Today both combined in the Sylviidae,
Itself a group of suspicious origins.

And how shall you be known to the world, now that you have been discovered?
For those that see you least you must bear the weight of
Ramphocaenus melanurus, or
In English speech, "Long-billed Gnatwren," both equally uninformative of your true nature.

Might not your *real* name at one time be proclaimed, which,
Once said, makes your presence a reality?
Oh, little *bbbbchik*,
Little *bbbbchik*,
Bbbbchik.

TABLE 5.6
Complete Inventory of Species Designated by the Expression *dái* in Aguaruna Naming Experiments (from a possible N = 176 species, 260 specimens)

Veniliornis affinis	22
Veniliornis passerinus	15
Celeus grammicus	10
Cymbilaimus lineatus	9
Celeus elegans	1
Celeus spectabilis	2
Automolus rufipileatus	3
Automolus sp.	2
Cyphorhinus arada	1
Eubucco richardsoni	1
Henicorhina leucosticta	1
Hylophylax sp.	1
Microcerculus marginatus	1
Myiodynastes sp.	1
Xenops minutus	1
Xiphorhynchus guttatus	1

more, if the name *dái* is applied to any other species, it is to woodpeckers of the genus *Celeus*, again a finding in concordance with data provided earlier. If there is a surprise, it is in the use of *dái* to designate the ant shrike, *Cymbilaimus lineatus*, a monotypic genus in South America. Is it possible that this species falls within *dái*'s denotative range, or might these responses represent simple mistakes? After all, informants, just like ethnobiologists, make errors all the time.

That informant error is likely to account for these facts seems highly likely when one looks at the naming responses associated with *Cymbilaimus*, as shown in table 5.7. The table reveals unambiguously that the monotypic ant shrike is generally designated by a single term, *tsejechík* (seventy-two responses). While this species bears some superficial resemblance to *Veniliornis* spp., the similarity is slight. Furthermore, all of the informants who use *dái* as a name for the ant shrike are women—additional evidence, given what we know about the sexual distribution of ornithological knowledge in this society, that the term is loosely and most likely mistakenly applied.

The examples thus far indicate variable knowledge associated with both sex and age in the classification of birds by the Aguaruna. None of these variations in category membership, however, reflects radically different systems. One must turn to the categorization of the local marsupials to find a case of what tentatively appear to be two parallel or complementary systems of classification where different speakers use the same terms for completely different spe-

TABLE 5.7

Complete Inventory of Aguaruna Naming Responses for Specimens of *Cymbilaimus lineatus* in the Naming Experiments Described in Text (from a possible N = 176 species, 260 specimens)

tsejechík	72
dái	9
pángka	4
píljuak	1
sawáke	2
shíik	5
takaíkit	2
tsanchiám	1
tsantsentsé	1
tsejémna	1

cies. These variant classifications do not appear to be accounted for by the age or sex of the informant.

The Opossum-Sorting Experiment

Six genera of opossums are represented in the local mammalian fauna of the Aguaruna area: the North American opossum, *Didelphis marsupialis* (characterized by a dark and a light phase); the woolly opossum, *Caluromys lanatus*; the water opossum, *Chironectes minimus*; the gray four-eyed opossum, *Philander opossum*; the brown four-eyed opossum, *Metachirus nudicaudatus*; and at least three species of the brown mouse opossum, *Marmosa* spp. (see Berlin and Patton 1979, in prep.).

Twenty informants (fifteen males, five females) participated in a naming and sorting experiment of prepared museum specimens of these six genera. Seventeen specimens were spread out on the same tables as described for the bird-naming experiments, with the following number of specimens per genus:

Didelphis marsupialis (white phase)	2
D. marsupialis (dark phase)	2
Marmosa spp.	5
Chironectes minimus	1
Caluromys lanatus	1
Philander opossum	3
Metachirus nudicaudatus	3

Informants were asked to group the specimens into piles with the request, "*apustá kumpají*" 'Put (it, them) with its (their) companion(s)', and then to name the resulting groups. Two informants, a younger male and female, did so poorly that their results were discarded (one called the large *Didelphis* a kind of 'rat' and the other labeled the woolly opossum with the term most informants use for the South American conocono, *Isothrix villosa*, a creature similar to a large rat).

Two partially distinct systems appear to be employed by the Aguaruna in their classification of the local opossum species, both of which are described in table 5.8. Focusing first on the similarities between System A and System

TABLE 5.8
Aguaruna Categorization of Opossums Indicating Two Complementary Systems of Classification
(from Berlin and Patton, in prep.)

Scientific Name	Aguaruna Name	Number of Responses	Gloss (if any)
	System A (10 informants)		
Didelphis (white phase)	*máyachachau*	10	
Didelphis (dark phase)	*nantú kujáncham*	8	'moon opossum'
	shing kujáncham	1	'genuine opossum'
	máyachachau	1	
Philander opossum	*jápacham*	3	
	tikísh kujáncham	3	'another opossum'
	nujánt kumpají	1	'nujánt's companion'
	kujáncham	2	(unspecified opossum)
Metachirus + *Marmosa*	*jápacham*	8	
	nujánt kumpají	1	'nujánt's companion'
	katip	1	'rat'
Caluromys lanatus	*nujánt*	9	
	kujáncham	1	(unspecified opossum)
Chironectes minimus	*namakía kujáncham*	6	'water/creek opossum'
	kujáncham	2	(unspecified opossum)
	máyachachau	1	
	System B (8 informants)		
Didelphis (white phase)	*nantú kujáncham*	5	'moon opossum'
	shing kujáncham	2	'genuine opossum'
	?	1	
Didelphis (dark phase)	*shing kujáncham*	6	'genuine opossum'
	nantú kujáncham	2	'moon opossum'
Philander opossum	*máyachachau*	6	
	jápacham	2	
Metachirus + *Marmosa*	*jápacham*	6	
Caluromys lanatus	*nujánt*	8	
Chironectes minimus	*namakía kujáncham*	6	'water/creek opossum'

B, one notes that two species, the woolly opossum (*Caluromys lanatus*) and the water opossum (*Chironectes minimus*), are fairly consistently classified as *nuját* and *inítia kujáncham*, respectively. These are clearly the most distinctive genera in the set. The long, fine hair of the woolly opossum covers most of its tail, unlike that of any of the other species present. The water opossum exhibits webbed hind feet and a streamlined body, which reflect its adaptation to a water habitat. The two could hardly be confused.

The conceptual treatment of the two genera of so-called four-eyed opossums is also similar in the two systems, with the term *jápacham* occurring as the preferred generic name in both cases.

The major and most significant difference between the two variant classifications is in the treatment of *Didelphis marsupialis* (both color phases) and *Philander opossum*. Speakers with System A unanimously attribute *Didelphis*'s white-phase form to a taxon called *máyachachau*, while the dark phase of the species is commonly called *nantú kujáncham*. *Philander opossum* is apparently poorly known in this system, for reasons that are difficult to explain, but the only nondescriptive term used, *jápacham*, ties it to the four-eyed opossums.

In contrast, speakers with System B almost universally treat *Philander* as *máyachachau*, with the two color phases of *Didelphis* usually being recognized as folk species of the bitypic *kujáncham*, namely, *nantú kujáncham* and *shing kujáncham*, respectively. These two contrasting schemes are better visualized diagrammatically as shown in figure 5.4. As mentioned earlier, the two variant conceptual treatments seen in the figure are not distributed in a way that suggests the differences are due to age or sex of informant. The women present are divided equally between the two versions, and both younger and older males exhibit either system. Nonetheless, each system appears to be well established, as can be seen from the sizable number of informants manifesting each version. As the grouping experiments were done independently by each subject, there is no reason to assume that the results represent an individual's aping of the groupings of his or her companions. One cannot escape the conclusion that if a person with System A uses the term *máyachachau* in a conversation with persons possessing System B, they will be thinking and talking about different creatures.

5.6 Some Factors Contributing to Cognitive Variation

The above data from Aguaruna ethnozoology reveal a good deal of patterned cognitive variation. It seems reasonable to conclude that underlying the differences described for the several cases of bird classification is informants' differential knowledge as a function of their sex and age, surely two of the most important factors in the distribution of ethnobiological knowledge generally (see Boster 1980; Hays 1974; Ellen 1979b:346).

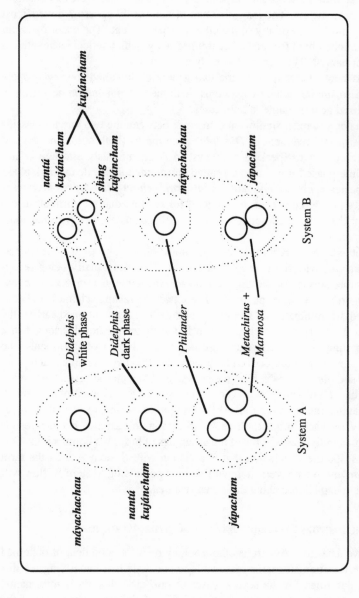

Figure 5.4 Diagrammatic representation of two competing systems of classification as exemplified by the Aguaruna conceptualization of four genera of opossums, *Didelphis*, *Philander*, *Metachirus*, and *Marmosa*. (After Berlin and Patton, in prep.)

Considering the case of the barbets, the folk generic categories of both men and women were shown to be closely equivalent, although males were more consistent in their naming responses than females. Likewise, the conceptual treatment of woodpecker species indicate quite similar categorizations, although some individuals (females and younger males) might be labeled as lumpers, treating the biologically polytypic woodpecker species as three monotypic folk generic categories. Older males, however, are splitters in that two of the biologically polytypic genera (*Celeus* and *Phloeoceastes*) are subdivided into four linguistically recognized subgeneric taxa, reflecting their expertise. Males appear to have greater knowledge of some rarely seen and secretive species, such as *Ramphocaenus melanurus*, but this is understandable because of men's greater familiarity with the local avifauna, which is in turn a reflection of their social roles as hunters.

However, no such general and obvious explanations account for the variant classifications found for the opossums. While it seems clear that the responses and various alternative sortings of these animals are patterned in ways that make them easy to describe, possible explanations for the variation observed are not available based on the data that my collaborators and I currently possess. It may be true that the Aguaruna have little need to develop a generally shared conceptual treatment for these animals. Neither *Philander* nor *Didelphis* are considered edible, and because of their nocturnal habits are perhaps rarely seen. However, both of these observations, rather than being legitimate explanations, represent ad hoc speculations lacking empirical support.

All of the examples considered thus far represent cognitive variation between men and women in the conceptualization of folk generic taxa. Differential distribution of ethnobiological knowledge as a factor of one's sex is more clearly demonstrated in the classification of folk specific and varietal taxa, especially species of cultivated plants, as shown in Boster's (1980) monographic research on Aguaruna manioc classification. While the primary emphasis of this work was to describe and explain differential knowledge among women's classification of this important crop, Boster first demonstrated the extent of the sexual cognitive division of labor regarding this species.

In a number of experiments using living specimens of manioc varieties, Boster showed that women consistently exhibited higher overall agreement on the names of varieties than men, noting that the "probability that the disparity between the rankings of men and women could have occurred by chance alone is effectively zero" (Boster 1980:109). Furthermore, some men refused even to participate in his experiments, stating that "it would be senseless to go through the exercise of trying to identify things [that] they knew nothing about" (ibid.). It is possible that something comparable to this extreme sexual division of knowledge about important cultivated plant species accounts in part for the variable naming results obtained by Sillitoe in his research on Wola identification of varieties of sweet potatoes and yams (Sillitoe 1983).

Another factor contributing to variation in naming is contextual (Ellen 1979b:348). This type of variation can also be usefully illustrated by citing Boster's research. In a series of more general naming experiments, Boster asked men and women to identify 102 distinct species of wild and cultivated plants growing along a preselected trail (see Stross 1973 for a similar procedure used in work on Tzeltal ethnobotany). A single manioc plant was included in the naming task. Boster describes how the context influenced the type of naming response obtained from his informants, as follows:

> All but two of the [thirty] male informants identified the manioc variety with [the folk generic term] *máma*. . . . When women were guided in the task by male assistants, seventeen of the twenty-five also identified the manioc with [*máma*], although eight identified it as a kind of *máma*. However, when women were guided by a female assistant, all but one of the seven identified the specimen as a kind of *máma* [the likelihood of this distribution occurring by chance has a p ≤ .0001]. (Boster 1980:54)

Aguaruna women, it seems, are unlikely to offer folk specific names for manioc in response to questions from men since they know that males are ignorant of the facts of the matter. A quite similar observation on the contextual appropriateness of type of response given is often encountered, as well, in the interaction of the ethnobiologist with native collaborators. Bulmer describes his own field experience in this regard:

> [One's informants] initially gear their responses to what they estimate to be the level of the field worker's sophistication. . . . If for example they realise that the field worker is knowledgeable about birds they are unlikely deliberately to hold back information about finer points of ornithological classification. But if they realise that he is an ignoramus they can hardly be expected to volunteer information that in their view he would not understand or appreciate. Thus [I have] been assured by more than one field worker that Highlanders among whom they have worked lump certain bird species in a single taxon (e.g., the common local species of cuckoo-dove, *Macropygia*). . . . In every case [I] inquired into personally the two cuckoo-doves are in fact terminologically distinguished. (Bulmer 1969:11)

Of equal importance to any of the above-mentioned factors leading to variable data in ethnobiological classification are the genuine differences in the distribution of particular species throughout some local flora or fauna as a reflection of differential ecological regions or zones in the environment. Berlin, Breedlove, and Raven (1974) found that many of the variant classifications of plant species among the Tzeltal are most likely explained by such ecologically based factors. A simple case will illustrate this point.

There are at least seven locally occurring species of butterfly bushes, *Buddleia* spp., in the municipality occupied by the Tenejapa Tzeltal. These species are unequally distributed throughout the area, with many occurring in the colder regions of 7,000 feet elevation, and fewer species occurring in the warmer areas below 3,500 feet elevation. In addition, two species, *B. skutchii* and *B. crotonoides*, are more abundant than the remaining taxa. Table 5.9 presents Tzeltal naming responses for the seven *Buddleia* spp. Some species are said to be "true exemplars" of the taxon while others are said to be "like or similar to true exemplars."[6] Table 5.9 reveals two stable folk generic taxa, *sak baj te'* lit. 'white-faced tree' (because of its bicolored leaves, the lower surface being strikingly gray-white in appearance) and *tzel pat te'* lit. 'angle-bark tree' (because of the squarish stems typical of this species). Informants from lower elevations recognize but a single folk generic taxon for the group with its focus on *Buddleia skutchii*. All remaining species are thought to be related to the prototype (*kol pajaluk sok sak baj te'*) but are not true members of the class. Informants from the colder areas, however, recognize another folk genus in addition to *sak baj te'*, *B. crotonoides* (the prototype) and *B. parviflora* as *tzel pat te'*, as seen in figure 5.5.

These two variant forms of categorization are most likely due to straightforward ecological considerations. *B. crotonoides* is poorly distributed in the warmer regions of the municipality and informants from this area do not commonly see it. In the colder habitats, *B. skutchii* and *B. crotonoides* are ob-

TABLE 5.9
Tzeltal Naming Responses for All Locally Occurring Species of Butterfly Bushes *Buddleia* spp. (slightly modified after Berlin, Breedlove, and Raven 1974:233–236)

	sak baj te'	*'Similar to' sak baj te'*	*tzel pat te'*
Buddleia skutchii	12	3	
B. americana	2	4	
B. nitida	1	1	
B. amplexicaulis	1	2	
B. sessiflora	1		
B. crotonoides		9	6
B. parviflora		1	
Vernonia leiocarpa		3	

Note: Numbers indicate individual botanical specimens identified at the time of collection.

6 The Tzeltal use of the term *batz'il* 'true, genuine' in these cases is not to be confused with the use of the attributive as it occurs as a modifier of subgeneric names, e.g., *batz'il iw* 'prototypical subgeneric taxon of the generic taxon *iw*' (*Persea* sp.), in contrast with *koyol iw* 'elongated fruited *iw*' (*Persea* sp.). In the case under discussion, the expression 'true' is used to distinguish those species that are thought to be prototypical exemplars of a folk generic taxon from species that are conceptually related but not full members of that named class. Laughlin (pers. comm.; Laughlin and Breedlove, in press) independently reports identical classificatory behavior among the Zinacantán Tzotzil, where the comparable phrase *yit'ix X* 'bastard X', in contrast to *batz'il X* 'genuine X', is quite commonly employed.

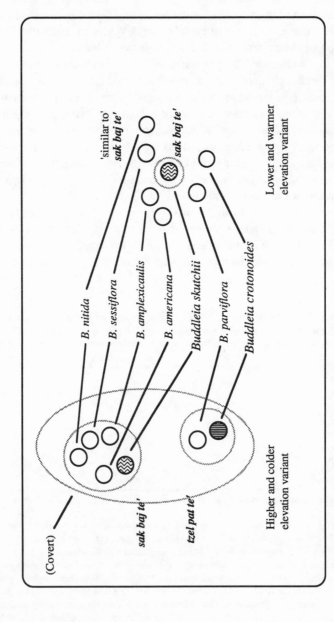

Figure 5.5 Diagrammatic representation of Tzeltal categorization of *Buddleia* spp., indicating two ecologically constrained variants apparently due to the differential distribution of the respective species.

served regularly, and their differences in leaf coloration (one strongly bicolored, the other only weakly so) contrast markedly.

Although there are a number of other important factors underlying the variation that emerges from the responses of informants in ethnobiological classification research (see especially the detailed discussions in Hays 1974 and Boster 1980), I will close this section by focusing on a factor that has not been given as much emphasis as it deserves. This is what Ellen appropriately calls "methodological indeterminacy." To what extent does the variation discovered reveal significant differences in the ways that one's informants classify plants and animals rather than "carelessness or oversight on the part of the ethnographer or weaknesses in the techniques employed" (Ellen 1979b:354)?

I will not attempt to address the issue of the degree to which investigators take seriously their research as fieldworkers and aim to minimize careless data collection. It is worthwhile to consider briefly, however, variation introduced as a reflection of the inadequacy of one's data-collection techniques. Consider, for example, the following case, pertaining once again to the Aguaruna classification of birds.

Our investigations reveal that, in addition to the differences in classification already described, a substantial number of bird species appear to be unknown to females, at least as measured by the types of naming experiments described above. The example of the long-billed gnatwren was one such case. But how is one to deal with data collected in the naming experiments that relate to the classification of the common and highly distinctive *Lipaugus vociferans*, the screaming piha? The naming responses for two well-prepared specimens of this bird are given in table 5.10. The table indicates that some males and proportionally many more females confuse *Lipaugus vociferans* with bird species that it resembles superficially, *saiyáng* (*Saltator maximus*), the buff-throated saltator, and *tututáng* (*Coccyzus melocoryphus*), the dark-billed cuckoo. Nonetheless, the large majority of men unambiguously recognize the screaming piha as *páipainch* (thirty-eight independent identifications). However, this term is never used by Aguaruna females as a naming response to either specimens of *Lipaugus* or specimens presented in *any* of the three bird-naming experiments.

On the basis of these data alone one might conclude that females lack a folk generic category for this species altogether. Such a conclusion, however, seems highly unlikely given the ubiquitous presence of the screaming piha in the area. By simply stepping into the forest on any day, one cannot avoid hearing the screamer's distinctive calls. Its name is an unambiguous onomatopoeic derivation of its cry [uweá uweá—**pái páich áa**—uweá, uweá—**pái páich áa**], characterized by de Schauensee as a "very loud three-note call preceded by [a] low gurgling sound unmistakable when once heard" (1970:269). Women (as well as all other informants) would likely be able to name the species unambiguously were they provided the added stimulus of

TABLE 5.10

Distribution of Naming Responses to Three Specimens of the Screaming Piha (*Lipaugus vociferans*) in Aguaruna Naming Experiments (see text for explanation)

	Sex	No.	Sex	No.
Most common terms				
páipainch	m	38	f	0
saiyág	m	2	f	2
tututáng	m	6	f	4
No knowledge or unique terms				
?	m	8	f	6
ikáncham			f	2
kuíntam			f	1
ukúnchkit	m	1		
ukúntuch	m	1		
suwísh	m	1		
wisuí			f	1
yukupáu			f	1

hearing a recording of its call (a technique employed productively by Jensen 1988 in his work among the Wayampí, and one that needs to be more widely applied). The methods used in the naming experiments, then, if limited as they were to the simple presentation of the prepared museum skins, are not always adequate to capture individuals' ethnobiological knowledge of even the most common species. Similar observations could be made on the identification of amphibians known first by their distinctive calls and perhaps only rarely seen.

For those species whose identification is largely visual, the use of photographs and drawings offset in part the problems associated with the distortions that occur with the presentation of stuffed skins. This is particularly relevant in data collection for mammals and the larger birds whose natural appearance is radically altered when these species are prepared as museum specimens.

Nonetheless, on the whole it is clear that, in spite of these drawbacks, common cultural patterns in the application of names for plants and animals in systems of ethnobiological classification emerge from careful and serious work with a substantial number of informants. Given that the experimental procedures employed are surely less than satisfactory, it seems likely that their imperfection would contribute to obscure rather than reveal patterns. That clear-cut patterns can be ascertained in spite of the inadequacy of the methods used implies a great deal about the strength of the biological order underlying, and reflected in, our informants' cognitive systems.

Not even the most pessimistic researchers would deny that patterns emerge from the morass of data collected in the course of fieldwork. The analysis of these patterns and the search for the explanations that best account for them are nevertheless subject to the margin of approximation and indeterminacy that, as Ellen has pointed out, will always be present for any ethnobiological description. A good approximation, however, is better than none, and as ethnobiological methods continue to be refined, our approximations will get even better.

CHAPTER SIX

Manchúng and *Bíkua*: The Nonarbitrariness of Ethnobiological Nomenclature

Nomina debent naturae rerum congruere.

—St. Thomas Aquinas

In establishing a harmony between a thing and its name, we conform to a psychic habit as old as humanity.

—J. Vendryès, *Language*, 1925

TAKE ANOTHER LOOK at the line drawings in figure 6.1. These are rough approximations of the drawings used in a famous experiment on sound symbolism described several decades ago by the great German gestalt psychologist Wolfgang Köhler (1929). In the study, subjects were asked to look at the drawings and to assign the nonsense words, *takete* and *maluma*, to the figure they thought most appropriate to each term. All of the subjects, and I predict the reader of this monograph as well, invariably paired the nonsense word *takete* with the sharp, angular figure and *maluma* with that drawn with free-flowing circular lines. While this appears to be so obvious as to at first merit little reflection, psychologists, linguists, philosophers, and even poets and literary critics, have struggled for years to develop an adequate theoretical explanation to account for this and similar phenomena.

My aim in this chapter is to relate some recent research in the general area of sound symbolism to the more specific issue of the nature of ethnobiological nomenclature, especially the nomenclature associated with taxa of generic rank. The general proposal that I will attempt to develop in the first part of the

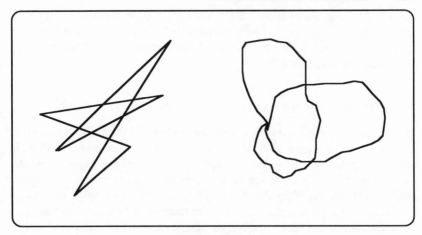

Figure 6.1 Geometric figure after Wolfgang Köhler's description of an experiment in sound symbolism.

chapter is a simple one: that the sounds that make up the generic names for creatures in folk biological systems of classification are often associated with their referents in a way that is less arbitrary than linguists generally believe to be the case in sound-to-meaning correspondences. The phonetic composition of terms for creatures, *qua* labels for living things, often reflect some aspect of the inherent qualities of the organisms being named, and, thus, serve as a useful mnemonic for the speaker in the cognitive management of a rather extensive ethnobiological lexicon.

The second part of the chapter will explore a similar theme as it relates to the nomenclature of plants, as well as that of animals. It will be suggested that many folk generic names are metaphorically descriptive of some features of the plant or animal species to which they are applied, this too serving as a useful semantic aid to memory.

The general inspiration behind these ideas is not new. There is a rich literature on the nature of sound symbolism as it relates to the origin of language, much of it verging on the edge of sheer fantasy (see especially Rosman 1982). Works specifically aimed at tracing the etymologies of terms for plants and animals in an equally speculative vein can be seen in the popular book by Potter and Sargent (1974).

It is not my goal to address the difficult topics associated with etymology or language change, although these issues must ultimately be examined if a more comprehensive understanding of the processes described here is to be attained. My more modest aim is to provide some synchronic data, from present-day ethnozoological and ethnobotanical lexicons, which suggest that a good portion, perhaps more than half, of the generic nomenclature employed in ethnobiological systems of classification is semantically transparent. This transparency draws on the productive features of the lexical semantics of language as well as the unconscious psychological associations of sound and meaning in human language generally.

6.1 EARLY EXPERIMENTS ON SOUND SYMBOLISM

It is important to place the presentation that I will make shortly in its historical context, even by means of an overly brief review. As Jakobson and Waugh succinctly put it, sound symbolism appears to be for human beings an innate recognition of the "natural similarity association between sound and meaning" (Jakobson and Waugh 1979:178). Sapir, to whom the systematic study of this association can be traced, at least for research in America, characterizes the phenomenon as "the expressively symbolic character of sounds quite aside from what the words in which they occur mean in a referential sense" (Sapir 1929:225).

Experimental research in the area can be assigned to two primary types, *analytic* studies and *word-matching* experiments (see I. K. Taylor 1963; Taylor and Taylor 1965, 1967). The so-called analytic studies generally require subjects either to match arbitrary nonsense words with visual stimuli (such as Köhler's drawings), or to make some semantic judgments about pairs of nonsense words in terms of one or several dimensions of connotative meaning.

Sapir's classic study on phonetic symbolism is an example of this latter class of experiments. Briefly, Sapir (1929) told subjects that two nonsense words, *mil* and *mal*, were the names of tables, and then asked them to state which name indicated the larger table. Subjects invariably chose *mal*. In an earlier experiment, Sapir asked subjects to associate the "imaginary words" *la*, *law*, and *li* with three tables of different size. Sapir claims "practically 100% success" with *li* meaning 'small table', *law* 'meaning 'large table', and *la* meaning 'middle-sized table', "a table *par excellence*" (Jakobson and Waugh 1979:185). Results of these early studies clearly show that certain sensations of relative size are regularly associated with vowel quality.

The second type of studies in sound symbolism, the so-called word-matching experiments, requires subjects to match pairs of real words from natural languages with denotatively equivalent words in some second, unknown language. The pairs of words utilized in these studies have almost invariably been antonyms.

An example of such an experiment can be found in the the the sets of expressions used in a study I conducted several years ago (Berlin 1976b). The instructions to subjects were as follows:

Listed below are a series of words from a Mayan language and from English. English words appear above the Mayan terms. Please match each of the two English words in each series with the Mayan word below it that you believe most likely represents the same meaning in English.

1)	long	short	2)	large	small
	nahtil	komol		ch'in	muk'ul
3)	broad	slender	4)	far	near
	silil	pamal		k'ubul	tihil
5)	intelligent	dumb	6)	flattened	wrinkled
	bolol	p'ihil		lechel	much'il

Several such sets were presented and results showed that subjects were able to make the correct matches in approximately 70 percent of the cases.

In spite of a number of justified criticisms of the experimental methods employed in studies using antonymic pairs (e.g., not employing native speakers to pronounce the words, not controlling adequately for the native languages of the subjects), the overall results show that subjects are able to match antonyms in a language they do not know with ones in a language they do know with much better than chance accuracy (see R. Brown and Nuttall 1959 and a large number of other experiments in this tradition reviewed by Jakobson and Waugh 1979).

While linguists and psycholinguists have accepted, at times grudgingly, these findings for antonymic pairs, there has never been any real support for the notion that sound symbolism might be a more widespread phenomenon, infecting, as it were, the lexicon of whole semantic domains. For such to be the case does not square well at all with modern linguistics textbook ideology on the arbitrariness of the association of sound and meaning in languages generally. (Recall the standard introductory linguistics-class example where one is instructed on the arbitrariness principle by comparing the words for *dog* in French, Chinese, and some other exotic language, and the professor asking rhetorically for some luckless soul in the class to propose an explanation for the linguistic facts based on sound symbolism.) Nonetheless, there is some evidence, admittedly scarce at the moment, that indicates the need for some qualification of this traditional view. It is to this evidence that I now turn.

6.2 ETHNOBIOLOGICAL SOUND SYMBOLISM IN HUAMBISA: BIRDS AND FISH

Join me in a short experiment. The following list of fifteen pairs of words are real names for birds and fish from a language spoken by a population of Indians of the Peruvian rain forest. In each pair, one word is the name of a fish and the other the name of a bird. Read each of the words aloud to yourself, and check the term in each pair that you believe sounds like the name of a bird. For help in pronunciation, keep in mind that the vowels are as in Spanish, with the exception that [e] is roughly like the last vowel in "ethnobiologist" (technically, the mid-unrounded central vowel represented as ɨ, "barred i"). The diacritic ['] indicates the stressed syllable in each word. Keep a record of your results for the discussion that follows.

1. chunchuíkit	máuts	9. yákakua	kasháikunim
2. chichikía	katán	10. tsútsum	wichíkuat
3. terés	takáikit	11. tukímp	kárnir
4. yawarách	tuíkcha	12. iyáchi	ápup
5. waíkia	kanúskin	13. tsárur	wáuk
6. kanímu	makakít	14. áau	tsapáum
7. chawít	kángka	15. wahák	apúp
8. katísh	waíkiach	16. táwai	kúmar

These sixteen pairs of terms, as well as thirty-four other sets, were used to conduct a larger experiment several years ago with six hundred University of California undergraduates. The set of fifty pairs was drawn randomly from the relatively complete inventories of simple bird and fish names collected during the conduct of ethnobiological research among the Huambisa, the Jivaroan population to which I have referred repeatedly in prior chapters.

All terms used in the experiment were unitary in their linguistic structure, i.e., they were linguistically analogous to words such as *robin, jay, crappie*, and *bass*. Linguistically complex words structurally analogous to compounds such as *mocking bird, king fisher, sting ray*, and *gold fish* were excluded from the sample. There are 175 linguistically simple names for birds in Huambisa and 85 such names for fish. The complete set of fifty pairs of terms used in the experiment is seen in table 6.1. They were typed as a randomly organized list and presented as a small pamphlet of three pages. As with the brief experiment in which the reader was asked to participate, students were told that each pair consisted of a bird name and a fish name, and that they were asked to select the term that they thought most likely to be the bird name in each pair. I then read the list, pronouncing each pair of terms twice. The whole experiment required approximately ten minutes to administer.

Analysis of the results of this simple experiment indicate that the Berkeley students were able to correctly select the name of a bird in each pair in 58 percent of the cases. This level of accuracy is not high, but is much higher than chance given the large number of individual comparisons involved.

What might account for the above findings? An obvious first clue is suggested by a linguistic analysis of those pairs of names where much higher than chance results were achieved. There are twenty-nine such pairs, with ranges of accuracy from a high of 98 percent to those just a bit higher than chance. The first sixteen pairs, with accuracy scores ranging from 98 percent through about 72 percent, are those chosen for the short experiment in which the reader was invited to participate at the beginning of this chapter. All of these twenty-nine pairs, rank ordered by their accuracy scores, are seen as table 6.2.

From a quick perusal of the test items, one might be led to think (as I did)

TABLE 6.1

Pairs of Huambisa Bird and Fish Names Used in Word-matching Experiment (see text for explanation)

1. chunchuíkit	máuts	26. kungkuí	chantsém
2. katísh	waikiách	27. kanímu	makakít
3. weáhai	tsakanána	28. hinumánch	sécha
4. taúsh	wáncha	29. kúpi	yuwímas
5. yákakua	kashíkunim	30. wahák	hápatar
6. súngka	maparátu	31. sánti	pútu
7. iyáchi	ápup	32. shári	étsa
8. shúwi	úushap	33. kunángket	pinínch
9. kántut	shingkián	34. táwai	kúmar
10. tsútsum	wichíkuat	35. kumpáu	shíru
11. pítsa	champerám	36. kunángkit	ungkuchák
12. wáikia	kanúskin	37. shanáshna	nukúmp
13. máchikan	isíp	38. titím	kuíntam
14. huitám	mamayák	39. tingkísh	káashap
15. píshi	páni	40. yasáng	kuntsít
16. chuíntam	suiyám	41. paumít	kíatsa
17. tampirúsh	sukuyá	42. chichikía	katán
18. tsárur	wáuk	43. tukímp	kánir
19. chíimpa	waunchíp	44. terés	takáikit
20. chúwi	tséep	45. áau	tsapáum
21. wapurús	yúsa	46. máshu	tsapakúsh
22. chawít	kángka	47. ispík	sháip
23. pirísh	kúum	48. tuukía	yantsahíp
24. yawarách	tuíkcha	49. púwa	aúnts
25. chanúngkerap	ímia	50. cháke	yáuch

that bird names are generally longer than fish names, and that people selected the correct name on this basis. Actually, bird and fish names are of comparable length when the total inventories for each domain are examined (see below). If there is a major difference, bird names differ from fish names in the somewhat greater proportion of monosyllabic terms for birds. Twenty-three single-syllable bird names compare with but three single-syllable fish names. Fifty-two percent of bird names are bisyllabic, closely comparable to the 61 percent of bisyllabic fish terms. The two lexicons are essentially identical in the relative distribution of three- and four-syllable expressions.

A closer look at the phonetic composition of those terms showing high levels of accuracy reveals a greater proportion of *high front vowels* in bird names than in fish names. Almost three-fourths (or 72 percent) of the bird names recognized with greater than chance accuracy include the high front vowel [i] in one or more syllables. The contrasting fish names in these pairs differ markedly. Less than half of them (44 percent) contain syllables with vowel [i].

TABLE 6.2
Twenty-nine Pairs of Huambisa Bird and Fish Names Used in Sound Symbolism Experiment, Rank Ordered by Accuracy Scores ≥ .50 (see text for explanation)

1. *chunchuíkit*	mauts (98%)
2. *chichikía*	katán (95%)
3. terés	*takáikit* (94%)
4. yawarách	*tuíkcha* (92%)
5. *waíkia*	kanúskin (89%)
6. kanímu	*makakít* (87%)
7. *chawít*	kángka (86%)
8. katísh	*waíkiach* (84%)
9. *yákakua*	kasháikunim (83%)
10. tsútsum	*wichíkuat* (82%)
11. *tukímp*	kárnir (79%)
12. *iyáchi*	ápup (78%)
13. tsárur	*wáuk* (77%)
14. áau	tsapáum (74%)
15. *wahák*	jápatar (78%)
16. *táwai*	kúmar (72%)
17. *chuíntam*	suiyám (70%)
18. *tingkísh*	káashap (73%)
19. kunángket	*pinínch* (67%)
20. *túukia*	yantsahíp (64%)
21. *kántut*	shingkián (65%)
22. kumpáu	*shíru* (65%)
23. *píshi*	páni (65%)
24. *kúpi*	yuwímas (59%)
25. kunángkit	*ungkuchák* (57%)
26. *weáhai*	tsakanána (53%)
27. paumít	*kiátsa* (53%)
28. *pirísh*	kúum (51%)
29. *chúwi*	tséep (51%)

Note: Correct answers in italics.

There is, furthermore, a remarkable distinction in the *syllabic distribution* of vowel [i] in bird and fish names in these pairs. Almost half of the bird names recognized with 58 percent or greater accuracy exhibits vowel [i] in the first syllable. In contrast, only two of the twenty-nine names for fish in these same pairs are formed with [i] in the first syllable. Fish names distinctly favor another first-syllable vowel, the low central vowel [a]. More than 55 percent of fish names in this set are formed in this manner.

Could it be that bird names are marked for [i] and that fish names are marked for [a], and, if this is the case, what is so birdlike about [i] and so fishy about [a]? In order to answer the first question, the full inventories of 175 bird and 85 fish names were examined to determine if the pattern seen in the test sample continued to hold for the complete Huambisa ethnoornithological and ethnoichthyological vocabulary.

Possible Factors at Work

Figure 6.2 displays the relative distribution of initial syllabic vowels for the complete inventory of Huambisa bird and fish names. The generalization suggested by the terms in the experimental inventory appears to hold: [i] is definitely more favored in the first syllable of bird names (33 percent of the full inventory), while names for fish markedly appear to avoid this vowel in the same position (fewer than 8 percent of fish names are formed with first syllable [i]). By contrast, 54 percent of fish names exhibit the central vowel [a] as the vocalic segment of the initial syllable, as compared to 36 percent in bird names.

A number of other important differences can be noted about the names for animals in these two zoological domains. Considering the full Huambisa vocabularies for both birds and fish, one observes that the obstruents [p], [t], [ts], [ch], and [k] occur as word-initial segments with about equal frequency. About 50 percent of the bird names takes one of these obstruents as an initial segment, and fish names show only a slightly higher proportion of 56 percent. However, the relative distribution of obstruents of *high acoustic frequency* (acute [p] before [i], [t], [ts], and [ch]) and the obstruent of *low acoustic frequency* (grave [k] before [a], [u], and [e]) is markedly distinct for fish and bird names, as can be seen in figure 6.3. Here we see that the bias toward the acoustically high frequency [i] in bird names is reinforced by the selection of comparable high frequency obstruents, while just the reverse is true for fish names. In the latter case, lower acoustic frequency [a] combines with the low acoustic frequency [k] as the favored sequence of segments.

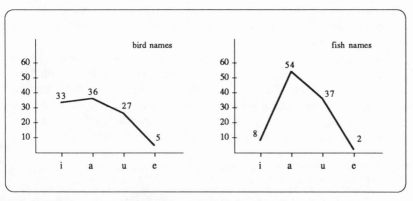

Figure 6.2 Proportional distribution of initial vowels in the complete inventory of linguistically simple names for birds and fishes in Huambisa.

	Relatively high	Relatively low
Bird names	(p = 12 before i) t = 16 ts = 7 ch = 20	(p = 11 before a, u) k = 20
Fish names	t = 3 ts = 6 ch = 4	p = 6 k = 29

p ≤ .0001, Fisher's Exact Test

Figure 6.3 Distribution of initial obstruents by relative acoustic frequency for all linguistically simple Huambisa bird (N = 86) and fish (N = 48) names. The vowel [i] occurs only once in fish names as the initial vowel segment of names that begin with one of the nonnasal obstruents.

Nasals also show distinctive distributional patterns in terms for fish and birds. More than 40 percent of the eighty-five fish names shows nasal stops in word-final position, either as the final segment or as the initial segment of the final syllable. In contrast, only 17 percent of the total inventory of bird names shows such a pattern for final nasals.

Furthermore, in comparison with birds, 18 percent of the fish names have continuants ([s], [sh], and [r]) as final consonants, while a meager 8 percent of the bird names show this pattern. On the other hand, about one-third of the bird names show word-final obstruents. The corresponding figure for fish names is 15 percent.

Finally, while a quarter of the fish names end with open syllables, nearly half of the bird names are so formed (49 percent). These contrasting distributional phonetic features allow one to build some expectations as to the prototypical shapes of bird and fish names in Huambisa. The two pairs of terms receiving the highest accuracy scores on the word-matching experiment come close to these prototypes: *chunchuíkit—máuts* and *chichikía—katán*.

6.3 Universal Sound Symbolism or Simple Onomatopoeia?

The striking phonetic differences in the composition of Huambisa bird and fish names suggest a number of possible interpretations. Experimental evidence indicates that certain sensations (movement, size, texture) are associated with the acoustic qualities of specific sound segments of natural languages. Jespersen provides evidence that the concept of 'quickness' is widely associated with front vowels, and [i] is the most productive in this regard, for example, Danish *kvik, livlig*, Swedish *pigg*, French *vite, vif, rapide*, Italian *vispo*, Japanese *kirikiri* (Jespersen 1933:299).

Swadesh has pointed out that the meaning association of the low central vowel [a] is "for something that moves on and on" (Swadesh 1970:114). Swadesh also contrasts the sound-symbolic association of voiceless obstruents such as [ts], [ch] with concepts such as 'sharp' as well as the abstract concept of 'rapid movement', both of which contrast with the 'heavy' and 'slow' continuity of nasal sounds.

The Huambisa data seem to suggest that, at least in this language, ethnozoological nomenclature linguistically marks the contrast of angular avian agility with smooth and continuous piscine flow. A universalist perspective would account for these associations in terms of abstract sound symbolism in Sapir's sense, or as Ohala would put it, "sound/meaning correlations where the meaning does not seem to be one that is capable of imitation by speech sounds" (Ohala 1983:5).

An alternative interpretation would suggest that the data are better understood as a result of simple onomatopoeia. In this view, the names of particular animals are simply human phonetic representations of the sounds that these organisms emit. Jespersen referred to such terms as 'echoic words' in that "the echoic word designates the being that produces the sound" (Jespersen 1964[1921]:399).

It is true that onomatopoeia plays a large role in Huambisa ornithological vocabulary. Berlin and O'Neill (1981) tape-recorded 206 Huambisa bird names and the corresponding human vocalizations of the birds' calls, and found that 34 percent of these names were onomatopoeic in origin. The disproportionate presence of [i] in Huambisa bird names might be interpreted primarily as onomatopoeia, which would in turn account for the higher than chance results of the word-matching experiment. Following this line of reasoning, my colleague Paul Kay, on first hearing several pairs of bird and fish names, exclaimed: "Oh, yeah, the bird names are the ones that go 'tweet-tweet'." Dwight Bolinger, after having read an earlier draft of this paper, made a similar observation: "Listen for onomatopoeia and what you will hear, when birds are concerned, will be high sounds" (Bolinger, pers. comm.).

Like most good intuitions, these observations contain some truth. While a substantial number of bird names of onomatopoeic origin are indeed formed with [i], many other onomatopoeic names are formed exclusively with vowels [a] and [u], as seen in table 6.3. Here we see that Huambisa takes full advantage of its low central and back vowels in the production of onomatopoeic bird names. Clearly, some other factors in addition to simple onomatopoeia appear to be at work in the folk ornithological lexicon and, as will be seen shortly, in

TABLE 6.3
Examples of Onomatopoeic Huambisa Bird Names Formed with Vowels [a] or [u]

Scientific Name	Huambisa Name	Vocalization*
Daptrius ater	shanáshna	[shá.shá.shá]
Ortalis guttata	wakáts	[wakatará, wakatará]
Aburria pipile	kúyu	[kúyu.kúyu.kúyu]
Opisthocomus hoazin	sāsā	[sā.sā.sā.sā.sā]
Aramides cajanea	kunchár	[kunchár.kunchár]
Ara manilata	kāyāk	[kiák.kiák.kiák.kiák]
Amazona ochrocephala	awarmás	[áura.áura.áura]
Crotophaga ani	kuákua	[sak. au. kúR]
Nyctibius aethereus	autám	[aúu. aúu. aúu]
N. griseus	aúju	[áuhu.áuhu.áuhu]
Trogon viridis	táwai	[táta.tá.tá.tá.tá.tá]
Ceryle torquata	tarásh	[tarásh. tarásh. tarásh]
Baryphthengus ruficapillus	yukúru	[hu.rú. hu.rú]
Bucco capensis	maukáatarar	[mo.ka.ta.rár]
Capito aurovirens	púr	[púrrr. púrrr. púrrr]
Pteroglossus flavirostris	kakarpát	[kár.kat.kár.kat.kár.kat]

* Linguistic representation of onomatopoeic vocalizations employs a practical orthography and only roughly approximates the actual phonetic qualities of the calls.

the fish lexicon as well. I suggest that one possible factor is abstract *size-sound symbolism*.

Of all the synaesthetic associations of sound and meaning, size-sound symbolism is perhaps the best established, building on Sapir's 1929 experiment and even earlier work (see Tolman 1887, 1904, historical sources courtesy of D. Bolinger). Ohala summarizes the acoustic parameters of size-sound symbolism as follows:

> Words denoting or connoting SMALL or SMALLNESS . . . tend to exhibit a disproportionate incidence of vowels and/or consonants characterized by high acoustic frequency. Words denoting or connoting LARGE use segments with low acoustic frequency. In consonants, voiceless obstruents have higher frequency than voiced because of the higher velocity of the airflow, ejectives higher than plain stops . . . and dental, alveolar, palatal and front velars higher than labials and back velars. In the case of vowels, high front vowels have higher F2 and low back vowels the lowest F2. (Ohala 1984:9)

If vowel quality plays a systematic part in abstract size-sound symbolism, it should be possible to test such an association quantitatively, provided that a standard metric be available. Fortunately, for birds, just such a metric (average length from beak to tail) has been recorded for all of the major species of birds in South America (de Schauensee 1970). The association of length (size) and vowel quality for the total inventory of 175 Huambisa bird names is shown on the left of figure 6.4. On the right, one finds the association of length and vowel quality for the extreme ends of the continuum. In both tests, the association of [i] with relative size of bird species is strongly confirmed.

Onomatopoeia and size-sound symbolism could, and probably do, work hand in hand, of course. As Kay might now respond, "O.K., so it's the *small* birds that go 'tweet-tweet'." Notice in fact the significantly higher number of bird names with [i] versus all other vowels (65 percent) in the top half of figure 6.4, namely denoting those birds that are 10 inches in length or less.

However, in examining bird names formed with [i], one finds that only about *half* of them are onomatopoetically derived, as seen from the list of terms given in table 6.4. These data clearly suggest that onomatopoeia alone cannot account for the association of size and vowel quality. A distinction is made here between *imitation* and *onomatopoeia*. Imitation is an effort to represent the sounds of audible events (e.g., the call of an animal) by whistling, humming, grunting, hissing, smacking, or clicking (cf. the whistled rendition of the call of the bobwhite quail, *Colinus virginianus*) and *onomatopoeia*. Onomatopoeia refers to efforts to represent the call of some audible event (e.g., the call of an animal) by employing the resources of the regular speech sounds of an individual's language, in combination with such paralinguistic processes as stress, intonation, tempo, and vocalic quality. An *onomatopoetic vocalization* of a particular animal's call and the name of that animal may be related

	Vowel quality			
	[i]	[e, a, u]	[i]	[e, a, u]
≤10"	60	32	≤7" 37	16
≥11"	35	48	14 ≥15"	30
	p = ≤ .001		p ≤ .0001	

Figure 6.4 Association of length of bird species and vowel quality in Huambisa ornithological lexicon

TABLE 6.4

Huambisa Bird Names Exhibiting Vowel [i] for Species ≤10 Inches in Length and
Their Approximate Human Vocalizations

Scientific Name	Size (inches)	Huambisa Name	Vocalization
Myrmotherula obscura	3.2	*chunchuíkit	[chí.chi.chí.chi]; voiceless, starts slowly, builds to rapid peak
Pipra coronata	3.2	*wisham	[whispered whistle]
Pipra pipra	4.0	*kaawia	No call
Sporphila sp.	4.2	*shaíp	[tsúng.tsúng.tsúng]
Cyanerpes spp.	4.2	*jimpíkit	[tsíp.tsíp.tsíp.tsíp]
Hylophalax naevia	4.2	pishipísh	[písh.pish.písh.pish]
Myrmotherula axilaris	4.2	kiátsa	[kiátsa.kiátsa.kiátsa]
Hypocnemis hypoxantha	4.0	*wakíach	[whistled imitation only]
Microcerculus marginatus	4.5	tingkísh	[tí.ti.ti.tí.ti.ti.tí.ti.ti]
Forpus xanthopterygius	6.0	nuínuí	[núi.nui.nui. núi.nui.nui]
Chlorophanes spiza	6.0	*ukúnchkit	[tsíng.tsíng.tsíng.tsíng]
Atticora spp.	6.0	*shúrpip	[mbís.mbís.mbís.mbís]
Glyphorynchus spirurus	6.5	*tushimp	[tsí.tsi.tsi]; voiceless
Thamnophilus schistaceus	6.5	chichikía	[chichikía.chichikía]
Chaetura spp.	6.0	*chiním	[shí.shi.shí.shi.shí.shi]
Icterus croconotus	6.0	juitám	[huí.huí huí.huí.huí]
Veniliornis passerinus	6.0	*nái	[kí.kí.kí.kí.kí.kí]
Touit huetii	6.0	shai	[shái.shái.shái]
Eubucco bourcierii	6.5	tíwa	[tí.wa.tí.wa.tí.wa]
Piranga rubra	6.5	píchurkik	[píchurkik.píchurkik]
Hoploxypterus cayanus	6.5	*tuentuí	No call
Formicarius colma	6.0	*chiwachíng	[pá.pi.re.re.re.re]
Laterallus melanophaius	6.0	*shíru	No call
Attila spadiceus	6.0	ukurpíp	[kuru.ku.pí.pí.pí.pí]
Grallaria dignissina	6.0	wíahai	No data
Tringa solitaria	6.0	*kiángkia	No call
Formicarius analis	6.1	tukímp	[tekímp.tekímp.tekímp]
Cymbilaimus lineatus	6.2	*tseretsíng	[whistled imitation]
Automolus spp.	6.5	*kuíntam	[chip.chip.twa.rú]
Actitis macularia	6.5	*piampía	[suí.suí suí.suí.suí.suí]
Pitylus grossus	6.5	*wichíkuat	[pis.pis.pisáá]
Capito niger	6.5	*takáikit	[tuntú. tuntú. tuntú]
Brotogeris cyanoptera	8.0	chimp	[chirím.chirím.chirím]
Icterus chrysocephalus	8.0	pikít	No information
Laniocera hypopyrrha	8.5	chíntam	[chuí.chuí.chuí]
Xiphorhynchus guttatus	8.5	*yukaíkua	[tsuá.tsuá.tsuá]
Saltator maximus	8.5	tukía	[tú.tu.tú.tu.tú.tu]
Pionopsitta barrabandi	10.0	muí	[muí.muí.muí.muí.muí]
Pyrrhura picta	10.0	kírus	[kíru.kíru.kíru.kíru]
Geotrygon saphirina	10.0	*pupuí	[whistled imitation]
Falco rifigularis	10.0	tsiártik	[tsi.tsi.tsi.tsi]
Lipaugus vociferans	10.5	páipainch	[kui.kui.pái.páinch.aaa]

Note: Vocalizations of bird calls are rough phonetic transcriptions of taped recordings made by
the author during formal interviews with three Huambisa males in 1979 and 1980 on the Santiago
River, Amazonas, Peru. Entries marked with an * are judged to be nononomatopoeic.

in at least one of two ways: (1) the vocalization may bear no resemblance to the name as in the stereotypic calls of certain domesticated animals, for example, the English vocalizations for the calls of the cat (*meow*), the dog (*woof-woof*), and the pig (*oink-oink*); (2) the vocalization may be similar to the name in that some or all of the speech sound of the name comprise a fragment of the vocalization (cf. the British-English name *cock* (synonym *rooster*) and the call, *cockadoodledoo*, or the name *bobwhite*, which is a complete phonological replication of the call of *Colinus virginianus*.) In the present treatment, a name is not considered to be onomatopoeic unless it can be demonstrated that native speakers, when phonologically vocalizing the name of some animal, produce vocalizations that bear a phonetic resemblance to the name itself. This definition is not shared by most linguists who use considerably more ambiguous and rarely stated criteria in determining whether a particular term shows onomatopoeia.

6.4 COMPARISON WITH OTHER ETHNOORNITHOLOGICAL VOCABULARIES

Are the patterns apparent in Huambisa ornithological nomenclature unique? In an effort to answer this question, I have been gathering data on a number of other languages for which relatively complete ethnoornithological vocabularies are available. Thus far, data from three unrelated languages have been compiled. Two languages are from South America, Wayampí (Tupian) and Apalái (Cariban). These materials are drawn from Jensen (1988). The third language is Tzeltal (Mayan) from southern Mexico (data from Hunn 1977).

The association of vowel quality with bird size in these three languages is given in figure 6.5 (Wayampí and Apalái) and table 6.5 (Tzeltal). In each of these three languages, the association of vowel quality with relative size is

Wayampí				Apalái	
		Vowel quality			
[i], [e]	[a], [o], [u], [I]			[i], [e]	[a], [o], [u], [I]
≤10"	48	18	≤10"	45	15
≥ 11"	35	35	≥ 11"	40	32
	p ≤ .005	[both by Fisher's Exact Test]		p ≤ .03	

Figure 6.5 Distribution of Wayampí (Tupian) and Apalái (Cariban) bird names by length of species and vowel quality. (Data from Jensen 1988)

TABLE 6.5

Distribution of Tzeltal Bird Names by Length of Species and Vowel Quality (data from Hunn 1977)

Name	Length (inches)	Scientific Name	Name	Length (inches)	Scientific Name
Stems with [i], [e]			Stems with [a], [o], [u]		
≤ 9 inches					
			tz'unun	3.5	'hummingbirds'
			xlux	5	*Catharus aurantii-rostris*
chayin	5	*Vireo flavoviridis*	xpurowok	7	*Scardafella* sp.
ulich	5	'swallows'	solsol	7	*Melozone biarcuatum*
xmayil	5	*Seiurus* spp.	x'ub	8	*Colinus virginianus*
p'itp'it	5	*Empidonax* spp.	k'orochoch	8	*Melanerpes formicivorus*
xch'ijt	5	*Vermivora* spp.	ot'ot'	9	*Amblycercus holosericeus*
chonchiw	6	*Zonotrichia capensis*			
toytoy	6	*Glaucidium* spp.			
wirin	7	'flycatchers' (in part)			
sik'	7	'swifts'			
k'usin	7	*Atlaptetes albinucha*			
tzokoy	7	*Campylorhynchus zonatus*			
kulkulina	8	*Agelaius phoeniceus*			
chochowit	8	*Saltator coerulescens*			
xch'e	8	*Dumetella carolinensis*			
k'owex[a]	8	*Pipilo erythrophthalmus*			
chiboriáno[b]	8	*Sturnella magna*			
tz'ijtil	8	*Dendrocopos villosus*			
purkuwich	9	*Caprimulgus vociferus*			
ti'	9	*Centurus aurifrons*			
≥ 10 inches					
			toht	9.5	*Turdus* sp.
			tukut	10	*Colaptes auratus*
chulin	10	*Melanotis hypoleucus*	kurunkuts	10.5	*Ottus* spp.
pu'kuy	11	*Nyctidromus albicollis*	stzumut	11	'doves'

TABLE 6.5 (*Cont.*)

Name	Length (inches)	Scientific Name	Name	Length (inches)	Scientific Name
Stems with [i], [e]			Stems with [a], [o], [u]		
			puyuch'	11	*Pionus* sp.
liklik	10.5	*Falco sparverius*	k'uk'	11	*Trogon* spp.
wanchil	10.5	*Dives dives*	xkuj	14	*Ciccaba virgata*
chiktawilon[b]	11	*Crypturellus*	xoch'	14.5	*Tyto alba*
		cinnamomeus	kutzukutz	16	*Momotus momota*
tuntzerek'[a]	12	*Dryocopus lineatus*	x'uman	18.5	*Geococcyx velox*
peya'[a]	17	*Psilorhinus morio*	pan	16–18	'toucans'
ch'ekek[a]	24	*Penelopina nigra*	jojkot	22.5	*Ortalis vetula*
xulem[a]	24	*Cathartes aura*	tza'los	24	*Coragyps atratus*
usel[a]	30	*Sarcoramphus papa*	joj	25	*Corvus corax*
			mo'	32	*Ara* spp.
			tuluk'	33–47	*Meleagris gallopavo*

Note: Length represents maximum length in inches for mature adults.
[a] Note possible scaled association of [e] versus [i].
[b] Likely loans from Spanish.
p ≤ .013 by Fisher's Exact Test.

confirmed, although not as strongly as with the Jívaro case, leading to the tentative conclusion that the Huambisa materials are not unique but form part of a wider pattern of sound symbolism found in ethnoornithological lexicons elsewhere.

6.5 FISH, AGAIN

The decisive argument for size-sound symbolism in ethnozoological vocabulary must ultimately be made by reference to animals whose sound-emitting abilities are nonexistent, or at least not auditorily noticeable by human beings. Here I wish to return once again to Huambisa fish. Unlike the case of birds, no standard metric exists for the measurement of the relative 'size' of fish species. (Which is 'larger'? The slender freshwater electric eel or the flat long-tailed stingray?) For want of a standard measurement, I have relied on simple length measurements from our ethnoichthyological research in investigating possible size-sound meaning associations in this domain.

Table 6.6 presents the distribution of Huambisa fish names by length of species and vowel quality for those species for which reliable length measurements could be obtained. Table 6.6 reveals that the patterns of size-sound symbolism observed for ornithological vocabulary appear to hold, as well, for the names of fish in Huambisa. What better names for the small angel fish and the minnowlike *Thoracocharix* than *ispík* and *jinumánch*? Likewise, can the assignment of the terms *tungkáu* and *múta* to the two large free-swimming doradid catfish be totally without psychological motivation?

TABLE 6.6
Distribution of Huambisa Fish Names by Length of Species and Vowel Quality

Name	Length (inches)	Scientific Name	Name	Length (inches)	Scientific Name
		Stems with [i]			Stems with [a], [u], [e]
≤ 10 inches					
íspik	2	Brachychalcinus nummus	kuntsét	3	Rivulus spp.
hinumánch	3	Thoracocharax stellatus	kantásh	4	Aequidens syspihes
kánir	3	Henonomus sp.	kusúm	4	Characidium spp.
kanúskin	3	Paragoniates alburnus	tsapakús	4	Leporinus striatus
yautsaháip	4	Moenkhausia cotinho	tsárur	4	Creagrutus spp.
máchikan	4	Tetragonopterus argenteus	maparátu	4	Centromochlus heckelii
shári	4	Panaque spp.	hápatar	5	Chaetostoma sp. nov.
yuwímas	5	Copeina guttatus	cháke	6	Hypostomus madeirae
kúnchi	5	Pimalotus spp.	mamayák	6	Astyanax spp.
shúwi	6	Lasiancistrus spp.	púwa	8	Microglanis parahybae
nukúmpi	7	Heptapterus sp.	wapurús	8	Cichlasoma bimaculatus
tampirúsh	7	Cynaptomus spp.	tsapáum	8	Triportheus angulatus
paumít	7	Myleus spp.	katán	10	Auchenipterus nuchalis
kátish	8	Leporinus spp.	terés	10	Trichomycterus sp.
chúwi	8	Crenicichla spp.			
kanímu	8	Erythrinus erythrinus			
kasháitum	8	Gladium sp.			
yutuí	8	Pimelodella spp.			
≥ 12 inches					
suiyám	12	Cynaptomus spp.	kumpáu	12	Rhamdia sp.
páni	12	Serrasalmus spp.	kúum	12	Curimata spp.
shingkián	12	Callichthys callichthys	hácham	12	Chaetostoma spp.
wampíkus	12	Ancestrorhynchus falcatus	yawarách	12	Curimata spp.
kugkuí	24	Hoplias malobarius	pápe	16	Duopalatinus olallae
kuír	24	Megalonema spp.	ápup	18	Pseudotylosurus angusticeps
titím	24	Soribum lima	karachám	20	Loricaria spp., Rhineloricaria spp.
numkúmpia	36	Synbranchus marmoratus	champerám	24	Cynodon gibbus
			kushám	24	Pimelodus ornatus
			wáncha	24	Gymnotus spp.
			kángka	30	Prochilodus spp.
			máuts	30	Pseudocetopsis sp.
			káshap	36	Potamotrygon sp.
			tunkáu	36+	'large river catfish'
			múta	36+	'large river catfish'

p = ≤ .05 by Fisher's Exact Test

Sources: Scientific determinations were provided by Camm C. Swift, Ichythyology Section, Los Angeles Museum of Natural History. Data from Berlin, Swift, and Stewart (in prep.).

Notes: Length represents maximum length in inches for matue adults. Estimates are based on data derived from informant elicitation and field collections.

6.6 CLOSING OBSERVATIONS ON HUAMBISA SOUND SYMBOLISM

The phonetic characteristics of the names of birds and fish in Huambisa tentatively suggest the workings of universal sound symbolic processes. First, birds and fish differ on the basis of the distribution of phonetic segments of high and low acoustic frequency. Bird names show a considerably larger number of segments of acoustically high frequency, which, it is claimed, connote quick and rapid motion (i.e., "birdness"). This contrasts with the lower-frequency segments in fish names, which lead to connotations of smooth, slow, continuous flow (i.e., "fishness").

Second, bird and fish vocabularies both demonstrate a prominent internal pattern of size-sound symbolism, where vowel quality and relative size are positively associated at high levels of statistical significance. Names of smaller birds and fishes commonly show high frequency vowel [i] stems, while larger birds and fish are referred to by names comprised of the lower-frequency vowels [a] and [u]. Comparable patterns of size-sound symbolism have been found in the ethnoornithological vocabularies of at least three other unrelated languages—Wayampí, Apalái, and Tzeltal—leading to the conclusion that the phenomenon is likely to be widespread and general.

Having come this far, one is led to look further at the other major groups of animals in Huambisa ethnozoology to determine to what extent patterns of sound symbolism might be documented for the zoological lexicon in general. This work has only begun, but some vague outlines are discernable at the present time and worth mentioning here.

Patterns of size-sound symbolism are productively exploited in the formation of names for frogs and toads. Thus the small, brightly colored and highly poisonous *Dendrobates* spp. are known by names such as *kíri*, *wirisám*, and *tápik*. The warty, black, lumbering toads of the genus *Bufo* are appropriately labeled *bung* and *mukúnt* while a large *Hyla* sp. is known as *purushám*. (Frogs as a group are covered in the following section.)

When one examines the names for invertebrates, some interesting patterns are apparent. Names for insects (*sensu lato*) in general are remarkable in that the occurrence of the midcentral vowel [e] ("barred ɨ") appears considerably high in comparison to other groups of animals. While bird and fish names show this vowel in an initial syllable in but 5 and 2 percent of the cases, respectively (see again figure 6.2), 17 percent of insect names contain [e] as their first vowel, for example, *éte* 'wasp', *tétse* 'kind of fly', *née* 'kind of beetle', *hempés* 'kind of insect that hovers like a hummingbird', *serén* 'kind of bee'. The percentage is not high, but the contrast between birds and fish is nonetheless considerable. Sound symbolism might be at work here as well, although it is heavily flavored with onomatopoeia, as can be easily appreciated by noting the distinct 'humming' sound produced by pronouncing a prolonged [ɨ], suggestive of the humming of insects.

Terms for butterflies appear to exhibit size-sound symbolism. *Wámpang* is the large iridescent morpho butterfly that glides slowly through the forest as a swatch of blue-purple light, while *wichíkip* refers to all remaining butterflies, but especially the small social, yellow-winged creatures that flash by in hordes as they rise from the sandy banks of jungle streams.

A plausible explanation of these findings has been elaborated by Ohala who, building on the work of Morton (1977), has proposed a universal and innate cross-species "frequency code . . . where high [fundamental frequency] signifies (broadly) smallness . . . and low [fundamental frequency] conveys [the meaning] of largeness" (Ohala 1984:12).[1]

In a perfect world, names for the creatures of nature should reflect their natural, inherent qualities. These data suggest that to a large extent, the Huambisa, and perhaps other peoples like them who maintain close ties with the natural universe, are unconsciously motivated to develop systems of zoological nomenclature whose sound-meaning associations take full advantage of the frequency code innate to many living species. As noted earlier, it is important to remember that Linnaeus, the greatest biological nomenclator of all times, intuitively shared this same view when, in considering the nature of generic names, claimed that all "should be apt in meaning, easy to say and remember, and pleasant to hear" (as cited in Stern 1959:8).

6.7 *"-r-"* IS FOR FROG

When I first presented the Huambisa sound symbolism data at a session of the Berkeley Linguistics Society meeting several years ago, Yakov Malkiel, the distinguished Romance philologist, approached me and suggested that a profitable area of research would be to explore the phonetic makeup of words for 'frog' in the world's languages. Based on his experience with Indo-European languages, Malkiel had the distinct impression that an exceptionally high number of names for 'frog' contained the sound [r], a phonetic segment known technically as a flapped or trilled alveolar liquid.

While the data are clearly scanty at the present time, it appears that Malkiel's intuitive observations on Indo-European may have wide application in languages of traditional societies as well. The alveolar trill [r], and the phonetically closely related lateral liquid [l], seem to be unconsciously drawn upon as the most appropriate sounds from the human speech inventory to serve as segments for the names of anurans (both frogs and toads), so that the names of these creatures are formed in this fashion in an extraordinary proportion of the languages examined. These data allow one to speak of substantive universal features of onomatopoeia comparable to universal size-sound symbolism.

It seems undebatable that the use of [r] and [l] in names for frogs and toads

---

[1] Ohala has suggested that the frequency code might also provide a framework for the interpretation of certain universals of intonation, facial expressions (in association with vocalization), as well as the anatomical sexual dimorphism of the vocal apparatus in human and nonhuman species.

is fundamentally onomatopoeic. Potter and Sargent devote one brief paragraph to the topic in their short survey of the etymology of words from nature: "In Aristophanes' *brekekekex koax koax* of the chorus of *The Frogs* we may hear a fine onomatopoetic rendering of the frog's croak. The Gk. word for 'frog' is *batrakhos*, and we may make a guess that this too began by being imitative. . . . This is true for O. E. *frogga*, seemingly a pet-form of O. E. *forse, frose*, a cognate of Modern German *Frosch*" (Potter and Sargent 1974:66). Potter and Sargent do not focus on the phonetic segments under consideration, but the examples that they provide indicate clearly that [r] carries a major load. To their list, of course, could be added Latin, Italian, and Spanish *rana*, Italian *ranocchio* and *rospo*, French *grenouille, rainette, crapaud*, Romanian *broasca*, and many others.

I recently compiled a list of names for toads and frogs in thirty-three non-Indo-European languages, mostly from the files of the South American Indian Languages Documentation Project, a University of California, Berkeley, and University of Pittsburgh research project devoted to collecting lexical and grammatical data on South American Indian languages. In my inventory, I listed all of the terms found in the source and then selected those languages that showed one or more names comprised of [r] or [l]. Of the thirty-three languages examined, thirty, or 91 percent of them, showed the suspected pattern for [r], [l] or both. These thirty languages, and the relevant forms, are given in table 6.7. Treating Ashéninka and Asháninka (Maipurean), on the one hand, and Huambisa [Wambisa] and Shuar (Jivaroan), on the other, as single cases due to their close genetic relationship, the proportion changes insignificantly.

It is clear that the inventories are incomplete, good scientific determinations for the large majority of the animals are missing, and one could always cite problems with investigators' various renderings of the sounds [r] and [l]. In addition, since most of the languages are from South America, it might be claimed that their similarity is due to either genetic relationship or lexical borrowing. While this factor is relevant to a small number of languages in the sample (see above), an examination of the several different language families represented should convince the reader that genetic affiliation is highly unlikely as a primary factor leading to the presence of [r] and [l] in the terms cited (unless one is talking in terms of time depths so remote as to be virtually impossible to document). Likewise, the massive geographic area covered makes historical contact and linguistic borrowing even more unlikely. Furthermore, the presence of terms with [r] and [l] in languages of different continents of the world should be decisive in ruling out genetic or historical factors as the fundamental reasons for the patterns observed.

Of course, a full test of the apparent specific association of [r] and [l] segments with words for 'frog' requires one to show that these sounds do not occur with a similar distribution in the names for other common creatures that

TABLE 6.7

Names for Frogs and Toads in Twenty-nine Languages Formed in Part by [r] or [l]

Frog or Toad Name	Gloss	Group, Location, and Language Famil
chancha miri	'white toad'	Amawaka (Panoan), Peru
okoro	'toad'	
kara'i	'toad of the spring'	
tokoro'	*Bufo* spp.	
anjobololo	'toad'	Araona (Takanan), Bolivia
lolololo	'toad'	
lolo	'large toad'	
masero	'toad'	Asháninka (Maipurean), Peru
soverokwi	'tadpole'	
pirinto	'large frog'	
masero	'toad'	Ashéninka (Maipurean), Peru
vratantatzi	'toad'	
patziri	'toad'	
pirim-piritzi	'toad'	
soverokwi	'tadpole'	
moorintzi	'toad'	
ovaratantatzi	'small toad'	
piviro	'toad'	
taayiri	'toad'	
kaampo nari	'toad'	
karava	'river frog'	
patzirikiri	'toad'	
tzinkemiro	'toad'	
chempivirito	'large toad'	
jeento-ri	'large toad'	
pirinto	'frog of the ox bow' (lake)	
tempo-nari	'toad'	
sap le'chue	*Dendrobates* sp.	Kayapa (Barbarkoan), Ecuador
porio	'tadpole'	Chayawita (Kawapanan), Peru
huapiro	'frog'	
huarira	'small frog'	
huari	'frog'	
huirin	'toad'	
tororo	'frog'	
koriapa	'small toad'	
zapurereba	'tadpole'	Wahibo (Wahivoan), Venezuela
purusham	'frog'	Wambisa (Xivaroan), Peru
wirisam	*Dendrobates* sp.	
karakaras	'toad'	
suakarep	'frog'	
kiria	'frog'	
muritu	'frog'	

'rog or Toad Name	Gloss	Group, Location, and Language Family*
hiriri	'toad, frog'	Ignaciano (Maipurean), Bolivia
valu	'large frog'	Inga (Kechua), Peru
k	*Cophixalus parkeri*	Kalam (Indo-Pacific), New Guinea
wlek	*Nyctimystes kubori*	
olea	'toad'	Kamarakotos (Karib), Venezuela
varoma	'frog'	
erek	*Hyla* spp.	Lacandon (Mayan), Mexico
ibero	'toad, frog'	Lokono (Maipurean), Surinam
ere	'frog'	Moseten (Mosetenan), Bolivia
lun'tei	'toad'	Movima (Movima), Bolivia
uaran'tei	'toad'	
ru, vrupe	'frog, toad'	Moxo (Maipurean), Peru?
oro-poro	*Litoria infrafrenata*	Nuaulu (Austronesian), Indonesia
ararai	*Litoria amboinensis*	
ere	*Platymantis papuensis*	
imæræ	*Leptodactylus* sp.	Piaroa (Piaroan), Venezuela
ure	*Leptodactylus knudzeni*	
uwari	'frog'	
o'kari	'frog'	
væræk'o	*Eleutherodactylus* sp.	
arakara	*Bufo* sp.	
'kæara	*Hyla crepitans*	
agwa	'frog'	Piro (Maipurean), Peru/Brazil
olo	'frog'	
ahwa	'frog'	
koli	'frog'	
wachri	'large frog'	
lojru	'frog'	
ula	'frog'	Rangi, Tanzania
gre	*Dendrobates* sp.	Shuar (Xivaroan), Ecuador
ururu	'toad'	Takana (Takanan), Bolivia
	'frog'	
uaretete	'small frog'	
aro'ma	'frog'	Taurepán (Kariban), Venezuela
reu-tuku	'toad	
alala'ke	'toad'	Terena (Maipurean), Brazil
ru'mo	'water frog'	
orabora	'small frog'	Warao (Warao), Venezuela

TABLE 6.7 (*Cont.*)

Frog or Toad Name	Gloss	Group, Location, and Language Family*
diasori	'frog'	
johara	'frog'	
siasori	'frog'	
borabora a natoro	'tadpole'	
akora	'toad'	
wareke	'small frog'	
karitoto'	'toad'	
welele	*Hyla multifasciata*	Wayampí (Tupian), French Guiana
epalaA	*Hyla leucophyllata*	
wiliwili	*Chiasmocleis shudikarensis*	
mulu	*Leptodactylus pentadactylus*	
muluwa	*Leptodactylus rugosus*	
alu	*Pipa pipa*	
palanaluway	*Phyllobates pictus*	
pilikAlA	*Bufo typhonius*	
pilikAlA'i	*Dendrophryniscus minutus*	
kunawalu	*Phrynohias resihifitrix*	
takIli	*Phyllomedusa tomopterna*	
takIlilu	*Phyllomedusa vaillantii*	
kululu	*Bufo marinus*	
kululuipApI	*Bufo guttatus*	
kwala	*Hyla dentei*	
kwala'i	*Hyla fasciata*	
kIlu	'frog'	
yakaleyu'i	*Hyla proboscidea*	
kuleyu'i	*Hyla granosa*	
yakaleyu'ilaanga	*Hyla ornatissima*	
mulutukupile	*Hyla rubra*	
tamelua	*Phrynohias venulosa*	
jero	'small toad'	Witoto Muinane (Witotoan), Peru
jirurungo	'tadpole'	
kokikurino	'small toad'	
maru	'toad'	Xevero (Kawapanan), Peru
xamorita	'toad'	
matovara	'tadpole'	Yukpa (Kariban), Venezuela

Sources: Amawaka: D'Ans 1972; Hyde, Russell, and Russell 1980; Araona: Pitman 1981; Ashénika: Kindberg 1980; Ashánika: Payne 1980; Kayapa: Lindskoog and Lindskoog 1964; Chayawita: Hart and Hart 1975; Wambis: Berlin and McDiarmid, in prep.; Ignaciano: Ott and Ott 1983; Inga: Landerman 1973; Kalam: Bulmer and Tyl 1968; Kamarakotos: Simpson 1940:301; Lacandon: Gongora-Arones 1987; Lokono: Pet 1987; Moseteno: Bil lolotti 1917; Movima: Judy and Judy 1962; Moxo: Marban 1894; Nuaulu: Ellen, Stimson, and Menzies 197 Piaroa: Zent 1989; Piro: Nies 1986; Matteson 1965; Rangi: Kesby 1986; Shuar: Salesianos Misionaros 192 Takana: Van Wynen and Van Wynen 1962; Taurepán: Simpson 1940; Terena: Butler and Butler 1969; Wara Basilio de Barral 1979; Wayampí: Lescure, Grenand, and Grenand 1980; Witoto Muinane: Minor and Min 1971; Xevero: Tessman 1930; Yukpa: Muñoz and Armato 1986.

* Orthography for South American Indian groups is that adopted by the South American Indian Document tion Project.

might equally well be so characterized because of their calls, for example, the names for crows or parrots in the languages of the world. Nonetheless, when more data are compiled from additional sources, I am quite convinced that Professor Malkiel will be shown to be correct. If the essence of any animal can be captured by the ways humans have chosen to refer to it, the frog confidently croaks its way to first place in line.

6.8 LEXICAL REFLECTIONS OF CULTURAL SIGNIFICANCE

While the nonarbitrary association of sound and meaning might be reflected in a people's ethnozoological vocabulary, this productive process will hardly be relevant to the ethnobotanical lexicon. Traditional peoples may talk to their plants, but their plants rarely talk back. Other linguistic devices must be invoked to make a people's language serve mnemonically in the management of the vocabulary of plants. In general, if the generic name of a particular plant species is descriptive of some feature or attribute of that species (e.g., *tulip tree*), one might suppose that the cognitive effort involved in associating the name with its proper referent will be lesser than if the name were totally semantically opaque, that is, in arbitrary association with its referent (such as *heather*). Of course, there are a considerable number of qualifications that have to be discussed if this proposed general tendency is to be considered valid.

In chapter 1, I suggested that the generic names for plants and animals in many languages could be grouped into at least three major classes—simple names, productive names, and unproductive names—building on a typology of lexical forms first proposed by Conklin (1962). Whatever terminology one employs to designate the three types of forms, it is clear that these categories mark expressions that vary along a dimension of analyzability from what I would like to call *semantically opaque* at one end of the scale to *semantically transparent* at the other end.

It now appears likely that the generic names for plants in many languages, and perhaps those for animals as well, might be arranged along this scale of semantic transparency. Furthermore, for reasons that are obvious, or that will become so shortly, the semantic transparency of some particular generic name appears to be largely an inverse function of the cultural importance of the species to which the name is applied. This claim is supported by the following kinds of data.

Table 6.8 shows the distribution of the 381 folk generic names for plants in Tzeltal that are of native origin (ignoring those terms that refer to recently introduced species and which are, for the most part, Spanish loanwords) across the four categories of cultural significance discussed in chapter 3.

Examples of terms that are semantically opaque include *ixim* 'corn' (*Zea mays*), *on* 'avocado' (*Persea* spp.), and *ich* 'chili pepper' (*Capsicum* spp.). Semitransparent terms are *tza' tuluk'* lit. 'excrement of turkey'; 'black sapote'

TABLE 6.8

Distribution of Names of Tzeltal Generic Plant Taxa in Terms of Their Semantic Transparency across the Four Major Categories of Cultural Significance as Discussed in Chapter 3

	Semantically Opaque	Partially Transparent	Transparent
Cultivated	21	5	1
Protected	18	10	7
Significant	49	67	61
Not treated	13	44	85
		N = 381, p = ≤ .001	

(*Diospyonos digyna*); *ichil ok* lit. 'leg of chili-pepper'; 'husk tomato' (*Lycopersicum esculentum*); and *yak' tz'i'* lit. 'dog's tongue' (*Eryngium ghiesbreghtii*). Transparent terms include expressions such as *ixim ak* lit. 'corn grass' (*Tripsacum lanceolatum*); *ch'ix te'* lit. 'spine tree' (*Cratageus pubescens*); and *ichil ak'* lit. 'itchy vine' (*Clematis dioica*).

The pattern underlying table 6.8 is more readily apparent in diagrammatic form, as shown in figure 6.6. Here we see clearly that the likelihood of a Tzeltal generic taxon being labeled by a simple, opaque word increases with its cultural importance—again, assuming that importance is a reflection, at least in part, of the degree of human intervention associated with the particular species. Nearly 80 percent of the cultivated plants (twenty-one) are named by linguistically unanalyzable words. Half of the protected plants (51 percent) receive simple names. Significant plants are less likely to be named by semantically opaque expressions (28 percent), while only thirteen nonmanaged folk genera are given such names, a mere 9 percent of the category.

The distribution of semantically semitransparent and transparent generic plant names is also predictable as a function of cultural importance. The semitransparent forms show a moderate tendency to refer to plants subjected to some degree of human intervention. Fully semantically transparent expressions are strongly associated with plant taxa that are only marginally managed, if at all.

Comparable data from an unrelated language that demonstrate the same principle as seen in the Tzeltal materials come from Ka'apor (Tupí-Guaraní family) of the eastern Amazonian region of Brazil's Pará and Maranhão states (Balée 1986). Balée recently conducted an important comparative study of five Tupian languages aimed at showing that the words for intensively managed plant species are more likely to be retained over time than those for species of plants that receive only some or little management. His study independently replicates and confirms the findings of Berlin, Breedlove, Laughlin, and Raven (1973) on the relationship of cultural significance and lexical retention in Tzeltal-Tzotzil ethnobotany.

As in the Tzeltal-Tzotzil comparison, Balée reasoned, building on Sapir's

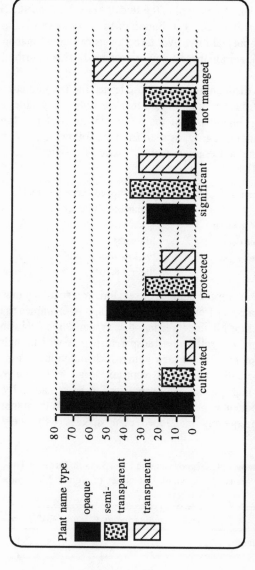

Figure 6.6 Proportional distribution of degree of semantic transparency of Tzeltal generic plant names over four major categories of cultural significance. (After Berlin, Breedlove, and Raven 1974)

(1916) suggestion about the relationship of the analyzability of a term and its relative age, that "one would expect that the terms for unmanaged plants would tend to be more analyzable than terms for managed plants" (Balée 1986:18). Given his linguistic knowledge of Ka'apor, Balée selected Ka'apor words that showed high and low degrees of lexical similarity with the other four Tupí-Guaraní languages used in the study (Araweté, Asurini, Tembé, and Wayampí), and examined the distribution of these 112 expressions, in terms of their linguistic analyzability, over three levels of human management: intensively managed, semimanaged, and unmanaged. This distribution is seen in table 6.9.

Balée makes no distinction among those terms that I would characterize as semantically semitransparent and those that are fully analyzable, although it would appear from his glosses of the forms that most of his "analyzable" forms are of the latter category, as seen from the following illustrative examples (where [e] is the midcentral vowel [ɨ] "barred-ɨ") (after Balée 1986, table 6).

tayahu-mera	'white-lipped peccary's tree'
tatu-mera	'armadillo's tree'
kangwaruhu-mera	'paca's tree'
saweya-mera	'rat's tree'
yashi-ka'a	'yellow-footed tortoise's herb'
tapi'i-ka'a	'tapir's herb'

What best accounts for the degrees of semantic transparency that have been shown in these examples from Tzeltal and Ka'apor—examples that could be multiplied several times with data from other systems? One plausible suggestion is that semantically relatively transparent names will be helpful in the cognitive management of plant taxa with which individuals less frequently interact. Psychologically, names for plant taxa dealt with regularly (the so-called intensively managed species) can afford to be semantically opaque in that their use is frequent enough for the speaker-hearer to learn them by rote. Conversely, infrequently mentioned plant species will likely be given

TABLE 6.9
Distribution of Names of Ka'apor Generic Plant Taxa in Terms of Their Semantic Transparency across Three Major Categories of Human Management (after Balée 1986)

	Unanalyzable (opaque)	Analyzable (transparent)
Intensively managed	22	1
Semimanaged	21	4
Nonmanaged	34	30
		N = 112, p = ≤ .001

names that aid the speaker-hearer in associating the proper name with its referent. Metaphorical allusion to some aspect of its appearance, or its association, imagined or real, with some place or creature, serve as linguistic cues to memory, for example, a leaf shaped like a dog's tongue, a seed pod thought to look vaguely like a penis, or a tree whose fruits are particularly relished by the collared peccary.

These views are not new, of course, having been discussed in a more general context by Zipf (1935, 1949), and C. H. Brown (1984a) and Brown and Witkowski (1983). What is relevant here is that the semantic resources of language are productively employed in what might be called the metaphorical mapping of the ethnobiological landscape. As such, prominent aspects of the organisms being named will be selected for linguistic recognition in a nonarbitrary fashion. Characteristic calls of particular creatures will form the stimuli for human vocalization, which in turn will be the source in many cases of the generic name itself. An unconscious appreciation of universal sound symbolism may work independently or hand in hand with onomatopoeia to form the basis for the names of other creatures. And, when appropriate, the productive use of language to form expressions that are literally or metaphorically descriptive of salient properties of the thing signified will also play a major role in the ethnobiological lexicon. In these various ways, the names for living things pulse with the life of the world of nature to which they have been, and continue to be, symbolically assigned.

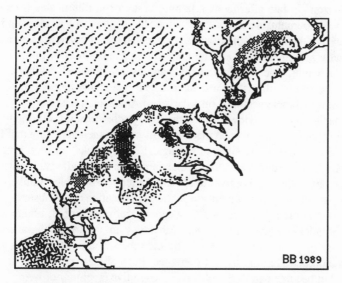

Manchúng and *bíkua* (*Tamandua tetradactyla* and *Cyclopes didactylus*), the collared and silky anteater, respectively.

CHAPTER SEVEN

The Substance and Evolution of Ethnobiological Categories

THE CENEPA RIVER takes a 90-degree turn at the small Aguaruna settlement of Huampami (Wampám), affording the observer standing on its northern bank an unobstructed view of the steep slopes that form the constrictive channel guiding the river's clouded waters southward to the Marañón and finally the Amazon. In late afternoon, a falling western sun illuminates the face of the broad mountainside like a great lamp, the contrasts of shadow and light emphasizing the rich complexity of a surface that one rarely notices at midday. Especially prominent now are the great forest giants, trees of thirty to forty meters in height, emerging in scattered patterns from the thick canopy as stark, gray-white shafts, ultimately tracing a jagged line along the eastern horizon, quiet but remarkable sentinels on a darkened Amazonian landscape.

In many ways, the view of ethnobiological classification outlined in the foregoing pages can be likened metaphorically to the mental picture that I have sketched above. The classifier of biological reality looks out on a great forested sea comprised of living things that number in the hundreds of thousands. On this vast surface, a comparatively small (but considerable) number of organisms stand out as forest giants to capture the attention of the observer, some so obvious in their presence that they can scarcely be ignored, others less so but nonetheless so striking when noted that they are unforgettable, and others yet whose presence is revealed only by the specialized understanding gained from the intimate familiarity of experience. Each of these plants and animals, destined to become part of the observer's cognitive inventory of living things, contrasts vividly with what remains, an undifferentiated background of life that passes by unconsidered, unseen, and unknown.

The many hundreds of distinctive groupings that do present themselves un-ambiguously for human recognition are, of course, themselves the result of the processes of biological evolution. The human observer, psychologically endowed with innate capacities for categorization, almost spontaneously per-ceives the readily recognizable patterns inherent in the ways that evolution has worked. This unconscious recognition of nature's plan ultimately emerges as the cognitive structure that we know as a society's system of ethnobiological classification. In reality, of course, there are several systems present, as has been pointed out numerous times here and elsewhere; but underlying them all one can discern a general pattern of both structure and content that allow for such systems to be characterized by a relatively small number of organizing principles, some of the most important of which have been outlined here.

7.1 TOWARD A SUBSTANTIVE INVENTORY OF ETHNOBIOLOGICAL CATEGORIES

Most of the widespread regularities concerning the categorization and naming of plants and animals by peoples of traditional, nonliterate societies discussed in the present outline are structural in nature. Hierarchic organization and rec-ognition of groupings of organisms of various degrees of affinity, unambigu-ous recognition of prototypical members of ethnobiological categories of ge-neric, specific, and intermediate rank, general patterns of nomenclature—all of these are features bearing on the structural organization of the categories of plants and animals into a cognitively cohesive framework.

Very little has been said about the possible substantive regularities that exist between systems of ethnobiological classification, regularities in the actual biological referents of the ethnobiological categories themselves. It is to the discovery of the substantive regularities in ethnobiological classification that I believe much future research must be addressed if one is ever to come close to being able to answer the fundamental questions raised in chapter 2, namely, of those species that exist in some local habitat, *which* are recognized and *why?* It is to this difficult subject that I turn now, closing with an outline of some of the ways in which one might begin to think about providing a dia-chronic dimension to the essentially synchronic typology that I have focused on thus far.

The identification of substantive regularities in ethnobiological classifica-tion is limited greatly by the natural biogeographical differences that charac-terize the various habitats in which traditional peoples are located in distinct regions of the world. To borrow Lenneberg and Roberts's term (1956), on a regional basis the language of experience of ethnobiology is much more con-strained than that found in the linguistic recognition of the sensation of color, or, for that matter, in the various ways of naming the genealogical nexus un-derlying one's relationships with one's kindred. Nonetheless, within broad biogeographic regions of the world, and in some limited cases, for groups of plants and animals with multicontinental distributions, it seems likely that substantive regularities in ethnobiological classification are likely to be found that are almost invariably recognized in all systems.

Consider the substantive regularity between the systems of ethnobiological classification of the Aguaruna of Peru and the Wayampí of Brazil, each with names for one or more of the several species of toucans found in their respective habitats. While these two groups are linguistically unrelated (unless, again, one moves to time depths of linguistic relationships well beyond those that can be established by currently available methods of linguistic reconstruction), each of them has singled out this particular group of birds and included it in their individual systems of ornithological classification. Not only are the species as a group recognized as a conceptual category (either named or covert), but also, the individual species are treated quite similarly in each language. A person with a knowledge of the conceptual structure of the Aguaruna classification of these birds would simply have to learn the Wayampí terms for their Brazilian counterparts in order to control with facility the latter system.

It seems immediately counterintuitive to argue that the recognition of these magnificent birds in each of these two systems, and in the many hundreds of others that could be cited, represents the results of the genetic linguistic relationships that unites what some authors have called the Paleo-Indian substrate that all South American Indians share (cf. Greenberg 1987). Rather, toucans become named fragments of these various ethnobiological systems precisely because the perceptual and behavioral characteristics of these creatures are so obvious that *not* to recognize them is essentially impossible.

Is it frivolous to imagine the development of a *substantive inventory* of the biological chunks of reality that make up the categories of individual systems of ethnobiological classification likely to be recognized, at least for restricted regions of the world? I do not believe that such an inventory of fundamental ethnobiological concepts has ever been proposed for anywhere in the world. Nonetheless, a start has been made for parts of Latin America, as seen in the diagnostic lexical questionnaire of the South American Indian Languages Documentation Project (Kaufman, Berlin, and Rodrigues 1988). This word list is made up of approximately nineteen hundred items, about a third of which refer to basic vocabulary (in Swadesh's sense). The remaining portions of the list are drawn from the domains of subsistence, social relations, and ethnobiological concepts. The items in this latter segment add up to approximately one thousand, around eight hundred of which refer to groupings of plants and animals that we believe are likely to be named in any individual ethnobiological system found in the region.

We have produced our inventory of ethnobiological concepts on the basis of a number of the considerations raised in chapter 2, several of which were first discussed briefly by Bulmer (1974a) and outlined more fully by Hunn (1977). In addition, our list has benefited from extended discussions with botanists and zoologists as well as our own intuitions and hunches based on personal experience from long-term fieldwork in Latin America.

As suggested in chapter 2, the first and perhaps most important consideration in determing the likelihood that a particular plant or animal will be named is the *taxonomic distinctiveness* (or *phenotypic salience* [Hunn 1989]) of the local species as determined by an analysis of the scientific classification of the flora and fauna of a particular area. Species that occur as members of relatively sparsely populated biological families, for example, the capybara (*Hydrochoerus*) and the rabbit (*Sylvilagus*), both monotypic genera in monotypic families, are good bets. Each of these animals stands out so starkly as to almost guarantee their linguistic recognition (see Berlin 1982).

A second factor considered is the *size* of the organism in relation to human beings (see Bulmer 1974a). Common sense demands that the larger the organism in comparison to humans, the more likely it will be recognized. Hunn (pers. comm.; 1989) is currently working on an algorithm for establishing this factor more formally.

Two additional factors that are also at work but much more difficult to evaluate accurately relate to the *prevalence* of individual species in the local habitat as well as their relative *ease of observation*. Attempting to gather good information on these parameters is difficult if not impossible for many species, given the few comprehensive studies of the flora and fauna of even the best-known areas of the world inhabited by traditional societies. Nonetheless, taken together, these several factors are likely to represent the most significant considerations leading to the naming of any biological species in a folk system of ethnobiological classification, not only for the South American case but universally.

Taking all of these properties into consideration—taxonomic salience, relative size, prevalence, and relative ease of observation—one can generate an inventory of potentially namable taxa that can be tested against actual systems of ethnobiological classification. Table 7.1 provides a small fragment of what a basic ethnobiological concept list might look like for the mammals of one relatively broad biogeographical region of the world, Amazonian South America. Parts of this list have already been evaluated against data drawn primarily from dictionary sources for a small number of Amazonian Indian languages. This retrospective testing sustains, in the main, our original notions about the cognitive salience of these organisms. However, the number of languages examined thus far is minuscule (fewer than thirty), and the dictionary sources used are quite unreliable biologically. Nonetheless, it is a start, and future fieldwork will provide a clearer picture of how well our proposed inventory accounts for the ethnobiological facts of any particular ethnobiological system of the area.

Most of the examples discussed in the preceding pages have focused on the higher vascular plants and vertebrate animals. Nonetheless, it appears that a

TABLE 7.1
Inventory of Mammal Genera Likely to Receive Linguistic Recognition in All Systems of Ethnobiological Classification of Amazonian South America*

Tapiridae 'tapir'	
Tapirus	'tapir'
Tayassuidae 'pigs'	
Tayassu pecari	'collared peccary'
T. tajacu	'white-lipped peccary'
Cervidae 'deer'	
Mazama	'deer'
Hydrochaeridae 'capybara'	
Hydrochaeris	'capybara'
Leporidae 'rabbit'	
Sylvilagus	'rabbit'
Bradypodidae 'sloths'	
Bradypus	'three-toed sloth'
Choloepus	'two-toed sloth'
Erethizontidae 'procupines'	
Coendou	'porcupine'
Chaetomys	'thin-spined porcupine'
Dasypodidae 'armadillos'	
Dasypus	'banded armadillo'
Cabassous	'naked-tailed armadillo'
Priodontes	'giant armadillo'
Myrmecophagidae 'anteaters'	
Cyclopes	'two-toed anteater'
Myrmecophaga	'giant anteater'
Tamandua	'collared anteater'
Primates and Callitrichidae 'monkeys and marmosets'	
Alouatta	'howler monkey'
Aotus	'nocturnal monkey'
Ateles	'spider monkey'
Brachyteles	'woolly spider monkey'
Cacajao	'ukari'
Chiropotes	'saki monkey'
Callicebus	'aiti monkey'
Cebus	'capuchin monkey'
Callimico	'marmoset'
Logothrix	'woolly monkey'
Pithecia	'macacus'
Saimiri	'squirrel monkey'
Callithrix	'short-tusked marmoset'

TABLE 7.1 (*Cont.*)

Saguinus	'pinchi'
Cebuella	'pygmy marmoset'

Dasyproctidae and Dinomyidae 'agoutis, pacas, and relatives'
Agouti	'paca'
Dasyprocta	'agouti'
Myoprocta	'acushi'
Dinomys	'false paca'

Procyonidae 'raccoons and affines'
Procyon	'raccoon'
Bassaricyon	'olingo'
Nasua	'coati'
Potos	'kinkajou'

Canidae 'dogs and affines'
Atelocynus	'short-eared dog'
Speothos	'bush dog'
Canis	'common dog'

Felidae 'cats'
Felis onca	'jaguar'
F. concolor	'cougar'
F. pardalis	'ocelot'
F. wiedii	'margay'
F. yagouarundi	'jagouarundi'

Platinistidae, Delphinidae, and Sirenia 'dolphins and manatee'
Inia	'Amazon dolphin'
Sotalia	'river dolphin'
Trichechus	'manatee'

Mustelidae 'weasels and affines'
Eira	'tayra'
Galictis	'huron'
Lutra	'river otter'
Mustela	'weasel'
Conepatus	'skunk'
Pteronura	'flat-tailed otter'

Sciuridae 'squirrels'
Sciurus	'squirrel'
Microsciurus	'dwarf squirrel'

Didelphidae 'opossums'
Caluromys	'woolly opossum'
Caluromysiops	'black-shouldered opossum'
Didelphis	'American opossum'
Glironia	'bushy-tailed opossum'

TABLE 7.1 (*Cont.*)

Chironectes	'water opossum'
Marmosa	'mouse opossum'
Metachirus	'brown four-eyed opossum'
Philander	'gray four-eyed opossum'

Cricetidae and Echimydae 'rats'
    Various genera (12), all likely to be grouped together with small degree of internal differentiation

Chiroptera 'bats'
    Various bat genera of the Desmontidae, Emballonuridae, Molossidae, Noctilionidae, Thyropteridae, Vespertilionidae, and Phyllostomidae, all likely grouped as single category and not differentiated

    * The content of this inventory is primarily a result of long-term consultation with my colleague James L. Patton, Museum of Vertebrate Zoology, University of California, Berkeley.

number of substantive generalizations can now be set forth on some of the most distinctive groupings of invertebrates likely to be recognized by human beings, to be tested against further empirical research. From a brief perusal of the few but careful and relatively comprehensive studies on ethnoentomology (Wyman and Bailey 1964 for the Navajo [see the insightful reanalysis of these same materials by Morris 1979]; Posey 1979, 1984; Hunn 1977; and, to some extent, P. Taylor 1990), it seems likely that in those regions of the world where such groupings are found, folk systems of classification will cognitively recognize, and in most cases, linguistically encode at least the following major morphotypes of arthropods, as seen in table 7.2.

Hunn (1977, 1982) has suggested that the internal cognitive differentiation of a number of these invertebrate groups will be motivated by practical considerations, for example: ''The detail applied [by the Tzeltal] to the classification of orthopterans [grasshoppers] may be explained in terms of the cultural significance of these insects'' (1977:288). While recognizing that cultural considerations will play some part in the degree to which several of these groups are further subdivided, it is hardly conceivable that such factors account for the recognition of the major morphotypes themselves, nor do I think Hunn would make such a claim. Rather, as with many vertebrate species, it is more likely that the overt or implicit recognition of the major groups shown in table 7.2, as well as many of the subdivisions that they encompass, is once again a reflection of the perceptually distinctive features of form and behavior that these creatures present to the human observer wherever they occur.

There are serious problems associated with collecting the necessary data to test the extent to which the biological categories represented in these basic concept lists will be lexically realized in actual systems of classification. As mentioned earlier, most of the materials that might be used must currently be

TABLE 7.2

Inventory of Major Morphotypes of Arthropods Likely to Be Named in Any Ethno-biological System of Classification if Representatives Are Found in the Local Habitat

Formicidae	'ants'
Eumenidae, Vespidae, Sphecidae	'wasps'
Apoidea	'bees'
Diptera, Braconidae	'flies'
Lepidoptera	'butterflies and moths'
Orthoptera	'grasshoppers'
Odonata	'dragonflies'
Cicadidae	'cicadas'
Parasitiformes	'ticks'
Blattidae	'roaches'
Coleoptera, Hemiptera	'beetles/bugs'
Curculionidae	'weevils'
Arachnida, Phalangida	'spiders'
Scorpionida	'scorpions'
Mallophaga, Siphonaptera, Thrombidiformes	'fleas, lice, and chiggers'
Lepidoptera, Diptera larva	'caterpillars'
Myriapoda, Diplopoda, Chilopoda	'millipedes'

drawn from dictionary sources or from collaborators whose primary interest is not ethnobiological. The drawbacks associated with such an approach have been amply discussed in reference to comparable surveys on higher-order life-form taxa such as that of Brown (1984a), both by Brown himself and his critics (see Randall and Hunn 1984). These problems become even more serious when one sets out to collect accurate data for taxa of generic and specific rank. It is clear that no serious test of a theory aimed at predicting which biological species will be named in any particular system can be achieved without new and ingenious ethnobiological fieldwork that is not so costly as to make rapid survey research impossible.

One way in which new fieldwork might be carried out would be to develop a traveling ethnobiological museum comprised of well-prepared botanical and zoological specimens accompanied by diagnostic color photographs, draw-ings, and, in the case of certain animals, taped sound recordings of typical calls. At some point, the relevant species incorporated in this transportable ethnobiological laboratory could be complemented by videotapes of the vari-ous species in their natural state, a procedure that would at least minimize problems associated with scale and perspective in the visual presentation of the respective species.

The goal would be to take the traveling museum into as many areas of the same region as possible and to conduct in-depth ethnobiological elicitation with the collaboration of linguists familiar with the native languages of several critically selected indigenous societies. Although this is clearly a much less than ideal program of field research, it would be possible to collect a good deal of highly reliable data on the basic outlines of different systems in a relatively short time (say ten years).

To some, such a proposal might, at first glance, appear somewhat futuristic, but over the last several years I have become convinced that, with a little luck, hard work, and willing collaborators, the future is today. Many of the necessary recordings of tropical birdcalls have already been produced by Jacques Villard (Villard 1980), a number of which were productively used by Jensen (1988) in his detailed description of Wayampí bird classification. Well-prepared herbarium specimens mounted permanently in plastic holders and placed in standard-sized notebooks are essentially indestructible and have recently been used in large numbers with many informants with considerable success (cf. Hays 1976, who used a field herbarium quite like the one just described, and Berlin, Berlin, et al. 1990). Portable computers and video equipment are no longer restricted solely to groups with operating budgets comparable to those of the U.S. Army or Shell Oil Corporation.

If accurate comparative materials can be obtained on the biological content of a major portion of plant and animal taxa in broad but regionally defined areas of the world, one may then be able to move toward the development of the much neglected diachronic dimension of ethnobiological classification. C. H. Brown's considerable efforts in this regard (C. Brown 1984a and several related papers) have been limited to sketching the probable linguistic encoding sequence for the higher-order taxa of life-form rank. It is apparent that most of his conclusions are basically sound, in spite of a host of criticisms concerning his definitions of what constitutes a life-form taxon in any particular case. Mounting a comparable effort for even a small fragment of the fundamental generic taxa of folk systems of classification on a worldwide scale would be a major undertaking.

But systems of ethnobiological classification do not exist in a synchronic vacuum, nor are they all the same in spite of strong structural as well as substantive similarities. Individual systems reflect not only the biological constraints of nature, but also the modifying processes of cultural history. A major productive area of future work in ethnobiological classification will be to explore the recent cultural-historical ramifications of ethnobiological knowledge as it can be ascertained by ethnobiologically sophisticated comparative anthropological and historical linguistic research.

As part of the South American Indian Languages Documentation Project, my collaborators and I have been exploring several ways in which scholars might examine the spatial distribution of linguistic data through the use of an interactive database-graphics tool called SAPIR (South American Prehistory Inference Resource),[1] a name we have given our protocol in recognition of the great linguist's statement of principles on the use of linguistic evidence for making cultural historical inferences (see Sapir 1916, 1936). The broader linguistic goals of the project will not be described here (see Berlin, Kaufman, and Miller 1987–88). Instead, I will focus on how the tool we are in the process of developing might be of use for the kinds of cultural-historical work in ethnobiology that can be productively carried out in the coming years, not only for South America but for anywhere in the world.

To paraphrase Robert Lowie, *distribution is the first guide to history*. There is perhaps no better way to grasp the possible historical significance of the words for a particular concept than to plot their distribution on a map, a procedure long recognized by scholars in many disciplines and, for South America, perhaps most notably employed by E. Nordenskiöld (1922). The resulting patterns may or may not, of course, be best accounted for on historical grounds, but their discovery is the first step in developing hypotheses that might account for them.

SAPIR will begin with a digitized image of the distribution of the approximately 350 distinct South American Indian languages (more correctly, the geographical distribution of the groups that speak these languages). Each language (many of which are discontinuous) is represented as a simple polygon that roughly shows the particular group's current geographic extension. Rivers, mountain ranges, country boundaries, and other geographic features can also be digitized and optionally turned on and off at the user's desire so as to maximize ease of viewing in certain contexts. Each polygon representing an Indian language will be associated with a lexical data file that includes the complete inventory of ethnobiological concepts described earlier, as well as many other types of linguistic, social, and cultural information.

SAPIR will enable the user to access, augment, and edit these databases through a scrollable, hierarchical list. As an extremely oversimplified example, imagine that one were interested in exploring the culture history of the (supposed) regionally universal ethnobiological concept 'collared peccary' (*Tayassu pecari*) in a portion of the Arawakan language family. After having selected "Arawakan" (the family), "Maipurean" (the subgroup), and "animals" (the domain) with appropriate and intuitively transparent commands, one would finally "click" on COLLARED PECCARY and immediately see the native terms (in technical linguistic orthograpy) for this concept appear on

---

[1] The database manager that is currently being developed for SAPIR is an extension of D. W. Miller's Great American History Machine (GAHM), which permits one to explore interactively the distributions of highly complex data on computer-generated maps. Miller's own particular application for GAHM allows him to examine geographic distributional characteristics of numerical data encoded in the U.S. census materials from 1840 to the present. While a good deal of development is yet to be carried out before SAPIR will have all of the power currently found in GAHM, the prospects for this specialized adaptation are extremely promising.

one's computer console, displayed at their appropriate locations on the map of South America. For ease of presentation, a hypothetical example is given in figure 7.1.

After having observed the distribution of these forms and having made the provisional assessment that two or more words for some concept, or set of concepts, are similar, the user might then want to link those forms as the first step in building a set of what we are now calling "linked polygons," that is, language areas thought by the cultural historian to be a higher-order unit by virtue of their sharing numerous similar words for the same concepts. This feature can be diagrammatically shown in figure 7.2.

The similarity judgments ("linkages") found between two or more terms for the same or similar concepts can vary from *total similarity, slight similarity*, to *distant similarity*. These judgments can be stored, retrieved, altered, and displayed, and several modes of linkage specification are being explored (e.g., shading, linking of centroids). In addition, SAPIR will allow one to annotate, store, and retrieve information on why the researcher thinks two or more concepts are similar. Equally important is that SAPIR will include a mode for displaying the *combined linkage results for any number of concepts*, providing an automated way of displaying the strength of similarity association between two or more regions.

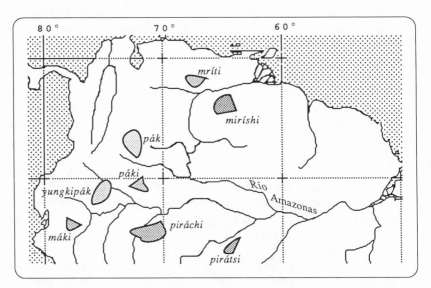

Figure 7.1 Hypothetical display of terms for the ethnobiological concept of 'collared peccary' (*Tayassu pecari*) in eight South American Indian languages of northwestern South America using some of the mapping capabilities of SAPIR (South American Prehistory Inference Resource). See text for explanation. (Base map by M. Lizarralde, 1989)

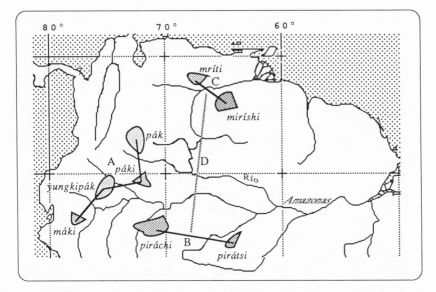

Figure 7.2 Hypothetical display of terms for the ethnobiological concept of 'collared peccary' (*Tayassu pecari*) in eight South American Indian languages of northwestern South America revealing similarity judgments by the cultural historian that yield four linked polygon sets (A–D). See text for explanation. (Base map by M. Lizarralde, 1989)

The linguistic and cultural historical answers that must be developed to account for the patterns revealed by this kind of research must, of course, be provided by the investigator. These distributional maps, however, will allow one to note empirical generalizations and form hypotheses that might best account for the distribution of these linguistic facts as they relate to the cultural history of the region in a fashion that might otherwise require many hundreds of hours employing more traditional but equally valid methods of scholarly research.

The questions, and partial answers, that might rapidly be generated employing SAPIR are quite numerous. As we saw in table 7.1, three major genera of armadillos are found in Amazonian South America, *Dasypus* spp. (including *Tolypeutes tricinctus*), *Priodontes giganteus*, and *Cabassous unicinctus*. Some languages, such as the Tupian-speaking Wayampí of French Guiana, treat these three categories as folk species of a polytypic genus *tatu* (see figure 3.4). The Aguaruna and Huambisa see them as three distinct folk genera, one of which is polytypic (i.e., *shushuí* with two folk species mapping to *Dasypus novemcinctus* and *D. septemcinctus*; *yangkúnt Priodontes giganteus*; and *tuwích Cabassous unicinctus*). What is the pattern observed in the conceptual treatment of this group for the whole South American region? What best accounts for the patterns?

Are the ubiquitous species of sloths, *Bradypus infuscatus* (the three-toed sloth) and *Choloepus hoffmanni* (the two-toed sloth), ever treated as separate folk genera in any system, or are they always conceptually grouped as folk species of an inclusive generic category? Why? What are the perceptual and biogeographical facts that place *Bradypus infuscatus* as the prototype of the folk generic?

Is there a pattern in the apparent association of *Jacamerops aurea*, the great Jacamar, with hummingbirds—a pattern found in widely dispersed languages of Greater Amazonia—and, if so, what are the perceptual facts that lead to this association (similar bill type?).

Is the sound-size symbolism noted for the Jivaroan, Tupian, and Carib languages borne out for the region as a whole? If, as I claim, the sound "r" is strongly associated with 'frog', might there not also be comparable patterns in the human speech sounds selected in rendering the names of other creatures?

In what ways can the distribution of ethnobiological vocabulary, so richly elaborated in traditional societies, provide clues to the patterns of population dispersals of the indigenous peoples? How different is the picture that one paints with the ethnobiological evidence from that arrived at by using, for example, data derived from Swadesh's standard basic vocabulary? What are the major *ethno*biogeographical regions of the area as determined by a careful analysis of the biogeographical record, and what is the interaction of biological and sociocultural factors that best accounts for these facts?

All of the above questions, of course, and the many others like them, are neither new nor surprising. They are, in fact, rather old-fashioned. What is perhaps innovative will be the analysis of extensive and carefully collected ethnobiological data with flexible computerized resources aimed at the development of a regionally based cultural historical understanding that has heretofore been lacking. More significantly, this effort will add some diachronic texture to the synchronic structure of ethnobiological classification that I believe has been absent in earlier work, my own being a prime example. This new time depth—even if it touches only on the relatively recent culture history of a region—will help place the cognitive significance of ethnobiological knowledge in proper developmental perspective, providing some indication of the biological and cultural processes that have been at work in the growth of ethnobiological systems of classification.

7.2 The Evolution of Ethnobiological Categories: Typological Speculations

Plants and animals evolve over time. The systems of ethnobiological classification that human beings come to develop to mirror evolution's work also change through time, although many anthropologists of quite different philosophical persuasions would choose not to call this development evolutionary.

Whatever terminology one adopts to discuss this difficult topic, there is a small but substantial body of data, much of it collected in the last few years, that indicates a good deal about some aspects of the typological growth of ethnobiological systems of classification.

Several years ago, I made a somewhat premature set of proposals on the typological diachronic elaboration of ethnobotanical nomenclature (Berlin 1972). The general gist of the argument was that in the earliest stages of development of ethnobotanical (but by implication, ethnozoological) classification, a system would be comprised solely of named generic taxa. Over time, the system would at first gradually expand horizontally. Plants and animals heretofore not named, but similar in their perceptual and behavioral characteristics to already-named folk genera, would be recognized linguistically by the process of generic name extension. The psychological processes here might best be characterized as *analogical*.

Later, taxa of life form and specific rank would develop, to be followed by the linguistic encoding of taxa of intermediate and varietal rank. Lastly, and quite late in the developmental sequence of the growing hierarchy, the taxon marking the rank of kingdom would be labeled. The general psychological processes of growth during these stages might be characterized as *hierarchical*, with increasing (downward) differentiation and (upward) generalization from a set of primary generic taxa that constituted the basic core of the system.

In my 1972 presentation, nothing much was said about the forces propelling a particular system along its way, except by passing reference to a "more general, technologically based theory of cultural evolution" and allusions to analogous ontogenetic processes observed in the acquisition of vocabulary by children (R. Brown 1958). The lame excuse for failure to provide even the glimpse of an explanatory theory was given in the one-liner, which I believe is a bad paraphrase of something similar once stated by Greenberg: "On the other hand, one usually searches for causal explanations only after one has observed something that might be interesting to explain" (Berlin 1972:84). There was, however, an implicit suggestion about the significance of the role of plant domestication in the relatively late linguistic recognition of taxa of subgeneric rank. Noting that varietal taxa appear near the end of the developmental sequence in ethnobotanical systems of classification, I claimed that

varietal [taxa] occur almost exclusively in the classification of important cultivars. . . . The control over nature that is required in selecting and maintaining a particular race of corn, beans, rice, chili-pepper, squash or what have you, morphologically distinct enough to merit habitual lexical designation, can be accomplished only by relatively advanced horticulturalists. . . . [O]ne should not expect to find varietal ethnobotanical nomenclature except in the languages of societies which practice rather refined methods of cultivation. Even in these languages, varietal names will be restricted to highly important groups of cultivated plants. (Ibid.:72)

These intuitions on the possible evolutionary significance of the recognition of subgeneric taxa were not to be made explicit until the research of Whistler (1976) and Waddy (1982a), to be followed Hunn and French (1984) and C. H. Brown (1985), all of whose work is discussed below.

As concerns the possibility that there might be some sequential relationship between taxa of life-form and subgeneric rank, the former perhaps being encoded linguistically before the latter, I speculated that

> I had at one time hoped to show that specific names become encoded in a language's ethnobotanical lexicon before the appearance of major life forms such as 'tree', 'vine', 'grass', and so on. The data that I have been able to gather . . . do not allow for a definitive answer as to which ethnobotanical [rank] may be prior. I know of no language which lacks at least some specific plant names, although there may have been languages . . . which lacked general life-form terms. (Ibid.:58)

The precious little detailed, cognitively sophisticated ethnobotanical fieldwork that had been carried out in the early 1970s had been conducted almost exclusively among horticultural peoples, many of them with centuries of experience in the domestication of plants (and animals). No comprehensive report had at that time been produced on the systems of ethnobiological classification of foragers or peoples whose traditional form of subsistence was not based on horticulture.

Since then, however, a number of exemplary studies on the systems of ethnobiological classification of nonagricultural societies have appeared (especially Whistler 1976; Hunn 1979, 1980, 1990; Hunn and French 1984; Turner 1974; Turner, Bouchard, and Kennedy 1981; Turner, Thomas, Carson, and Ogilvie 1983; Waddy 1983, 1988; Fowler 1972; Felger and Moser 1985). In addition, a number of comparative papers bearing on the theoretical significance of ethnobiological data from such societies for the development of ethnobiological classification have appeared and have been widely read and debated (see especially C. H. Brown 1985, 1986 with commentary; Hunn and French 1984; Headland 1983, 1986).

These new materials, which I will discuss below, point to the fact that, with the striking exception of the Seri, the recognition of folk species in the ethnobiological systems of traditional nonagricultural peoples is essentially nonexistent. Life-form taxa, however, are well established in virtually all such systems (Brown 1984a). If these data are supported by additional research, it seems clear that subgeneric taxa almost certainly follow the development of named life-form taxa, contrary to what I first suggested given the data available to me in the early 1970s (viz. above). This would lead one to speculate now on an encoding sequence for ethnobiological taxa like the one given in figure 7.3.

Thus, it now seems likely that the cognitive motivation for the recognition of subgeneric taxa in the first place is tied directly to the emergence of plant

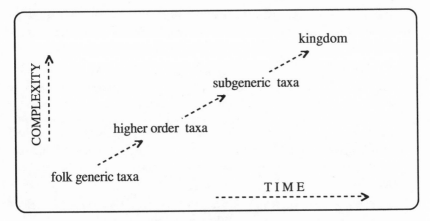

Figure 7.3 Hypothetical diachronic sequence for lexical recognition of major ethnobiological ranks.

domestication and must be quite late in the evolution of systems of ethnobiological classification generally.

Evidence for the Paucity of Folk Specific Taxa in Foraging Societies

One of the first detailed studies to appear on the plant classification systems of nonhorticultural peoples was that of Turner (1974) among the Haida, Bella Coola, and Lillooet Indians of British Columbia, Canada. Turner notes that "specific and varietal categories . . . are much less significant than generic categories. In fact, there are no plant segregates in Haida, Bella Coola, or Lillooet which could be interpreted as varietal names. . . . [N]o specific taxa exist in Bella Coola . . . and only a few examples of lexically recognized specific taxa can be found in Haida and Lillooet" (Turner 1974:139). "Few" is an overstatement. In Skidegate Haida, from an inventory of 154 generic plant taxa, only one is found to be polytypic, mapping to several species of tobacco. In a closely related dialect of Haida, with 167 generic plant taxa, only 7 are polytypic. Most of these seven are bitypic. The largest, *stsakwm*, includes six subgeneric members, all varieties of *Amelanchier alnifolia*, namely,

> *stsekwm-úl* 'real saskatoons' [prototype of the genus]
> *nek'nakw'-úkw'sa7* 'rotten-berries'
> *spekpek* 'white'
> *swelhkwa7-ú7sa7* [no gloss]
> *stl'exelús* 'sweet-eye'
> *stex-lús* 'bitter-eye'

In a comparable study carried out among the Nitinaht, a Nootkan language of the Wakashan language family of the same general area, Turner makes similar observations.

> Specific-level taxa are scarcely represented and varietal level taxa are not represented at all. . . . There is only one example of [a] 'generic' level plant taxon [from an inventory of about one hundred generic taxa] in Nitinaht that is further subdivided into a 'specific' level. . . . That is *quaway*, salmonberry, which is differentiated nomenclaturally into its different colour forms: golden, ruby, and dark purple. . . . [T]his scarcity of 'specific' level and total lack of 'variety' folk taxa is consistent with the situation existing in other Northwestern languages. (Turner, Thomas, Carlson, and Ogilvie 1983:49)

Another important study of nonagricultural peoples, this one in the area of historical reconstruction, is that of Whistler (1976). Whistler's comprehensive comparative study of the ethnobiological systems of classification of the Patwin branch of the Wintun language family, perhaps one of the largest aboriginal groups in California, indicates unambiguously that specific taxa were poorly developed or essentially nonexistent. Whistler's innovative research was based on an analysis of the extensive lexical materials available for several dialects of Patwin collected by ethnologists and linguists working with California Indians in the early part of the century (Barrett, Kroeber, de Angulo, Radin, Snyder, Morgan), data from the "extensive field notes and indices of linguists working under the auspices of the Survey of California Indian Languages (E. Bright [1951–1952], Ultan [1961–63], and Whistler [1975–1976])" (Whistler 1976:20). In addition, Whistler had access to the detailed comparative "natural history wordlists of C. Hart Merriam for Patwin-speaking groups, gathered at scattered intervals from 1903 to 1936" (ibid.:20).[2]

The results of his comparative study led Whistler to the following conclusions concerning specific taxa in Patwin.

> The really overwhelming fact about the structure of Patwin taxonomies is their preponderance of monotypic taxa of generic rank. Fowler (1972), working on reconstruction of the Numic system of ethnobiology, discovered a similar dominance of monotypic generics among the Numic groups, which also had a subsistence pattern of hunting and gathering. This coincidence raises the question of whether all hunting-gathering societies will show a similar pattern. (Ibid.:48)

To my knowledge, Whistler was the first scholar to note the possible association between form of subsistence and the paucity of taxa of specific rank and to make this suggestion in print. Unfortunately, his insight was not seriously evaluated until a decade later.

---

[2] The materials are now published as Merriam (1980); see Berlin (1981) for a review. Whistler's methodology is an exemplary model for persons interested in carrying out historical reconstruction on ethnobiological systems of classification.

The data supporting Whistler's claims are straightforward. Of the 189 folk generic taxa recognized in the Kabalmen dialect of Patwin, 6 are polytypic (3 percent). The Tebti dialects, with 211 folk genera, subdivide 8 with named subgeneric classes (4 percent). Finally, the River dialects, with 171 folk genera, possess only 2 polytypic generics (less than 1 percent of the total).

Whistler is aware of the several complicating factors associated with the reconstruction of vocabulary in heavily acculturated groups, a point raised by a number of the commentators on C. H. Brown's recent speculations (Brown 1985; especially Bulmer 1985), and this is a point to which I will return directly. Thus, he states

> For the Patwin . . . the issue boils down to deciding whether the dearth of taxa of specific rank is due to loss early in the decay of the language and culture, or whether the taxa were never there in the first place. The pattern of the Patwin taxonomies seems to indicate that the latter is the more correct assumption, which might in turn suggest that non-agricultural societies in general may have extremely high percentages of monotypy, considerably higher than the 85 per cent or so reported by Berlin for agricultural societies. (Ibid.:49)

Fowler's extensive comparative work among the Numic peoples of the Great Basin of the United States reveals the same patterns as described for aboriginal California. Fowler notes that specific taxa

> occur in all Numic schemes, but with far less frequency than generics [and] are less stable than generics. . . . They comprise a productive and sometimes idiosyncratic class, with forms often varying from informant to informant within a single language, sub-cultural area or speech community. . . . [I]ndividuals [are] uncertain as to whether to handle some forms as taxonomic subordinates to generics, or as their taxonomic equivalents; i.e., as other generics [and coordinate to them]. In this latter case, informants feel that the modifiers contained in some of these forms call attention to plant and animal similarities rather than to sub-groupings [*sic!*]. (Fowler 1972:228)

In addition, Fowler notes that of the small number of specific categories that can be found, few exhibit wide distributions that might allow for them to be reconstructed,

> in spite of the presence of like semantic principles leading to their formation, i.e., the use of color, size . . . attributives. . . . [O]nly the forms for snowshoe hare as 'white (jack)rabbit', *tosa-kamme*, rattlesnake perhaps as 'rock snake', *to-kog^wa* and gopher snake/water snake as *pasi-ko* . . . show sufficient phonological similarities and distributional patterns as to suggest proto-Numic reconstruction. (Ibid.:231)

A third important body of data on a nonhorticultural people comes from Australia. Waddy has recently published a theoretically significant series of papers (Waddy 1982a, 1982b, 1983) and a two-volume monograph (Waddy 1988) on the plant and animal classification of the Anindilyakwa of Groote Eylandt, Australia. This work is important in a number of respects, not the least of which being its careful attention to ethnobiological data collection based on rather full and comprehensive botanical and zoological voucher collections (see Waddy 1988, vol. 2; and Levitt 1981). In addition, the Anindilyakwa are an important test case for the developing proposal on the significance of form of subsistence and the paucity of specific taxa in that "they, more than most Australian Aboriginal groups, have retained not only their enthusiasm for traditional subsistence activities, but a great deal of knowledge associated with these" (Bulmer 1985:54). They do not possess, or so it seems, a seriously degenerated system of classification due to acculturation. Waddy's description of subgeneric taxa shows that

> in comparison with the data on plants presented by Berlin, Breedlove, and Raven (1974) and by Hays (1974), there are extraordinarily few labelled taxa of specific rank in Anindilyakwa. One example is the group of grasses with awned seed *dingarrkwa*. *Dukwulyadada dingarrkwa*, meaning 'white seeds,' refers to *Aristida browniana* and *dumurrijungwa dingarrkwa*, meaning 'black seeds', refers to *Pseudopogonatherum irritans*, neither of which has particular cultural significance. . . . Other examples of specific taxa found in the plant kingdom are big-leaved/small-leaved (3 generic taxa) and good/bad (of no use) (1 generic taxon). (Waddy 1988:72)

In discussing the Anindilyakwa classification of animals, she states:

> Labelled subgeneric divisions are rare in the animal kingdom, as in the plant kingdom. Binomially labelled specific taxa in the animal kingdom are limited to the 'real' one [i.e., linguistic marking of the prototypical species], though I have recently heard the distinction good/bad applied to sea cucumbers. In most instances where more than one scientific species is included in the one Anindilyakwa taxon, the differences between the species are recognized though not labeled. (Ibid.:80)

Waddy's description of Groote Eylandt ethnobiology recognizes a combined total of some six hundred generic plant and animal taxa. The number of subgeneric taxa reported is less than 5 percent of this figure. This leads Waddy to conclude, clearly independently of Whistler's identical observation on Californian foragers made a decade earlier, that

> the Aborigines of Groote Eylandt were hunters and gatherers who relied largely on fish and turtles, some land animals and on bush fruits and roots. They ate few seeds and no leafy vegetable matter. It will be interesting to see if other hunter-gatherer societies also have such a sparsity of folk specifics. If so it would support my contention that folk specifics and folk varietals may have developed largely in societies where agriculture plays a significant role in the economy and there is a subsequent need to make finer distinctions within a taxon. This seems to be a corollary of Berlin,

Breedlove and Raven's finding that the proportion of folk specifics is much higher among cultivated plants than among other plants. (Waddy 1982a:72)

A final example of a detailed ethnobiological description of another traditionally foraging group has been provided by Hunn, who over the last fifteen years has been conducting ethnozoological and ethnobotanical research among the Sahaptin of the state of Washington (Hunn 1979, 1980, 1990; Hunn and French 1981). As with Turner's and Waddy's research, Hunn's work is well grounded in conscientious ethnobiological fieldwork (1,050 voucher plant collections representing 30 percent of the vascular flora of the region and nearly 200 collections of animal specimens), as well as field and handbook identifications of the vertebrate and invertebrate fauna following well-established ethnobiological procedures (Hunn 1977:17–38). In addition, Hunn worked with numerous Sahaptin speakers of several dialects and was particularly concerned with issues of informant variation.

The Sahaptin system of ethnobiological classification recognizes 236 folk generic ethnozoological taxa and 213 generic ethnobotanical categories, for a total generic inventory of 450 groups. However, as with the other traditionally foraging societies discussed thus far, the Sahaptin have a minuscule number of subgeneric taxa:

While the basic role of the folk generic core of folk biological classification systems is clearly evident in the Sahaptin case, the existence of a well defined hierarchy of folk taxa involving 3–6 folk taxonomic *ranks*, as detailed by Berlin *et al.* . . . is scarcely evident in the Sahaptin system. The *specific* rank, the hallmark of which is the systematic use of binomial nomenclature in naming specific contrast sets, is not evident in the Sahaptin material. Binomial nomenclature . . . is consistently applied to subdivide no more than 2% of the recorded Sahaptin folk generic taxa. . . . [Since life-form taxa in Sahaptin are also problematic] Sahaptin may represent a stage of development approximating the 'one-level hierarchy' composed entirely of folk generic taxa that Berlin proposed as the earliest phase of evolutionary elaboration of taxonomic nomenclatural systems. (Berlin 1972; Hunn 1980:3–4)

A major comparative survey bearing on the relation of ethnobiological classification and form of subsistence has recently been conducted by C. H. Brown (1985). Brown conducted his survey in order to test the hypothesis that "binomial names, such as English *blue oak* and *shingle oak*, are common in folk taxonomies of cultivators but rare in those of hunter-gatherers" (1985:iv). In addition to some but not all of the groups discussed above, Brown includes a good number of earlier, nonethnobiologically sophisticated sources (e.g., Chamberlain 1908, 1964).

Although his argument is marred by a number of methodological and conceptual errors, Brown's claims are generally correct, as the above data might suggest. The most significant problem with Brown's interpretation is his failure to distinguish the ethnobiological ranks of the taxa he chooses to classify as "binomial." Given the above observations on the significance of rank and hierarchical elaboration, it is crucial that one be able to determine the ethnobiological rank of the categories to which the terms in question apply. As Headland points out in a candid critique of Brown's survey:

> The question to ask, is not what percentage of a peoples' biological taxa are binomials, but what percentage of the *specific* taxa are binomials. For Brown to substantiate his hypothesis that hunter-gatherers lack binomials in their biological terminology, he must, in my opinion, limit himself to data which discriminate specific from generic taxa and then calculate only the percentage of the specific labels which are binomials. Generic taxa must be excluded from his statistical calculations in every language compared. (Headland 1985:58)

I believe that Brown's intention was to focus on folk specific taxa (*sensu* Berlin), as a companion article that appeared a year later in the same journal demonstrates (Brown 1986), although this goal is simply implicit in his earlier piece. Nothing in his 1985 data, however, can be interpreted as seriously contradicting the proposal that nonhorticultural peoples have developed few if any subgeneric taxa as part of their ethnobiological systems of classification of plants and animals.

Geoghegan's Speculations on Ndumba

If it is likely that the systems of ethnobiological classification of simple foragers have yet to develop any significant number of specific taxa, or if this ethnobiological rank is, at least, poorly elaborated, while the systems of horticultural peoples are clearly complex with large numbers of polytypic generic classes, the question arises, what evidence is available concerning the transition from the simpler to the more complex systems? No ethnobiological description of a people moving from foraging to what might be called "incipient agriculture" has ever been carried out. It is likely, according to many ethnographers, that no such society currently experiencing this transition exists anywhere in the world today. If such groups are to be found at all, one might look to the so-called fringe peoples on the western and eastern slopes of the densely populated areas of the New Guinea highlands such as the Hewa (Hays, pers. comm.). While there is little doubt that, in general, human systems of subsistence show a progression from hunting-gathering to horticulture, it is quite unlikely that the details of this process will ever be understood from evidence collected among present-day peoples.

Nonetheless, it is at least worthwhile to consider some of the likely factors involved in this transition, especially as it relates to ethnobiological classification, provided it be clearly recognized that our speculations are, at best, plausible guesses based on fragmentary evidence and, perhaps more importantly, as my colleague John Rowe might quietly mutter, if one does not spend too much time on the topic in the process.

To my knowledge, one system, that of the Ndumba of New Guinea, has been suggested as an example of how a once-foraging people might have begun to move toward the elaboration of the set of polytypic generic taxa that is the "hallmark" of a horticulturally based society. It will be recalled that Ndumba ethnobotanical classification shows a particularly aberrant hollow curve as regards the frequency of specific contrast sets of two, three, and four members. It is precisely this feature that Hays chose to comment on at length in a number of publications that show the Ndumba system to be at variance with a number of the principles of ethnobiological classification that I had proposed earlier (cf. Hays 1979, 1983). For greater ease in following the argument, figure 7.4 shows a comparison of the distribution of polytypic generics for the Ndumba with that of the Tzeltal, Wayampí, and Aguaruna, groups whose frequency distributions approximate those expected in terms of the Willis curve, as discussed in chapter 3.

In chapter 3, I indicated that Ndumba is notable in its aberrance from Willis's general principles of numbers of taxa per group, with an exceptionally low number of subgeneric contrast sets of two and three members, but considerable numbers of taxa of greater size. Geoghegan (1976), who was the first to take notice of Ndumba's uniqueness in this respect, proposed a novel interpretation that relates to the development of ethnobiological classification generally.

Geoghegan stated his argument in roughly the following way. When a society begins to develop horticulture, it will first begin to divide a few selected culturally important cultivated plants into a small set of polytypic generic taxa.

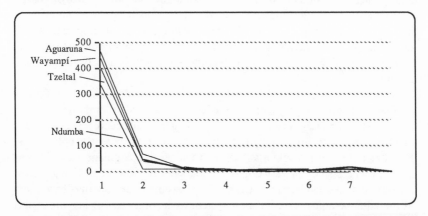

Figure 7.4 Frequency distribution of generic taxa in four systems of ethnobotanical classification in terms of numbers of specific taxa included in sets with 1 (monotypic genus) to ≥7 members. Numbers of taxa per set taken from table 3.3.

Specific differentiation in this group of plant taxa will occur quite rapidly, and large numbers of specific plant taxa will be formed, or, as I would like to say it now, literally, *invented*. On the other hand, generic polytypy will progress more slowly among the less important plants. When Geoghegan plotted the (logarithmic) distribution of polytypic genera for the Ndumba, he noted that

> a very large number of monotypic folk genera (333 in all) and a small number of polytypic genera . . . show an extremely high degree of polytypy [hence the relatively curious shape of the hollow curve with its disproportionate number of 2-typic, 3-typic, and 4-typic taxa]. . . . The excessively higher number of monotypic genera could be taken as pointing to the taxonomy being in a relatively early stage of development compared to [Tzeltal or Aguaruna]. If the majority of the polytypic genera are of high cultural significance (e.g., cultigens), then I would take these data as supporting my . . . extension of Berlin's arguments concerning the growth of folk taxonomies: namely, that the *subdivision of folk generics into specific taxa during the early development of a taxonomy takes place most rapidly among the folk genera of greatest importance, and relatively slowly among those of lesser significance.* (Geoghegan 1976:478, emphasis added)

As plausible as Geoghegan's proposals might seem, they do not appear to be borne out by the data. First, Ndumba is not characterized by an "excessively higher number of monotypic genera" than one finds proportionally in most systems. Ndumba, with a P value of .14 is next to Wayampí and Taubuid (each with P = .15), followed closely by Tzeltal (P = .17). Second, when one examines the full inventory of Ndumba polytypic genera, one discovers that the inventory is split roughly in half between the cultivated forms (twenty-five cultivated folk genera versus twenty-seven noncultivated generics), hardly the majority that Geoghegan was looking for to confirm his hypothesis. Furthermore, while the cultivated generics show somewhat higher numbers of highly polytypic forms (eight taxa encompassing ≥ ten folk species versus three sets for the noncultivated classes), the distribution of contrast sets with two through nine members is not significantly different between the two groups.

What *is* strange about the Ndumba materials is the deviation from the expected Willis distribution, with its considerably deflated N for the sets of two, three, and four members (recall again the standard Willis curve). I now believe that this can be explained, in part, by the nature of Hays' botanical collections. His major goal in his important monograph on this Highland New Guinea people was the study of variation in ethnobotanical knowledge. Using a sample of five males and five females, he aimed to determine patterns of variation in the ethnobotanical classification system by having each of his informants independently view and name a standardized field herbarium of 517 plant specimens that he had collected from the region, an enormous undertaking resulting in over five thousand informant identifications.

Nonetheless, the sample of 374 species in 261 genera, did not approach the total number of species for the region as a whole. While Hays made every effort to "sample all of the possible eco-niches within the various vegetation communities . . . trying to make my collections as broadly representative of the local flora as possible within my limited resources" (Hays 1974:180), it is certain that this sample falls far short of the total species diversity for the higher plants for this region of the New Guinea highlands. As a consequence, it is quite likely that had more general collections been carried out with an effort toward developing a comprehensive flora of the area, clearly outside Hays's aims, then the number of polytypic folk genera with fewer members would also likely increase significantly. This observation gains support by Hays's own candid observation that

> by no means all of the plant names *discovered* in Ndumba occurred as *naming responses*; indeed, out of the total lexicon of 1,249 names which might have been applied to the plants collected, only 602 actually were applied. . . . [However] with the aid of various reference works . . . I am confident of the referents of some 249 plant names not [used in the naming tasks]. . . . [Nonetheless], the 'totally unknown' quantity of Ndumba ethnobotanical nomenclature is about [32 percent]. (Ibid.:186, 188, emphasis added)

Thus, while the Ndumba might have been thought of as candidates for data on the transition from foraging to horticulture, they now seem unlikely as an appropriate test case. The question remains, however: What does best account for the paucity of subgeneric taxa in the systems of nonagricultural peoples that are found in the world today or whose historical reconstructed systems of classification show little or no evidence of specific taxa?

Utilitarian Explanations on Form of Subsistence and Ethnobiological Classification

The most recent speculations, and that is what they must be called, come from Hunn and French (1984) and C. H. Brown (1985). Both proposals are neofunctionalist and build on the unconfirmed observation that foragers will exhibit systems of ethnobiological classification that include fewer named generic groupings than those of horticulturalists. Hunn and French state their argument as follows:

> [It] is likely that hunter-gatherers will have smaller folk biological inventories [of generic taxa] than subsistence farmers in the same habitat. This accords with an otherwise curious fact that Kalahari San hunter-gatherers are *more selective* of the plants they use than nearby agricultural Bantu. . . . They can afford to be more selective because of the low population densities and high mobility. Subsistence farmers are subject to periodic crop failures . . . at which times they are forced to rely on wild foods the hunting-gathering San consider inedible. Their sheer numbers force them to recognize a wider range of species as of potential use than is true of

the San. If this hypothesis is correct, the increased reliance on binomial naming [i.e., the recognition of folk specific taxa] may be understood as a response to the need for an expanded ethnobiological repertoire. (Hunn and French 1984:89)

Brown independently makes a similar claim, again stating that the size of foragers' systems of ethnobiological classification are smaller than those of horticulturalists.

[Farmers'] knowledge of plants and animals is typically vastly greater than that of noncultivators. To understand this, one need only refer to the fact observed above that foragers of biologically rich areas do not necessarily develop plant and animal taxonomies larger than those of hunting and gathering peoples of biologically poorer regions. . . . A major benefit of agriculture is that it supports population densities many times greater than those that can be maintained by a foraging way of life. . . . Of course, this benefit becomes a liability if broad *crop failure* occurs. In such an event, as Lee [1979:180–181] suggests, small-scale farmers must exploit wild plant and animal resources more intensively than hunters and gatherers, since there are vastly more mouths to feed. Consequently, expanded knowledge of and interest in wild plants and animals [and the consequent development of subgeneric taxa] may be essential to the existence of small-scale agricultural groups. (C. H. Brown 1985:49, emphasis added)

In evaluating these arguments, it should be noted that there is very little, if any, ethnobiological evidence that would support the observation that foragers *in the same habitats* as agriculturalists have significantly lower inventories of generic taxa, a point noted earlier in chapter 3. In Brown's paper, no hunter-gatherer system is paired with an agricultural group that resides in the same habitat, with the exception of the Philippine Tasaday and Agta, for whom comparison with other Philippine groups is made. The data are hardly comparable, however, in that neither of these groups has been studied in detail.

The Tasaday, the famous recently discovered "Stone Age population" whose identity as a so-called primitive people is in serious doubt (Headland 1989; Berreman 1991), have not been accorded detailed ethnobiological description. As Bulmer cogently writes:

The report on the Tasaday (Yen 1976) is by a highly competent ethnobotanist but is based on no more than six weeks' fieldwork, using an interpreter. It further appears that Yen was (very rationally) primarily concerned to identify *plants*, not, as Brown was in his four-day Huastec study, to elicit *vocabulary*. [In addition], the fact that there were at the time only 13 adult Tasaday and that the total size of their speech community . . . seems unlikely to be larger than a few score persons might surely be expected to have some consequence for the scale of their lexicon in folk biological as well as other domains. (Bulmer 1985:54)

Another possible group living in a tropical habitat that might be used for comparision are the Agta of the Philippines. Although this group has adopted agriculture, there is good evidence that this is a relatively recent cultural change. Headland, who has lived for many years with these people and who has conducted preliminary ethnobotanical work among them, stoutly disagrees with Brown's analysis of his own data. In spite of the fact that Headland has not carried out extensive ethnobotanical survey work among the Agta, I calculate, on the basis of his 1985 report (as well as Headland, pers. comm.), that the Agta inventory of plant generic taxa approaches four hundred, and would likely go higher with systematic ethnobotanical data collection, especially given Fox's (1953) account of around six hundred folk generic taxa for the Pinatubo Negritos of the Zambales range of Luzon, a people similar in many ways to the Agta. Both of these figures (four hundred generic taxa for the Agta, six hundred for the Pinatubo Negritos) correspond closely to the approximately six hundred or so folk genera found among the advanced horticultural Taubuid residing in the same general region (Pennoyer 1975). (That Conklin's inventory of nine hundred-plus generic taxa for the Hanunóo has never been matched by *any* horticultural group in the world living in comparably rich tropical forest habitats should not be taken as detracting from the five hundred upper limit of folk generic taxa found for most horticultural peoples studied thus far in tropical forest regions.)

Brown, in incorporating Headland's new materials for the Agta, now notes that "the [Agta] case, then, contradicts my suggestion that extensive use of binomial labels is required when taxonomies are large . . . hunter-gatherers may be able to sustain higher levels of interest in a larger number of biological classes than can farmers. Why this should be so is far from clear at present" (Brown 1985:62). The other nonhorticultural groups listed in Brown's survey occupy areas of the world where the natural biological diversity is considerably lower than the humid tropics, or they have been in contact with Western civilization for hundreds of years, or both. Most of these groups, as Bulmer (1985) points out, have not been seriously studied, and none have been investigated by ethnobiologists. It should not be surprising that the inventories reported for these peoples should be smaller than those reported from well-studied horticultural societies.

If we can take as general fact that the relative size of the generic inventory of foragers and horticulturalists occupying the same habitat has not been demonstrated to be substantially different, given the above considerations, we are still confronted with the apparent dearth of specific taxa in the systems of the former and the possible explanations that might account for it.

A Perceptual-Cognitive Evaluation of Form of Subsistence and the Recognition of Folk Specific Taxa

The Hunn-French-Brown argument in brief suggests that cultivators are driven to expand their knowledge of wild plant (and animal?) diversity directly as a result of peoples' utilitarian concerns with the implications of major failures in food production due to the vicissitudes of bad weather, crop pests, or the like. In their own words:

> Subsistence farmers are subject to periodic crop failures . . . at which times they are forced to rely on *wild foods*. If this hypothesis is correct, the increased reliance on binomial naming [i.e., the development of specific taxa] may be understood as a response to the need for an expanded ethnobiological repertoire. (Hunn and French 1984:89, emphasis added)

> [The benefit of higher population density] becomes a liability if broad crop failure occurs. In such an event small-scale farmers must exploit *wild plant and animal resources* more intensively than hunters and gatherers, since there are vastly more mouths to feed. Consequently, expanded knowledge of and interest in wild plants and animals [i.e., the consequent development of specific taxa] may be essential to the existence of small-scale agricultural groups. (Brown 1985:49, emphasis added)

There seems to be little doubt that domestication led, and continues to lead, to the creation of folk specific taxa. It also follows that a cognitively qualitative difference manifests itself as part of the process of human beings' conscious construction and manipulation of new and perceptually different forms of life. Based on this qualitative difference in their interaction with living things—a kind of interaction that is in many respects consciously experimental—individuals begin to take what might be called a second, more careful look at nature. People begin to be more systematic in the way they deal with the biological world. Regions of the biological space that they had known all along as undifferentiated generic gestalten are now looked upon in greater detail, perhaps even submitted to *close study*. Heretofore unnoticed objective differences are recognized explicitly for the first time. Two closely related but unimportant species, at one time unremarkable from a cognitive point of view, now become worthy of linguistic recognition—as distinct parts of what was once a single folk generic taxon.

Hunn and French and Brown would argue that the driving force behind this new curiosity about nature and the formation of novel specific categories is the simple utilitarian need to develop some kind of famine food resource center in the event of major crop failures. This view is a moden restatement of the functionalist position of Malinowski, who saw ethnobiological knowledge as the quintessence of primitive pragmatism, to paraphrase Morris (1983). From this perspective, ''The road from the wilderness to the savage's belly and consequently to his mind is very short. For him the world is an indiscriminate background against which there stands out the useful, primarily the edible, species of animals and plants'' (Malinowski 1974:44). One figuratively finds a world peopled with emerging horticultural societies hard at work, scouring the forest for potentially edible plants that can be labeled as folk species. These are the potentially edible leaves, roots, and berries that might be readily available when the gods failed to bring the rain.

While it may be impossible to adequately test the utilitarian argument for the expansion of folk specific taxa in horticultural societies, some clues can be gained by examining the nature of folk specific contrast sets for groupings of non-cultivated or less explicitly managed plant resources for traditional cultivators today. Plausibility of the strict utilitarian proposal is gained if it can be shown that a large proportion of wild plants are recognized as folk specific taxa in ethnobiological systems of classification primarily because of their edibility, even if this edibility is resorted to on a nonregular basis (i.e., during times of food shortages). However, the functionalist explanation is weakened if it is found that folk species that refer to wild or weakly managed plant resources are known primarily for their nondietary cultural significance.

Tables 7.3 and 7.4 present data on the primary cultural value of all recognized folk species documented for both a seed-cultivating and root-cultivating horticultural society, the Tzeltal and Aguaruna. Folk species are grouped first by their level of human management (cultivated, protected, significant, not treated for the Tzeltal; cultivated, significant, not treated for the Aguaruna) and then further classified as to their value as edible or non-edible plants.

Tables 7.3 and 7.4 show a strong correlation between edibility of folk species and degree of cultural management. Most weakly managed forms are not considered important at all because of their potential food value. Surely the conceptual recognition of these noncultivated forms does not occur primarily because people are concerned about the unpredictability of bringing in a bountiful harvest, as Hunn, French, and Brown would argue the case. The majority of these wild species have little dietary importance and many have only mini-

TABLE 7.3

Association of Edible and Nonedible Folk Species, with Level of Cultural Management, for the Tzeltal of Mexico

Value of Folk Species as Food	Cultivated	Protected	Significant	Not Treated
Edible	106	5	21	0
Nonedible	8	8	73	15

Note: Chi-square = 127, p ≤ .001.

TABLE 7.4

Association of Edible and Nonedible Folk Species, with Level of Cultural Management, for the Aguaruna of Peru

Value of Folk Species as Food	Cultivated	Significant	Not Treated
Edible	128	57	0
Nonedible	11	117	37

Note: Chi-square = 156, p ≤ .001.

mal direct adaptive significance. While several can be used for house construction, cordage, and other material goods, many are valued as the source of the seeds for the production of particularly pleasing necklaces, as adornments for religious shrines, and for other nonmaterialistic functions. More importantly, many of the nonmanaged folk species are striking in their perceptual distinctiveness, for example, the various types of bromiliads or ferns. Rather than suggesting that peoples' second look at nature is motivated by rumbling stomachs, the facts suggest that the biological differences noted are those that most directly express themselves as part of the plan of nature, provided, of course, that one is looking closely enough to discern it.

The Seri: A Counterexample

Both the utilitarian and cognitive positions on folk species and form of subsistence in systems of ethnobiological classification are tied to the modification of plants and animals by the processes of domestication. The facts to be explained take the form of a hypothesis framed as a standard implicational statement: *if* a system exhibits well-established taxa at the rank of folk species, *then* the basic form of subsistence will be founded on agriculture (or by implication, animal husbandry). The Seri of Mexico provide a clear and unambiguous counterexample to this hypothesis and cast serious doubt on its validity as currently formulated.

The Seri reside in the hot and arid desert regions of the Mexican Sonoran coast and islands of the Gulf of California. Average annual rainfall in the region ranges from no more than 100 to 250 mm. Rainfall is "extremely uneven from year to year, and is unpredictable in the driest portions of the region. No perennial rivers or streams flow into the sea and nonindustrial agriculture in such a region is not feasible" (Felger and Moser 1985:20). After contact with the Spanish in the colonial period, some Seri moved inland and "from time to time accepted an agricultural life. . . . Most of the Seri, however, remained hunter-gatherers" (ibid.:87).

In spite of their nonagricultural form of subsistence, the Seri exhibit a system of ethnobotanical classification that conforms closely to that which one has come to expect in well-established horticultural populations. Felger and Moser's excellent ethnobiological description of the group makes this fact unambiguously clear. In a region with about five hundred vascular species, one notes that the "total Seri flora of 427 plant names can be grouped into 310 ethno-genera (folk genera). Eighty-two percent (255) of the ethno-genera are monotypic; the remaining nearly 18 percent (55) are polytypic (two or more ethno-species) and contain 127 ethno-species. . . . Ethno-varietal distinctions occur only among [the highly culturally significant] *Opuntia arbuscula* . . . [one of the edible prickly pear cactuses] and *Pectis* [a wildflower with edible fruits in the sunflower family]" (1985: 62).

The proportion of monotypic to polytypic folk genera among the Seri, 18 percent, conforms closely to the polytypy ratio found for other horticultural groups in diverse parts of the world (see again table 3.5 and the discussion of the widespread 80:20 generic monotypy-polytypy ratio). Also, the distribution of numbers of polytypic folk generic taxa generally conforms to that expected by the standard Willis curve (see figure 3.8a), although the total number of monotypic genera may be a bit low.

Nomenclaturally, Seri polytypic genera show an unmarked prototypical member for the focal folk species while other species of the genus are designated by classic binomial expressions, for example, *zazjc* (*Castela polyandra*); *zazjc caacöl* (*C. emoryi*) lit. 'large zazjc'; *heel* (*Opuntia violacea*); *heel cooxp* (*O. ficus-indica*) lit. 'white heel'. These patterns are familiar ones that have been documented time and again for numerous other groups and are in no way unexpected.

The Seri case forces a reconsideration of the relationship of the presence of folk species to form of subsistence. The most obvious step is to reexamine the data from the several other nonhorticultural groups described above. Are these systems aberrant in some systematic way? I have suggested earlier (Berlin 1972) that as folk systems of classification devolve, as a result of lesser and lesser direct contact with the living world, subgeneric taxa are the first to be lost (cf. the degenerate rank of folk species in American English folk botany). Given the persistent pressures of acculturation, one might claim that, while the groups from the Northwest Coast (Sahaptin, Nootka, Nitanat), California (Patwin), the Great Basin (Numic groups), and Australia (Groote Island) at one time possessed well-established folk species such as those found among the Seri, they have lost them as a result of Western influence and a subsequent decline in their aboriginal cultural knowledge. While such an interpretation is plausible, it appears to me unlikely that the processes of acculturation could so uniformly obliterate taxa of specific rank in societies of noncultivators in quite different environments and geographic regions of the world while leaving intact the specific taxa of horticultural peoples who have been in contact for at least as long or longer. If processes of acculturation worked to systematically reduce the numbers of folk specific taxa in a regular fashion, one would not expect to find the consistent 80:20 generic polytypy ratio so typical of traditional systems everywhere, many of which have been in contact with the Western world for centuries. Rather, one might suppose that at least some of these systems would show far fewer folk species than they actually do.

On the basis of the Seri case, one is drawn to the less than satisfactory conclusion that the presence of well-established folk species does not unambiguously signal that the processes of domestication have been set in motion. While it still appears likely that specific taxa appear late in the evolution of systems of ethnobiological classification, and that domestication plays a major role in leading to their development, the Seri clearly manifest the same intense interest in looking closely at nature as do experimental horticulturalists. Why this should be so cannot be answered by the data at hand. Given the relationship of lexical retention to cultural significance (as discussed in chapter 3), the Seri materials might be illuminated by first determining the degree of management of the plant species included in polytypic generics, and then carrying out a detailed historical linguistic reconstruction of plant lexicon to establish the extent to which the polytypic generic taxa found at the present time represent an ancient part of Seri lexicon or are a more recent innovation. Nonetheless, the Seri remain a major ethnobiological puzzle that can be resolved only by the collection of new data, not only among this group but among other non-cultivating populations elsewhere.

7.3 EPILOGUE

The evidence presented in the preceding chapters supports a general family of hypotheses about the nature of human categorization of plants and animals. Underlying them all is the view that human beings are drawn by some kind of innate curiosity to those groupings of plants and animals that represent the most distinctive chunks of biological reality. This human curiosity about the world is no doubt adaptive, in the broadest sense, but the mass of evidence presented here strongly suggests that people are not *simply* curious about those parts of the world of nature that might be of some direct utilitarian value to them.

The perceptually distinctive chunks that stand out as living landmarks, like the great forest giants of the tropical forest, guide the observer through and over the biological landscape. These landmarks are, of course, the folk genera that form the basis of all systems of ethnobiological classification.

But, as I once claimed, since many of these signposts are so obvious that they almost cry out to be named, the kind of interest required of the human observer might best be characterized as a kind of passive curiosity. Things are noticed, but the cognitive effort involved is really not very much; to be seen and remembered, none of these chunks requires hours of Cain's "close study." Even less is entailed if some notable property of the plant or animal can be captured by the names that people ultimately assign them, building on the processes of sound symbolism and metaphorical description.

But it is also clear that changing social conditions led at some point to the development of humans' passive curiosity about nature into what must have been the first efforts at genetic engineering. This closer look at biological reality led naturally enough to the development of the folk species found in ethnobiological systems of classification, in spite of what now appears to be the contrary data presented by the Seri case. Any evidence that might be brought to bear on the psychological and cultural processes involved in this major qualitative change in our appreciation of biological diversity will represent a significant contribution to ethnobiological science and be appreciated by all who have seriously contemplated the wonder of Nature's plan.

References

Anderson, E. N. 1972. *Essays on South China's Boat People*. Taipei: The Orient Cultural Service.

Atran, S. 1983. Covert Fragmenta and the Origin of the Botanical Family. *Man* 18: 51–71.

Atran, S. 1985. The Nature of Folk Botanical Life-Forms. *Amer. Anthro.* 87: 298–315.

Atran, S. 1987a. Ordinary Constraints on the Semantics of Living Kinds: A Commonsense Alternative to Recent Treatments of Natural-Object Terms. *Mind and Language* 2: 27–63.

Atran, S. 1987b. The Essence of Folkbiology: A Reply to Randall and Hunn. *Amer. Anthro.* 89: 149–52.

Atran, S. 1988. *Whither the New Ethnography?* Paper presented at King's College Conference on Complex Cultural Categories. Cambridge University.

Atran, S. 1990. *Cognitive Foundations of Natural History*. London: Cambridge University Press.

Balée, W. 1986. "Special" Factors in the Comparative Phytosystematics of Tupí-Guaraní. Bronx: New York Botanical Garden. Unpublished manuscript.

Balée, W., and C. Daley. 1987. Ka'apor Resin Classification. Bronx: New York Botanical Garden. Unpublished manuscript.

Barral, B. 1979. *Diccionario Warao-Castellano, Castellano-Warao*. Caracas.

Bartlett, H. H. 1916. The Botanical Work of Edward Lee Greene. *Torreya* 16: 151–75.

Bartlett, H. H. 1940. The Concept of Genus. I. History of the Generic Concept in Botany. *Bull. Torrey Bot. Club* 67: 349–62.

Basilio de Barral, M. 1979. *Diccionario Warao-Castellano, Castellano-Warao*. Caracus: Universidad Catolica Andres Bello.

Berreman, G. D. 1991. The Incredible "Tasaday": Deconstructing the Myth of a "Stone Age" People. *Cultural Survival Quart.* 15: 3–45.

Bentham, G., and J. D. Hooker. 1885. *Genera Plantarum*. London: Reeve and Company.

Berlin, B. 1970. *A Preliminary Ethnobotanical Survey of the Aguaruna Region of the Upper Marañón River Valley, Amazonas, Peru*. Washington, D.C.: Report to the Wenner-Gren Foundation for Anthropological Research.

Berlin, B. 1972. Speculations on the Growth of Ethnobotanical Nomenclature. *Lang. and Soc.* 1: 51–86.

Berlin, B. 1973. The Relation of Folk Systematics to Biological Classification and Nomenclature. *Ann. Rev. Ecol. and Systematics* 4: 259–71.

Berlin, B. 1974. Further Notes on Covert Categories and Folk Taxonomies: A Reply to Brown. *Amer. Anthro.* 76: 327–31.

Berlin, B. 1976a. The Concept of Rank in Ethnobiological Classification: Some Evidence from Aguaruna Folk Botany. *Amer. Ethnol.* 3 (special issue on Folk Biology): 381–99.

Berlin, B. 1976b. A Study in Tzeltal Sound Symbolism. University of California, Berkeley. Unpublished manuscript.

Berlin, B. 1978a. Ethnobiological Classification. In *Cognition and Categorization*, edited by E. Rosch and B. Lloyd, 9–26. Hillsdale, N.J.: Lawrence Erlbaum Associates.

Berlin, B. 1978b. Bases Empíricas de la Cosmología Aguaruna. In *Ethnicidad y Ecología*, edited by A. Cherif, 15–26. Lima: Centro de Investigación y Promoción Amazónica.

Berlin, B. 1981. Review of *Indian Names for Plants and Animals among California and other Western North American Tribes* by C. Hart Merriam, assembled and annotated by Robert F. Heizer. *Language* 57: 245–46.

Berlin, B. 1982. Predicting Discontinuities in Ethnobiological Classification. University of California, Berkeley. Unpublished manuscript.

Berlin, B. 1986. Comment on The Growth of Ethnobiological Nomenclature by C. H. Brown. *Curr. Anthro.* 27: 12–13.

Berlin, B. In prep. *A Comparative Ethnobiological Dictionary of the Jivaroan Languages of Peru and Ecuador.*

Berlin, B., and E. A. Berlin. 1975. Aguaruna Color Categories. *Amer. Ethnol.* 2 (special issue on Intra-Cultural Variation): 61–87.

Berlin, B., and E. A. Berlin. 1983. Adaptation and Ethnozoological Classification: Theoretical Implications of Animal Resources and Diet of the Aguaruna and Huambisa. In *Adapative Responses of Native Amazonians*, edited by R. B. Hames and W. T. Vickers, 301–28. New York: Academic Press.

Berlin, B., and P. Kay. 1969. *Basic Color Terms: Their Universality and Evolution.* Berkeley: University of California Press.

Berlin, B., and R. W. McDiarmid. In prep. Aguaruna and Huambisa Classification of Reptiles and Amphibians.

Berlin, B., and J. O'Neill. 1981. The Pervasiveness of Onomatopoeia in the Jivaroan Language Family. *J. Ethnobiol.* 1: 95–108.

Berlin, B., and J. L. Patton. 1979. *La Clasificación de los Mamíferos de los Aguaruna, Amazonas, Perú.* Berkeley: Language Behavior Research Laboratory and Museum of Vertebrate Zoology.

Berlin, B., and J. L. Patton. In prep. *Mammals of the Aguaruna and Huambisa, Amazonas, Peru.*

Berlin, B., E. A. Berlin. D. E. Breedlove, T. Duncan, V. Jara, R. M. Laughlin, and T. Velasco. 1990. La Herbolaria Médica Tzeltal-Tzotzil. Tuxtla Gutiérrez, Chiapar, Mexico: Instituto Cultura Chiapaneco.

Berlin, B., J. Boster, and J. O'Neill. In prep. *Huambisa Bird Classification.*

Berlin, B., J. Boster, and J. P. O'Neill. 1981. The Perceptual Bases of Ethnobiological Classification: Evidence from Aguaruna Folk Ornithology. *J. Ethnobiol.* 1: 95–108.

Berlin, B., D. E. Breedlove, and P. H. Raven. 1966. Folk Taxonomies and Biological Classification. *Science* 154: 273–75.

Berlin, B., D. E. Breedlove, and P. H. Raven. 1968. Covert Categories and Folk Taxonomies. *Amer. Anthro.* 70: 290–99.

Berlin, B., D. E. Breedlove, and P. H. Raven. 1973. General Principles of Classification and Nomenclature in Folk Biology. *Amer. Anthro.* 75: 214–42.

Berlin, B., D. E. Breedlove, and P. H. Raven. 1974. *Principles of Tzeltal Plant Classification*. New York and London: Academic Press.

Berlin, B., D. E. Breedlove, R. M. Laughlin and P. H. Raven. 1973. Lexical Retention and Cultural Significance in Tzeltal-Tzotzil Ethnobotany. In *Meaning in Mayan Languages*, edited by M. S. Edmonson, 143–64. The Hague: Mouton.

Berlin, B., T. Kaufman, and D. Miller. 1987–88. South American Indian Languages Documentation Project at UC-Berkeley. *SSILA Newsletter* 6: 4.

Berlin, B., P. Kay, and W. Merrifield. 1985. Color Term Evolution: Recent Evidence from the World Color Survey. Unpublished manuscript.

Berlin, B., P. Kay, and W. P. Merrifield. In prep. *The World Color Survey: Further Evidence on the Universality and Evolution of Basic Color Terms*.

Berlin, B., C. Swift, and D. Stewart. In prep. *Principles of Huambisa Fish Classification*.

Bessy, C. 1908. The Taxonomic Aspect of the Species Question. *Amer. Nat.* 42: 218–24.

Bibolotti, B. 1917. *Moseteno Vocabulary and Treatises*. Evanston, Ill.: Northwestern University Press.

Black, M. 1954. *Problems of Analysis (Collected Essays)*. Ithaca, N.Y.: Cornell University Press.

Blackwelder, R. E. 1967. *Taxonomy: A Text and Reference Book*. New York: John Wiley and Sons.

Boas, F. 1911. Introduction. In *Handbook of American Indian Languages*, edited by F. Boas, 1–83. Washington, D.C.: Government Printing Office.

Boster, J. 1980. How Exceptions Prove the Rule: An Analysis of Informant Disagreement in Aguaruna Manioc Identification. Ph.D. diss., University of California, Berkeley.

Boster, J. 1986. "Requiem for the Omniscient Informant": There's Life in the Old Girl Yet. In *Directions in Cognitive Anthropology*, edited by J.W.D. Dougherty, 177–98. Urbana: University of Illinois Press.

Boster, J. 1987. Agreement between Biological Classification Systems Is Not Dependent on Cultural Transmission. *Amer. Anthro.* 89: 914–19.

Bousfield, J. 1979. The World Seen as a Colour Chart. In *Classifications in Their Social Context*, edited by R. F. Ellen and D. Reason, 195–220. London: Academic Press.

Bright, E. 1951–52. *Patwin Field Notes*. Berkeley: Department of Lingusitics, University of California.

Bright, J. O., and W. Bright. 1965. Semantic Structures in Northwestern California and the Sapir-Worf Hypothesis. *Amer. Anthro.* 67: 249–58.

Brown, C. H. 1974. Unique Beginners and Covert Categories in Folk Biological Taxonomies. *Amer. Anthro.* 76: 325–26.

Brown, C. H. 1977. Folk Botanical Life-Forms: Their Universality and Growth. *Amer. Anthro.* 79: 317–42.

Brown, C. H. 1979a. Folk Zoological Life-Forms: Their Universality and Growth. *Amer. Anthro.* 81: 791–817.

Brown, C. H. 1979b. Growth and Development of Folk Botanical Life-Forms in the Mayan Language Family. *Amer. Ethnol.* 6: 366–85.

294 · References

Brown, C. H. 1981a. More on Folk Zoological Life-Forms. *Amer. Anthro.* 83: 398–401.

Brown, C. H. 1981b. Growth and Development of Folk Botanical Life-Forms in Polynesian Languages. *J. Polynesian Soc.* 90: 83–110.

Brown, C. H. 1982. Folk Zoological Life-Forms and Linguistic Marking. *J. Ethnobiol.* 2 (1): 95–112.

Brown, C. H. 1984a. *Language and Living Things: Uniformities in Folk Classification and Naming.* New Brunswick, N.J.: Rutgers University Press.

Brown, C. H. 1985. Polysemy, Overt Marking, and Function Words. *Lang. Sci.* 7: 283–332.

Brown, C. H. 1984c. Life-Forms From the Perspective of *Language and Living Things*: Some Doubts About the Doubts. *Amer. Ethnol.* 11: 589–93.

Brown, C. H. 1985. Mode of Subsistence and Folk Biological Taxonomy. *Cur. Anthro.* 26: 43–62.

Brown, C. H. 1986. The Growth of Ethnobiological Nomenclature. *Cur. Anthro.* 27: 1–18.

Brown, C. H. 1987. The Folk Subgenus: A New Ethnobiological Rank. *J. Ethnobiol.* 7: 181–92.

Brown, C. H., and S. Witkowski. 1982. Growth and Development of Folk Zoological Life-Forms in the Mayan Language Family. *Amer. Ethnol.* 9: 97–112.

Brown, C. H., and S. Witkowski. 1983. Polysemy, Lexical Change, and Cultural Importance. *Man* 18: 72–89.

Brown, R. 1958. How Shall a Thing Be Called? *Psych. Rev.* 65: 14–21.

Brown, R., and R. Nuttall. 1959. Methods in Phonetic Symbolism Experiments. *J. Abnorm. Soc. Psych.* 59: 441–44.

Brunel, G. 1974. Variation in Quechua Ethnobiology. Ph.D. diss., University of California, Berkeley.

Bruner, J. S., J. J. Goodnow, and G. A. Austin. 1956. *A Study of Thinking.* New York: John Wiley and Sons.

Buck, R., and D. Hull. 1966. The Logical Structure of the Linnaean Hierarchy. *Sys. Zool.* 15: 97–110.

Bulmer, R.N.H. 1965. Review of *Navajo Indian Ethnoentomology* by L. C. Wyman and F. L. Bailey. *Amer. Anthro.* 67: 1564–67.

Bulmer, R.N.H. 1967. Why Is the Cassowary Not a Bird? *Man* 2: 5–25.

Bulmer, R.N.H. 1968. Worms That Croak and Other Mysteries of Karam Natural History. *Mankind* 6: 621–39.

Bulmer, R.N.H. 1969. *Field Methods in Ethnozoology with Special Reference to the New Guinea Highlands.* Department of Anthropology and Sociology. University of Papua New Guinea, Roneo.

Bulmer, R.N.H. 1970. Which Came First, the Chicken or the Egg-Head? In *Échanges et communications, mélanges offerts à Claude Lévi Strauss à l'occasion de son 60ème anniversaire*, edited by J. Pouillon and P. Maranda, 1069–91.The Hague: Mouton.

Bulmer, R.N.H. 1974a. Folk Biology in the New Guinea Highlands. *Soc. Sci. Inform.* 13: 9–28.

Bulmer, R.N.H. 1974b. Memoirs of a Small Game Hunter: On the Track of Unknown

Animal Categories in New Guinea. *J. d'Agricul. Tropicale Botan. Appliquée* 21: 79–99.

Bulmer, R.N.H. 1978. Totems and Taxonomy. In *Australian Aboriginal Concepts*, edited by L. R. Hiatt, Canberra: Australian Institute of Aboriginal Studies.

Bulmer, R.N.H. 1979. Mystical and Mundane in Kalam Classification of Birds. In *Classifications in Their Social Contexts*, edited by R. F. Ellen and D. Reason, 57–80. London: Academic Press.

Bulmer, R.N.H. 1985. Comment on *Subsistence and Ethnobiological Nomenclature* by C. H. Brown. *Cur. Anthro.* 26: 54–55.

Bulmer, R.N.H. 1986. The Unsolved Problems of the Birds of Leviticus. Department of Anthropology, University of Auckland.

Bulmer, R.N.H., and J. I. Menzies. 1972–73. Karam Classification of Marsupials and Rodents. *J. Polynesian Soc.* 81: 472–92, 82: 86–107.

Bulmer, R.N.H., and M. J. Tyler. 1968. Karam Classification of Frogs. *J. Polynesian Soc.* 77: 333–85.

Bulmer, R.N.H., J. I. Menzies, and F. Parker. 1975. Kalam Classification of Reptiles and Fishes. *J. Polynesian Soc.* 84: 267–307.

Burton, M., and L. Kirk. 1979. Sex Differences in Masai Cognition of Personality and Social Identity. *Amer. Anthro.* 81: 841–73.

Cain, A. J. 1956. The Genus in Evolutionary Taxonomy. *Sys. Zool.* 5: 97–109.

Cain, A. J. 1958. Logic and Memory in Linnaeus's System of Taxonomy. *Proc. Linn. Soc. London* Session 169: 144–63.

Cain, A. J. 1959a. Taxonomic Concepts. *Ibis* 101: 302–18.

Cain, A. J. 1959b. The Post-Linnaean Development of Taxonomy. *Proc. Linn. Soc. London* 170: 234–44.

Cancian, F. 1963. Informant Error and Native Prestige Ranking in Zinacantan. *Amer. Anthro.* 65: 1068–75.

Castetter, E. F. 1935. *Uncultivated Native Plants Used as Sources of Food*. Ethnobiological Studies in the American Southwest. Albuquerque: University of New Mexico Press.

Castetter, E. F. 1944. The Domain of Ethnobiology. *Amer. Nat.* 78: 158–70.

Chafe, W. 1965. *Meaning and the Structure of Language*. Chicago: University of Chicago Press.

Chamberlain, R. V. 1908. Animal Names and Anatomical Terms of the Gosiute Indians. *Proc. Acad. Nat. Sci. Philadelphia* 60: 74–103.

Chamberlain, R. V. 1964. *The Ethno-Botany of the Gosiute Indians of Utah*. New York: Kraus Reprint Corporation.

Chambers, A. 1972. Patterns of Acquisition of Conifer-Evergreen Tree Names. Unpublished manuscript.

Clayton, W. D. 1972. Some Aspects of the Genus Concept. *Kew Bull.* 27: 281–87.

Clayton, W. D. 1974. The Logarithmic Distribution of Angiosperm Families. *Kew Bull.* 29: 271–79.

Clayton, W. D. 1982. The Genus Concept in Practice. *Kew Bull.* 38: 149–53.

Clifford, J. 1988. *The Predicament of Culture*. Cambridge, Mass.: Harvard University Press.

Clifford, J., and G. Marcus, eds. 1986. *Writing Cultures*. Berkeley: University of California Press.

Colby, B. N. 1966. Ethnographic Semantics: A Preliminary Survey. *Cur. Anthro.* 7: 3–32.

Conklin, H. C. 1954. The Relation of Hanunóo Culture to the Plant World. Ph.D. diss., Yale University.

Conklin, H. C. 1962. The Lexicographical Treatment of Folk Taxonomies. *Inter. J. Amer. Ling.* 28: 119–41.

Conklin, H. C. 1980. *Ethnographic Atlas of Ifugao: A Study of Environment, Culture, and Society in Northern Luzon*. New Haven, Conn.: Yale University Press.

Cowan, S. T. 1962. The Microbial Species. *Sym. Soc. Gen. Microbiol.* 12: 433–55.

Croat, T. 1978. *Flora of Barro Colorado Island*. Stanford, Calif.: Stanford University Press.

Cronquist, A. 1968. *The Evolution and Classification of Flowering Plants*. New York: Houghton Mifflin.

D'Ans, A. M. 1972. *Repertorios Etno-Botanico y Etno-Zoologico Amahuaca (Pano)*. Peru: Centro de Investigacion de Lingüística Aplicada.

Darwin, C. 1859. *On the Origin of Species by Means of Natural Selection*. London: Murray.

Dentan, R. K. 1970. Labels and Rituals in Semai Classification. *Ethnol.* 9: 16–25.

de Schauensee, R. M. 1970. *A Guide to the Birds of South America*. Wynnewood, Penn.: Academy of Natural Sciences of Philadelphia.

Descola, P. 1988. *La Selva Culta: Simbolismo y Praxis en la Ecología de los Achuar*. Quito: Abya-Yala y Instituto Francés de Estudios Andinos.

Diamond, J. M. 1966. Zoological Classification System of a Primitive People. *Science* 151: 1102–4.

Diamond, J. M. 1972. *Avifauna of the Eastern New Guinea Highlands*. Cambridge, Mass.: Nuttal Ornithological Club.

Dorsey, J. O. 1884. *Omaha Sociology*. Washington, D.C.: Smithsonian Institution Press.

Dougherty, J.W.D. 1975. A Universalist Analysis of Variation and Change in Color Semantics. Ph.D. diss., University of California, Berkeley.

Dougherty, J.W.D. 1978. Salience and Relativity in Classification. *Amer. Ethnol.* 5: 66–80.

Dougherty, J.W.D. 1979. Learning Names for Plants and Plants for Names. *Anthropological Linguistics* 21: 298–315.

Dournes, J. 1973. Chi-Chê: La Botanique des Srê. *J. Agricul. Trop. Botan. Appliquée* 20: 1–189.

Dwyer, P. 1976. An Analysis of Rofaifo Mammal Taxonomy. *Amer. Ethnol.* 3: 425–45.

Dwyer, P. 1984–85. Other People's Animals: Two Examples from New Guinea. *Search* 15: 321–27.

Eigenmann, C. 1922. *The Fresh-Water Fishes of Northwestern South America*. Mem. Carnegie Mus. Nat. History, vol. 7.

Ekdahl, M., and N. Butler. 1969. *Terêna Dictionary*. Arquivo Lingüístico. Brasília: Instituto Lingüístico de Verano.

Ekdahl, E. M., and N. Butler. 1979. *Aprenda Terêna*, vol. 1. Brasilia: SIL.

Ellen, R. F. 1975. Variable Constructs in Nuaulu Zoological Classification. *Soc. Sci. Inform.* 14: 201–28.

Ellen, R. F. 1978. Restricted Faunas and Ethnozoological Inventories in Wallacea. In *Nature and Man in South East Asia*, edited by P. A. Stott, 142–64. London: School of Oriental and African Studies, University of London.

Ellen, R. F. 1979a. Introduction. In *Classifications in Their Social Context*, edited by R. F. Ellen and D. Reason, 1–32. London: Academic Press.

Ellen, R. F. 1979b. Omniscience and Ignorance: Variation in Nuaulu Knowledge, Identification and Classification of Animals. *Lang. in Soc.* 8: 337–64.

Ellen, R. F. 1986. Ethnobiology, Cognition, and the Structure of Prehension: Some General Theoretical Notes. *J. Ethnobiol.* 6: 83–98.

Ellen, R. F., A. F. Stimson, and J. I. Menzies. 1976. Structure and Inconsistency in Nuaulu Categories for Amphibians. *J. Agricul. Trop. Botan. Appliquée* 23: 125–38.

Ellen, R. F., A. F. Stimson, and J. I. Menzies. 1977. The Content of Categories and Experience: The Case for Some Nuaulu Reptiles. *J. d'Agricul. Trop. Botan. Appliquée* 24: 3–22.

Felger, R. S., and M. B. Moser. 1985. *People of the Desert and Sea*. Tucson: University of Arizona Press.

Ford, R. I. 1978. Ethnobotany: Historical Diversity and Synthesis. In *The Nature and Status of Ethnobotany*, edited by R. I. Ford. Anthropological Papers, Museum of Anthropology, University of Michigan, no. 67, pp. 33–49. Ann Arbor: University of Michigan Press.

Foster, G. M. 1979. Brief Communications. *Human Organization* 38: 179–183.

Fowler, C. S. 1972. Comparative Numic Ethnobiology. Ph.D. diss., University of Pittsburgh.

Fowler, C. S., and J. Leland. 1967. Some Northern Paiute Native Categories. *Ethnol.* 6: 381–404.

Fox, R. B. 1953. The Pinatubo Negritos: Their Useful Plants and Material Culture. *Philippine Journal of Science* 81: 173–414.

Frake, C. O. 1961. The Diagnosis of Disease among the Subanun. *Amer. Anthro.* 63: 11–32.

Frake, C. O. 1962. The Ethnographic Study of Cognitive Systems. In *Anthropology and Human Behavior*, edited by T. Gladwin and W. C. Sturtevant, 72–93. Washington, D.C.: Anthropological Society of Washington.

Friedberg, C. 1968. Les méthodes d'enquête en ethnobotanique. *J. d'Agricul. Trop. Botan. Appliquée* 15 (7–8): 297–324.

Friedberg, C. 1970. Analyse de quelques groupements de végétaux comme introduction à l'étude de la classification botanique Bunaq. In *Échanges et communications: mélanges offerts à Claude Lévi-Strauss à l'occasion de son 60ème anniversaire*, edited by J. Pouillon and P. Maranda. The Hague: Mouton.

Furbee, L., and R. A. Benfer. 1983. Cognitive and Geographic Maps: Study of Individual Variation among Tojolabal Indians. *Amer. Anthro.* 85: 305–334.

Gardner, P. M. 1976. Birds, Words, and a Requiem for the Omniscient Informant. *Amer. Ethnol.* 3: 446–68.

Garro, L. 1986. Intracultural Variation in Medical Knowledge: A Comparison between Curers and Non-curers. *Amer. Anthro.* 88: 351–70.

Geertz, C. 1973. *The Interpretation of Cultures*. New York: Basic Books.

Geoghegan, W. H. 1976. Polytypy in Ethnobiological Classification. *Amer. Ethnol.* 3: 469–80.

Gery, J. 1977. *Characoids of the World*. Neptune City, N.J.: T.F.H. Publishers, Inc.

Gilmour, J., and S. Walters. 1964. Philosophy and Classification. In *Vistas in Botany*, vol. 4, *Recent Researches in Plant Taxonomy*, edited by W. Turrill, Oxford: Pergamon Press.

Glick, L. B. 1964. Categories and Relations in Gimi Natural Science. *Amer. Anthro.* 66: 273–80.

Gongora-Arones, E. 1987. *Etnozoología Lacandona: La Herpetofauna de Lacanjá-Chansasab*. Ixtapa, Veracruz, México: Instituto Nacional de Investigaciones sobre Recursos Bióticos, Number 13.

Goodenough, W. H. 1957. Cultural Anthropology and Linguistics. In *Seventh Annual Roundtable of Linguistics and Language Studies*, edited by P. Garvin, 167–73. Washington D. C.: Georgetown University.

Gould, S. J. 1979. A Quahog Is a Quahog. *Nat. Hist.* 88: 18–26.

Greenberg, J. H. 1987. *Language in the Americas*. Stanford, Calif.: Stanford University Press.

Greene, E. L. 1888. Botanical Literature, Old and New, II. *Pittonia* 2: 251–60.

Greene, E. L. 1894. Correct Nomenclature VII. *Erythea* 2: 12–13.

Greene, E. L. 1983[1909]. *Landmarks in Botanical History*, edited by F. N. Egerton. Stanford, Calif.: Stanford University Press.

Gregg, J. 1954. *The Language of Taxonomy: An Application of Symbolic Logic to the Study of Classificatory Systems*. New York: Columbia University Press.

Gregg, J. 1967. Finite Linnaean Structures. *Bull. Math. Biophysics* 29: 191–206.

Grenand, P. 1980. *Introduction à l'étude de l'univers Wayãpi*. Paris: Société d'Études Linguistiques et Anthropologiques de France.

Guppy, H. B. 1906. *Observations of a Naturalist in the Pacific*. London.

Hage, P., and K. Hawkes. 1975. Binumarien Color Categories. *Ethnol.* 14: 287–300.

Hage, P., and W. Miller. 1976. "Eagle" = "Bird": A Note on the Structure and Evolution of Shoshoni Ethnoornithological Nomenclature. *Amer. Ethnol.* 3: 481–87.

Haiman, J. 1980. Dictionaries and Encyclopedias. *Lingua* 50: 329–57.

Hallpike, K. 1976. Is There a Primitive Mentality? *Man* 11: 253–70.

Hallpike, K. 1979. *Foundations of Primitive Thought*. Oxford: Oxford University Press.

Harnad, S., ed. 1987. *Categorical Perception: The Groundwork of Cognition*. Cambridge: Cambridge University Press.

Harner, M. 1972. *The Jívaro*. Berkeley: University of California Press.

Harrington, J. P. 1947. Ethnobiology. *Acta Amer.* 5: 224–47.

Harris, M. 1968. *The Rise of Anthropological Theory*. New York: Crowell.

Harshburger, J. W. 1896. Purposes of Ethnobotany. *Bot. Gazette* 21: 146–54.

Hart, G., and H. L. Hart. 1975. *Vocabulario Chayahuita*. Datos Etnolingüísticos. Lima: Instituto Lingüístico de Verano y Ministero de Educación.

Hays, T. E. 1974. Mauna: Explorations in Ndumba Ethnobotany. Ph.D. diss., University of Washington, Seattle.

Hays, T. E. 1976. An Empirical Method for the Identification of Covert Categories in Ethnobiology. *Amer. Ethnol.* 3: 489–507.

Hays, T. E. 1979. Plant Classification and Nomenclature in Ndumba, Papua New Guinea Highlands. *Ethnol.* 18: 253–70.

Hays, T. E. 1982. Utilitarian/Adaptationist Explanations in Folk Biological Classification: Some Cautionary Notes. *J. Ethnobiol.* 2: 89–94.

Hays, T. E. 1983. Ndumba Folk Biology and General Principles of Ethnobiological Classification and Nomenclature. *Amer. Anthro.* 85: 592–611.

Hays, T. E., and J. E. Laferriere. 1987. Recent Doctoral Dissertations of Interest to Ethnobiologists. *J. Ethnobiol.* 7: 223–33.

Headland, T. N. 1981. Taxonomic Disagreement in a Culturally Salient Domain: Botany Versus Utility in a Philippine Negrito Taxonomic System. M.A. thesis, University of Hawaii.

Headland, T. N. 1983. An Ethnobotanical Anomaly: The Dearth of Binomial Specifics in a Folk Taxonomy of a Negrito Hunter-Gatherer Society in the Philippines. *J. Ethnobiol.* 3: 109–20.

Headland, T. N. 1985. Comment on *Mode of Subsistence and Ethnobiological Nomenclature* by C. H. Brown. *Cur. Anthro.* 26: 57–58.

Headland, T. N. 1986. Why Foragers Do Not Become Farmers: An Historical Study of a Changing Ecosystem and Its Effect on a Negrito Hunter-Gather Group in the Philippines. Ph.D. diss., University of Hawaii.

Headland, T. N. 1989. Primitives or Poseurs. *The Sciences* 29: 8.

Healey, C. J. 1978–79. Taxonomic Rigidity in Biological Folk Classification: Some Examples from the Making of New Guinea. *Ethnomedizin* 5: 361–84.

Helfman, G. S., and J. Randall. 1973. Palauan Fish Names. *Pac. Science* 27: 136–53.

Holman, E. W. 1985. Evolutionary and Psychological Effects in Pre-Evolutionary Classifications. *J. Classification* 2: 29–39.

Holmberg, A. 1969. *People of the Long Bow.* New York: American Museum of Natural History.

Hopkins, N. A. 1980. Amuzgo Ethnobotanical Structure and Terminology. Paper presented at the annual meetings of the American Anthropological Association, Washington, D. C.

Hughes, G. E., and M. J. Cresswell. 1968. *Introduction to Modal Logic.* London: Methuen.

Hull, D. 1970. Contemporary Systematic Philosophies. *Ann. Rev. Ecol. and Systematics* 1: 19–53.

Hunn, E. 1975. Cognitive Processes in Folk-ornithology: The Identification of Gulls. Language Behavior Research Laboratory. Berkeley: University of California.

Hunn, E. 1976. Toward a Perceptual Model of Folk Biological Classification. *Amer. Ethnol.* 3: 508–24.

Hunn, E. 1977. *Tzeltal Folk Zoology: The Classification of Discontinuities in Nature.* New York: Academic Press.

Hunn, E. 1979. The Abominations of Leviticus Revisited: A Commentary on Anomaly in Symbolic Anthropology. In *Classifications in Their Social Context*, edited by R. F. Ellen and D. Reason, 103–16. London: Academic Press.

Hunn, E. 1980. Final Project Report to the National Science Foundation, Technical Description of Project Results, Sahaptin Ethnobiology.

Hunn, E. 1982. The Utilitarian Factor in Folk Biological Classification. *Amer. Anthro.* 84: 830–47.

Hunn, E. 1987. Science and Common Sense: A Reply to Atran. *Amer. Antho.* 89: 146–49.

Hunn, E. 1989. Four Factors Governing the Cultural Recognition of Biological Taxa. Unpublished manuscript.

Hunn, E. 1990. *Columbia Plateau Indian Ethnography*. Seattle: University of Washington Press.

Hunn, E., and D. French. 1981. *Lomatium*: A Key Resource for Columbia Plateau Native Subsistence. *Northwest Science* 55: 87–94.

Hunn, E., and D. French. 1984. Alternatives to Taxonomic Hierarchy: The Sahaptin Case. *J. Ethnobiol.* 3: 73–92.

Hutchinson, J. 1959. *The Families of Flowering Plants*. 2 vols. Oxford: Oxford University Press.

Huxley, T. 1869. *The Classification of Animals*. London: Churchill and Sons.

Hyde, S., R. Russell, and M. C. Russell. 1980. *Diccionario Amahuaca* (edición preliminar). Lima: Ministero de Educación y Instituto Lingüístico de Verano.

Isbrücker, I.J.H. 1980. *Classification and Catalogue of the Mailed Loricariidae*. Amsterdam: Institut voor Taxonomische Zoölogie, Universiteit van Amsterdam.

Jakobson, R., and L. R. Waugh. 1979. *The Sound Shape of Language*. Bloomington: University of Indiana Press.

Jenkins, J. T. 1936. *The Fishes of the British Isles*. London: Warne and Co.

Jensen, A. A. 1988. *Sistemas Indígenas de Classificação de Aves: Aspectos Comparativos, Ecológicos e Evolutivos*. Belém: Museu Paraense Emílio Goeldi.

Jespersen, O. 1921. *Language: Its Nature, Development, and Origin*. London: Allen and Unwin.

Jespersen, O. 1933. Symbolic Value of the Vowel i. In *Selected Papers of O. Jespersen in English, French, and German*, edited by O. Jespersen, 283–303. Copenhagen: Levin and Munksgaard.

Judy, R., and J. E. Judy. 1962. *Vocabulario Movima y Castellano*. Vocabularios Bolivianos. Cochabamba, Bolivia: Instituto Lingüísticso de Verano, Ministerio de Asuntos Campesinos y Ministero de Educación y Bellas Artes, Oficialía Mayor de Cultura, Departamento de Arqueología y Folklore.

Kaufman, T., B. Berlin, and A. Rodrigues. 1988. A Comparative Grammatical and Lexical Questionnaire for the Study of South American Indian Languages. South American Indian Languages Documentation Project Archives, Universities of California and Pittsburgh.

Kay, P. 1966. Comment on *Ethnographic Semantics: A Preliminary Survey* by B. N. Colby. *Cur. Anthro.* 7: 20–23.

Kay, P. 1971. Taxonomy and Semantic Contrast. *Language* 68: 866–87.

Kay, P. 1975. A Model-Theoretic Approach to Folk Taxonomy. *Soc. Sci. Inform.* 14: 151–66.

Kay, P. 1987. The Deconstructionist Hall of Mirrors. Unpublished manuscript.

Kempton, W. 1981. The Folk Classification of Ceramics: A Study of Cognitive Prototypes. New York: Academic Press.

Kesby, J. 1986. Rangi Natural History: The Taxonomic Procedures of an African People. New Haven, Conn.: Human Relations Area Files, Inc.

Kindberg, L. 1980. Diccionario Ashánica (edición provisional). Documento de Trabajo. Yarinacocha, Pucallpa, Peru: Instituto Lingüístico de Verano.

Köhler, W. 1929. Gestalt Psychology. New York. Liveright Publishing Corp.

Krisologo B., P. J. 1965. Diccionario Español-Wa-Jibi (Guahibo). Caracas: Instituto Caribe de Antropología, Fundación La Salle de Ciencias Naturales.

Lakaatos, I., and A. Musgrave, eds. 1970. Criticism and the Growth of Knowledge. London: Cambridge University Press.

Lakoff, G. 1973. "Hedges": A Study in Meaning and the Logic of Fuzzy Concepts. J. Phil. Logic 2: 458–508.

Lakoff, G. 1987. Women, Fire, and Dangerous Things. Chicago: University of Chicago Press.

Lakoff, G., and M. M. Turner. 1988. More Than Cool Reason. Chicago: University of Chicago Press.

Lamarck, J. B., and A. P. Candolle. 1815. Flore française. 6 vols. Paris: Desray.

Landerman, P. 1973. Vocabulario Quechua del Pastaza. Yarinachocha, Pucallpa, Peru: Instituto Lingüístico de Verano.

Larson, J. L. 1971. Reason and Experience: The Representation of Natural Order in the Work of Carl von Linné. Berkeley: University of California Press.

Laughlin, R., and D. E. Breedlove. In press. The Flowering of Man: An Ethnobotany of the Tzotzil of Zinacantan. Washington, D.C.: Smithsonian Institution Press.

Lave, J. 1981. How "They" Think. Contem. Psych. 26: 788–90.

Leach, E. 1976. Social Anthropology: A Natural Science of Society? Proc. Brit. Acad. No. 62. Oxford: Oxford University Press.

Lee, R. B. 1979. The !Kung San. Cambridge: Cambridge University Press.

Leech, E. 1974. Semantics. Harmondsworth, U.K.: Penguin Books.

Lefebvre, C. 1972. Quechua Ethnobotany. Unpublished manuscript.

Lenneberg, E., and J. Roberts. 1956. The Language of Experience: A Study in Methodology. Supplement to Inter. J. Amer. Ling. 22: 2.

Lescure, J., F. Grenand, and P. Grenand. 1980. Les amphibiens dans l'univers Wayãpi. J. Agricul. Trop. Botan. Appliquée 28: 247–61.

Lévi Strauss, C. 1966. The Savage Mind. London: Weidenfeld and Nicolson.

Levitt, D. 1981. Plants and People: Aboriginal Uses of Plants on Groote Eylandt. Canberra: Australian Institute of Aboriginal Studies.

Lindroth, S. 1983. The Two Faces of Linnaeus. In Linnaeus: The Man and His Works, edited by T. Frängmyr, 1–62. Berkeley: University of California Press.

Lindskoog, J. N., and C. A. Lindskoog. 1964. Vocabulario Cayapa. Serie de Vocabularios Indígenas "Mario Silva y Aceves." Quito: Instituto Lingüístico de Verano y Ministerio de Educación Pública.

Linnaeus, C. 1751. Philosophia Botanica. Stockholm: G. Kiesewetter.

Linton, R. 1936. The Study of Man. New York: Appleton-Century-Crofts.

Lionni, L. 1977. Parallel Botany. Translated by P. Creagh. New York: Knopf.

Locke, J. 1848. *An Essay Concerning Human Understanding*. London: Tegg.

Majnep, I. S., and R.N.H. Bulmer. 1977. *Birds of My Kalam Country*. Auckland: Auckland University Press.

Malinowski, B. 1974. *Magic, Science and Religion*. London: Souvenir Press. (Original ed. 1925).

Mandelbrot, B. 1956. On the Language of Taxonomy: An Outline of a "Thermostatistical" Theory of Systems of Categories with Willis (Natural) Structure. In *Information Theory*, edited by C. Cherry, 135–45. London: Butterworths.

Marban, P. 1894. *Arte de la Lengua Moxo*. Leipzig: B. G. Teubner.

Marcus, G., and J. Fischer. 1986. *Anthropology as Cultural Critique*. Chicago: University of Chicago Press.

Martin, G. 1990. Comparative Ethnobotany of Mixe and Chinantec. Ph.D. diss., University of California, Berkeley.

Mathews, H. 1983. Context Specific Variation in Humoral Classification. *Amer. Anthro*. 85: 826–46.

Matteson, E. 1965. *The Piro (Arawakan) Language*. Berkeley: University of California Press.

Mayr, E. 1942. *Systematics and the Origin of Species from the Viewpoint of a Zoologist*. New York: Columbia University Press.

Mayr, E. 1949. The Number of Species of Birds. *Auk* 63: 64–69.

Mayr, E. 1957. Species Concepts and Definitions. In *The Species Problem*, edited by E. Mayr, 122. Washington, D.C.: American Association for the Advancement of Science.

Mayr, E. 1969. *Principles of Systematic Zoology*. New York: McGraw-Hill.

Mayr, E. 1981. Biological Classification: Toward a Synthesis of Opposing Methodologies. *Science* 214: 510–15.

Mayr, E. 1982. *The Growth of Biological Thought: Diversity, Evolution, and Inheritance*. Cambridge, Mass.: Harvard University Press.

Mayr, E., E. S. Linsley, and R. Usinger. 1953. *Methods and Principles of Systematic Zoology*. New York: McGraw-Hill Book Company, Inc.

Merriam, C. H. 1980. *Indian Names for Plants and Animals among California and Other Western North American Tribes*. Berkeley: Archaeological Research Facility, Department of Anthropology, University of California.

Minor, E. E., and D. H. Minor. 1971. *Vocabulario Huitoto Muinane*. Yarinacocha, Pucallpa, Peru: Serie Lingüística Peruana. Instituto Lingüístico de Verano.

Morgan, B. 1932. Phonemic and Preliminary Morphemic Analysis of River Patwin. M.A. thesis, University of California, Davis.

Morris, B. 1976. Whither the Savage Mind? Notes on the Natural Taxonomies of Hunting and Gathering People. *Man* 11: 542–57.

Morris, B. 1979. Symbolism and Ideology: Thoughts Around Navajo Taxonomy and Symbolism. In *Classifications in Their Social Context*, edited by R. E. Ellen and D. Reason, 117–38. London: Academic Press.

Morris, B. 1983. The Pragmatics of Folk Classification. *J. Ethnobiol*. 4: 45–60.

Morton, E. W. 1977. On the Occurrence and Significance of Motivational-Structural Rules in Some Bird and Mammal Sounds. *Amer. Nat*. 111: 855–69.

Muñoz, H. O., and J. Armato. 1986. *Léxico Yukpa-Español Español-Yukpa*. Maracay: IUPEMAR.

Murray, S. O. 1983. Group Formation in Social Science. Edmonton, Alberta, Canada: Linguistic Research, Inc.

Nelson, G. J., and N. I. Platnick. 1981. Systematics and Biogeography: Cladistics and Vicariance. New York: Columbia University Press.

Nies, J. 1986. *Diccionario Piro*. Yarinacocha, Pucallpa, Peru: Instituto Lingüístico de Verano.

Nordenskiöld, E. 1922. Deductions Suggested by the Geographical Distribution of Some Post-Columbian Words Used by the Indians of South America. *Comparative Ethnographical Studies* 4. Göteborg, Sweden.

Ohala, J. 1982. The Frequency Code and Its Effect on Certain Forms of Speech and Facial Expressions. In *International Congress of Linguistics*, edited by International Congress of Linguistics Editorial Committee, 199–208. Tokyo: International Editorial Committee, ICL.

Ohala, J. 1983. Cross-Language Use of Pitch: An Ethological View. *Phonetica* 40: 1–18.

Ohala, J. 1984. An Ethological Perspective on Common Cross-Language Utilization of FO of Voice. Berkeley: Phonology Laboratory, Department of Linguistics, University of California. Unpublished manuscript.

Ott, W., and R. Ott. 1983. *Diccionario Ignaciano y Castellano, con Apuntes Gramaticales*. Cochabamba, Bolivia: Instituto Lingüístico de Verano y Ministerio de Educación y Cultura.

Panoff, F. 1972. *Maenge Gardens: A Study of Maenge Relationship to Domesticates*. Ph.D. diss., Australian National University, Canberra.

Paso y Troncoso, F. del. 1886. La Botánica Entre los Nahuas. *Annal. Mus. Nacion. Mexico* 3.

Patton, J. L., B. Berlin, and E. A. Berlin. 1982. Aboriginal Perspectives of a Mammal Community in Amazonian Peru: Knowledge and Utilization Patterns of the Aguaruna Jívaro. In *Mammalian Biology in South America*, edited by M. Mares and H. H. Genoways, 111–28. Pittsburgh: Pymatuning Laboratory of Ecology.

Payne, D. L. 1980. *Diccionario Ashénica-Castellano*. Yarinachocha, Pucallpa, Peru: Documento de Trabajo. Instituto Lingüístico de Verano.

Pelto, P. J., and G. H. Pelto. 1975. Intra-Cultural Diversity: Some Theoretical Issues. *Amer. Ethnol.* 2: 1–18.

Pennoyer, F. D. III. 1975. Taubuid Plants and Ritual Complexes. Ph.D. diss., Washington State University, Pullman.

Pet, W.J.A. 1987. Lokono Kian: The Arawak Language of Suriname: A Sketch of Its Grammatical Structure and Lexicon. Ph.D. diss., Cornell University, Ithaca, N.Y.

Pitman, M. 1981. *Diccionario Araona-Castellano*. Riberalta, Bolivia: Instituto Lingüístico de Verano.

Posey, D. A. 1979. Ethnoentomology of the Gorotire Kayapó of Central Brazil. Ph.D. diss., University of Georgia, Athens.

Posey, D. A. 1984. Hierarchy and Utility in a Folk Botanical Taxonomic System: Patterns in the Classification of Arthropods by the Kayapó Indians of Brazil. *J. Ethnobiol.* 4: 123–34.

Potter, S., and L. Sargent. 1974. *Pedigree: The Origin of Words from Nature*. New York: Taplinger.

Pullam, G. K. 1989. The Great Eskimo Vocabulary Hoax. *Natural Language and Linguistic Theory* 7: 275–81.

Putnam, H. 1975. *The Meaning of 'Meaning.'* Minneapolis: University of Minnesota Press.

Randall, R. 1976. How Tall Is a Taxonomic Tree? Some Evidence for Dwarfism. *Amer. Ethnol.* 3: 543–53.

Randall, R. 1987. The Nature of Highly Inclusive Folk Botanical Categories. *Amer. Anthro.* 89: 143–46.

Randall, R., and E. Hunn. 1984. Do Life Forms Evolve or Do Uses for Life? *Amer. Ethnol.* 11: 329–49.

Raunkiaer, C. 1934. *The Life Forms of Plants and Statistical Plant Geography*. Oxford: Oxford University Press.

Raven, P. H., B. Berlin, and D. E. Breedlove. 1971. The Origins of Taxonomy. *Science* 174: 1210–13.

Romney, A. K., and R. D'Andrade. 1964. Cognitive Aspects of English Kin Terms. *Amer. Anthro.* 66: 146–70.

Romney, A. K., and S. Weller. 1988. *Systematic Data Collection*. Newbury Park, Calif.: Sage Publications.

Rosch, E. 1973. On the Internal Structure of Perceptual and Semantic Categories. In *Cognitive Development and the Acquisition of Language*, edited by T. E. Moore, 44. New York: Academic Press.

Rosch, E. 1977. Human Categorization. In *Studies in Cross-Cultural Psychology*, edited by N. Warren, 1: 1–49. London: Academic Press.

Rosch, E. 1978. Principles of Categorization. In *Cognition and Categorization*, edited by E. Rosch and B. Lloyd, 28–49. Hillsdale, N.J.: Lawrence Erlbaum Associates.

Rosch, E. 1981. Prototype Classification and Logical Classification: The Two Systems. In *New Trends in Cognitive Representation: Challenges to Piaget's Theory*, edited by E. Scholnick, 73–86. Hillsdale, N.J.: Lawrence Erlbaum Associates.

Rosch, E., C. B. Mervis, W. Gray, D. Johnson, and P. Boyes-Braem. 1975. Basic Objects in Natural Categories. *Cog. Psych.* 8: 133–56.

Rosch, E., C. Simpson, and R. S. Miller. 1976. Structural Basis of Typicality Effects. *J. Exper. Psych.* 2: 491–502.

Rosman, J. 1982. *Onomatopoeia and Word Origins*. Austin, Texas: Privately published.

Salesianos Misioneros. 1924. Diccionario Jíbaro-Castellano y Castellano-Jíbaro. *Bol. Acad. Nac. Hist.* 9.

Sankoff, G. 1971. Quantitative Analysis of Sharing and Variability in a Cognitive Model. *Ethnol.* 10: 389–408.

Sapir, E. 1916. Time Perspective in Aboriginal American Culture: A Study in Method. In *Selected Writings of Edward Sapir*, edited by D. G. Mandelbaum, 389–461. Berkeley: University of California Press.

Sapir, E. 1929. A Study in Phonetic Symbolism. *J. Exper. Psych.* 12: 225–39.

Sapir, E. 1936. Internal Linguistic Evidence Suggestive of the Northern Origin of the Navajo. *Amer. Anthro.* 38: 224–35.

Sapir, E. 1938. Why Anthropology Needs the Psychiatrist. *Psychiatry* 1: 7–12.

Shaw, A. 1966. *J. C. Willis' Dictionary of Flowering Plants and Ferns*. Cambridge: Cambridge University Press.

Sillitoe, P. 1980. Confusions in the Classifications: How the Wola Name Their Plants. *Ethos* 45: 133–56.

Sillitoe, P. 1983. *Roots of the Earth*. Manchester, England: University of Manchester.

Simpson, G. G. 1940. The Principles of Classification and a Classification of Mammals. *Bull. Amer. Mus. Nat. Hist.* 85.

Simpson, G. G. 1961. *Principles of Animal Taxonomy*. New York: Columbia University Press.

Smith-Bowen, E. 1954. *Return to Laughter*. New York: Harper Brothers.

Sneath, P., and R. Sokal. 1973. *Numerical Taxonomy*. San Franciso: W. H. Freeman.

Starr, M., and H. Heise. 1969. Discussion of W. Wagner, *The Construction of a Classification*. In *Systematic Biology*, edited by National Research Council, 92–99. Washington, D.C.: National Research Council, National Academy of Sciences.

Stern, W. 1959. The Background of Linnaeus' Contribution to the Nomenclature and Methods of Systematic Biology. *Sys. Zool.* 8: 4–22.

Steudel, S. 1855. *Synopsis Plantarum Graminearum*. Stuttgartiae: J. B. Matzler.

Stochl, J., and R. E. Hadel. 1975. *A Dictionary of Central American Carib*. 3 vols. Belize City: Belize Institute of Social Research and Action.

Stross. 1975. Variation and Natural Selection as Factors in Linguistic and Cultural Change. In *Linguistics and Anthroplogy: In Honor of Carl F. Voegelin*, edited by M. D. Kinkade, K. R. Itale, and O. Warner, 607–32. Lisse: Peter de Ridder Press.

Stross, B. 1973. Acquisition of Botanical Terminology by Tzeltal Children. In *Meaning in Mayan Languages*, edited by M. S. Edmonson, 107–41. The Hague: Mouton.

Sturtevant, W. C. 1964. Studies in Ethnoscience. *Amer. Anthro.* 66: 99–113.

Swadesh, M. 1970. *The Origin and Diversification of Language*. Chicago: Aldine and Company.

Taylor, K. I. 1963. Phonetic Symbolism Reexamined. *Psych. Bull.* 60: 200–209.

Taylor, K. I., and M. M. Taylor. 1965. Another Look at Phonetic Symbolism. *Psych. Bull.* 64: 413–27.

Taylor, K. I., and M. M. Taylor. 1967. Phonetic Symbolism in Four Unrelated Languages. *Canadian J. Psych.* 16: 344–56.

Taylor, K. I. 1972. Sanuma (Yanomama) Food Prohibitions: The Multiple Classification of Society and Fauna. Ph.D. diss., University of Wisconsin, Madison.

Taylor, P. M. 1984. "Covert Categories" Reconsidered: Identifying Unlabeled Classes in Tobelo Folk Biological Classification. *J. Ethnbiol.* 4: 105–22.

Taylor, P. M. 1987. *The Ethnobiology of the Tobeloese People*. Smithsonian Contributions to Anthropology. Washington, D.C.: Smithsonian Institution Press.

Tessman, G. 1930. *Die Indianer Nordost-Perus: Grundlegende Forschungen für eine systematische Kulturkunde*. Hamburg: Friederischen, de Gruyter & Co.

Thompson, R. 1972. A Yucatec Plant Taxonomy. University of Texas, Austin. Unpublished manuscript.

Tolman, A. 1887. The Laws of Tone Color in the English Language. *Andover Rev.* 7: 326–37.

Tolman, A. 1904. Symbolic Value of English Sounds. In *Views about Hamlet*. New York: Houghton Mifflin.

Tournefort, J. P. de. 1700. *Institutiones sei Herbarie*. 3 vols. Parisiis: Typographia Regia.

Trager, G. "Cottonwood"-"Tree": A Southwestern Linguistic Trait. *Inter. J. Amer. Ling*. 9: 117–18.

Turner, N. 1974. Plant Taxonomic Systems and Ethnobotany of Three Contemporary Indian Groups of the Pacific Northwest (Haida, Bella Coola, and Lillooet). *Sysis* 7: 1–107.

Turner, N. J. 1986. Intermediate Level Folk Plant Categories in Thompson and Lillooet Interior Salish. British Columbia Provincial Museum. Victoria, B.C. Unpublished manuscript.

Turner, N. J. 1987. General Plant Categories in Thompson and Lillooet, Two Interior Salish Languages of British Columbia. *J. Ethnobiol*. 7: 55–82.

Turner, N. J. 1988. "The Importance of Rose": Evaluating the Cultural Significance of Plants in Thompson and Liliooet Interior Salish. *Amer. Anthro*. 90: 272–90.

Turner, N. J., and M.A.M. Bell. 1973. The Ethnobotany of the Southern Kwakiutl Indians of British Columbia. *Economic Botany* 27: 257–301.

Turner, N. J., R. Bouchard, and D.I.D. Kennedy. 1981. Ethnobotany of the Okanagan-Colville Indians of British Columbia and Washington. *Occ. Pap. Brit. Col. Prov. Mus*. 21. Victoria, B.C.

Turner, N. J., J. Thomas, B. F. Carlson, and R. T. Ogilvie. 1983. Ethnohistory of the Nitinaht Indians of Vancouver Island. *Bri. Colum. Prov. Mus*. 24. Occ. Paper Series.

Tversky, A., and I. Gati. 1978. Studies of Similarity. In *Cognition and Categorization*, edited by E. Rosch and B. Lloyd, 81–98. Hillsdale, N.J.: Lawrence Erlbaum Associates.

Tyler, S. 1987. *The Unspeakable: Discourse, Dialogue and Rhetoric in the Postmodern World*. Madison: University of Wisconsin Press.

Ullman, S. 1963. Semantic Universals. In *Universals of Language*, edited by J. H. Greenberg, 217–62. Cambridge, Mass.: MIT Press.

Ultan, D. 1961–63. Patwin Field Notes and Indices. Department of Linguistics, University of California, Berkeley. Unpublished manuscript.

Van Wynen, D., and M. G. Van Wynen. 1962. *Tacana y Castellano*. Vocabularios Bolivianos. Cochabamba, Bolivia: Instituto Lingüístico de Verano.

Vickers, W. T., and T. Plowman. 1984. *Useful Plants of the Siona and Secoya Indians of Eastern Ecuador*. Chicago: Field Museum of Natural History.

Villard, J. 1980. An Inventory of Tropical Bird Species Accompanied by Recorded Bird Calls. Laboratory of Zoology: Universidade de Campinas, São Paulo, Brazil.

Waddy, J. A. 1982a. Biological Classification from a Groote Eylandt Aborigine's Point of View. *J. Ethnobiol*. 2: 63–77.

Waddy, J. A. 1982b. Folk Biology and the Northern Territory Science Curriculum. In *Applied Linguistics of Australia, Occasional Papers* 5: 80–87. Applied Linguistics Association of Australia.

Waddy, J. A. 1983. Groote Eylandt Ethnobiology: Plants and Animal Foods on Groote

Eylandt. In *Groote Eylandt* (rev. ed.), edited by E. K. Cole, 15–21. Bendigo: Keith Cole Publications.

Waddy, J. A. 1988. *Classification of Plants and Animals from a Groote Eylandt Aboriginal Point of View* (2 vols.). Darwin: Australian National University.

Wagner, W. 1969. The Construction of a Classification. In *Systematic Biology*, edited by National Research Council, Washington, D.C.: National Academy of Sciences.

Walsh, D. S. 1979. Patterns of Metaphor in Rága Plant Nomenclature. Paper presented at the 49th Congress of the Australian-New Zealand Society for the Advancement of Science. Auckland, New Zealand.

Walters, S. M. 1986. The Name of the Rose: A Review of the Ideas on the European Bias in Angiosperm Classification. Tansley Review Paper 6, *New Phytologist* 104: 527–46.

Watson, J. G. 1928. Malayan Plant Names. *Malayan Forest Records* 5: 17–77. Singapore.

Weller, S. 1983. Data on Intra-cultural Variation: The Hot-Cold Concept. *Hum. Organ.* 42: 249–57.

Weller, S. 1984. Consistency and Consensus among Informants: Disease Concepts in a Rural Mexican Village. *Amer. Anthro.* 86: 341–51.

Weller, S. 1987. Shared Knowledge, Intracultural Variation, and Knoweldge Aggregation. *Amer. Behav. Sci.* 31: 178–93.

Werner, O. 1969. The Basic Assumptions of Ethnoscience. *Semiotica* 1: 329–38.

Werner, O. 1970. A Lexemic Typology of Navajo Anatomical Terms, I: The Foot. *Inter. J. Amer. Ling.* 36: 247–65.

Whistler, K. 1975–1976. Patwin Field Notes and Indices. Department of Linguistics, University of California, Berkeley. Unpublished manuscript.

Whistler, K. 1976. Patwin Folk-taxonomic Structures. M.A. thesis, University of California, Berkeley.

Wierzbicka, A. 1972. *Semantic Primitives*. Frankfurt: Athenaeum.

Wierzbicka, A. 1980. *Lingua Mentalis*. New York: Academic Press.

Wierzbicka, A. 1984. Apples Are Not a "Kind of Fruit": The Semantics of Human Categorization. *Amer. Ethnol.* 11: 313–28.

Wierzbicka, A. 1985. *Lexicography and Conceptual Analysis*. Ann Arbor, Mich.: Karoma Publishers.

Williams, C. B. 1946. Yule's Characteristic and the Index of Diversity. *Nature* 157: 482.

Williams, C. B. 1947. The Logarithmic Series and the Comparison of Island Floras. *Proc. Linn. Soc. London* 158: 104–108.

Williams, C. B. 1949. Jaccard's Generic Coefficient and Coefficient of Floral Communities in Relation to the Logarithmic Series. *Ann. Botany* 13: 53–58.

Williams, C. B. 1951. A Note on the Relative Size of Genera in the Classification of Plants and Animals. *Proc. Linn. Soc. London* 162: 171–75.

Williams, C. B. 1964. *Patterns in the Balance of Nature*. London: Academic Press.

Willis, J. C. 1907. Some Evidence Against Natural Selection. *Annals Peral.* 84: 1–17.

Willis, J. C. 1922. *Age and Area*. Cambridge: Cambridge University Press.

Willis, J. C. 1940. *The Course of Evolution*. Cambridge: Cambridge University Press.

Willis, J. C. 1949. The Birth and Spread of Plants. *Boissiera* 8.

Witkowski, S. R., C. H. Brown, and P. K. Chase. 1981. Lexical Encoding Sequences and Language Change: Color Terminology Systems. *Amer. Anthro.* 83: 13–27.

Wyman, L. C., and F. L. Bailey. 1964. *Navaho Indian Ethnoentomology.* University of New Mexico Publications in Anthropology. Albuquerque: University of New Mexico Press.

Wyman, L. C., and S. K. Harris. 1941. *Navajo Indian Medical Ethnobotany.* Bul. 366, Anthro. Series. Albuquerque: University of New Mexico Press.

Yen, D. E. 1976. The Ethnobotany of the Tasaday, II: Plant Names of the Tasaday, Manobo Blit and Kemato Tboli. In *Further Studies on the Tasaday*, edited by D. E. Yen, and J. Nance, 137–58. Makati, Rizal, Philippines: Panamin Foundation.

Young, J. C., and L. Garro. 1982. Variation in the Choice of Treatment in Two Mexican Communities. *Soc. Sci. and Med.* 16: 1453–65.

Yule, C. U. 1924. A Mathematical Theory of Evolution Based on the Conclusions of Dr. J. C. Willis. *Phil. Trans. Bull.* 213: 21–87.

Yule, C. U., and J. C. Willis. 1922. Some Statistics of Evolution and Geographical Distribution of Plants and Animals. *Nature* 109: 177.

Zent, T. 1989. Piaroan Faunal Inventory. Unpublished manuscript.

Zipf, G. K. 1935. *The Psycho-Biology of Language.* Boston: Houghton Mifflin.

Zipf, G. K. 1949. *Human Behavior and the Principle of Least Effort.* Cambridge, Mass.: Addison-Wesley.

Author Index

Index of Scientific Names

Index of Ethnoscientific Names

Subject Index

Achuar, 6
acoustic qualities, 241
adaptive strategies, 149
age, 199, 206, 209, 219–221, 223
agriculturalists, 284
Agta, 62, 164, 284–285
Aguaruna, 6–7, 10, 19–20, 27, 30, 32, 39,
    45, 48, 72–74, 78, 89, 90–92, 98–100,
    104, 108, 115, 119, 120, 121, 123–129,
    141, 144–146, 153, 162–163, 167, 170–
    171, 173, 175, 177–178, 181, 183, 188,
    191–192, 207–225, 229–230, 260, 262,
    271, 281–282, 287
Aguaruna ethnozoology, 223
Amawaka, 252
ambiguously affiliated generics, 172
Amuzgo, 164
Anindilyakwa, 98–100, 176, 179–180, 185,
    194, 278
antonymic pairs, 235
anurans, 250
Apache, 140
Araona, 252
Arawakan, 269
Arawete, 258
arbitrariness principle, 235
armadillos, 271
armored catfishes, 133
association of sound and meaning, 235, 255
Asháninka, 251–252
Ashéninka, 251–252
Asurini, 258
asymmetries of ethnobiological taxonomies,
    173

basic level categories/objects, 70–75, 77–78
Batak, 55
Bella Coola, 98, 275
binomials, 60
binomial structure, 116–117
biological discontinuities, 53
biological ranges, 207–209, 219
biological reality, 53, 80, 290
bird names, 236–245
birds, 7, 9–10, 32, 45

box diagrams, 36–38, 41

Cantonese, 108
Cantonese ethnoichthyology, 170
capacities for categorization, 261
categorization, 20, 26, 31–34, 36
categorization and nomenclature, 54
categorization of plants and animals, 53
category resemblance, 70
causal explanations, 273
Chayawita, 252
Chinantec, 98, 129
classical notions of genera, 106
classification, 3–51, 135–167, 171–172, 179–
    194
cognitive competence, 73
cognitive inventory of living things, 260
cognitive variation, 203–206, 223, 225
cognitively distinct classifications, 213
color, 106–107
complex plant names, 58
configurational category, 61
continuants (in sound symbolism), 240
contrasting generic taxa, 144
contrast set, 19, 28, 143, 169–170, 173–174
covert life forms, 176–177
cross-cultural perspective, 13
cue validity, 70
cultivated plants, 106, 273, 278, 281
cultivated plant species, 225
cultural evolution, 273
cultural factors (in the recognition of ethno-
    biological taxa), 118, 119
cultural knowledge, 199–200
cultural significance as a factor in recognized
    folk taxa, 72, 77, 80, 118, 255–256, 266,
    278, 282, 287, 290
cultural-historical work, 269

decided gaps, 83–84
degrees of similarity, 82
Dene, 43, 45, 200, 203
denotative meaning, 201
diagrammatic conventions in ethnobiological
    theory, 36–37, 40–42, 44, 48–50